WITHDRAWN

Eastern Arabian Frontiers

EASTERN ARABIAN FRONTIERS

by
J. B. KELLY

FREDERICK A. PRAEGER, *Publisher*
NEW YORK · LONDON

228576

Frederick A. Praeger, Publisher
64 University Place, New York 3, N.Y., U.S.A.
77–79 Charlotte Street, London W.1, England

Published in the United States of America in 1964
by Frederick A. Praeger, Inc., Publisher

Library of Congress Catalog Card Number: 64-13137

Printed in Great Britain

DS
227
K4.

Contents

Preface	page 7
Acknowledgements	11
List of Tribes and Arabic Terms	13
List of Abbreviations used in the Text and Footnotes	15
Note on the Spelling of Arabic Names	15
Introduction	17
I. The Region in Dispute, its Economy and its Inhabitants	25
II. The Wahhabi Period, 1800–1869	51
III. The Ascendancy of Zaid ibn Khalifah, 1871–1909	91
IV. Frontier Negotiations and Saudi Ambitions, 1909–1949	107
V. The Development of the Frontier Dispute, 1949–1954	142
VI. The Interim Régime in the Disputed Areas, 1954–1955	175
VII. The *Saudi Memorial* of 1955	207
Conclusion	260
Appendix A: The Arbitration Agreement of 30 July 1954	281
Appendix B: The Submissions on *Zakat* in the *Saudi Memorial*	293
Index	305

Maps

The Buraimi Oasis   16
Eastern Arabia, showing the various frontier
   claims   *at the end of the book*

Preface

The delimitation of the eastern frontier of Saudi Arabia with her neighbours, Qatar, the Trucial Shaikhdoms, and the Sultanate of Muscat and Oman, has been a major issue in the politics of the Arabian peninsula for the past three decades. Of late years, under the appellation of 'the Buraimi Oasis dispute', it has attained international dimensions, mainly as a consequence of its having become a subject of acute disagreement between Britain and Saudi Arabia, and, more recently, of investigation by the Secretary-General of the United Nations. It has not only caused a diplomatic rupture of six years' duration between Britain and Saudi Arabia—although the ostensible reason for the latter's breaking off relations was the Suez crisis of 1956—but it has at times strained the Anglo-American alliance through Britain's insistence upon checking Saudi Arabia's territorial ambitions and the United States' reluctance to see any offence given the Saudi Government.

Inevitably, the frontier question has been subject to misunderstanding and misrepresentation. It seems almost impossible nowadays for events to be seen from any point of view except that of partisan interest. Thus, the frontier issue has been variously portrayed as a struggle between rival oil companies, American in Saudi Arabia, British in the littoral states, as the striving of Saudi Arabia to fulfil her 'manifest destiny' to rule Arabia from sea to sea, and, of course, as the last flicker of a fading imperialism before the inexorable spread of Arab nationalism. Doubtless there are elements of all these present, but the frontier question also has an identity of its own, removed from them. Its roots go back more than a century and a half, and its persistence into the twentieth century has little to do with oil exploitation, imperialism, or Arab nationalism, however much these factors have inflamed it in our day. The basic issue is that of the continued existence of small states in the face of the attempts of their more powerful neighbours to absorb them.

Indeed, one might properly assert that this has been the principal

Preface

question at issue in the Arabian peninsula since the Second World War. Saudi Arabia in 1949 advanced a claim of such magnitude to the territory of the Shaikhdom of Abu Dhabi as to jeopardize its very existence. In the nineteen-fifties she threatened the integrity of the Sultanate of Muscat and Oman by her support of the Imamate movement, which broke out in open revolt in 1957. Iraq in the summer of 1961 laid claim to the sovereignty of Kuwait, declaring the principality to be part historically of her territory. Egypt in the mid-nineteen-fifties supported Saudi Arabia's bid to extend her eastern frontier to the southern coast of the Persian Gulf and into Oman, but later shifted her attention to the Yemen and changed her tactics to those of direct intervention. Her goals, however, remained constant: possession of the Gulf oil-fields and the fulfilment of the old aspirations of Mehemet Ali to control the Gulf and Red Sea routes to the East.

Up to date the independence and territorial integrity of the Gulf states have been upheld by Britain, acting also from a historical compulsion. Since the early nineteenth century she has consistently opposed, for their sakes and the sake of her own strategic and commercial interests in the area, the extension of Saudi, Turkish, Persian, Egyptian or Iraqi rule over them. They, for their part, have shown little disposition to welcome such rule, whether proposed in the name of revivalism, irredentism or nationalism. How long they will continue to maintain their independence will, in the absence of any other arrangement, depend largely upon how long Britain is able, or allowed, to defend them. The course of events in the Arabian peninsula shifts as regularly, if not with the same predictability, as the movements of its nomadic tribes with the seasons. Egypt and Saudi Arabia have fallen out over the issue of republican versus monarchical government in the Yemen, but more particularly over Egyptian ambitions in the peninsula. Britain and Saudi Arabia have been reconciled. The frontier question in Eastern Arabia may, for all practical purposes, have reached its final stage. Whether it has will depend ultimately upon the destiny that awaits Saudi Arabia.

I have endeavoured in the present study to place the frontier question in its historical setting as well as to give as full an account as possible of the dispute between Saudi Arabia and Britain in recent years. The areas to which Saudi Arabia lays claim, and their tribal composition, are described in Chapter I, their history and that of Saudi expansion in Eastern Arabia in the nineteenth century, in

Preface

Chapters II and III. The revival of Saudi power in this century and the negotiations before the Second World War to define the frontier are recounted in Chapter IV. Chapters V and VI deal with events from the assertion of the new frontier claim by Saudi Arabia in 1949 to the failure of the attempt to settle the issue by arbitration in 1955. The bases for the 1949 Saudi claim, as set forth in the memorial presented by the Saudi Government to the arbitration tribunal in 1955, are examined in Chapter VII; and a résumé of events from 1955 to the resumption of Anglo-Saudi diplomatic relations in January 1963 is given in the Conclusion.

My own interest in the frontier question arose out of investigations that I have made, over the past ten years, into the history of British policy in the Persian Gulf and Eastern Arabia in the nineteenth century, mainly in the India Office and Foreign Office Records. The results of this work I hope to publish in the near future. I owe a considerable debt of gratitude to a number of people who have helped me during this time, and I wish that it were possible to acknowledge my debt to them here. I am particularly grateful to the Institute of Commonwealth Studies, University of Oxford, for the encouragement and support given me during my three years (1955–1958) as Senior Research Officer there; and to Professor Ann K. S. Lambton, O.B.E., Professor of Persian in the University of London, who read the present book in manuscript and made many valuable criticisms and suggestions. Needless to say, any faults or errors that the book contains are solely mine. I should like also to take this opportunity to express my appreciation of the kind assistance given me over the years in locating books and records by Mr. Stanley C. Sutton, C.B.E., Librarian of the India Office (Commonwealth Relations Office), and by Mr. Douglas Matthews, formerly assistant India Office Librarian and now Librarian of the Home Office. Finally, I wish to thank the Social Science Research Council of New York and the American Council of Learned Societies for their generosity in awarding me, through their Joint Committee on the Near and Middle East, a research grant in 1960–1 which enabled me to gather the major proportion of the material for this study. They are, of course, in no way responsible for its contents or for any of the opinions expressed in it.

J.B.K.

Ann Arbor, Michigan
February 1963

Acknowledgements

I wish to express my gratitude to the authors and publishers concerned for permission to quote from the following books and articles:

Wilfred Thesiger, *Arabian Sands*, Longmans, Green and Co., Ltd., 'A Further Journey across the Empty Quarter', *Geographical Journal*, CXIII, and 'Desert Borderlands of Oman', *Geographical Journal*, CXVI, Royal Geographical Society; H. R. P. Dickson, *The Arab of the Desert*, Bertram Thomas, *Arabia Felix* and *Alarms and Excursions in Arabia*, Geo. Allen and Unwin, Ltd.; Sir John Glubb, *War in the Desert*, Hodder and Stoughton, Ltd.; H. St. J. B. Philby, *The Empty Quarter*, Constable and Co., Ltd.; and Sir Anthony Eden, *The Memoirs of Anthony Eden: Full Circle* (U.S. edn.), Houghton Mifflin Co.

I wish also to thank the Controller of Her Majesty's Stationery Office for permission to reproduce the arbitration agreement and exchange of notes between the United Kingdom and Saudi Arabia of 30 July 1954 (Cmd. 9272).

List of Tribes and Arabic Terms

1. TRIBES

Al Bu Sa'id
Al Bu Shamis[1]
Awamir (sing. Amiri)
Baluchi
Bani Bu Ali
Bani Ghafir (also known as Miyayihah)
Bani Hina
Bani Ka'ab
Bani Kalban
Bani Qitab
Bani Riyam
Bani Ruwaihah
Bani Yas
Dhawahir
Duru'
Ghafalah
Hajariyin
Hirth
Ifar
Manahil (sing. Manhali)
Manasir (sing. Mansuri)
Maqabil
Mazari' (sing. Mazrui)
Murrah (sing. Murri)
Na'im
Qawasim (sing. Qasimi)
Rashid[2]

[1] Al Bu Shamis are technically a branch of the Na'im, but are usually classed as a separate tribe. The Na'im proper are made up of the other two branches, Al Bu Khuraiban and Khawatir.

[2] The Rashid are divided into the Bait Imani and Bait Kathir.

2. ARABIC TERMS

amil, tax collector
amir, commander
arif, lesser tax collector
baghlah, large sailing vessel
dirah (pl. *diyar*), tribal range
falaj (pl. *aflaj*), underground water conduit
farizah, monetary allowance
fidawi, armed retainer
gaidh, date harvest

List of Tribes and Arabic Terms

hayyal, deep-sea fishing
hijra, agricultural settlement
ikramiyah, presents given in return for *zakat*
imam, leader (esp. in spiritual matters)
jizyah, poll-tax levied on the 'people of scripture', i.e. Christians, Jews, Sabaeans and Zoroastrians
kharaj, tribute, land tax
khaur, coastal inlet
mutawwa', strict believer
muzakki, *zakat*-collector
naib, deputy or lieutenant
nisab, taxable minimum
qadi, judge

qaim-maqam, deputy governor
qaza, lesser administrative district in the Ottoman Empire
sabkhah, salt flat
sanjaq (Turkish), sub-province, second-largest administrative unit in Ottoman Empire
sharha, gift
Shari'ah, the law of Islam
tamimah, paramount shaikh
tarifa, adherent, comrade
vali, governor of a *vilayet*
vilayet, province, largest administrative unit in Ottoman Empire
wali, see *vali*
zakat (or *zakah*), alms tax

List of Abbreviations Used in the Text and Footnotes

F.O.: Foreign Office Records, London.

I.O.: India Office Records, London.

Saudi Memorial: Memorial of the Government of Saudi Arabia: Arbitration for the Settlement of the Territorial Dispute between Muscat and Abu Dhabi on the one side and Saudi Arabia on the other, A.H. 1374/A.D. 1955.

U.K. Memorial: Arbitration Concerning Buraimi and the Common Frontier between Abu Dhabi and Sa'ūdi Arabia: Memorial submitted by the Government of the United Kingdom of Great Britain and Northern Ireland, 1955.

Note on the Spelling of Arabic Names

For the sake of simplicity, Arabic names have been spelt without any diacritical marks. The Arabic letter '*ain* has been represented by ', when it occurs in the middle or at the end of a word.

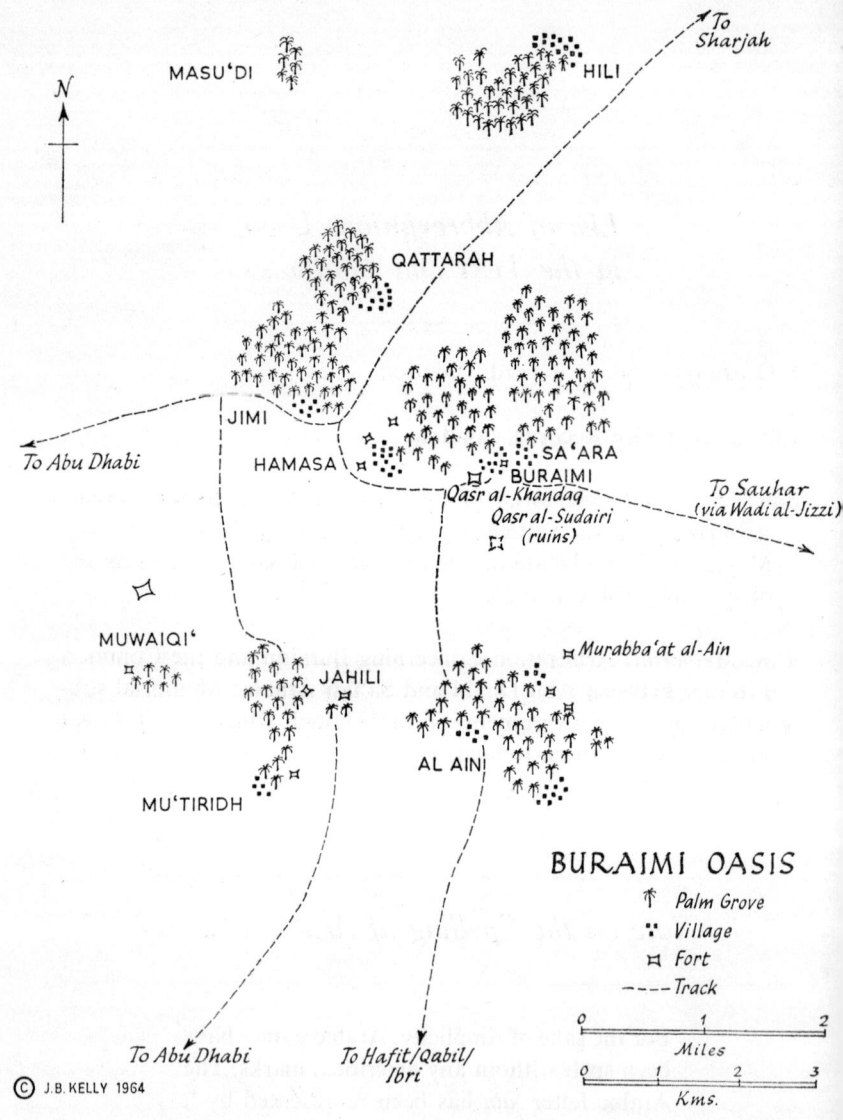

Introduction

'In Asia,' Lord Curzon once remarked, '... there has always been a strong instinctive aversion to the acceptance of fixed boundaries, arising partly from the nomadic habits of the people, partly from the dislike of precise arrangements that is typical of the oriental mind, but more still from the idea that in the vicissitudes of fortune more is to be expected from an unsettled than from a settled Frontier.'[1] Frontiers are few and far between in Eastern Arabia. Most of the region is desert, uninhabited except for a few nomadic tribes. The settled populations dwell far apart: in the oases of Hasa, Liwa and Buraimi, in the ports and fishing villages along the coasts of Hasa, Qatar and Trucial Oman, and in the mountain valleys and coastal towns of Oman. The way of life is primitive. Society is predominantly tribal in structure, government is patriarchal in character, and the economy, even today, is still largely a subsistence one, dependent upon fishing, pearling, and pastoral and agricultural pursuits. Only a small part of the region has ever been mapped or surveyed in any detail.

The only internationally agreed territorial frontiers existent in Eastern Arabia today are those of Saudi Arabia with Kuwait and Iraq, laid down in 1922–3 when Britain was the mandatory power in Iraq, and, of more recent origin, the Saudi-Qatar frontier and some sectors of the boundaries of the Trucial Shaikhdoms with the Sultanate of Muscat and Oman. None of these frontiers has yet been formally demarcated on the ground. Elsewhere there are only what might be termed *frontières de convenance*, shadowy lines which serve to mark off the jurisdiction of one ruler from that of another. Thus, for years past, the respective jurisdictions of the rulers of Saudi Arabia, Qatar and Abu Dhabi were considered to meet in the area

[1] 'Frontiers', *The Romanes Lecture, 1907*, Oxford, 1907, p. 49.

Introduction

at the foot of the Qatar peninsula. Further east, the limits of Saudi authority were held by the Saudi Government to correspond roughly with the northern and eastern edges of the Rub' al-Khali, the 'Empty Quarter'; while the border of the Sultanate of Muscat and Oman with the Trucial Shaikhdoms lay more or less along the spine of the Hajar Mountains, from the Buraimi Oasis northwards to the Musandam peninsula.[1]

Until recent years there was little disposition on the part of the rulers concerned to give these lines any more substance. The concept of territorial sovereignty in the Western sense did not exist in Eastern Arabia. A ruler exercised jurisdiction over a territory by virtue of his jurisdiction over the tribes inhabiting it. They, in turn, owed loyalty to him and not to the shaikhdom, amirate or sultanate in which they dwelt. Political allegiance to a territorial unit, such as is implicit in the European states system, is unknown to the Arabian tribesman. His loyalty is personal to his tribe, his shaikh, or a leader of greater consequence, and not to any abstract image of the state. In so far as he conceives of a territorial loyalty, it is to his domestic abode, his wells, his gardens, his palm trees, or, in the case of the nomad, his *dirah*, or tribal grazing ground. A claim to jurisdiction over him, therefore, amounts to a claim to jurisdiction over the land he occupies. In the case of the settled populations of the seaports or oases such claims do not normally give rise to any difficulties. Applied to nomadic tribes, however, they almost inevitably produce complications.

While the pattern of movement of a nomadic tribe is normally fixed, it may alter slightly, or even dramatically, with changes in the grazing brought about by drought or other causes. For a ruler to claim possession of the area over which a tribe roams, on the grounds that it owes loyalty to him, is tantamount, in theory, to his claiming possession of an area not only of considerable size but also one whose limits may fluctuate, sometimes to a large degree. In practice, however, such claims are usually limited to the tribe's home range, or *dirah*, to which it may or may not possess exclusive rights. But a tribe's loyalty is not always constant. It may be, and sometimes is, withdrawn from one ruler and transferred to another, or even withheld completely. Where it is transferred, the tribe's new ruler is as likely as not to lay claim to its *dirah*. Since it is just as likely that the tribe's former ruler will refuse to recognize its defection or

[1] See Map 2 at end.

Introduction

relinquish his claim to its *dirah*, the territory in question becomes an object of dispute.

Territorial disputes of this nature, and others arising from historical causes, have long been a feature of Eastern Arabian politics; but although they were a source of friction between the rulers involved in them, only occasionally did they provoke an open conflict. The vast stretches of desert that, in many cases, separated these rulers from one another greatly hindered the active prosecution of territorial claims on the far marches of their dominions, and served to limit clashes of authority among them to tribal raiding and counter-raiding. Over the past two decades, however, this order of things has been fast changing, chiefly because of the exploitation of oil in Saudi Arabia, Kuwait and Qatar. The traditional economies of these states, and to a lesser degree, those of their southern neighbours, the Trucial Shaikhdoms and the Sultanate of Muscat and Oman, have been dislocated. Tribal life in the deserts has been disturbed by the migration of tribesmen to work in the oil-fields, and by the advent of modern desert transport, which has diminished the Baduin's reliance on the camel. Modern transport has also overcome the barriers once interposed by sand dune and salt flat, and together with the unexpected access of wealth from oil revenues has enabled rulers to close the gap that formerly existed between their pretensions to authority and the actual extent of their power to control the territories over which they claimed jurisdiction. The inevitable result has been to invest the question of frontier definition with an urgency which it did not previously possess.

The question came to a head in the autumn of 1949, when Saudi Arabia put forward a claim to sovereignty over the greater part of the territory lying between the base of the Qatar peninsula and the south-eastern corner of the Persian Gulf. The claim was embodied in a Note from the Saudi Government to the British Government on 14 October 1949, which declared the eastern frontier of Saudi Arabia to lie, in the first instance, along a line beginning on the west coast of Qatar, well up the Bay of Salwah, and running across the peninsula, to end on the east coast above the inlet known as Khaur al-Udaid; and, in the second instance, to begin on the southern coast of the Persian Gulf, two kilometres east of Bandar al-Mirfa, and to run south-westwards for a short distance, and then east and north to a point beyond the Buraimi Oasis.[1]

[1] For the exact definition of the frontier, see below, pp. 144–5, and Map 2 at end.

Introduction

Three states were directly affected by the Saudi claim: the Shaikhdom of Qatar, the Shaikhdom of Abu Dhabi, and the Sultanate of Muscat and Oman. The first of these states, Qatar, is a low, flat and arid peninsula projecting into the Gulf from the Arabian mainland. It has an area of about 8,000 square miles and a population of some 55,000. The capital, Dauhah, on the east coast, is a fishing village made prosperous overnight through the discovery of oil on the western side of the peninsula. The ruling family of the shaikhdom is the Al Thani, which came to power in the second half of the nineteenth century. The Saudi claim threatened Qatar with the loss of a belt of territory several miles deep, north of the *frontière de convenance*, which ran across the base of the peninsula, roughly from the head of the Bay of Salwah to the northern shore of Khaur al-Udaid.

Saudi Arabia's claim held far more serious implications for the Shaikhdom of Abu Dhabi. Abu Dhabi is one of six principalities lying along the southern coast of the Gulf, which, together with a seventh, Fujairah, facing the Gulf of Oman, make up the Trucial States or Trucial Oman. Four-fifths of Abu Dhabi's territory was embraced by the Saudi claim, including the Liwa Oasis, the ancestral home of the shaikhdom's ruling family, the Al Bu Falah section of the Bani Yas tribe. From Liwa the Bani Yas colonized Abu Dhabi Island in the eighteenth century, and the Al Bu Falah later made it their capital. The present Al Bu Falah ruler is Shaikh Shakhbut ibn Sultan, who succeeded to power in 1928. Abu Dhabi in the nineteenth century was a fairly important maritime state, while on land the authority of the Al Bu Falah shaikhs extended as far west as Khaur al-Udaid. They acquired a foothold in the Buraimi Oasis in the eighteen-twenties, and from the middle of the century onwards they controlled several of the settlements. The total area of the shaikhdom, the largest of the Trucial States, is about 25,000 square miles. The size of the population is unknown, but it may be 20,000. Revenues until recently were very small. Abu Dhabi, like the other Trucial Shaikhdoms, has suffered from the decline of the pearling industry, and its economy, until the recent discovery of oil deposits, both inland and off-shore, was dependent upon fishing, date cultivation and pastoral pursuits.

The implied inclusion of the Buraimi Oasis in the Saudi Government's claim—'implied' because the oasis was not specifically mentioned in the Note of 14 October 1949—affected also the Sultanate

Introduction

of Muscat and Oman, for the oasis lies on the Sultanate's frontier with Abu Dhabi and its sovereignty is divided between them. Muscat and Oman are ruled by the Al Bu Sa'id dynasty, which came to power in the middle of the eighteenth century. The present Sultan is Saiyid Sa'id ibn Taimur, who succeeded to the throne in 1932.

Until the accession of the Al Bu Sa'id, government in Oman had been theocratic, spiritual and temporal power being vested in an *imam*, elected by the tribes, most of whom were of the Ibadiya sect of Islam. The founder of the Al Bu Sa'id line, Ahmad ibn Sa'id, was elected Imam in 1749, but his successors, with one or two exceptions, repudiated the Imamate, thereby divesting political authority in Oman of its religious sanction, and ruled as secular lords with the title of 'saiyids', while by Europeans they were called 'sultans'. The Imamate fell into abeyance, and except for a brief interval in the nineteenth century it was not revived until 1913.

Through the enterprise of the Al Bu Sa'id Muscat became the leading maritime state of Arabia in the nineteenth century, and a great entrepôt of the trade of the Persian Gulf with India, Africa and the Red Sea. The Al Bu Sa'id's control of the East African coast from Dar es Salaam northwards, and their possession of the adjacent island of Zanzibar, also made them the great entrepreneurs of the Arab slave trade. In the latter half of the century a decline in their fortunes set in, brought about partly by the separation of Zanzibar from the Sultanate in 1861, and partly by the loss of revenue suffered through the abandonment of the slave trade between 1845 and 1873. The political consequences of this decline for the Al Bu Sa'id were serious: they lost the support of a number of the inland tribes, and in this century they were faced with the revival of the Imamate outside the Al Bu Sa'id line. Nowadays the revenues of the Sultanate are limited. The economy depends upon agriculture and fishing. In area the Sultanate is about 80,000 square miles, and its population is said to number perhaps half a million.

The Kingdom of Saudi Arabia, the protagonist in the frontier question, is the creation of the late King Abdul Aziz ibn Abdur Rahman Al Sa'ud, better known as King Ibn Sa'ud. Though its roots go back to the eighteenth century, and to a movement of religious reform which will be described later, the modern state of Saudi Arabia dates from 1902, when Ibn Sa'ud returned from exile in Kuwait to recover Riyadh, the capital of Najd and the home of the Al Sa'ud, from the rival dynasty of Ibn Rashid of Jabal Shammar,

Introduction

to the north, and to restore Saudi rule in Central Arabia. A decade later he dispossessed the Turks of the province of Hasa, on the Gulf coast, and at the close of the First World War he emerged as Sultan of Najd and Hasa. In the next few years he completely overthrew the Rashidis, annexed Jabal Shammar, and conquered the Hijaz. In 1927 he was accorded recognition as King of the Hijaz, Najd and its dependencies. He went on to extend his dominions to the southern edge of the Rub' al-Khali and to the borders of Yemen, and in 1932 he proclaimed himself King of Saudi Arabia. Today, the kingdom comprises nearly 1,000,000 square miles of territory. Its population, at the most conservative estimate, is 5,000,000. Its wealth from oil revenues is proverbial. It overshadows the other states of Arabia.

By asserting a territorial claim against Qatar and Abu Dhabi the Saudi Government created a situation in which Great Britain was legally bound to intervene. The seven Trucial Shaikhdoms—Abu Dhabi, Dubai, Sharjah, Ajman, Umm al-Qaiwain, Ras al-Khaima and Fujairah—stand in a special treaty relationship to the British Government by virtue of a series of agreements, entered into over the last century and a half and principally directed towards the suppression of piracy and the slave trade in the Gulf and adjacent waters, and the maintenance of peace and security at sea. The most important of these engagements, the Treaty of Maritime Peace in Perpetuity of 4 May 1853, bound the Trucial Shaikhs to observe a permanent truce at sea amongst themselves and empowered the British Government to watch over and enforce the truce. Later in the century the shaikhs agreed to entrust the conduct of their foreign relations to Britain, and not to alienate any portion of their territories to another power without British sanction. All of these obligations were accepted by the Al Thani Shaikhs of Qatar also in a treaty concluded on 3 November 1916.

A legal obligation, therefore, devolved upon the British Government to take note of Saudi Arabia's claim in 1949, and to act for the Shaikhs of Qatar and Abu Dhabi in any situation that might arise from that claim. There were, however, other considerations. Britain was responsible for maintaining the maritime peace of the Gulf along those stretches of the Abu Dhabi and Qatar coastlines which were claimed by Saudi Arabia. Oil companies, which were partly British in ownership, had concessionary agreements with these states

Introduction

and with the Sultanate of Muscat and Oman. Finally, there was almost a historical compulsion upon the British Government to uphold, as they had in the past, the integrity of these states against pretenders to their sovereignty, pretenders who, over the last century and a half, have included Persians, Turks, Egyptians and Saudis.

No comparable legal obligation existed towards the Sultanate of Muscat. On the other hand, Britain had maintained particularly friendly relations with the Sultanate since the late eighteenth century, when the reigning Sultan had allied himself with Britain in the war with France. Successive Al Bu Sa'id Sultans in the nineteenth century co-operated with the British Government in the suppression of piracy, the promotion of commerce, and the elimination of the slave trade from Arabian and African waters. In return, the Al Bu Sa'id had received the backing of the British Government in opposing their enemies abroad and in maintaining their rule in Oman. In 1891 the reigning Sultan gave an undertaking similar to those given by the Trucial Shaikhs not to alienate any portion of his territory to another power without British approval. It was only natural that the present Sultan, when confronted in 1949 with Saudi Arabia's territorial claim, should ask for and receive British support.

Britain rejected Saudi Arabia's claim late in 1949 and the two countries entered into negotiations to see whether some kind of reasonable compromise between the Saudi claim and those of the three littoral states might be achieved. The negotiations, carried on in Jeddah, London and Dammam from 1949 to 1952, proved fruitless, and in August of the latter year the Saudi Government attempted a forcible solution of the frontier problem by dispatching an armed force to seize a village in the Buraimi Oasis. This violation of Abu Dhabi and Muscat sovereignty was resisted by the rulers of those states and by the British authorities in the Gulf, and a blockade was later imposed upon the Saudi force. Negotiations on the frontier were eventually resumed by the British and Saudi Governments, and they culminated in an agreement on 30 July 1954 to submit the dispute to impartial arbitration by an international tribunal. The arbitration collapsed in September 1955, for reasons which will be explained later.[1] A month later the Shaikh of Abu Dhabi and the Sultan of Muscat, with British support, resumed direct control of the Buraimi Oasis. A frontier with Saudi Arabia, based upon an assessment of what seemed reasonable and legitimate in the claims of the

[1] See below, Chapter VI.

Introduction

contending parties, was declared by the British Government, and the Saudi Government were warned against making any unauthorized crossing of that line.

Efforts have been made by the two governments since 1955 to find an agreed solution of the frontier problem, both by direct negotiation and through the good offices of the Secretary-General of the United Nations, acting in his personal capacity. These efforts were impaired by the absence of normal diplomatic relations between Britain and Saudi Arabia from November 1956, when they were broken off by the Saudi Government as a protest against the Anglo-French intervention in Egypt, until January 1963. From their public pronouncements since 1955 the Saudi Government would not appear to have modified their territorial claim of 1949 in any way. Nor is there anything to indicate that the British Government have altered their opposition to that claim. The views of both governments on the question of the sovereignty of the region in dispute were set forth by them in memorials submitted to the arbitration tribunal in 1955. These memorials, and more particularly the United Kingdom memorial, have formed the basis of the present study. The information that they contain has been supplemented to a considerable extent with other material on the history of the disputed region and on the development of the frontier dispute since 1949. The nature and origin of this material is indicated in the Preface and at various places in the body of the work.

CHAPTER I

The Region in Dispute, its Economy and its Inhabitants

That part of Arabia which lies to the east of Qatar, between the southern shore of the Persian Gulf and the northern rim of the Rub' al-Khali, the Empty Quarter, is largely a depressing waste of sand dune, salt flat and gravel plain. It consists, broadly speaking, of a coastal tract with an off-shore chain of islands, and a desert hinterland. The islands begin off the coast of Qatar and end to the north-east of Abu Dhabi town, which itself stands on an island. The coastal tract, a succession of sand and gravel plains interspersed with *sabkhah*, or salt flat, runs from the foot of Qatar eastwards to Abu Dhabi, and then turns north-eastwards, extending to beyond Ras al-Khaima, the northernmost of the Trucial Shaikhdoms, where it is forced into the sea by the massive cliffs of the Musandam peninsula, which juts into the entrance to the Persian Gulf. The desert hinterland behind the coast is dominated by sand dunes, which grow more formidable in size as they approach the Rub' al-Khali. There are two fairly large oases in the region, Liwa, in the middle of the desert hinterland, and Buraimi, at its eastern edge, by the foothills of the western Hajar.

The Hajar Mountains of Oman run in a curve south-eastwards from the Musandam peninsula, along the easternmost edge of Arabia, to the Indian Ocean. Their inward slopes flatten out into a stony steppe that ends at the Rub' al-Khali. The Rub' al-Khali fills the bulk of Eastern Arabia from the coastal region in the north to the highlands of the Hadhramaut in the south and the steppes of Oman to the east. In its southern reaches it is a waterless expanse of sand. Its northern, and larger, portion is made up of towering sand hills and is known to the Baduin who frequent it as 'al-Ramlah' or

The Region in Dispute, its Economy and its Inhabitants

'al-Rimal'—'the sands'. A northward extension of the Rub' al-Khali, the Jafurah, thrusts up towards the Persian Gulf coast to the west of Qatar, its base lying roughly along a line from the Jabrin Oasis in the west to the Sabkhat Matti in the east, and its apex almost touching the Gulf coast north of Uqair.[1]

The region whose sovereignty is claimed *in toto* by Saudi Arabia and in varying proportions by the Shaikhdoms of Qatar and Abu Dhabi and the Sultanate of Muscat, commences in the west at the foot of the Qatar peninsula and extends eastwards between the Gulf coast and the Rub' al-Khali to the Buraimi Oasis.[2] For convenience it may be divided, as it was for the purposes of the arbitration in 1955, into the 'western areas', comprising the bulk of the disputed territory, and the Buraimi region, i.e. the Buraimi Oasis and its immediate vicinity.

The area at the base of Qatar is known as the Jiban (sing. *jaub*, a depression). It is made up, as its name suggests, of a series of depressions, running south-south-eastwards from the head of the Bay of Salwah. Major R. E. Cheesman, who in 1921 was the first European to visit it, and H. St. J. B. Philby, who explored it more thoroughly in 1932, both came to the conclusion that the Jiban had originally been an estuary of the sea, and that Qatar, at some time in its geological past, had been an island.[3] 'The desert plain runs out flat and uncompromisingly to the fringe of a chasm, whose intricate outline of low cliffs has evidently been fashioned from the sea in ancient times,' wrote Philby of his first sight of the Jiban after crossing the northern Jafurah from Hufuf.[4]

'... As I looked upon the cliffs of the valley and the great expanse of salt-flats that stretched out before and below us, I could not resist the conclusion that the broken, sinuous line of the former encircled an ancient estuary, while the latter could not but be an old floor of the sea, from which the waters had receded to their present line on either side of the Qatar promontory. That was surely once an island as Bahrain is today, for the salt plain (in parts actually lower than sea-level) runs right across its base from sea to sea.'[5]

---

[1] See Map 2 at end.
[2] A strip of the coast to the west of Abu Dhabi is not in dispute. For the exact limits of the opposing claims, see below, pp. 144–5, 153, and Map 2 at end.
[3] See Cheesman, *In Unknown Arabia*, London, 1926, p. 39, and Philby, *The Empty Quarter*, London, 1933, pp. 41 and 46–47.
[4] *Empty Quarter*, p. 41.
[5] Ibid., pp. 46–47.

The Region in Dispute, its Economy and its Inhabitants

The line of salt flat, or *sabkhah*, is not continuous but is broken in places by sand hills and rocky outcrops. North of the *sabkhah*, the high ground, which marks the beginning of Qatar proper, is easily discernible. In the west, just above Salwah Oasis, where the Saudi Government maintains a frontier post, rises the hump of Jabal Nakhsh, the southernmost point of the Jabal Dukhan, the low range of hills which runs down the western side of Qatar.

At the eastern foot of the peninsula, inland from Khaur al-Udaid, the land is broken and scored by wadis. Bertram Thomas, who passed through it after his great crossing of the Rub' al-Khali from Dhufar in 1931, described it as 'quarry-like country of extreme desolation'.[1] Near the coast the land flattens out into sand and gravel plains. The coastal region south of Khaur-al-Udaid, to a depth inland of about twenty miles, is called the Aqal. It is a rolling expanse of sand with several wells. To the east of it is a gravel plateau, rising gently from west to east, called the Mijan. The Mijan also contains a number of wells, which, like those of Aqal, are used by Bani Yas and Manasir tribesmen who graze their herds here or visit the coast in the winter to fish. The main camel route from Abu Dhabi to Qatar also passes this way.

On its eastern side the Mijan falls away in a sharp escarpment to the great salt plain known as the Sabkhat Matti. Thirty miles or more broad at the sea's edge, the Sabkhat Matti extends inland in long streaks for about sixty miles. Much of it is impassable, especially after rain, but across its southern arms there are a few tracks which can be used by camels and motor vehicles. The coastline at the foot of Qatar is deeply indented with *khaurs*, or inlets. The northernmost, Khaur al-Udaid, is traditionally regarded as marking the boundary between the Shaikhdoms of Qatar and Abu Dhabi. On its southern shore are the ruins of the settlement of Udaid, founded by Bani Yas from Abu Dhabi in the early nineteenth century and abandoned by them later in the century. Next to Khaur al-Udaid is a broad bay, Khaur al-Duwaihin, and further to the east, a smaller inlet, Dauhat al-Nakhlah. Beyond Dauhat al-Nakhlah is a shallow bay, Dauhat al-Sila', whose shoreline is formed in part by the Sabkhat Matti.[2]

South of the Mijan and west of the Sabkhat Matti, for a distance of forty to fifty miles are steppe, salt flat and rolling sand hills, with occasional wells. As Bertram Thomas saw it, 'The steppes were dusted with gravel of jasper and gypsum, pebbles of black, white, red

[1] *Arabia Felix*, London, 1932, p. 293.   [2] See Map 2 at end.

The Region in Dispute, its Economy and its Inhabitants

and green that shone in the sun; the northern salt plains were studded by innumerable small shells in an early stage of petrification; the gullies in the sand-hills were here and there bright green with *haram* [salt bush] scrub, or pink and white with patches of gypsum rubble. . . .'[1] This area, which Philby calls 'the lesser Jiban',[2] lies at the eastern end of the Jaub, the great depression that cuts across the Jafurah Desert from the Jabrin Oasis in the west and divides the sands of the Jafurah from those of the Rub' al-Khali to the south. At the southern edge of the lesser Jiban lies the well of Bunaiyan, on the fringe of the first ranges of high red sand hills which mark the beginning of al-Rimal and the Rub' al-Khali in general.[3] A line of wells stretches all the way westwards up the Jaub: they are, according to Philby,[4] 'a favourite line of tribal concentration in seasons of favourable rain-fall' for the Murrah tribe of the Rub' al-Khali. Major Cheesman was told by his Murri guide that Bir Aziz wells, which Philby places 'perhaps two days' journey or rather less south-west of Bunaiyan',[5] were considered to mark 'the boundary between the Jafura and Al Rimal deserts. They would also be used by Oman tribes raiding towards Jabrin and, of course, by the Jabrin raiders returning the call.'[6]

In February 1948, Wilfred Thesiger, the last of the great Arabian travellers, crossed the Jafurah from Jabrin and struck across the southern reaches of the Sabkhat Matti to enter the Dhafrah from the west.

'We decided we must make a detour and cross these salt-flats near their head, otherwise the camels might become inextricably bogged, especially after the recent heavy rain. They would only have to sink in as far as their knees to be lost. Camels are always bad on greasy surfaces, so we fastened knotted cords under their feet to stop them from slipping. Here the salt-flats were divided into three arms by crescent-patterned drifts of sterile white sand. The flats themselves were covered with a crust of dirty salt which threw up a glare into our faces and, even through half-closed eyes, stabbed deep into my skull. The camels broke through this crust and floundered forward through liquid black mud. It took us five unpleasant anxious hours to get across.

[1] *Arabia Felix*, p. 282. [2] *Empty Quarter*, p. 87. [3] See Map 2 at end.
[4] *Empty Quarter*, loc. cit. [5] Ibid. [6] *In Unknown Arabia*, p. 243.

The Region in Dispute, its Economy and its Inhabitants

'On the far side we camped among undulating, utterly lifeless white sands, where even the salt-bushes were dead and their stumps punctured our naked feet like needles. It was eleven days since we had left Jabrin. . . .

'Next morning, after travelling for twelve miles across flat white sands, we came to a succession of dune-chains, each of which, when approached from the west, showed up in turn as a wavy silver-blue wall, three to four feet high, running out of sight to north and south along the top of an orange-red slope a mile wide. Their farther sides fell away into a jumble of hollows. They gradually became larger and more complicated and developed into high but uniform dune-ranges and swelling downs, full of crescent-shaped hollows and deep potholes. The steeper sides of many of these hollows showed marks where water from the recent heavy rain had flowed down, and in some places the crust formed by the rain had been pitted by hailstones. Here we found grazing and noticed the tracks of hares, fennec foxes, honey badgers, and monitor lizards.'[1]

'Al-Dhafrah' is the name generally applied to the whole desert region to the east of the Sabkhat Matti, between the Gulf coast to the north and the Rub' al-Khali to the south. It is made up of several definable regions: the Taff, or coastal tract, in the north, the Bainunah in the west, Ramlat al-Hamra in the east, and between them, and extending southwards from the Taff to the Rub' al-Khali, a succession of districts called, in order, Saruq, Qufa, Bitanah, Liwa, Batin and Kidan.[2]

The Taff, which extends from the Sabkhat Matti eastwards to Abu Dhabi to a depth inland of about fifteen miles, is, for most of its length, low-lying and marshy. *Sabkhah* occurs frequently, and there are occasional limestone ridges. The waters off-shore are rendered hazardous to navigation by an intricacy of islands, shoals and reefs. Many of the islands are barren and waterless, while others have sufficient vegetation on them to make it worth while for tribesmen to bring sheep and camels across from the mainland for grazing. Some have rain-water tanks and are used throughout the year, particularly during the pearling season in the summer, by fishermen of the Rumaithat and Qubaisat sections of the Bani Yas. A few islands, like Dalma and Ghaghah, have stone buildings, and used to have, until the decline of the pearl trade, small settled populations. Now, only Dalma, where the Shaikh of Abu Dhabi maintains an *amir*, or

---

[1] *Arabian Sands*, London, 1959, pp. 241-2.   [2] See Map 2 at end.

The Region in Dispute, its Economy and its Inhabitants

local representative, is permanently inhabited. A century ago the more easterly islands were known as the East India Company's Islands, a name given them when the first survey of the Arabian coast was made in the early eighteen-twenties. The name seems now to have disappeared. Historically, the whole archipelago has been regarded as coming under the control of Abu Dhabi. Two of the islands, Sir Bani Yas and Yasat, are named after the principal tribe of the shaikhdom, the Bani Yas.

The western portion of the Taff, for a distance of about sixty-five miles eastwards from the Sabkhat Matti, is sometimes called the Taff-Bainunah, from the region lying immediately behind it. The Bainunah, the westernmost district of the Dhafrah, is an area of undulating sand dunes which extend inland for about forty miles.[1] It has a number of rather brackish wells and is used for winter grazing by the Baduin of the region. To the east of the Bainunah, in the central Dhafrah, the dunes are larger, and they increase in height as they recede from the coast. Between the coast and the Liwa Oasis, fifty miles to the south, are three separate belts of dune country, Saruq, Qufa and Bitanah. In the hollows of the dune chains here lie wells of sweet water and clumps of palm trees. To the south of Liwa, in the districts called Batin and Kidan, the dunes are even higher. Batin, or Batin-Liwa ('the hinterland of Liwa'), measures about thirty miles in depth. Its dunes are golden-yellow in colour with white salt flats running between them. Salt-bush, upon which camels can feed, grows freely on the dunes, but the wells of Batin are salt and the area is sparsely populated. Kidan, to the south of it, is the last stretch of the Dhafrah before the Rub' al-Khali. The dunes here are white or golden in colour, and they are easily distinguishable from the red sands of the Empty Quarter behind them.

Liwa Oasis is the very heart of the Dhafrah.[2] It stretches in an arc from south-west to south-east and measures from forty to fifty miles across. It consists of high white and golden dunes with small gravel depressions among them, in which lie wells of good water and groves of palm trees. Although the existence of Liwa was known to the outside world from the first half of the nineteenth century, no European had laid eyes upon the oasis until Wilfred Thesiger passed

---

[1] Some authorities hold that the Taff and Bainunah do not properly form part of the Dhafrah but are external to it.
[2] The form of the name is sometimes given as 'al-Jiwa', but the inhabitants call it 'al-Liwa'.

The Region in Dispute, its Economy and its Inhabitants

through it in 1948. Thesiger first arrived on the southern outskirts of Liwa in December 1946, after his remarkable secret crossing of the Rub' al-Khali from Mughshin. He did not think it wise at that time to venture any further north.

'Ibn Saud's tax-collectors were in Dhafara and the Rabadh, collecting tribute from the tribes; and there were Rashid, Awamir, Murra, and some Manahil to the north of us.

'We had to avoid all contact with Arabs other than the Rashid, and if possible even with them, so that news of my presence would not get about among the tribes, for I had no desire to be arrested by Ibn Saud's tax-collectors and taken off to explain my presence here to Ibn Jaluwi, the formidable Governor of the Hasa. Karab from the Hadhramaut had raided these sands the year before, so there was also a serious risk of our being mistaken for raiders, since the tracks of our camels would show that we had come from the southern steppes. . . . Hamad [a Rashidi shaikh] told me that Liwa belonged to the Al Bu Falah of Abu Dhabi. He said that they were still fighting Said bin Maktum of Dibai, and that, as there was a lot of raiding going on, the Arabs would be very much on the alert.'[1]

Fifteen months later, in March 1948, Thesiger again approached Liwa, this time, as has been seen, from Jabrin and the Jafurah, after his second crossing of the Empty Quarter by way of the western sands. He now had no hesitation about entering the oasis, but he could not linger there. '. . . Our camels were exhausted and we ourselves were worn out. Our food was nearly finished and it was difficult to buy anything here but dates.'[2] Passing rapidly through the centre of the oasis, Thesiger pressed on for the coast, and eventually reached Abu Dhabi.

The following October he was back on the Trucial Coast, and in November he was able to explore Liwa at leisure. He travelled the whole length of the oasis from east to west and counted fifty-two settlements.

'Most of them are inhabited by the Bani Yas, but the Manasir own the groves to the east of Tharwaniya which are however smaller

[1] *Arabian Sands*, p. 137. Cf. 'Across the Empty Quarter', *Geographical Journal*, CXI, 6–7. The Saudi tax-collectors were a small party under Ibn Shushan, who camped for a time at al-Aqaila in the Bainunah and collected taxes from some Manasir there. Ibn Shushan also sent collectors to Liwa, but they came back empty-handed.
[2] *Arabian Sands*, p. 243. See also, 'A Further Journey across the Empty Quarter', *Geog. Journ.*, CXIII, 21–46.

The Region in Dispute, its Economy and its Inhabitants

and less important than those to the west. These Arabs live in rectangular cabins built of palm fronds and placed for the sake of coolness on the downs above the palm groves. Two or three cabins are usually enclosed by a high fence and inhabited by a family. . . . Palms are planted along the salt flats, close under the high steep-sided dunes and in hollows in the sands, and the groves are fenced in. Other fences are built along the dune tops to control the movement of the sand, which in a few places has partly buried some of the trees. The palms are carefully spaced and evidently well tended and their dates are reputed to be of good quality. The water is fresh and found at depths of from 7 to 20 feet, the deepest wells providing the best water, but there is nowhere any cultivation other than that of the date palms, probably owing to the salt near the surface of the ground. The Liwa Arabs own some camels and a few donkeys and goats. . . . They all owe allegiance to the Abu Fallah shaikhs of Abu Dhabi.'[1]

Later estimates of the number of Liwa settlements, by the Assistant Political Agent, Trucial Oman, and by a Petroleum Development (Trucial Coast) survey party, placed them at forty-two.[2] Only thirteen are inhabited the year round: the rest are occupied in the summer for the date harvest but deserted in the winter. The more populous of the permanently inhabited villages are, from west to east, al-Mariyah al Gharbiyah, Qutuf, Kaiyyah, Mazaira'ah, Qarmidah, Shah and Sabkhah.[3] At the height of the date season the population of all the Liwa settlements is said to be anywhere between 619 and 755 families, or roughly 2,500–3,000 persons.[4]

Ten forts are scattered through the oasis, all of them in a dilapidated state or in ruins. Several were destroyed at the time of the Qatar-Abu Dhabi war in the eighteen-eighties. The population of Liwa is composed almost exclusively of Bani Yas and Manasir. They have lived amicably together for more than a century, tending their palm trees, grazing their herds in the nearby deserts, and fishing together off the coast and islands to the north. Intermarriage between them is frequent. Jurisdiction over Liwa is exercised by the Shaikh of Abu Dhabi, who maintains a *wali*, or governor, at Mariyah village.

[1] 'A Further Journey . . .', *Geog. Journ.*, CXIII, 39–40.
[2] For a comparison of these estimates, and that of a member of the Desert Locust Survey who visited Liwa in 1952, see *U.K. Memorial*, II, Annex E, no. 1.
[3] The remaining permanent settlements are Shidiq al-Kalb, Latir, Dhuwaihir, Dhafir, Mariyah and al-Yaif.
[4] See *U.K. Memorial*, loc. cit.

The Region in Dispute, its Economy and its Inhabitants

He is assisted by a *qadi*, or judge, and a *muzakki* who collects a levy from the Bani Yas on their dates.

East of Liwa is the Ramlat al-Hamra, the last district of the Dhafrah in the east. It is a country of broad, sandy plains, broken by salt flats, wide valleys and occasional hills. Sweet-water wells are numerous and the grazing is good. Ramlat al-Hamra terminates in the south near Umm al-Zamul, in the Rub' al-Khali, beyond which lie the notorious quicksands of Umm al-Samim ('the mother of poison') at the edge of the Oman steppes. On the north Ramlat al-Hamra merges with the Khatam, an ill-defined area which belongs neither to the coastal strip nor to the Dhafrah. Roughly wedge-shaped in outline, the Khatam consists of heavy sand dunes which extend northwards between Abu Dhabi town in the west and the Buraimi Oasis in the east, southwards to the Ramlat al-Hamra, and eastwards to the edge of the Dhahirah province of Oman. It abounds in wells of good water, and in the winter months it is thronged by tribesmen from the surrounding districts seeking pasturage for their herds.

The Buraimi Oasis lies in the plain of al-Jau at the northern edge of the Dhahirah, close by the foothills of the western Hajar, and roughly equidistant from Abu Dhabi in the west and Sauhar in the east. The oasis is more or less circular in outline and about six miles in diameter. For water it depends upon the run-off from the Hajar and from the Jabal Hafit, a solitary, batholithic pile rising out of the plain immediately to the southwards. The water is brought to the oasis in underground channels, or *aflaj*. One *falaj*, or channel, normally serves only one village, although it may run under another. There are nine villages or settlements—Buraimi, Sa'ara, Hamasa, al-Ain, Jimi, Hili, Qattarah, Mu'tiridh and Muwaiqi'.[1] Buraimi and Hamasa are inhabited principally by the Na'im tribe, Sa'ara by Na'im and a large number of Bani Jabir, Najadat and Dhawahir. All three villages come under the authority of the Sultan of Muscat. The other six are populated principally by Dhawahir, and to a lesser extent, by Bani Yas and other tribesmen. They are under the authority of the Ruler of Abu Dhabi. Attached to the villages are date plantations and gardens where fruit and cereals are grown.

Several forts or the ruins of forts dot the oasis. The most imposing of these is the Qasr al-Khandaq ('the castle of the moat') on the

---

[1] See Map 1. Buraimi and Sa'ara are sometimes lumped together as one village.

south side of Buraimi village. Built a century and a half ago by the early Wahhabi, or Saudi, invaders of Buraimi, it has been maintained in fair repair ever since. In the open ground before it, raised lines of earth and rubble mark the site of the former Qasr al-Sudairi, built by the Wahhabis at some time after 1853 and destroyed after their expulsion from the oasis in 1869. In the centre of Buraimi village stands the Qasr al-Hillah, formerly the residence of the paramount shaikh of the Na'im and now occupied by the Sultan of Muscat's *wali*. At the eastern end of al-Ain village stands a large fort erected by the Ruler of Abu Dhabi in 1897, and on the plain in front of it is the fort of Murabba'at al-Ain, built in 1950 by Shaikh Zaid ibn Sultan, brother of the present Ruler and his governor in the oasis. A few miles to the south of Buraimi, at the foot of Jabal Hafit, are the villages of Hafit and Qabil, whose politics and economics are closely bound up with those of Buraimi.

Buraimi Oasis serves as a centre of trade for the Baduin of the Khatam, Ramlat al-Hamra and upper Dhahirah. The oasis itself produces dates, fruits, vegetables and livestock, while in its markets are offered for sale rice, coffee, sugar, cloth and a variety of other goods brought in through the ports of the Trucial Coast, mainly Dubai, and to a lesser extent through Sauhar on the Gulf of Oman. Buraimi's economic importance, however, derives as much, if not more, from its situation as a centre of communication as from its size and fertility. It has long been regarded as the northern gateway to the Sultanate of Muscat and Oman, which extends eastwards from this point, along the mountain chain of the Hajar, to the Indian Ocean, and southwards, across the steppes of the Hamra Duru' and Jaddat Harasis, and the sand and gravel plains of the Huqf, to Dhufar on the southern coast of Arabia.

'On the Trucial Coast,' Thesiger noted on one of his visits to Buraimi, 'they talk of visiting Oman when referring to Buraimi, whereas in Buraimi, and indeed generally throughout this part of Arabia, Oman is used to mean the Jabal al Akhadar and the settled country lying to the west of it and to the south of Jabal Kaur. . . .'[1] Camel and motor-vehicle tracks lead into Buraimi from Abu Dhabi in the west and from Dubai, Sharjah, and the other towns of Trucial Oman from the north. A much-used track runs eastwards from Buraimi through the Wadi al-Jizzi, which cuts through the Hajar due east of the oasis, to Sauhar and the towns of the Batinah coast.

[1] 'Desert Borderlands of Oman', *Geog. Journ.*, CXVI, 168, n. 68.

The Region in Dispute, its Economy and its Inhabitants

There is no other practicable route across the Hajar for eighty miles to the southwards, so that communication between the upper Dhahirah and the Batinah, and eventually, Muscat, is normally maintained by way of Buraimi and the Wadi al-Jizzi, though for motor transport the longer but easier route through the Wadi al-Qaur, further north, is preferred. The tracks southwards from Buraimi run through towns like Dhank and Ibri, along the western flanks of the Hajar, and beyond them to Bahlah, Nizwa, and the other towns of inner Oman that lie in the shadow of the Jabal Akhdhar.

The population of the western areas and the Buraimi region is almost wholly tribal in organization. It may be divided, broadly speaking, into settled and nomadic. The settled population lives mainly in Abu Dhabi town and in the oases of Liwa and Buraimi. A few live on Dalma Island. No rigid line can be drawn, however, between sedentary and nomadic tribesmen. Most of them dwell for part of the year, usually the summer, in the oases, where they tend their palms and gather the date harvest, or on the coast and islands, where they engage in fishing and pearling. For the remainder of the year they roam the Dhafrah with their herds, their wanderings being subject to the state of the grazing. The territory over which a tribe habitually roams is known as its *dirah* or *dar*. In many parts of the Arabian peninsula a tribe's exclusive right to its *dirah* is recognized by all, and another tribe will wander into the area without permission at its peril. In the Dhafrah there are no such exclusive rights to *diyar*, or ranges, nor is there any exclusive ownership of wells. The two principal tribes, the Bani Yas and the Manasir, share the Dhafrah and its wells amicably, and they also allow elements of other tribes to graze their herds there.

Economically, the tribes of the region are self-sufficient, though their standard of living is a very meagre one. Liwa produces barely enough dates to meet the needs of its inhabitants, who must rely upon Abu Dhabi for other essentials. Abu Dhabi, in turn, depends upon Buraimi for fruit and dates. In the desert the pasturage for camels, sheep and goats is dependent upon a capricious rainfall. Although the waters of the Gulf still provide the people of the Trucial Shaikhdoms with fish, the pearling trade, which was once their principal means of buying necessities like rice, sugar, coffee and cloth from abroad, has fallen into decay. To some extent the loss from this

The Region in Dispute, its Economy and its Inhabitants

source has been made up by payments to the Trucial Shaikhs by oil companies for concessionary rights. For the tribes of the Dhafrah their natural outlets of trade are Abu Dhabi town and Dalma Island; for those of the Khatam and eastern Ramlat al-Hamra it is Buraimi. No trade is carried on with Saudi Arabia. The nearest Saudi commercial centres lie more than 300 miles to the west of Liwa and more than 400 miles from Buraimi. The unit of currency in the region is the Maria Theresa dollar or the Indian rupee, not the Saudi *riyal*.

The most numerous and ubiquitous tribe to be found in the disputed territory is the *Bani Yas*. They live mainly in Abu Dhabi town, in Liwa, in Buraimi, and on the coast and islands. Numbers of Bani Yas live also in the other Trucial Shaikhdoms, particularly Dubai and Sharjah. Others again are scattered throughout the Gulf and even as far away as the coast of East Africa. Although the Bani Yas are not a tribe in the sense that they can trace their descent from an eponymous ancestor, they have nevertheless been so closely welded together as a federation for at least three centuries that they can fairly be regarded today as a cohesive tribe. Their numbers were estimated in Lorimer's *Gazetteer of the Persian Gulf* in 1908 at 10,000–12,000, and the nomadic sections were described by him as 'one of the most compact and powerful tribes of Trucial 'Omān; their range is practically co-extensive with the territories of the Shaikh of Abu Dhabi, the basis of whose power they are'.[1]

Today the Bani Yas number about 8,000, of whom 1,700 are Baduin, mainly of the Mazari' section. All the nomadic Bani Yas roam the Dhafrah and adjacent areas. The Bani Yas comprise fourteen major sections and six minor. Eight of the major sections dwell wholly or mainly in the disputed region. They are: *Al Bu Falah, Hawamil, Maharibah, Mazari', Al Mishaghin, Qubaisat, Rawashid* and *Rumaithat*. The other six major sections are:

Al Bu Falasah, who constitute the ruling family of Dubai;
Al Bu Muhair, who live mainly in Dubai, Sharjah and Ras al-Khaima;
Sudan, who are distributed throughout Trucial Oman and Qatar, and who are sometimes regarded as a separate tribe; and
Al Murur, Qumzan and *Subais*, most of whom live at Dubai.

Elements of all six sections are found also in the disputed areas, at

[1] J. G. Lorimer, *Gazetteer of the Persian Gulf*, '*Omān and Central Arabia*, 2 vols., Calcutta, 1908–15, II, 1932.

The Region in Dispute, its Economy and its Inhabitants

Abu Dhabi, in the Liwa and Buraimi Oases, in the Khatam and Taff, and on the islands. The six minor Bani Yas sections are: *Al Bu Amin, Araifat, Duhailat, Halalmah, Khamarah* and *Thumairat*.

Al Bu Falah are the smallest, and at the same time the leading, section of the Bani Yas. It is to this section that the family which has ruled Abu Dhabi for the last two centuries belongs. Al Bu Falah are to be found at Liwa, Buraimi and Abu Dhabi town. The *Hawamil* and *Maharibah* dwell mainly at Liwa, where they own palm trees and herds of sheep and goats. A third of the Maharibah are Baduin who winter elsewhere in the Dhafrah. The *Mazari'* are the principal Baduin section of the Bani Yas.[1] During the summer months they are to be found at Liwa, where they own a good number of the date palms, or on the pearling banks. In the winter they roam the Dhafrah, and sometimes the base of the Qatar peninsula, with their herds. They have been known to go as far afield as Hasa in search of grazing. *Al Mishaghin* are a small, almost wholly Baduin, section, which frequents the Khatam and Taff. The *Qubaisat* and *Rumaithat* are the principal fishing and pearling sections of the Bani Yas. The majority of the Qubaisat have their homes at Liwa, where they own palms, sheep and goats. It was they who founded the settlement of Udaid, on the southern shore of the *khaur* of that name, in the early nineteenth century. The *Rumaithat* dwell in Abu Dhabi and on the islands off the coast. They are almost exclusively fishermen and pearlers, though a number of families spend the summer months at Buraimi. A similar life is led by the *Rawashid*, who live also in Abu Dhabi town and on the islands.[2]

Liwa Oasis is the ancestral home of the Bani Yas. They occupy twenty-four out of its forty-two settlements, including eleven of the thirteen permanent ones, mainly in the central portion of the oasis, and they share control of several of the others with the Manasir. At the height of the *gaidh*, or date harvest, there are said to be 1,500–1,800 Bani Yas in Liwa. Most of them, however, spend the greater part of the summer on the pearl banks, which stretch across the lower Gulf from the tip of the Qatar peninsula, in a great arc

---

[1] There are also Mazari' living in the mountains of the Musandam peninsula and others on the coast of East Africa. What connexion they may have with the Mazari' of the Dhafrah has not been determined.

[2] The Rawashid are confused by the authors of the *Saudi Memorial* of 1955 (I, Chapter III, para. 41) with the Rashid, or Rawashid, of Southern and Eastern Arabia. The *Memorial* also states erroneously (I, Chapter III, para. 51) that the Murur section are connected with the Murrah of the Rub' al-Khali.

The Region in Dispute, its Economy and its Inhabitants

southwards and eastwards to Dubai. The main pearling season, the *Ghaus al-Kabir*, or 'great diving', begins in April and lasts until early October.[1] Between a quarter and a third of the vessels and crews on the banks come from the Trucial Coast, the remainder from Qatar and Bahrain. No Saudi fishermen or vessels participate in the pearl fishery of the lower Gulf. There is no large settled population on the coast between Qatar and Abu Dhabi devoted wholly to fishing and pearling. The pearling fleets rely for their crews upon Baduin and others from the interior. In the case of the Bani Yas who own palms at Liwa, one or more male members of each family have to be left behind in the pearling season to harvest the dates. Where this is not possible, the tribesmen return from the banks in time for the *gaidh*.

The harvest over, most of the Bani Yas depart from Liwa. The camel-owning Baduin, mainly Mazari' and some Maharibah, make for the Taff, the Bainunah, the Ramlat al-Hamra, and sometimes Qatar and Hasa, to graze their herds. Other Bani Yas go fishing in the shallow waters off the coast, usually by trawling or by setting nets across the mouths of creeks. Most of the catch is dried and exported to Europe through Dubai. Some tribesmen find work in the winter months with one or another of the oil companies in the Gulf, usually Petroleum Development (T.C.) Ltd., the Qatar Petroleum Company, or the Arabian-American Oil Company (ARAMCO).

It is a commonplace in south-eastern Arabia that the Bani Yas of the disputed region look to the Al Bu Falah shaikhs as their rulers, and have done so for at least two centuries. This fact had never been challenged before Saudi Arabia put forward her frontier claim in 1949. The basis of that claim, as later enunciated by the Saudi Government, and more particularly in the memorial submitted by them to the arbitration tribunal in 1955, was the loyalty of the tribes of the region to Saudi Arabia and her historical title to it. Even then, however, the Saudi Government did not claim the allegiance of the bulk of the Bani Yas, but only that of the Mazari' section. On the other hand, they denied that the tribe as a whole were loyal to the Al Bu Falah. As set out in the *Saudi Memorial* of 1955, the claim to the allegiance of the Mazari' was made, not upon the basis of a historical connexion, but upon a statement by a Mazrui tribesman and a few instances of tax-collecting by Saudi officials among the Mazari'. None of this evidence, as will be seen later, is particularly

[1] Two shorter seasons, *Khanchiyah* and *Raddah*, respectively precede and follow the main season.

The Region in Dispute, its Economy and its Inhabitants

convincing. Even if it were more substantial, it could hardly outweigh the historical evidence or the testimony of competent modern observers, like Thesiger, to the effect that the Bani Yas, including the Mazari', have for generations borne unswerving allegiance to the Al Bu Falah.[1]

Next to the Bani Yas, the most important tribe dwelling in the western areas is the *Manasir*. No fewer than six Manasir tribes are known to exist in the Middle East: three are in Iraq, one in Jordan, one in Asir in western Arabia, and one in eastern Arabia.[2] None of them has any connexion today with any of the others. The Manasir of Eastern Arabia are distributed through Trucial Oman, Qatar and Saudi Arabia. No paramount shaikh wields authority over these widely dispersed elements, which, as a general rule, consider themselves subject to the ruler in whose territory they reside. Most of the Manasir of Trucial Oman live in the western areas in dispute. Others live in the Shaikhdoms of Dubai, Sharjah and Ras al-Khaima. In all, the Manasir of Trucial Oman and Qatar number about 4,000, of whom some 2,800 live in the disputed areas. These latter are made up of three principal sections, *Al Bu Mundhir*, *Al Bu Rahmah* and *Al Bu Sha'ar*, and two smaller sections, *Al Bu Khail* and *Al Bu Hamir*.[3]

Because they are essentially nomadic the Manasir's pattern of distribution alters constantly with the years. Generally speaking, it is determined by the annual cycle of winter grazing in the Dhafrah and summer harvesting of dates at Liwa, or pearling in the waters of the lower Gulf. It is an existence, in short, very similar to that of the nomadic or semi-settled Bani Yas, with whom the Manasir share the grazing of the Dhafrah, the palms of Liwa, and the pearls of the southern banks. Nor has it changed much in the last century and a half. A report on both tribes, prepared by a British political officer in the Gulf in 1818, says of them:

'They have small date groves dispersed among their sand hillocks, which yield a scanty supply of fruit, and amidst which they live during the summer, until their crop is consumed. In this season the

[1] For an examination of the submissions with respect to the Bani Yas in the *Saudi Memorial*, see below, Chapter VII.

[2] There are also Manasir in the Sudan.

[3] These last two are sometimes identified as part of the Bani Yas. (See, e.g., *Saudi Memorial*, I, Chapter III, para. 49.)

The Region in Dispute, its Economy and its Inhabitants

water is very brackish, and in the wintry months the shepherds ascend Lahsa [Hasa] and Qutar, to find pasture for their cattle.'[1]

Nowadays almost all the Al Bu Mundhir, Al Bu Rahmah and Al Bu Sha'ar in the western areas own palms and huts at Liwa. They inhabit thirty-six of the forty-two settlements in the oasis, eighteen of them exclusively. They also have palms in the Bitanah and Saruq to the north of Liwa, and in the Khatam, away to the north-east. Numbers of them go pearling with the Bani Yas in the summer, normally in Bani Yas boats, since few Manasir today possess their own vessels. Many of the pearl fishers return to Liwa in midsummer for the date harvest. Afterwards, the Manasir disperse to other parts of the western areas with their herds, leaving only a dozen families behind in the oasis. Before they leave they seal their wells to prevent other Baduin, particularly Awamir, from using them. The Al Bu Rahmah and Al Bu Sha'ar from the eastern settlements usually make for the Ramlat al-Hamra and the Khatam; the Al Bu Mundhir from the central and western settlements make for the Bainunah and Taff. Some Al Bu Mundhir, often accompanied by Al Bu Rahmah, travel to Qatar or Hasa in search of pasturage. More than half of the Al Bu Mundhir have migrated to Hasa in this century. Those who still own palms at Liwa visit them annually for the date harvest, while others may drift back into the Dhafrah at times for grazing. Their chief is Qirran ibn Mani', who has resided permanently in Hasa for many years. The principal shaikhs of the Al Bu Rahmah are Sa'id and Hamad ibn Mubarak and Nasir ibn Sa'id ibn Suwaid; and of the Al Bu Sha'ar, Muhammad and Rashid ibn Khadim.

The two smaller Manasir sections, Al Bu Khail and Al Bu Hamir, lead a slightly different existence from that of the other three. Only about two-thirds of the Al Bu Khail own palms—in Liwa, the Khatam and the Buraimi Oasis—and their main grazing ground is in the Khatam, west of Buraimi. They function as carriers, by camel, of people and goods from Abu Dhabi to Buraimi, particularly during the summer when numbers of families from Abu Dhabi seek relief from the oppressive heat of the coast in the groves and gardens of the oasis. Al Bu Hamir, who are smaller still in number—fifty families to the Al Bu Khail's 150—lead a largely nomadic existence

---

[1] [I.O.] *Selections from the Records of the Bombay Government, new series, no. 24: the Persian Gulf*, Bombay, 1856, p. 16, 'Brief Notes on Oman, Muskat, Bahrein . . .', by Capt. R. Taylor, Assistant Political Agent in Turkish Arabia.

The Region in Dispute, its Economy and its Inhabitants

in the Khatam and Ramlat al-Hamra. A few own palms in Buraimi. The principal shaikh of the Al Bu Khail is Amir ibn Mubarak, and of the Al Bu Hamir, Abdullah ibn Baruk.

In the late nineteen-forties the Saudi Government brought direct pressure to bear upon the Manasir living in the western areas to persuade them to pay taxes to Saudi *amils*, or collectors. Such *amils* had been visiting the Dhafrah at infrequent intervals since 1926 to gather taxes from tribesmen, mainly Manasir, who customarily spent part of the year in Hasa.[1] Their visits became more frequent after 1945, presumably because the *amils* were seeking evidence to support a future claim that the Saudi Government had exercised jurisdiction over the Manasir and over the western areas in general for some time past. As an inducement to the tribesmen to pay, the *amils* offered them *ikramiyah*, the traditional presents in return, of a value far in excess of the tax demanded. This *ikramiyah* was paid in the form of cash. Several of the Manasir, who as a whole are very poor, accepted the offer, but the majority rejected it on the grounds that their traditional loyalty lay to the Al Bu Falah Ruler of Abu Dhabi. The claim to the allegiance of the Manasir was eventually put forward by the Saudi Government at the Dammam Conference in 1952, and it was elaborated three years later in the *Memorial* presented by Saudi Arabia to the arbitration tribunal.

It depended almost wholly upon statements from tribal leaders and upon evidence of tax-collecting among the Manasir. The statements from the tribal leaders, who were four in number and came from the Al Bu Mundhir and Al Bu Rahmah sections, were supposed to relate to the question of allegiance. In fact, only two of them did so: the others referred to tax-collecting and camel-stealing. The evidence of tax-collecting hardly supported the large construction placed upon it, viz., that the Saudi Government have regularly collected tax from the Manasir of the disputed areas for the past forty to fifty years.[2] There is little doubt that the Al Bu Mundhir section is divided in its loyalty: that portion (more than half) which has lived mainly in Saudi Arabia for about forty years past looks to King Sa'ud as its ruler, while the remainder, who live primarily in the Dhafrah, look to the Al Bu Falah Ruler of Abu Dhabi, Shaikh Shakhbut ibn Sultan. Most of the Al Bu Rahmah and all of the Al Bu Sha'ar, Al Bu Khail

---
[1] For the origin of these visits, see below, pp. 115–21.
[2] For an examination of both the statements and the evidence of tax-collecting, see below, Chapter VII.

and Al Bu Hamir also follow Shaikh Shakhbut. The Al Bu Falah can point to a long and close association with the Manasir. So close was it in the early nineteenth century that the report made in 1818, cited earlier, speaks of the Bani Yas as being 'divided into three branches; one called Beniyas, another Manasir, and a third Owaimir [Awamir]'. Since that time the Manasir have consistently supported the Bani Yas and the Al Bu Falah shaikhs in their struggles with other tribes and rulers in Trucial Oman, and the Al Bu Falah, in turn, have been held responsible by the other Trucial Shaikhs for the conduct of the Manasir. Most recently, the Manasir, among other tribes, fought for the Al Bu Falah in their war with the neighbouring Trucial Shaikhdom of Dubai.

'The Abu Falah', Thesiger noted during a stay at Buraimi in 1948 with Shaikh Zaid, the brother of Shaikh Shakhbut, 'command considerable respect among the tribes. During their recent war against the richer Bin Maktum family of Dibai and the Bani Katab tribe, they could count on contingents from the Bani Yas, Manasir, Dhuwahir, Bu Shams, Na'im and Al Kathir to offset the mercenaries hired by their opponents.'[1] The Abu Dhabi-Dubai war lasted from 1945 to 1948, and the principal engagement took place in January 1948, when, as Thesiger records, 'a raiding party 300 strong from Dibai had fallen upon and exterminated a Manasir encampment on the edge of the Hamra sands, killing fifty-two of them and losing five themselves'.[2] The actual site of the engagement was Ruwaihah, and most of the Manasir killed were of the Al Bu Rahmah and Al Bu Sha'ar sections. Despite the fact that Ruwaihah lies in territory which Saudi Arabia, a year later, was to claim as hers, and despite the slaughter of tribesmen who were to be claimed, at the Dammam Conference in 1952, as Saudi subjects, the Saudi Government took not the slightest notice of the event at the time.

Elements of tribes other than the Bani Yas and Manasir are to be found from time to time in the western areas in dispute. They are for the most part Murrah, Manahil, Rashid or Awamir. None of these tribes, with the possible exception of the Awamir, can be regarded as permanently inhabiting the region. The *Murrah* are a powerful tribe that roams over large tracts of the Rub' al-Khali and

[1] 'A Further Journey across the Empty Quarter', *Geog. Journ.*, CXIII, 41.
[2] 'A Further Journey ...', *Geog. Journ.*, CXIII, 39.

The Region in Dispute, its Economy and its Inhabitants

the Jafurah. They may be classed today as a Saudi tribe, though for years they resisted the authority of Ibn Sa'ud. In times of good rainfall they used to visit the Dhafrah and the other western areas, but the grazing in the Dhafrah has been poor of late years and hardly any of them have been seen in the region since 1948. The *Manahil* originate in the Hadhramaut, where the majority of them still live. Some families have, in past years, drifted up into the Dhafrah for grazing, but hardly any have been seen there since 1948. Thesiger, on his way to Liwa in November 1948, came upon some Manahil who were returning from raiding Manasir in the oasis.[1] Most of these nomadic Manahil consider themselves Saudi in allegiance. The *Rashid* (Rawashid or Rashid Al Kathir) also have their homeland in southern Arabia, to the north of the Hadhramaut. Their numbers are small, only 300 men, according to Thesiger, who describes them as 'among the most authentic of the Bedu, the least affected by the outside world'.[2] They are said to know the Rub' al-Khali, especially in its central and eastern portions, better than any other tribe, and Rashidi guides accompanied Thesiger on both of his crossings of the sands. Some of them live in the central sands while others occasionally visit the Dhafrah, though few have been seen there in the last dozen years. Most of the Rashid have by now acknowledged the authority of Saudi Arabia.

'The *'Awamir* [writes Thesiger] came originally from the Hadhramaut where a portion of the tribe still inhabits the Quff oases. ... From there they spread eastwards as far as Oman and established a number of villages under Jabal al Akhdhar, which the tribe still holds. Some years ago the 'Awamir were the dominant power in the south-eastern sands. However, as security improved in the North with the extension of Ibn Sa'ud's influence over the powerful Murra tribe, many of them moved up into the Dhafara. . . .'[3]

The central or Baduin division of the Awamir has been on the move northwards from the Hadhramaut since the turn of the nineteenth century. The group that settled in Oman, mainly around Nizwa, in Oman proper, and on the Batinah Coast, has been there for at least a century. They number today about 3,000 souls and acknowledge one paramount shaikh, or *tamimah*, Khamis ibn

[1] 'Desert Borderlands of Oman', *Geog. Journ.*, CXVI, 141.
[2] *Arabian Sands*, p. 54.
[3] 'Desert Borderlands of Oman', *Geog. Journ.*, CXVI, 141. Philby, too, classes the Awamir as an Omani tribe. (See 'Britain and Arabia', *Nineteenth Century and After*, CXVII, 583.)

The Region in Dispute, its Economy and its Inhabitants

Rashid ibn Nasir, who resides at Qala, a few miles from Nizwa. The Baduin division of the Awamir is possibly 2,000–3,000 strong. It is highly unsettled and most erratic in its wanderings. Sometimes its members will seek grazing in the eastern Dhafrah or the Khatam, or even as far west as the Bainunah. Then they will disappear from these areas for several seasons, wandering back into Oman or southwards into the sands. In the summers they tend to concentrate in the vicinity of the Buraimi Oasis. A few Amiri families are usually to be found in Muwaiqi' settlement. Some of them go to Liwa for the date harvest.

A strong hostility has long existed between the Awamir and the Duru' of the Oman steppes. In 1942 it flared into open warfare after the Duru' had raided the Awamir south of Liwa. The *tamimah* of the Baduin Awamir, Salim ibn Hamad ibn Rakkadh, eventually withdrew from the fighting into Saudi Arabia, taking some of his tribesmen with him. When he returned in 1948, he found that the tribe had chosen a new *tamimah*, Salim ibn Musallim ibn Hamm. Ibn Rakkadh set out to recover the leadership of the tribe, and he succeeded to the extent of winning back some of his former followers. His frequent and prolonged absences in Saudi Arabia after 1948, however, alienated the bulk of the tribe, who refused to allow him to resume active leadership. The result was, as Thesiger reported in 1950, that the Baduin Awamir were divided in their loyalties. 'Salim bin Hamad [ibn Rakkadh] . . . has placed himself and a part of his tribe, mostly of Al Badr, under Ibn Saud. They live in Dhafara and the western sands. The 'Awamir living in northern Oman and in the Hamra sands follow Salim bin Ham and acknowledge the Al Bu Falah as their overlords.'[1]

The Awamir's connexion with the Al Bu Falah goes back to the early nineteenth century. At that time it was sufficiently close for them to be described as a branch of the Bani Yas. In 1848 they helped the Al Bu Falah to expel the Wahhabis from the Buraimi Oasis, and in 1889 they fought for the Al Bu Falah in their war with Qatar. Like the Manasir, the Awamir have for generations been regarded in Trucial Oman as being the responsibility of the Ruler of Abu Dhabi. When the tribe was left leaderless by the defection of Ibn Rakkadh during the war with the Duru', a number of its members sought out Shaikh Zaid ibn Sultan, the Ruler's brother, at Buraimi, and were advised by him to appoint Ibn Hamm *tamimah*. Ibn Hamm

---
[1] 'Desert Borderlands', *Geog. Journ.*, CXVI, 163, n. 15.

The Region in Dispute, its Economy and its Inhabitants

composed the quarrel with the Duru' by a series of annual truces from 1955 onwards, and a final settlement was reached in 1960 through the mediation of Zaid ibn Sultan. Ibn Rakkadh, through his frequent sojourns in Saudi Arabia, provided the Saudi Government with an excuse to advance a claim, in their memorial to the arbitration tribunal, to the allegiance of the Awamir. As with the Manasir, the claim was made on the grounds of declarations of allegiance and instances of tax-collecting. There was no reference to any historical connexion with the Al Sa'ud, presumably because there had been none. The declarations of allegiance were from Ibn Rakkadh and an Amiri tribesman. At the time of making his declaration, Ibn Rakkadh was receiving money from the Saudis. The signatory of the other declaration was a camel thief. The evidence of tax-collecting was wholly illusory.[1] Ibn Rakkadh has since returned to live with the tribe, thus healing the breach between its sections, and, outwardly at least, he professes loyalty to Zaid ibn Sultan.

Most of the permanent inhabitants of the Buraimi Oasis, who number about 6,000, belong to one or the other of two tribes, the *Dhawahir* and the *Na'im*. There is, in addition, a floating population of Baduin at all seasons of the year, but more particularly in the summer, when the oasis is thronged by hundreds of tribesmen from the surrounding deserts. The *Dhawahir*, who constitute the largest segment of the settled population, were probably among the original inhabitants of the oasis. Certainly their name (sing. Dhahiri) suggests a long connexion with the adjoining province of al-Dhahirah. They occupy five of the villages—Jimi, Hili, Qattarah, Mu'tiridh and al-Ain. Their tribal organization is complex and difficult to disentangle.[2] Their principal shaikhs are Sultan ibn Surur and Mani' ibn Muhammad of Mu'tiridh. The Dhawahir live primarily by the cultivation of their date groves and gardens, though a few own camels which they graze in the Khatam nearby.

Politically, the Dhawahir have been subservient to others for at least two centuries. In the eighteenth century the dominant position

[1] See below, pp. 221–2.
[2] The main sections seem to be: Daramikah, Al Ali ibn Sa'id, Kuwaitat Sharasharah, Hazazmah, Hawadith, Arrar, Mutawa'a, Sharainah, Matarish, Shabit and Masafirat. Sometimes the Najadat are reckoned to be part of the Dhawahir, but they were once a section of the Na'im. The Nuwasir, too, whose origin is unknown, are claimed to belong to the Dhawahir.

45

The Region in Dispute, its Economy and its Inhabitants

in the oasis was held by the Na'im, while for intervals from 1800 until 1869 both tribes were subject to the Wahhabis of Najd. In these years the Al Bu Falah of Abu Dhabi acquired land and other property in the oasis, and by the eighteen-forties they had come to exercise some sort of political control over the Dhawahir, usually by supporting them against their rivals, the Na'im. For a time, after the withdrawal of the Wahhabis in 1869, the Dhawahir may have enjoyed a restricted independence, but by the last decade of the century they had become fully subject to Zaid ibn Khalifah, the greatest of the Al Bu Falah rulers. Lorimer's *Gazetteer of the Persian Gulf* stated in 1908 that 'a regular tribute . . . is paid him by the Dhawahir who are numerically a majority in the oasis'.[1] From the turn of the century onwards the paramount shaikh of the Dhawahir, Ahmad ibn Muhammad ibn Hilal of Jimi village, served the Al Bu Falah Ruler as his *wali* in the oasis. On his death in 1936 a general power of superintendence over the headmen of the Dhahiri villages was vested by the present Ruler, Shaikh Shakhbut ibn Sultan, in the *wali* of al-Ain, Ibrahim ibn Othman. When he died in 1946 Shakhbut's brother, Zaid, became the Abu Dhabi governor in the oasis.

A great deal of property, in the form of date groves, gardens and houses, is owned in the Dhahiri villages by the Al Bu Falah. Most of the land in Hili and Qattarah is owned by them and they have holdings in Jimi, Mu'tiridh and al-Ain. All the land in the settlement of Muwaiqi', where Shaikh Zaid has his headquarters, and that at Mas'udi and Jahili, are owned by the ruling family.[2] Other Bani Yas, mainly Rawashid, Al Bu Muhair and Mazari', own various smallholdings in the villages, particularly in al-Ain, Qattarah and Muwaiqi'. A few families from other tribes also dwell in the Dhahiri villages: Awamir and Manasir (of the Al Bu Khail and Al Bu Hamir sections) in Muwaiqi', a handful of Omani tribesmen in Jimi.

During the time that the Saudis had a force in the oasis, i.e. from 1952 to 1955, they made repeated attempts to seduce the Dhawahir from their traditional allegiance to the Al Bu Falah. They met with some success: several of the Dhawahir took Saudi money and certain members of the shaikhly families, among them the grandsons of Ahmad ibn Hilal, the former Abu Dhabi *wali*, gave declarations of

---

[1] *Gazetteer*, II, 264.
[2] See Map 1. The principal landowners are Shaikhs Zaid, Hazza' and Khalid ibn Sultan, and Muhammad ibn Khalifah, who also owns the date groves at Ghail, to the south of Mu'tiridh.

The Region in Dispute, its Economy and its Inhabitants

allegiance to Saudi Arabia in return. These defections permitted the Saudi Government to claim the Dhawahir as adherents in their *Memorial* to the arbitration tribunal in 1955. The evidence presented in support of the claim, however, was very flimsy. They had not been able to secure declarations from the principal Dhahiri shaikhs, Sultan ibn Surur and Mani' ibn Muhammad, although, as the shaikhs themselves told the arbitration tribunal in September 1955, they had offered large sums of money in exchange.[1]

The *Na'im*, the second and politically more important tribe dwelling in the Buraimi Oasis, occupy the villages of Buraimi, Sa'ara and Hamasa. They have no connexion with the Na'im of Qatar and Bahrain, who broke away from the main body of the tribe long ago. There are Na'im in the Trucial Shaikhdoms of Ras al-Khaima, Sharjah and Ajman, and the present Ruler of Ajman is a first cousin of the former *tamimah* of the Na'im of Buraimi. Originally, the Na'im were composed of three main branches, *Al Bu Khuraiban, Khawatir* and *Al Bu Shamis*. In this century, however, as a consequence of the antipathy that has long existed between the Al Bu Khuraiban and the Khawatir, on the one hand, and the Al Bu Shamis, on the other, the Al Bu Shamis have acquired a separate tribal identity. The name 'Na'im' is usually reserved for the Al Bu Khuraiban and Khawatir alone, although there is no hard and fast rule on this score, and the Al Bu Shamis will often be grouped with the others under the heading of 'Na'im'. The *dirah* of the Na'im takes in part of the Khatam and stretches along the western flanks of the Hajar Mountains, from Buraimi to Dhank. Inside the oasis, the villages of Buraimi and Sa'ara belong to the Al Bu Khuraiban, Hamasa to the Al Bu Shamis. Together they number about 1,500 souls. Al Bu Khuraiban also live at Hafit, about eighteen miles to the south of Buraimi, which they share with the Khawatir.[2] The town of Dhank is divided between Al Bu Khuraiban and Al Bu Shamis. Al Bu Shamis are also settled in the defiles at the western end of the Wadi al-Jizzi, to the east of Buraimi. Both the Al Bu Khuraiban and Al Bu Shamis have Baduin elements. These are not true Baduin in the sense that they wander far afield in search of pasturage. Instead, they remain the year round in the vicinity of their settlements. The Baduin Al Bu Khuraiban wander near Hafit, the Baduin Al Bu Shamis, between al-Sunainah, about thirty miles to the southwards, Dhank and Qabil.

[1] See below, p. 189.
[2] The remainder of the Khawatir live at Ras al-Khaima on the coast.

The Region in Dispute, its Economy and its Inhabitants

Despite their separateness of identity, the Al Bu Shamis, Al Bu Khuraiban and Khawatir have customarily acknowledged the authority of a single *tamimah*. For generations he has invariably been the head of the Al Hamuda clan of the Al Bu Khuraiban of Buraimi village. The most recent *tamimah* was Saqr ibn Sultan, who decamped to Saudi Arabia late in 1955, after the expulsion of the Saudi police detachment from the oasis. With him went Rashid ibn Hamad, chief of the settled Al Bu Shamis of Hamasa and a fervent adherent of the Saudi cause.[1]

In the eighteenth century the Na'im would appear to have acknowledged, though somewhat distantly, the authority of the rulers of Oman. On the arrival of the first Wahhabi invaders in 1800 the tribe submitted to them, and in the next few years they adopted the Wahhabi practice of Islam. Throughout the period of the Wahhabi occupations of Buraimi (1800–69) they alternately bore with Wahhabi rule and rebelled against it. After the withdrawal of the Wahhabis, they were for a time their own masters, although they acknowledged the overlordship of the Sultan of Muscat and their *tamimah* acted as his representative in the region. Before the century was out the power of the Na'im in the Buraimi area had been circumscribed by that of Zaid ibn Khalifah of Abu Dhabi, and they thereafter stood in a position of dependence upon him until his death in 1909. After that date the *tamimah* recovered some of his former standing, and he received an allowance from the Sultan of Muscat in return for representing him in the area. Yet his influence never matched that of Ahmad ibn Hilal of the Dhawahir, the Abu Dhabi *wali*, and it was not until Ahmad's death in 1936 that the then *tamimah*, Saqr ibn Sultan, at last assumed a commanding position. A decade later direct Al Bu Falah authority was re-asserted in the oasis by Zaid ibn Sultan from which time Saqr again suffered a decline in influence.

Like the other Na'imi shaikhs, Saqr professed allegiance, though not of a particularly reliable variety, to the Sultan, Saiyid Sa'id ibn Taimur, in exchange for an annual allowance supplemented by

---

[1] The other principal shaikhs of the Na'im are:
Muhammad ibn Ali ibn Awwad of the Al Bu Khuraiban of Hafit;
Ahmad ibn Muhammad al-Salf of the Khawatir of Hafit;
Muhammad ibn Salimin ibn Rahmah of the Baduin Al Bu Shamis of al-Sunainah; and
Matar ibn Salim al-Azizi, Hamad ibn Ahmad al-Yahyayi, and Hamad ibn Salim al-Wahshi of the Al Bu Shamis of Dhank.

The Region in Dispute, its Economy and its Inhabitants

presents on his visits to the capital. In 1948 he and Rashid ibn Hamad, the Al Bu Shamis chief of Hamasa, joined with the other shaikhs of the Buraimi region in re-affirming their allegiance to the Sultan in writing, in the presence of the Sultan's Minister of the Interior. Saqr was confirmed in his position as *tamimah*, and the shaikhs all swore that they would communicate with the Sultan only through him. A year later Saudi Arabia put forward her claim to the disputed region, and Rashid ibn Hamad began intriguing with the Saudis to give the claim some substance. It was he who guided the Saudi force into Buraimi in August 1952, and for the next three years he acted as the Saudis' chief agent for suborning the shaikhs of the Buraimi region. Saqr ibn Sultan withstood the pressure from the Saudis for two years before he, too, yielded to their inducements in the late summer of 1954.[1]

It is hardly surprising that the Saudi Government put forward, in their *Memorial* of 1955, a claim to the allegiance of the Na'im. It was supported by declarations of loyalty from Saqr ibn Sultan, Rashid ibn Hamad and several minor Na'imi shaikhs. The statements of the last were of no significance because the signatories lived outside the areas subject to arbitration. The *Memorial* also claimed the oasis for Saudi Arabia on the grounds of past occupation. The obstacle presented by the fact that the last Saudi occupation had ceased in 1869 was overcome by asserting that there had been no *animus reliquendi* on the part of the Saudi Government. The Na'im, it was said, had been Saudi subjects ever since the initial Saudi conquest of Buraimi at the close of the eighteenth century, they had remained steadfast in their loyalty after 1869, and they had held the oasis in trust for the Saudis until they resumed direct control of it in 1952.[2] The argument overlooked the fact that only the central portion of the oasis was occupied by the Na'im, the remainder being inhabited by the Dhawahir, who were subject to the Al Bu Falah.

Although they had less apparent reason for doing so, the Saudi Government also asserted a claim on historical grounds to the Dhafrah and the other western areas.

'... The Saudi State originally acquired sovereignty over the territories here in dispute prior to the year 1800; and ... since that time it has manifested over them an authority sufficiently effective and continuous ... to maintain its rights in full vigor.'[3]

---

[1] For these events, see below, Chapters V and VI.
[2] See, e.g., *Saudi Memorial*, I, Chapter IV, paras. 240, 248 and 342.
[3] *Saudi Memorial*, I, Chapter VI, para. 21.

The Region in Dispute, its Economy and its Inhabitants

'From 1795 to 1873, with three scattered exceptions all prior to 1849, a Saudi governor held Buraimi. . . . For approximately the same period a colleague held Hofuf and the province of Hasa. Between the two of them, they held for their master in Najd the whole expanse of territory—including all the "western areas" of the present proceeding—which separated their respective headquarters.'[1]

Obviously, the history of the region holds the key to much of what is involved in the present frontier dispute, and it is necessary, therefore, to go back to the first penetration of the region by the Saudis, *c.* 1800, in order to be able to determine whether their claim of 1949 has any historical justification.

[1] *Saudi Memorial,* I, Chapter VI, para. 23.

CHAPTER II

The Wahhabi Period, 1800–1869

Little is known of the history of the western areas in dispute before the seventeenth century. The region is sometimes classified, under the name *al-Gharbiyah*, as the westernmost of the provinces into which Oman is traditionally divided. It is more usual, however, to consider Oman as ending at the province of *al-Shamal* ('the northern'), i.e. the present-day Trucial Coast. An Omani chronicle, *Kashf al-Ghummah* ('The Dispeller of Grief') makes mention of the Bani Yas tribe as holding sway in the Dhafrah in the early seventeenth century.[1] A century later, according to the same source, their power extended eastwards to the edge of the Dhahirah province of Oman. The chronicle records that, shortly before his election in 1724, the Imam of Oman, Muhammad ibn Nasir, 'went to el-Dhâhireh and collected a numerous force there, with which he marched westwards. . . . Passing through the districts of el-Na'im, he collected men from that tribe and the Benú-Yas. . . .'[2]

The Bani Yas at this time dwelt mainly in the Liwa Oasis, where they tended their palms and grazed their herds in the adjacent deserts, journeying frequently to the coast and islands for fishing and pearling. About 1761 they discovered water on Abu Dhabi Island, which then became their principal seat, although the ruling Al Bu Falah shaikh, Dhiyab ibn Isa, continued to reside at Liwa until his death in 1793. His successor, Shakhbut ibn Dhiyab, soon afterwards made Abu Dhabi the capital of the shaikhdom. The way

[1] The *Kashf al-Ghummah*, by Shaikh Sirhan ibn Sa'id, was translated by Lieut.-Col. E. C. Ross and published under the title of 'Annals of Oman' in the *Journal of the Asiatic Society of Bengal*, Vol. XLIII, in 1874. It traces the history of Oman from earliest times to A.D. 1728. The reference to the Bani Yas is on pp. 162–3.

[2] 'Annals of Oman', *Journ. As. Soc. Bengal*, XLIII, 177–8.

The Wahhabi Period, 1800–1869

of life of the Bani Yas a couple of decades later was described in the report by the British Assistant Political Agent in Turkish Arabia (present day Iraq) in 1818, already mentioned, as follows:

'The Beniyas are a pastoral clan, of the province of Oman. They inhabit a part of its northernmost district, called Sir, which is of a very sandy, barren soil. It is divided into three branches: one called Beniyas, another Manasir, and a third Owaimir [Awamir]. Those who dwell in the interior possess camels of the finest breed; while those on the coast have boats of a light construction, each carrying four persons, and equipped for fishing; the produce of which is taken to the town of Lahsa [Hasa] for sale.... They have small date groves dispersed among their sand hillocks, which yield a scanty supply of fruit, and amidst which they live during the summer, until their crop is consumed. In this season, the water is very brackish, and in the wintry months the shepherds ascend Lahsa and Qutar, to find pasture for their cattle.'[1]

The Buraimi Oasis was inhabited by Omani tribes long before the *hijira*. At the close of the eighteenth century its principal inhabitants were, as they are today, the Na'im and the Dhawahir. Both tribes were involved in the political life of Oman, the Na'im as a member of the Ghafiri faction, the Dhawahir as a member of the opposing Hinawi faction. The Hinawi-Ghafiri schism, which still endures today, probably goes back to the original settlement of the country between the ninth century B.C. and the sixth century A.D. The Hinawi tribes, in general, are identifiable with the earlier Qahtani, or Yemeni, tribes from south-western Arabia, the Ghafiri with the later Nizari tribes from the north. The epithets 'Hinawi' and 'Ghafiri', however, are of more recent origin, dating from the early eighteenth century, when a struggle between the *tamimahs* of the Bani Hina and Bani Ghafir tribes for the succession to the Imamate of Oman developed into a civil war, which eventually enlisted into the opposing camps nearly every tribe in the country.

Oman had for centuries been ruled as a virtual theocracy. Half, at least, of the tribes were of the Ibadiya sect of Islam, and were accustomed to elect, from among their leading *tamimahs*, an Imam, who was vested with both spiritual and temporal authority over the tribes. When the contest for the Imamate between the *tamimahs* of the Bani Hina and the Bani Ghafir broke out, most of the Ibadi tribes rallied to the former's support, most of the Sunni, or orthodox

[1] [I.O.] *Bombay Selections, XXIV*, p. 16.

The Wahhabi Period, 1800–1869

Muslim, tribes to the latter's. The war dragged on until 1737, when the Ghafiris called upon Nadir Shah of Persia for aid. He gave it readily, and before long a Persian army had made itself master of most of the country. The Persians soon made it clear that they had come to stay, and they were not evicted until 1744, when Ahmad ibn Sa'id, the governor of Sauhar on the Batinah Coast, drove them out of Muscat. Five years later Ahmad was elected Imam of Oman, and with his accession began the reign of the Al Bu Sa'id dynasty, which has continued to the present day.[1]

According to the Omani chronicler, Salil ibn Razik, the Imam Ahmad ibn Sa'id's power 'extended from the end of Ja'alan as far as Tawwam'[2]—the ancient name for the Buraimi Oasis. Up to the time of his death in 1783, however, Ahmad does not appear to have maintained a *wali* in the oasis, although his predecessors, the Ya'ariba Imams of Oman, had done so in the seventeenth century.[3] Ahmad's son, Sultan, who came to power in 1792–3, later subdued the Na'im and ruled the Dhahirah through his relative, the *tamimah* of the Bani Jabir, the most powerful of the Ghafiri tribes.[4]

In the year 1800 the Wahhabis, as the Saudis were then known, made their first appearance east of the Jafurah Desert. The Wahhabis took their name from Muhammad ibn Abdul Wahhab, an eighteenth-century religious reformer in Central Arabia. His efforts to persuade his fellow countrymen to return to a strict observance of the fundamental principles of Islam captured the sympathy of the Al Sa'ud shaikhs of Dara'iya in Najd. With their backing, Ibn Abdul Wahhab's doctrines steadily gained acceptance in Najd until, by the last quarter of the century, the tribes had been welded together, under the leadership of the Al Sa'ud—whose ruling shaikh had now

---

[1] As mentioned earlier (p. 21), none of Ahmad's successors, with the exception of his son, Sa'id, who exercised his temporal power for only a year, and Azzan ibn Qais, a later member of the cadet branch of the family, ever aspired to the office of Imam. Most Europeans persisted, however, until well into the nineteenth century, in calling the ruler of Muscat, 'Imam'. For Azzan ibn Qais, see below, pp. 86–89.

[2] Salil ibn Razik's chronicle, which covers the history of Oman to 1856, was translated and edited by the Rev. G. P. Badger, and published under the title of *The Imâms and Seyyids of 'Omân* (London: Hakluyt Society, 1871). There is reason to believe that the earlier part of the work contains much of the *Kashf al-Ghummah*. The quotation is from p. 166.

[3] See 'Annals of Oman', *Journ. As. Soc. Bengal*, XLIII, 162.

[4] Col. S. B. Miles, 'Biographical Sketch of the Life of Seyyid Sultan bin el Imam Ahmad', *Persian Gulf Residency Annual Administration Report, 1887–88*, pp. 23 and 25.

The Wahhabi Period, 1800–1869

become Imam of the new movement—in a religio-military confederacy, the principal objects of which were proselytism and plunder. The combined success of Ibn Abdul Wahhab's preaching and the Al Sa'ud's political leadership has been explained by the leading European apologist of the Wahhabi movement in our day in these terms:

'The innate fanaticism of a desert people could be stirred under the influence of a great idea to galvanise its dissident elements into common action in a common cause, and . . . such a cause could be maintained so long as the great idea remained actively operative and the fanaticism was kept at white heat.'[1]

In the case of Wahhabism the fuel required was 'constant aggression and expansion at the expense of those who do not share the great idea'.[2] A similar judgement was rendered by an acute observer of Arabian politics in the last century:

'Wahhâbeeism, in fact, apart from certain speculative notions respecting the Supreme Being,—in the main perfectly in accordance with the theology of the Kurân,—may be defined as a politico-religious confederacy, which legalises the indiscriminate plunder and thraldom of all peoples beyond its own pale. This . . . is fully borne out by the intolerant proceedings of its adherents, not only in Nejd, but wherever they succeeded in establishing their ascendancy.'[3]

By the close of the eighteenth century the Wahhabis had spread beyond the confines of Najd and absorbed the province of Hasa, lying along the Gulf coast. In the next few years they swept northwards into Turkish Iraq, where in 1801 they perpetrated the frightful sack and massacre of Karbala, westwards into the Hijaz, where in 1803 they terrorized Mecca for several weeks and two years later occupied the city, and south-eastwards into Oman and the Pirate Coast, as the Trucial Coast was then called. Buraimi was seized in the spring of 1800 by a force of 700 cavalry and camel-riders under the command of the Wahhabi general, al-Hariq. Control of the forts in the oasis was quickly wrested from their occupants, the Na'im and Dhawahir, and al-Hariq proceeded to erect a new fort, the Qasr al-Subarah, in the middle of the oasis. For the next eighteen years Buraimi was to serve the Wahhabis as a base from which to plunder Oman and to exact tribute from the Al Bu Sa'id Sultans.

Two circumstances, aside from the preponderance of force that they were able to bring to bear upon Oman at certain periods, were

[1] H. St. J. B. Philby, *Arabia*, London, 1930, p. 181.   [2] Ibid.
[3] Badger, *Imâms and Seyyids of 'Omân*, p. lxv.

The Wahhabi Period, 1800-1869

in large measure responsible for the Wahhabis' retaining their hold on Buraimi for this period. One was the appeal made by Wahhabi doctrine, with its emphasis upon sectarian intolerance and its implied licence to plunder, to the more predatory and lawless tribes of northern Oman. The other was the Wahhabis' skilful exploitation of the religious and political differences that divided the tribes of the region, notably the antagonism between Ibadi and Sunni and the rivalry of the Hinawi and Ghafiri factions. The Na'im of Buraimi, a Sunni and Ghafiri tribe, readily became adherents of what has been termed, in a somewhat inflated metaphor, 'the Arabian Reformation'. Other eager, if not particularly devout, converts to the Wahhabi movement were the Qawasim of Sharjah and Ras al-Khaima. A Sunni and Ghafiri tribe, the Qawasim were bitter enemies of the Ibadi Al Bu Sa'id rulers of Oman, who had several times chastised them severely for raiding across the neck of the Oman promontory. They were also given to savage acts of piracy at sea which had caused European mariners to name the southern shore of the Gulf the 'Pirate Coast'. Under the spur of their new-found religious ardour the Qawasim embarked upon a systematic campaign of piracy after 1808, which had as its prime object the enrichment of themselves and their masters, the Al Sa'ud of Dara'iya, and, as its secondary purpose, the destruction of the maritime strength of the Sultan of Muscat.

Because of the preoccupation of the Wahhabi Amir with the Hijaz in the years after 1803 Oman did not feel the full weight of Wahhabi power until 1808. Towards the close of that year a new *naib* or lieutenant, Mutlaq al-Mutairi, was sent to take charge of the outpost at Buraimi with a strong reinforcement of troops. His coming, according to the historian of the Ibadiya, Abdullah ibn Humaid al-Salimi, 'was a long and bitter punishment and a great calamity. Shaikh Nasir ibn Abi Nabhan recorded that he made it lawful to shed the blood of the Muslims [i.e. the Ibadiya], claiming that they were polytheists and calling upon the people to accept his doctrines. He records also that anybody who did not accept Wahhabism, their women and children were sent into captivity and their property was plundered. Another annalist puts it on record that true Muslims were treated as polytheists and made to pay the *jizyah* [poll tax] and the *kharaj* [land tax].'[1]

[1] *Tuhfat al-Ayyan fi Sirat Ahl Oman*, 2 vols., Cairo, 1928-31, II, 187. The author of this work, whose title may be translated as 'The Treasures of the Elders about the History of the People of Oman', was one of the prime movers in the revival of the Ibadi Imamate in the early years of this century.

The Wahhabi Period, 1800–1869

By far the worst visitation suffered by Oman during the years that Mutlaq al-Mutairi was at Buraimi was a raid organized by three sons of the Wahhabi Amir in 1812. Travelling from Hasa by sea—the route through the Dhafrah being rendered unsafe by the hostility of the Bani Yas—they landed at Ajman, on the Pirate Coast, and made their way inland to Buraimi accompanied by the Na'imi Shaikh of Ajman. Their arrival in the oasis, according to the Omani chronicler, Salil ibn Razik, was not welcomed by the inhabitants:

'They [the Amir's sons] then assaulted the fort and afterwards encamped in the surrounding open country. During the night the el-Khadrâ [settled population] surprised them, killing many of the followers of Tûrky and Faisal [the Amir's sons] who thereupon took to flight.'[1]

After extricating themselves from this awkward situation, the Amir's sons, in company with Mutlaq al-Mutairi and a mixed force of tribesmen, struck at the towns of the Batinah Coast, looting, burning and killing as they went. They did not stop until they had laid waste eastern Oman as far as Ras al-Hadd.[2] They then returned to Najd with their booty and Mutlaq al-Mutairi followed them shortly afterwards.

A new *naib*, Abdul Aziz ibn Ghardaqah, was ordered to Buraimi at the close of 1812 to take his place. He and the force accompanying him had scarcely crossed the Dhafrah when they were attacked by the Bani Yas and their allies. Two hundred were slain in the battle, including Ibn Ghardaqah himself.[3] Mutlaq was ordered back to Buraimi to re-establish the Wahhabi position, but his days in Oman were numbered. Salil ibn Razik relates:

'When Mútlaq reached el-Bereimy he found that most of the Arabs and Hadhr were opposed to him, chiefly owing to the large demands which had already been made upon them for wars and

---

[1] *Imâms and Seyyids*, p. 318. The authors of the *Saudi Memorial*, in their account of this episode (Vol. I, Chapter IV, para. 54), derived from the same source, make no mention of the attack and render the above passage as, 'Upon their arrival allegiance was sworn to them by Al Bu Shamis, by other members of the tribe of Nu'aim, and by Bani Ka'b.'

[2] See *Imâms and Seyyids*, pp. 312–20. The nineteenth-century manuscript history of the Al Sa'ud by Othman ibn Bishr, *Unwan al-Majid fi Tarikh Najd* ('The Title of Glory: the History of Najd'), which covers the history of the dynasty up to 1851, also contains a description of the devastation wrought by the Amir's sons (see Vol. I, pp. 152–3). Ibn Bishr says that the expedition was wholly unauthorized by the Amir (loc. cit.).

[3] Ibn Bishr, I, 154, and *Imâms and Seyyids*, p. 325. Salil ibn Razik calls him 'Ibn Azdakah'.

The Wahhabi Period, 1800–1869

invasions; hence the wealthy among them pleaded poverty, and the brave feigned cowardice. However, he persevered in coaxing and plying them on their weak side until they yielded. . . .'[1]

Some time later, in 1813, while on his way to raid the Sharqiyah, the eastern province of Oman, Mutlaq was ambushed by Al Hajariyin tribesmen and slain.

Early in 1819 the Wahhabi occupation of Buraimi came to an end. Mehemet Ali Pasha of Egypt, on the orders of the Ottoman Sultan, had launched a campaign against the Wahhabis in 1811, to drive them from the Hijaz and the Holy Cities of Mecca and Madinah. Seven years later, in September 1818, his son, Ibrahim Pasha, stormed and took Dara'iya, the Wahhabi capital, razed it to the ground, and sent the Amir Abdullah ibn Sa'ud a captive to Constantinople, where he was beheaded. On the fall of Dara'iya the commander of the Wahhabi garrison at Buraimi, Battal al-Mutairi, the brother of Mutlaq, found himself beset, on the one side, by the forces of his former associates, the Shaikhs of Sharjah and Ajman on the Pirate Coast, and, on the other, by those of the Sultan of Muscat, Sa'id ibn Sultan. According to a contemporary report, 'Buttal followed the more prudent measure of surrendering to the Imaum [of Muscat]; and the Chiefs of the district of Brimee [Buraimi] have sworn allegiance to the Imaum whose officer now retains possession of the place.'[2] Battal was taken into the Sultan's service and the following year he repaid the debt by saving the Sultan's life on a joint British-Omani expedition against the Bani Bu Ali of Ja'alan, Wahhabi proselytes. Buraimi was meanwhile garrisoned by a force from Muscat.

The British had been interested in the Persian Gulf since the early seventeenth century, when the East India Company began trading with Persia. In the next century and a half they successively broke the Portuguese monopoly of the Gulf's commerce, established factories at Bandar Abbas, Basra and Bushire, and resisted French and Dutch

---

[1] *Imâms and Seyyids*, p. 326.
[2] [I.O.] Bombay Secret Proceedings, Vol. 41, Consultation of 21 July 1819, Capt. G. F. Sadlier to Gov.-in-Co., Bombay, 15 May 1819. See also, G. F. Sadlier, *Diary of a Journey across Arabia*, Bombay, 1866, p. 8. Sadlier, the first European to cross Arabia from east to west, was at Muscat on his way to Hasa and Najd, on a mission to Ibrahim Pasha, when Battal arrived from Buraimi.

The Wahhabi Period, 1800–1869

attempts to evict them from the area. By the close of the eighteenth century, however, the Company's trade with Persia and Turkish Arabia had fallen away to such an extent that the Company was considering withdrawing its factories from the Gulf altogether. At this juncture the purely commercial interest in the Gulf was replaced by new political and strategic considerations. The French occupation of Egypt in the summer of 1798 awakened in the Company's government in India fears of a French attack upon their Indian possessions by way of the Gulf and Persia. A treaty was quickly concluded with Saiyid Sultan ibn Ahmad of Muscat in October 1798, and renewed in 1800, by which he engaged not to give any aid to the French. A treaty of alliance against the French was also concluded with the Shah of Persia in 1801.

By 1810 the French threat in the East had vanished, but a new problem confronted the British Indian authorities in the Gulf, that of Qasimi piracy. Indian and European shipping alike had suffered from the Qawasim's depredations after 1808, and even the Company's armed cruisers were not immune from attack by their dhows. At the close of 1809 the Government of Bombay dispatched an expedition to the Pirate Coast to destroy the Qasimi war fleet. The expedition's commander was also instructed to render what aid he could to the Sultan of Muscat to save Oman from conquest by the Wahhabis, and to prevent Muscat and its maritime resources from being converted to piratical purposes. At Shinas, on the coast of the Gulf of Oman, at the beginning of 1810, the British had their first brush with the Wahhabis when they stormed and took a fort, seized earlier by the Qawasim, with Wahhabi backing, as a preliminary to a descent on the Batinah Coast.

Though it received a setback from the expedition of 1809–10, Qasimi piracy was not crushed, and by 1816 it had broken out anew with even greater ferocity. A second expedition was sent against the principal Qasimi port of Ras al-Khaima late in 1819, after the collapse of Wahhabi power in Eastern Arabia. At the close of the expedition in 1820 the Qawasim, and their allies on the Pirate Coast, were made to sign a treaty in which they agreed to forswear piracy for ever, and to co-operate with the British Government in India in suppressing it in the Gulf. The Shaikhs of Abu Dhabi and Bahrain, though not considered piratical by the British, were also admitted to the treaty at their own request. The Company's Resident at Bushire, on the Persian coast, was entrusted with the responsibility

The Wahhabi Period, 1800–1869

of enforcing the treaty, and his title was later changed to that of 'Political Resident in the Persian Gulf'.

Under the treaty the Shaikh of Abu Dhabi was held responsible for the coast from Dubai westwards to Qatar, and on several occasions after 1820 he was brought to account by the Political Resident for piracies committed by denizens of that coast. The shaikhdom was described in 1820 by an officer of the military force stationed in the Gulf after the expedition in these terms:

'The coast from *Gutta* [Qatar] to *Buthabi* [Abu Dhabi] is described as flat, bare and only approachable by the lightest boats. . . . Buthabi is the seat of the Beni Yas Arabs, situated on a small island separated by a channel from the Coast. . . . The Coast inhabitants amount to about 2,000 men of the Beni Yas; 3,000 reside at Thufra [Dhafrah] near Buthabi with Shaikh Suggur [Saqr], brother to Shaikh Shakhbooth. The former are fishermen and traders, the latter are cultivators of the date, etc. They are by some collectively estimated at 7,000 or 8,000 men.'[1]

Another report on Abu Dhabi, made in 1829 by one of the officers of the Bombay Marine employed on the survey of the Gulf,[2] runs:

'Aboothabee, in lat. 24° 29′ 21″ N., long. 54° 32′ 20″ E., is situated on a sandy island, and is the principal place of the Beniyas Tribe, and the residence of their Chief, Shaikh Tahnoon. The tribe consists of about two thousand four hundred men; but there are, of the Monasir and other tribes, near five thousand more, who acknowledge his government. These mostly reside in the interior, at several places in a district called Ruffthra [Dhafrah]. At Aboothabee the inhabitants are about twelve hundred generally, although much increased in the pearl season, consisting of people of the above tribes, and a number of Banians, who are traders and goldsmiths.

'The present Chief, Shaikh Tahnoon, is a fine looking man, possessing much of that open and hospitable frankness generally attributed to the Arab, and is, I think, attached to the English, both from inclination as well as interest. He is a firm ally of the Imaum of

---

[1] [I.O.] Bombay Pol. Proc., Range 385, Vol. 4, Consuln. of 25 April 1821, Report by Major Colebrooke, 1 September 1820.

[2] The Bombay Marine, the armed branch of the East India Company's maritime service, undertook the first survey of the Gulf in 1820, starting at Ras Musandam, at the entrance to the Gulf, and working westwards around the coast. No European sailors had ventured into the waters west of Abu Dhabi before this.

The Wahhabi Period, 1800–1869

Muskat, and by far the best of the Shaikhs on this coast. His tribe, the Beniyas, is one of the principal in Arabia, and is an independent race.'[1]

In the same year as this was written, an agreement defining their respective jurisdictions was drawn up between Shaikh Tahnun and Shaikh Sultan ibn Saqr of Sharjah, through the agency of the latter's kinsman, the Qasimi Shaikh of Lingah on the Persian coast. 'Their boundaries were fixed,' ran the agreement, 'and their territories and peoples defined: From Rumss to Deruh belonging to Shaikh Sooltan and from Debaye [Dubai] to Bidda [Dauhah in Qatar] to Shaik Tahnoon.'[2]

Rivalry between the Bani Yas and the Qawasim of Sharjah and Ras al-Khaima dominated the politics of the Pirate Coast for half a century after 1820. As the Qawasim were also at odds with the Al Bu Sa'id Sultans of Muscat, it was only natural that Abu Dhabi and Muscat should gravitate towards each other. The place where their interests met physically was the Buraimi Oasis, where the Al Bu Sa'id dominions ended and those of the Al Bu Falah began. Shakhbut ibn Dhiyab had been supplanted in the chieftainship of Abu Dhabi by his son Muhammad in 1816, and Muhammad, in his turn, was deposed by his brother, Tahnun, in 1820. From about that time onwards the elderly Shakhbut spent most of his time at Buraimi. He acquired such an influence over the Dhawahir that in 1839 his son Khalifah, the successor of Tahnun, remarked in a letter to the Political Resident in the Gulf, 'You are aware that the country of Zuweier [Dhawahir] belongs to my father Shakboot, and that the date groves are common to them and us.'[3]

The assertion of Al Bu Falah authority in the oasis was resented by the Na'im, who considered themselves masters of the oasis and who were still Wahhabi in sentiment. Since they were related to the Na'im of Ajman on the coast, and since the Shaikh of Ajman was a client of the powerful Sultan ibn Saqr of the Qawasim, it was inevitable that he should support the Na'im against the Al Bu Falah and the Al Bu Sa'id. Towards the close of 1820 the Na'im of Buraimi rose against the Sultan Sa'id ibn Sultan, besieged his garrison in the forts,

---

[1] [I.O.] *Bombay Selections*, *XXIV*, pp. 547–8, 'Memoir Descriptive of the Navigation of the Gulf of Persia', by Capt. G. B. Brucks.

[2] *U.K. Memorial*, II, Annex B, no. 3, Residency Agent, Sharjah, to Resident in Gulf, 17 June 1829.

[3] *U.K. Memorial*, II, Annex B, no. 5, Khalifah ibn Shakhbut to Capt. S. Hennell, n.d. [August–September 1839].

The Wahhabi Period, 1800-1869

and called upon their kinsmen at Ajman to aid them.[1] Sultan ibn Saqr immediately offered to mediate in the dispute, and largely through his agency an agreement was concluded between the Sultan and the Na'im whereby the Buraimi forts were declared to be neutral. Not long afterwards Sultan ibn Saqr occupied the forts, on the pretext of looking after the interests of the Na'im. A new agreement was concluded between him and the Sultan in December 1824, to which Tahnun ibn Shakhbut of Abu Dhabi was also made a party. The first article of the new agreement read:

'It appearing that the occupation of the Towers at Brymee by the followers of Shaikh Sooltan has afforded just cause of complaint to the Imam [i.e. the Sultan], the former Chieftain consents to abandon and demolish those Towers, and to abstain in future from rebuilding any fortification whatever at Brymee or in the neighbourhood of the Imam's frontier, who likewise engages to destroy any Towers or places of strength at the same place or in its neighbourhood.'[2]

There is no record of the forts having been destroyed, and the inhabitants of Buraimi would appear to have lived for some years thereafter in a state of uneasy security, created by the tripartite rivalry of Al Bu Sa'id, Qawasim, and Al Bu Falah.

The smouldering Al Bu Falah-Qasimi hostility flared up in the early eighteen-thirties in a bitter war, fought by land and sea, between the two confederations, bringing misery and suffering to both. Herds were depleted, plantations destroyed, towns burned, and, worst of all, fighting on the pearl banks led to the fishery's being abandoned year after year, cutting the tribes off from their sole resource for the purchase of necessities from abroad. Driven to extremes by the war, and more particularly by a sustained siege of Abu Dhabi town by the Qawasim in 1833-4, the Bani Yas at the outset of 1835 had recourse to a desperate measure to try to recoup their losses—nothing less than a wholesale attack upon the seaborne trade of the Gulf. The outbreak was quelled by the Indian Navy squadron[3] in the Gulf, and the Bani Yas were made to restore the plunder taken and to compensate their victims.

As a means of relieving the distressed condition of the Pirate Coast, as well as preventing the repetition of such an outbreak, the

[1] [I.O.] Factory Records: Persia and Persian Gulf, Vol. 32, Gov.-in-Co., Bombay, to Court of Directors, 17 January 1821, citing reports from Lieut.-Col. N. P. Warren, O.C. British troops in Gulf.
[2] *U.K. Memorial*, II, Annex B, no. 2.
[3] The Bombay Marine was renamed the Indian Navy in 1830.

The Wahhabi Period, 1800–1869

Political Resident in the Gulf, Captain Samuel Hennell, suggested to the shaikhs that they observe a truce on the pearl banks in the summer of 1835. They agreed, the truce was signed on 21 May 1835, and the Trucial System was born. The maritime truce was renewed annually until 1843, when it was signed for a ten-year period, and when this expired a permanent treaty of maritime peace, to be watched over and enforced by the British Government, took its place. The old Pirate Coast from this time forward may be called the 'Trucial Coast', although the name itself did not gain currency until later in the century. The Shaikh of Abu Dhabi signed the various truces as the ruler responsible for the western portion of the Trucial Coast, from his border with Dubai westwards to Khaur al-Udaid. His authority over that place was demonstrated in 1837 when he forced the Qubaisat section of the Bani Yas, who had fled to Khaur al-Udaid two years earlier to avoid paying their share of the compensation for the piratical outbreak of 1835, to return to Abu Dhabi. Khalifah ibn Shakhbut destroyed the settlement that they had built, and prevented anyone from settling there afterwards.

Wahhabi rule in Central and Eastern Arabia was re-established between 1824 and 1834 by a new Wahhabi Amir, Turki ibn Abdullah Al Sa'ud. In the former year he expelled an Egyptian garrison from Riyadh, to the south of Dara'iya, and made it the new capital of Najd. Hasa was retaken in 1830, and Turki then turned his attention eastwards and southwards to Bahrain, Qatar and Oman. His great need, it seems, was for money, and in 1831 he forced the Shaikh of Bahrain to resume payment of the *zakat*, or alms-tax,[1] which had been paid to the Wahhabis two decades earlier. The disturbed condition of the Trucial Coast, where the Bani Yas and the Qawasim were locked in their struggle for supremacy, and of Oman, where a rival member of the Al Bu Sa'id was endeavouring to overthrow the ruling Sultan, seemed to offer even greater opportunities for extortion. Late in 1832 Turki ordered Umar ibn Ufaisan, the governor of Hasa, who had led a raid upon Buraimi in 1828, to march once more upon the oasis, seize it, and install a permanent garrison there. Ibn Ufaisan left Hasa in January 1833 with 3,000 men and reached Buraimi the following month. He immediately preferred a demand for *zakat* upon the Sultan of Muscat, Saiyid Sa'id ibn Sultan, on pain

[1] See below, pp. 76–79, and Appendix B.

The Wahhabi Period, 1800–1869

of devastating Oman. The Sultan yielded and agreed to pay *zakat* of 5,000 Maria Theresa dollars to the Amir Turki. Ibn Ufaisan left for Hasa in the latter half of 1833, taking with him booty to the amount of $M.T. 15,000 and 300 camels, and leaving behind a garrison of seventy men at Buraimi.

For the next six years, by dint largely of skilfully exploiting tribal factionalism in northern and Trucial Oman, the Wahhabis remained in occupation of Buraimi. Reporting upon the position of Muhammad ibn Abdul Aziz, the garrison commander, in 1834, the British Residency Agent at Sharjah observed: 'The people of Ras al Khaimah are devoted to Abdul Aziz whose policy lies in fomenting divisions and quarrels between the different Shaikhs. Otherwise, were any union to subsist among them it would be impossible for a handful of Wahibi soldiers to hold the whole province of Oman in such subjection as it now is.'[1] Muhammad ibn Abdul Aziz was succeeded as *naib* at Buraimi by Sa'ad ibn Mutlaq, son of the famous Mutlaq al-Mutairi. Shortly after his arrival Sa'ad marched with 3,000 levies to attack the Al Hajariyin tribe of inner Oman, to avenge the death of his father. The outcome of the expedition is described by Lieutenant J. R. Wellsted of the Indian Navy, who was the first European to penetrate the interior of Oman, in his *Travels in Arabia*, published in 1838.[2]

'But the tribe he had destined to destruction, receiving intelligence of this movement two hours before he made his appearance, they collected eight hundred men, all who were then present, to oppose him. These were well armed, and the Sheikh's [Sa'ad's] threats that he would afford no quarter urged them to their best efforts. Notwithstanding their unequal numbers, they attacked the Wahhabis so unexpectedly, and with such fury, that they drove them from the field, and after slaying a great many, compelled the others to seek for safety in flight.'

Sa'ad ibn Mutlaq had no better success in managing the tribes of the Buraimi region. His cavalier treatment of the shaikhs and his increasingly exorbitant demands for *zakat* made his position at Buraimi more and more precarious in the next two years. The Qawasim of Sharjah and Ras al-Khaima, formerly the Wahhabis' principal accomplices in piracy, shunned him, and the Sultan of Muscat refused any longer to pay tribute to Riyadh. At the outset of 1839 Sa'ad left Buraimi for Najd. The Al Bu Shamis and other

[1] [F.O.] Persian Gulf Residency Files, Book LXXXVII, letter dated 1 April 1834.　　[2] London, 2 vols., I, 96–97.

Na'im in the oasis, who had suffered most heavily from his exactions, rose against the Wahhabi garrison and drove it out.

It was a favourable moment for such an act of defiance. Mehemet Ali Pasha of Egypt had again undertaken the conquest of Central and Eastern Arabia, and at the close of 1838 his forces overran Najd and Hasa and took the Amir Faisal, son and successor of Turki ibn Abdullah, prisoner. The Na'im, however, were a long way from being completely set free by this victory. Khurshid Pasha, the Egyptian commander in Arabia, sent Sa'ad ibn Mutlaq back to Trucial Oman in March 1839, with a force of 150–200 men, to re-occupy Buraimi in the name of the Pasha of Egypt. Landing at Sharjah, Sa'ad sent a demand to the Na'im to deliver up the oasis. They, according to a contemporary source, 'nobly replied that they would rather bury themselves in its ruins than give it up, and lost no time in applying to the Beniyas Chief, as also Syud Hamood bin Azan of Sohar, for support to meet the common enemy'.[1]

Saiyid Hamud ibn Azzan, head of the collateral branch of the Al Bu Sa'id and ruler of Sauhar, had long been at odds with the Sultan, Saiyid Sa'id, but he was reconciled to him at the end of 1839 in the face of the Egyptian threat. Hamud responded to the Na'im's appeal by sending 200 men under the command of his brother to Buraimi, and the Sultan, who was then at Zanzibar, sent a message to the Na'im, encouraging them to hold out against Sa'ad ibn Mutlaq, and promising them aid.[2] In July the Resident in the Gulf, Captain Hennell, arrived at Sharjah to inquire into Sa'ad ibn Mutlaq's activities. He found an emissary from the Na'im waiting for him, to ask for protection against the Wahhabi-Egyptian agent. Hennell, who had already sent a warning to Khurshid Pasha not to attempt to extend his authority over the shaikhdoms in treaty relations with the British Government, now told Sa'ad ibn Mutlaq that he would be well advised to return to Najd. To the emissary of the Na'im Hennell gave supplies of rice and ammunition, and he assured him that British protection would be extended to his tribe for as long as the crisis caused by the arrival of the Egyptian army on the shores of the Gulf lasted. The Resident also promised to send an agent to reside at Buraimi for the same length of time.[3]

---

[1] [I.O.] *Bombay Selections, XXIV*, p. 446.
[2] [I.O.] *Bombay Selections, XXIV*, pp. 229 and 446.
[3] [I.O.] Enclos. to Bombay Sec. Letters, Vol. 14, enclos. to Sec. Letter 89 of 18 July 1839, Hennell to Chief Secretary, Bombay, 10 July 1839.

The Wahhabi Period, 1800–1869

Saʻad ibn Mutlaq took his departure from the Trucial Coast soon afterwards. Almost as soon as he had gone Khalifah ibn Shakhbut of Abu Dhabi attacked the Naʻim with a mixed force of Manasir, Bani Yas and Bani Qitab tribesmen. Taken to task by the Resident for violating a promise he had given in July not to hamper the Naʻim in their efforts to oppose Saʻad ibn Mutlaq and the Egyptians, Khalifah replied by asserting that the Naʻim had provoked him.

'I have to inform you of the affairs with the Naiem with whom I agreed to oppose Saed bin Mutluk in order that he should be able to get no footing in Oman. The people in this direction were all unanimous but after Saed bin Mutluk had left these people put themselves in opposition to me, showing their hostility by plundering my people, three of whom were killed, and 50 Camels stolen. They forgot all benefits conferred by me, such as presents of gunpowder and lead and my having assisted them in their war against Bin Mutluk. After having stolen these things they made a foray into the country of my people the Zuweier [Dhawahir] tribe, destroying their date groves and cutting off their water. You are aware that the country of the Zuweier belongs to my father Shakboot, and that the date groves are common to them and us.'[1]

Hennell effected a reconciliation between the Dhawahir and the Naʻim on 9 January 1840, when he met the leading shaikhs of both tribes at Ajman on the Trucial Coast. The reconciliation was helped by his having earlier insisted that Khalifah ibn Shakhbut pay compensation for his attack. The Dhahiri shaikhs, despite their reluctance to enter into any engagement which might impair their connexion with the Manasir and the Mazariʻ section of the Bani Yas, agreed to the Resident's proposal that they enter into a defensive alliance with the Naʻim 'against all enemies whatever'.[2] The Naʻimi and Dhahiri shaikhs were given money, rice, powder and lead, and when they left for Buraimi late in January they were accompanied by an officer of the Resident's staff, Captain Atkins Hamerton, who was to advise them on the defence of the oasis.

Hamerton, the first European to see Buraimi, found the forts in a woeful state of repair, and Buraimi town, after six years of Wahhabi

[1] *U.K. Memorial*, II, Annex B, no. 5, Khalifah ibn Shakhbut to Resident, n.d. [August–September 1839].

[2] [I.O.] Enclos. to Bombay Sec. Letters, Vol. 19, enclos. to Sec. Letter 10 of 28 February 1840, Hennell to Chief Secretary, Bombay, 12 January 1840 (No. 2 Sec. Dept.).

The Wahhabi Period, 1800–1869

occupation, 'in a state of dilapidation'.[1] 'The Naim', he reported, 'are now evidently much reduced in numbers, and sunk in consequence among the tribes of Oman. The Suamis [Al Bu Shamis] of Byreemee formerly mustered four thousand men, and they do not now amount to more than eight hundred.' The principal shaikhs of the Al Bu Shamis were Muhammad and Sulaiman ibn Abdullah and Hamud ibn Surur, and of the Al Bu Khuraiban, Hamad ibn Saif and Ali ibn Hamud. The last-named, who lived at al-Sunainah, well south of the oasis, was acknowledged as *tamimah*, as all the heads of the Al Hamuda clan have been since that time. 'All these tribes', Hamerton remarked, 'united for the defence of Byreemee when it was supposed that Said ibn Mutluk intended to take it, on the part of Khoorshed Pasha.'

Control of the Buraimi Oasis in the years after 1840 was shared by the Na'im, who held the forts, and Khalifah ibn Shakhbut of Abu Dhabi. 'Be it known to you,' the Na'imi shaikhs wrote to the Residency Agent at Sharjah in August 1841, 'that Shaik Khaleefa bin Shakboot on his return from the neighbourhood of Ras-el-Khymah proceeded to the districts of the Zoowahir [Dhawahir] and sent for us to meet him. For a long time we refused but... we at last have had an interview with him, and have consented, as the Nakeels of the naeem Tribe ... to make Peace. Shaik Khaleefa has made himself responsible for the conduct of the Munasir, Moojara [Mazari'], Joowahir [Dhawahir] Tribes, and the followers of Sultan bin Syf (the Imam's Governor of Shinas).'[2]

Three years later the Residency Agent reported Shaikh Khalifah and the Na'im to be still on good terms.

'Sheikh Khuleefa bin Shackboot and his forces consisting of horsemen and Camel men set out from Aboothabee on the commencement of the hot weather. I heard of their being at Brymee and that all the Naim tribes, the Al boo-Shamis and Al boo Khureyban and the other Bedouin Tribes such as the Beni Kuttub [Qitab], Beni Kaab, Ghuflah and Zowahir, the whole had entered into engagements with him and became united with him as one. It appears to

---
[1] [I.O.] Bombay Sec. Proc., Vol. 135, Consuln. of 20 May 1840, Hamerton to Hennell, 27 March 1840. Hamerton's report, in a shortened version, is reprinted in *Bombay Selections XXIV*.
[2] *U.K. Memorial*, II, Annex B, no. 7, Muhammad ibn Abdullah and Hamud ibn Surur to Mullah Husain, 12 August 1841.

The Wahhabi Period, 1800–1869

me that at the present time there is not throughout the interior one Bedouin tribe opposed to him.'[1]

Another contemporary source states of Khalifah ibn Shakhbut's sojourn at Buraimi in the summer of 1844:

'Other tribes, too, did he manage to win over to his side,—indeed he appears to have conciliated the whole of the people he met with; for Syud Humood bin Azan, Chief of Sohar, quitted his territories, and repaired to Brymee to meet him; Syud Kahtan bin Syf, the Governor of Shinas, hastened to wait upon him; and with one and all was he said to have entered into a close and strict confederacy.'[2]

The prime reason for the banding together of the tribes and rulers of northern Oman in the latter half of 1844 was the threat of a possible Wahhabi re-occupation of Buraimi. The Egyptians had begun to retire from Najd in the summer of 1840, and their total withdrawal from Arabia was made a condition of the Convention of Alexandria in November–December 1840, and of the general settlement of the Eastern Question at the London Conference in 1841. Behind them in Najd the Egyptians left a puppet ruler, Khalid ibn Sa'ud. He was reported in October 1841 to be contemplating an attack upon Trucial Oman, but it never materialized, largely because the Resident in the Gulf dispatched one of his officers to the Amir's camp to warn him against embarking on such an enterprise.[3] At the end of 1841 Khalid was overthrown by another member of the Al Sa'ud, Abdullah ibn Thunaiyan. He announced shortly afterwards that he intended to send Sa'ad ibn Mutlaq back to Oman to retake Buraimi. The news made the Na'imi shaikhs at once claim that they were under British protection. 'The Brymee Shaikhs claimed', states a contemporary account, '. . .a species of connection with the British Government, which, although not absolutely subsisting, was possibly adduced in the hope that, if Abdoolla bin Sooneyan were ignorant of the truth, he might be deterred from interfering in their concerns from fear of the supposed alliance.'[4]

Abdullah ibn Thunaiyan, however, was in no position to make good his threats. In June 1843 he yielded power to the Amir Faisal ibn Turki on the Amir's return from captivity in Cairo. Faisal, who was to become the greatest of the Saudi rulers of the later nineteenth

[1] *U.K. Memorial*, II, Annex B, no. 9, Mullah Husain to Resident, 8 October 1844.
[2] [I.O.] *Bombay Selections XXIV*, p. 486.
[3] [I.O.] *Bombay Selections XXIV*, pp. 450–1.
[4] [I.O.] *Bombay Selections XXIV*, p. 453.

The Wahhabi Period, 1800–1869

century, soon made it clear that he intended to re-impose Wahhabi rule wherever it had existed before. Within a month of his return he sent messengers to the shaikhs of Trucial Oman to inform them that he was sending back Sa'ad ibn Mutlaq as his *naib* at Buraimi. It was not welcome news. '... The Chiefs of Brymee, Humood bin Suroor and Mahomed bin Abdoolla,' runs an official report of the time, 'addressed letters in November 1843 to the Resident, stating their belief in the earnestness of the Wahabee ruler's intimation, and requesting the aid and support of the British Government in order to repel the invaders.'[1] They were informed in reply that the protection extended to them earlier had lapsed on the withdrawal of the Egyptians from Arabia, and that the British Government had no intention of interfering in the internal politics of Arabia further than was necessary to maintain the peace of the Gulf. It had been a cardinal principle of British policy in the Gulf, ever since the costly and unnecessary Bani Bu Ali expeditions into southern Oman in 1820–1, not to become militarily involved on the Arabian mainland, and that principle was to hold good until well into the twentieth century. Any coercive measures that were necessary to preserve order along the coasts of Arabia were limited to naval actions.

Unfortunately for northern Oman, and more particularly for the inhabitants of Buraimi, Khalifah ibn Shakhbut died early in 1845, and the confederacy of the tribes that he had organized disintegrated. Sa'ad ibn Mutlaq returned to Buraimi in February 1845, at the head of a force of 700 men, and dispossessed the Na'im of the forts.[2] His main object, as in previous years, was to wring tribute from the Sultanate of Muscat by menaces and bloodshed. $M.T. 20,000 was immediately demanded of the Regent of Muscat, Saiyid Thuwaini ibn Sa'id, and $M.T. 5,000 of the ruler of Sauhar, Hamud ibn Azzan. Saiyid Thuwaini begged for time to refer the demand to his father, the Sultan, at Zanzibar. Sa'ad agreed to wait, but almost immediately he broke his pledge, ravaged the Batinah Coast, and

[1] [I.O.] *Bombay Selections XXIV*, p. 454.
[2] In one of the numerous attempts made in the *Saudi Memorial* of 1955 to lengthen the duration of the Wahhabi occupations of Buraimi in the nineteenth century, the authors state (Vol. I, Chapter IV, para. 164): 'The Imam Faisal sent Sa'd ibn Mutlaq al-Mutairi to Buraimi as Amir in 1844....' Reports from Hasa and Buraimi at the time state, on the contrary, that Sa'ad departed from Hasa on 13 January 1845, and arrived at Buraimi on 7 February. See [I.O.] Board's Collections, Vol. 2107, Colln. 98713, enclos. to Bombay Pol. Letter 44 of 30 April 1845, Hennell to Chief Secy., Bombay, 14 February–11 March 1845 (Nos. 83–116 Pol. Dept.).

The Wahhabi Period, 1800–1869

killed or carried off a number of women. When Thuwaini protested, it is related, 'the only reply he received was one couched in terms most overbearing and tyrannical; indeed the Wahabee Lieutenant seemed bent on something more than the mere venting of empty words and threats....'[1] Hamud ibn Azzan yielded to Sa'ad's threats. '... Rather than witness the horrid scenes of bloodshed and slaughter that must inevitably have followed, had he with his poor resources dared to encounter the powerful Wahabee, he made good the tribute demanded.'[2]

At this juncture, the Political Resident intervened, setting the cruisers of the Gulf squadron to patrol the Batinah Coast to stiffen Thuwaini's resistance, and sending warnings to both Sa'ad ibn Mutlaq and the Amir Faisal to cease their attacks upon Oman. A settlement was later reached on the basis of Thuwaini's agreeing to pay tribute of $M.T. 5,000 per annum to Riyadh and to give Sa'ad ibn Mutlaq personally $M.T. 2,000.

In the next two years the Wahhabi *naib*'s brutalities and extortions alienated nearly every tribe in northern and Trucial Oman. 'Chief after chief', states one account, 'conceived a hatred against him, and ranged themselves in opposition to his cause. Of the maritime chiefs, one alone, (the Chief of Amulgavine [Umm al-Qaiwain]) remained staunch to his side.'[3] The Na'im were particularly bitter in their opposition to him. Sa'ad attempted in 1846 to seize control of the town of Dhank, which was ruled by the Al Bu Khuraiban branch of the tribe, but they were so determined to stop him that they went to the length of concluding a defensive alliance against him with their longstanding rivals, the Al Bu Shamis. The *tamimah* of the Na'im also sought assistance from Hamud ibn Azzan of Sauhar. Saiyid Hamud at this time was engaged in an abortive attempt to revive the Imamate, and to persuade the *mutawwa's* of Oman, the more fanatically doctrinaire of the Ibadiya, to elect him to the office. Despite their religious differences with the Na'im—who were Sunni Muslims—the *mutawwa's* and Hamud ibn Azzan responded to the appeal.

[1] [I.O.] *Bombay Selections XXIV*, p. 217.
[2] [I.O.] *Bombay Selections XXIV*, p. 457. A sustained effort is made in the *Saudi Memorial* to disguise the real nature and purpose of the Wahhabi occupations of Buraimi. Thus, in their account of Sa'ad ibn Mutlaq's return to Buraimi and subsequent behaviour, drawn from the same source as that given here, the authors merely remark: '... Discussions took place between Thuwaini and Sa'd ibn Mutlaq regarding relations between the Saudi State and Muscat....' (*Saudi Memorial*, I, Chapter IV, para. 165).
[3] [I.O.] *Bombay Selections XXIV*, p. 457.

The Wahhabi Period, 1800–1869

'... Towards the close of the year [it is recorded] so strong was the party in league against Syud bin Mootluk, so precarious did he feel his position to be,—for reports had reached the Ameer [Faisal] that he was appropriating to himself a considerable portion of the treasure he had collected—that he meditated proceeding in person to Nujd, to wait upon his master, and try to dispel from his mind all credence in the evil reports so freely circulated against him. A day had even been fixed for his departure from Brymee, when the unexpected arrival of messengers with letters from the Ameer— "confirming him in his position, but desiring him to send without delay any ready money he might have in his possession"—led to the sudden abandonment of the plan, and the despatch of a considerable sum to Nujd. ...'[1]

The respite, however, was only a brief one. Early in 1847 Sa'ad was called back to Najd to explain why the Wahhabi position on the frontier of Oman had deteriorated so rapidly in the short time that he had been at Buraimi.

In his absence the situation of the Wahhabi garrison at Buraimi itself grew critical. 'In the Fort of Brymee,' reported the Political Resident in the Gulf in September 1847, 'the Deputy of Ameer Fysul, Ul Ujajee (who commands the stronghold), is compelled to trust entirely to his astute management of the feuds and passions of the surrounding Tribes for the maintenance of the moderate degree of authority he still possesses.'[2] A few months later the Amir Faisal tried to relieve the situation by sending a new *naib* with reinforcements to Buraimi. It made little difference to the Wahhabi position, as the Resident reported in April 1848.

'Considering ... that Abdool Rahman, the individual sent from Lahsah [Hasa] to relieve Al Ajajee was compelled to apply to the Shaik of Bahrein to transport him and his few followers by Sea owing to the disturbed state of the Desert not permitting them to proceed by land, no great apprehensions are entertained of any considerable addition to the small party of Nedgdees now in Brymee.'[3]

---

[1] [I.O.] *Bombay Selections XXIV*, p. 458.
[2] *U.K. Memorial*, II, Annex B, no. 10, Hennell to Chief Secy., Bombay, 9 September 1847.
[3] *U.K. Memorial*, II, Annex B, no. 42, Hennell to Chief Secy., Bombay, 28 April 1848. The authors of the *Saudi Memorial* state (I, Chapter IV, para. 171) that Abdur Rahman made the journey in 1847. They do not say whether it was by sea or land, but they do claim that he 'proceeded to his post with a

The Wahhabi Period, 1800-1869

Communication with Najd across the Dhafrah was at this time impossible for the Wahhabis. Sa'ad ibn Mutlaq had been forced to send the spoils he had collected in Oman to Riyadh by sea, and he himself took the same route when he returned to Najd in 1847. Indeed, the Wahhabis had not been able at any time since the beginning of the century to establish a single post in the Dhafrah or to exert any authority over the region between the Jafurah Desert and the Buraimi Oasis. The reason for this failure was simply the uncompromising hostility borne them by the Bani Yas. 'Even during the height of the Wahabee ascendency,' wrote Samuel Hennell, who knew the Arabian shore and its politics better than did any other Resident in the nineteenth century, 'this Tribe always maintained its independence and refused to pay the Zakat or Tithes claimed by the head of that Sect.'[1]

In the late spring of 1848 the Wahhabi *naib* at Buraimi, Muhammad ibn Saif al-Ajaji, tried to force payment of *zakat* from Hamud ibn Azzan of Sauhar by dispatching a punitive force against him. The force was trapped in the Wadi al-Jizzi by Hamud's son, Saif, with the aid of Na'im of the Al Bu Khuraiban division, and put to flight.[2] At this, Shaikh Sa'id ibn Tahnun of Abu Dhabi, supported by contingents of the Awamir and Mazari', and later, the Dhawahir, advanced to attack the Wahhabi garrison in the Buraimi forts. From the east, Saiyid Saif ibn Hamud of Sauhar closed in upon the oasis with the Na'im. On 17 June al-Ajaji abandoned the smaller fort, the Qasr al-Subarah, and three days later, by which time the besieging forces had been joined by contingents from the Bani Ka'ab and the Bani Qitab, he was forced to surrender the main

---

retinue of only twenty men, an entirely adequate number for this assignment in times of peace'. As their authority for this statement they cite Ibn Bishr, *Tarikh Najd*, II, 117. But Ibn Bishr writes: 'The Imam [Faisal] sent a force to Oman under the command of Abdur Rahman ibn Ibrahim, a native of Manfuhah, and he ordered the Amir Ahmad ibn Muhammad al-Sudairi to give them twenty men from al-Hasa. . . .'

[1] *U.K. Memorial*, II, Annex B, no. 4, Hennell to Chief Secy., Bombay, 7 May 1839. Writing of the period 1845-8, the authors of the *Saudi Memorial* state (I, Chapter IV, para. 164): 'Buraimi was not a simple frontier outpost garrisoned by conquerors in a foreign land; it was part and parcel of the State to which it adhered, a provincial capital in full standing.' With 400 miles of hostile territory lying between Buraimi and the nearest Wahhabi centre in Hasa it is difficult to visualize the oasis in quite these terms.

[2] [I.O.] Bombay Pol. Proc., Range 392, Vol. 58, Consuln. 25 of 20 September 1848, Mullah Husain (Residency Agent, Sharjah) to Resident, 25 Jumada II 1264/29 May 1848.

fort, the Qasr al-Khandaq. Saif ibn Hamud's men garrisoned the forts while Shaikh Sa'id ibn Tahnun encamped in the Dhahiri villages.[1]

Rumours that the Amir Faisal might try to send a force south from Hasa to regain control of Buraimi led Sa'id ibn Tahnun later to replace the Omani garrison in the forts with his own men, under the command of Hamud ibn Surur of the Al Bu Shamis. 'He likewise', reported the Residency Agent at Sharjah, 'commanded all the Bedowin Tribes at present acknowledging his authority, such as the Beni Kuttub [Qitab], ul Ghiflah [Ghafalah], Ul Awamir, and Al Muzareeh [Mazari'], to assemble and take up a position at Khutun [the Khatam] between Aboothabee and Brymee. . . .'[2] The Residency Agent further reported that Sa'id ibn Tahnun 'sent his Cousin Mahomed ben Syf to the Elders of the Moonasir and Moozareeh Tribes residing at Liwa and . . . they have come to Aboothabee to visit him and have entered into a close alliance with him: as far as I can ascertain they have engaged to remove with their families from Liwa and settle at Zaffrah [Dhafrah] between Aboothabee and Brymee that in the event of the Forces of Fysul ben Turkee [Faisal ibn Turki] invading these parts they, with the Tribe of the Beniyas, may engage them before they reach Brymee.'[3]

An attempt was made by Faisal in October 1848 to send a force across the Dhafrah, after he had failed to persuade the Trucial Shaikhs of Sharjah and Dubai to lend him ships for its transport by sea. The force, commanded by Sa'ad ibn Mutlaq, was ambushed in the Dhafrah and cut to pieces by Sa'id ibn Tahnun's tribesmen, Sa'ad ibn Mutlaq barely escaping with his life to Sharjah. There he managed to assemble a force from the remnants of al-Ajaji's garrison, and from the followers of the Qasimi ruler, Sultan ibn Saqr, who was jealous of the growing power of Sa'id ibn Tahnun. The Wahhabi's efforts to retake Buraimi, however, were of no use, and the Amir Faisal was driven, at the close of 1848, to appeal to the Resident in the Gulf to support his *naib* and to restrain the maritime

---

[1] [I.O.] Bombay Pol. Proc., Range 392, Vol. 59, Consuln. 25 of 20 September 1848, Mullah Husain to Resident, 12–18 Rajab 1264/14–20 June 1848; Vol. 63, Consuln. 32 of 22 November 1848, Mullah Husain to Resident, 23 Rajab–10 Sha'ban 1264/23 June–12 July 1848. See also *U.K. Memorial*, II, Annex B, nos. 11–12.

[2] [I.O.] Bombay Pol. Proc., Range 393, Vol. 1, Consuln. 37 of 31 December 1848, Mullah Husain to Resident, 25 Shawwal 1264/24 September 1848. See also *U.K. Memorial*, II, Annex B, no. 13. [3] Ibid.

The Wahhabi Period, 1800-1869

tribes of Trucial Oman from interfering with the passage of supplies to him by sea from Hasa.[1]

Faisal also appealed, to greater effect, to his overlord in Arabia, the powerful Sharif of Mecca, Muhammad ibn Aun. An emissary from the Sharif arrived at the Residency in the Gulf in March 1849 with a letter from the Sharif which ran:

'I beg to acquaint you, with reference to Bin Saood Fysul, that he is a subject of the [Ottoman] Sultan; and it is not concealed from you that there were Forts belonging to him in Oman; and the Al Boo Saeed [Al Bu Said] and [Said ibn] Tahnoon ejected him from them; and he pays into the Treasury of the Sultan 17,000 Rials; and he referred the matter to me, and reported to me the hostilities of Bin Tahnoon, and the Al Boo Saeed, and represented that Bin Tahnoon is on an Island at sea, and there is no means of access to him. I beg to inform you that Bin Saood is a subject of the Sultan; and my hope from you is that you will not sanction opposition to him. I have not chosen to protract my communication as you are not perfectly conversant in the Arabic Tongue. Shereef Ali comes to you on my part, from whose mouth you will receive accounts.'[2]

Sharif Ali told the Resident that Faisal had made the disturbances in Trucial Oman the excuse for not remitting the usual amount of tribute to Mecca, and that he had asked the Sharif to intercede for him with the Shaikh of Abu Dhabi. On his way to Bushire to see the Resident Sharif Ali had stopped in Trucial Oman, and he had managed to induce Sa'id ibn Tahnun to give up the Buraimi forts to Sa'ad ibn Mutlaq.[3] Faisal himself wrote to the Resident shortly afterwards, asking him to restrain Sa'id ibn Tahnun from making trouble for his *naib* in the future.[4]

The new Wahhabi occupation of Buraimi was more short-lived than any of the others. Sa'ad ibn Mutlaq left the oasis, never to return, in the spring of 1850, and Sa'id ibn Tahnun promptly laid siege to the Qasr al-Subarah and Qasr al-Khandaq, now held by Sa'ad's successor, Ibn Battal. Supported by the Manasir, Mazari',

---

[1] [I.O.] Bombay Pol. Proc., Range 393, Vol. 6, Consuln. 7 of 1 March 1849, Faisal to Major Hennell, 30 Muharram 1265/27 December 1848.
[2] [I.O.] Bombay Pol. Proc., Range 393, Vol. 10, Consuln. 14 of 2 May 1849, Muhammad ibn Aun to Resident, 11 Dhu'l-Qa'dah 1264/9 October 1848.
[3] Hennell to Chief Secy., Bombay, 12 March 1849 (No. 75 Pol. Dept.), enclosed with above letter.
[4] [I.O.] Bombay Pol. Proc., Range 393, Vol. 24, Consuln. 25 of 31 October 1849, Faisal to Hennell, 15 Jumada I, 1265/9 April 1849.

The Wahhabi Period, 1800–1869

Al Bu Shamis, and a detachment of horse sent by the Sultan of Muscat, Sa'id ibn Tahnun kept the Wahhabi garrison blockaded throughout the summer.[1] In November, joined by the Qasimi chieftain, Sultan ibn Saqr, Shaikh Sa'id forced Ibn Battal to capitulate.[2]

At the close of the year Faisal himself arrived on the frontiers of Qatar with a large force which he had originally collected for the invasion of Bahrain. Unwilling, apparently, to advance into Trucial Oman, he contented himself with telling an emissary of Sultan ibn Saqr of Sharjah that he regarded the Qasimi chief's co-operation with Sa'id ibn Tahnun as responsible for the fall of Buraimi, and that he would hold him to account for it. The only effect of this threat was to unite the Bani Yas and the Qawasim in a defensive league against the Amir. It was later joined by the Shaikh of Dubai.[3] Deterred by the combination, Faisal turned his attention back to Bahrain. Here he was handicapped in his plans to invade the island principality by the lack of ships, so he appealed, as was becoming his wont whenever his pretensions to overlordship in Eastern Arabia exceeded his ability to realize them, to the Resident in the Gulf for support, saying that all he wanted from Bahrain was the renewed payment of *zakat*. He was told in reply that the British Government did not recognize Wahhabi authority over any of the maritime states of Eastern Arabia, which had been dealt with as independent shaikhdoms for over thirty years.[4] A settlement was eventually reached between Faisal and the Shaikh of Bahrain, through the mediation, ironically enough, of Sa'id ibn Tahnun of Abu Dhabi.[5]

*

[1] [I.O.] Enclos. to Bombay Sec. Letters, Vol. 110, enclos. to Sec. Letter 49 of 17 September 1850, Mullah Husain to Resident, 23 April 1850.
[2] [I.O.] Enclos. to Bombay Sec. Letters, Vol. 106, enclos. to Sec. Letter 16 of 17 February 1851, Hennell to Chief Secy., Bombay, 21 December 1850 (No. 490 Pol. Dept.). See also *U.K. Memorial*, II, Annex B, no. 16. Lorimer, *Gazetteer of P. Gulf*, I, 708, states incorrectly that the attack of November was 'apparently fruitless'. The *Saudi Memorial* of 1955 does not mention it.
[3] [I.O.] Bombay Pol. Proc., Range 393, Vol. 64, Consuln. of 2 July 1851, Mullah Husain to Hennell, 9 April 1851. Mullah Husain was a witness to the agreement signed on that day.
[4] [I.O.] Enclos. to Bombay Sec. Letters, Vol. 101, enclos. to Sec. Letter 71 of 17 September 1851, Hennell to Chief Secy., Bombay, 24 June 1851 (No. 205 Sec. Dept.), enclosing Faisal to Hennell, 31 May 1851.
[5] [I.O.] Enclos. to Bombay Sec. Letters, Vol. 101, enclos. to Sec. Letter 73 of 2 October 1851, Hennell to Chief Secy., Bombay, 9 August 1851.

The Wahhabi Period, 1800–1869

By the beginning of 1853 Faisal felt secure enough to try once more to retake Buraimi. In January of that year he dispatched his son Abdullah, with an imposing force, southwards from Hasa. Abdullah reached Buraimi late the following month, and he peremptorily ordered all the Trucial Shaikhs to attend upon him without delay. 'He came', says an account written at the time, 'in the character of arbiter and redresser of wrongs suffered by his children (the Shaikhs) in Oman.'[1] His principal object, however, seemed to be to plunder the Sultanate of Muscat.

'Scarcely had Abdoolla bin Fysul arrived, ere he sent forth demands for the immediate cession of Sohar, and the payment of tribute so large in amount that it was plain he sought but a pretext, in the refusal that must of necessity follow, to attack and lay waste the districts of Batinah. . . . A blow, it was manifest, was about to be aimed at His Highness' [the Sultan's] dominions, that would imperil their safety, and endanger their integrity.'[2]

The Sultan, Saiyid Sa'id, was away at Zanzibar, where he now spent most of his time, leaving his son, Thuwaini, whose qualities of intellect and spirit were hardly conspicuous, as his regent in Oman. Thuwaini was incapable of presenting any kind of opposition to Abdullah ibn Faisal, so, well aware of this, Sa'id ibn Tahnun took the lead in saving Oman from the Wahhabis.

On arrival at Buraimi with the other Trucial Shaikhs to wait upon Abdullah, Sa'id set himself the task of dissuading the Amir's son from attacking the Batinah Coast. At the same time he wrote to Thuwaini, urging him to send all his available troops to Sauhar, at the eastern end of the Wadi al-Jizzi. It is not certain whether these measures would have had much effect had it not been for the arrival on the Trucial Coast, in late March, of the Political Resident, Captain A. B. Kemball, who had come to negotiate the Treaty of Maritime Peace in Perpetuity with the Trucial Shaikhs. Learning of Abdullah ibn Faisal's activities, and of Sa'id ibn Tahnun's efforts to stop him, Kemball ordered two cruisers to patrol the Trucial and Batinah Coasts, and sent letters to the Trucial Shaikhs gathered at Buraimi, requiring their immediate presence on the coast to sign the treaty. The measures had their effect: at the beginning of April Abdullah sent his lieutenant, Ahmad al-Sudairi, to Sauhar, in company with Sa'id ibn Tahnun, to treat with Thuwaini. An agreement was reached some time afterwards, providing for the payment

[1] [I.O.] *Bombay Selections XXIV*, p. 232. [2] Ibid.

The Wahhabi Period, 1800–1869

by the Sultan of *zakat* of $M.T. 12,000 per annum, plus a lump sum of $M.T. 60,000. In return, Abdullah guaranteed, on behalf of his father, the territorial integrity of the Sultanate. As Sa'id ibn Tahnun afterwards remarked to Captain Kemball, the price was high but the alternative was the dismemberment of the Sultanate.[1] Abdullah did not linger long at Buraimi. Despite his claim that he had come to settle disputes among the shaikhs, no such settlements were made. When he departed for Najd he left behind a garrison under the command of Ahmad al-Sudairi.

In view of the renewed imposition of *zakat* upon the Sultanate of Muscat, it might be appropriate at this point to examine the nature of this levy, which was imposed by the Wahhabi Amir upon all the littoral states of Arabia at one time or another in the nineteenth century. The authors of the *Saudi Memorial* of 1955 are at pains to distinguish between what they call 'true Islamic *zakah*'[2] which, they say, is collected in Saudi Arabia today, and the payments made to the Wahhabi Amirs by the rulers of the Gulf principalities a century ago.

'The large sums paid to the Saudi State during the nineteenth century were lump payments made by the political head of a foreign state as a form of tribute; they bore no relation to true *zakah*. . . . As Ibn Bishr, the Arab historian, points out, the collecting of the true *zakah* was carried out faithfully by the Saudi State during the same period in which revenue, sometimes called *zakah*, was being obtained from the tributary states of the Persian Gulf.'[3]

Whether or not the tax collected today in Saudi Arabia under the name of *zakat* is the *zakat* of the Koran and the *Shari'ah* is a question that will be examined elsewhere.[4] But it is quite erroneous to say

---

[1] The agreement is characterized by the authors of the *Saudi Memorial* as being 'conspicuous for its lack of harshness' (Vol. I, Chapter IV, para. 185). Whether it was or not is largely a matter of opinion, dependent upon one's view of the Wahhabi Amir's right to exact money from the Sultan of Muscat under threat of force, and of his intentions in sending his son to Buraimi with a large force. What is less contestable is the part played by Sa'id ibn Tahnun and Capt. Kemball in forcing Abdullah to modify his demands. Of this, it might be added, the *Memorial*'s authors make not the slightest mention, even though their account is drawn from the same source as that used for the account given above, viz., [I.O.] *Bombay Selections XXIV*, pp. 232–3.

[2] The word may be spelt '*zakah*' or '*zakat*'. The former spelling is used in the *Saudi Memorial*.

[3] *Saudi Memorial*, II, Appendix B, Part 2.

[4] See below, Appendix B.

The Wahhabi Period, 1800-1869

that a distinction was made in the nineteenth century—and to imply that Ibn Bishr made such a distinction—between the payments made by the rulers of the Gulf states and so-called 'true *zakat*'.

The basis of the Wahhabi state was, in theory, religious. The Saudi Amir was also *imam*, or spiritual leader of his people. In the return to the primitive simplicity of Islam, which was the moving spirit behind Wahhabism, the *zakat* was reconstituted as the basis of taxation in the Wahhabi state. To those outside of Najd who were converted to the new orthodoxy, the payment of *zakat* at first appeared as a religious duty. To those who rode to war under the banner of the Wahhabi Amir, however, the levying of *zakat* became an end in itself, and its payment was enforced upon all, even upon those who, like the Ibadiya of Oman, refused to subscribe to the doctrines of the reformed faith. Its character, in short, became that of an exaction rather than a voluntary religious offering, as indeed its payment within Najd, from almost the beginning of the Wahhabi movement, had been construed as a duty to the Saudi Amir rather than as a pious act. *Zakat* was being paid unwillingly by the Sultan of Muscat and the Shaikh of Bahrain in the first decade of the nineteenth century, at the same time as it was being paid willingly by the Na'im of Buraimi and the Qawasim of the Pirate Coast. It is hardly likely that the parties concerned drew any distinction between these payments, other than that created by the degree of coercion used in obtaining them. Nor is it likely that the Wahhabi Amir differentiated sharply between the *zakat* collected from his subjects in Najd, where it had been exacted from the first from the willing and the recalcitrant alike, and the *zakat* gathered by his forces beyond Najd from new adherents or unregenerate opponents.

The *zakat* prescribed by the Koran and the *Shari'ah* carried no implications of political authority or territorial sovereignty.[1] That this was understood by those who paid *zakat* to the Wahhabi Amir out of religious conviction is clear from the following extract from a report in 1805 on the Qawasim living on the Persian coast of the Gulf:

'Shaikh Gadeef [Qadhib] of Lingua on the Persian side of the Gulph is a Joassim by birth, uncle of Sultan ben Suggur of Rasul Khameh on the Arabian shore, and a Wahabee by religion and pays tribute to Sahood, the present leader of that rising sect; but living on the coast of Persia he calls himself, when it suits his pur-

[1] See below, Appendix B.

The Wahhabi Period, 1800–1869

pose, a Persian subject, tho' he obeys no order but what pleases him.'¹

When *zakat* was paid unwillingly, as in the case of the Sultan of Muscat and the Shaikh of Bahrain, its real character was more that of *Danegeld*, i.e. tribute exacted under threat of invasion, and as such it also carried no implication of territorial sovereignty but only that of superior force on the part of the exactor. The point is well illustrated by the case of Bahrain.

The attempt made by the Amir Faisal in 1851 to invade Bahrain was only one of several attempts made by him and his predecessors to conquer the island. It was frustrated, as were the others, largely by the intervention of the Resident in the Gulf, and a settlement was eventually reached, as mentioned earlier, through the mediation of Sa'id ibn Tahnun of Abu Dhabi. By it, the Shaikh of Bahrain agreed to pay Faisal *zakat* of $M.T. 4,000 annually. A little time later an envoy from Faisal, Abdur Rahman ibn Ibrahim, the man who had tried to relieve the Wahhabi garrison at Buraimi early in 1848, visited the Resident, Colonel Hennell, at Bushire. He had been sent to ask whether the British authorities in the Gulf would object to Faisal's enforcing payment of the *zakat*, if the ruler of Bahrain failed to keep the agreement. He was told by Hennell that the British Government would not allow the independence of Bahrain to be subverted on any pretext whatever, and that they did not recognize the Amir's pretensions to authority over the maritime states of the Gulf. To his superiors, however, Hennell expressed the opinion that it would be as well, for the sake of maritime peace in the Gulf, if the Shaikh of Bahrain were to maintain the payments.

'I am by no means satisfied that it would be a bad policy on the part of the Government to exert its influence with the Bahrein Sheik to induce him to pay the "zukat" or tithe to the Wahabee Ruler with regularity; taking care, however, that it was understood this payment was strictly considered *in a religious light*, as made to the Imam or Chief Priest of the Wahabee Sect, *and not as Tribute, and that it implied no acknowledgement of subjection.*'²

Three years later Shaikh Muhammad ibn Khalifah, the ruler of Bahrain, discontinued the payments, alleging that Faisal was

¹ [I.O.] Board's Collns., Vol. 192, Colln. 4155, Capt. David Seton (Res. at Muscat) to Gov.-in-Co., Bombay, 14 August 1805.

² [I.O.] Enclos. to Bombay Sec. Letters, Vol. 102, enclos. to Sec. Letter 73 of 2 October 1851, Hennell to Chief Secy., Bombay, 9 August 1851 (No. 258 Sec. Dept.). Italics added.

The Wahhabi Period, 1800–1869

intriguing to gain possession of Bahrain by supporting some rival members of the Al Khalifah family, who had taken refuge at Dammam. Faisal moved to attack Bahrain in 1854, but once again the island was saved by British intervention. The crisis was settled by the conclusion of an agreement in May 1855 between Muhammad ibn Khalifah and the refugees at Dammam. Provision was made in the agreement that if Faisal should forgo that part of the *zakat* from Bahrain that was raised by a tax on the estates of the refugees, the tax would not be imposed by Muhammad ibn Khalifah. The Resident, Captain Kemball, was present at the conclusion of the agreement, but he declined a request by both parties that he act as a witness to it, because, as he afterwards explained, the question of Bahrain's independence was not involved.

'To this note, though cognizant of the fact, I declined of course to affix my attestation, or to become in any way a party, observing that *the tribute given to Ameer Fysul, being purely of a religious character*, did not concern the Government, the more particularly that *its payment was not held to imply any territorial jurisdiction*.'[1]

In this respect, at least, it is clear, the *zakat* paid by the Shaikh of Bahrain, and by other Gulf rulers, to the Wahhabi Amir in the last century resembled the classical *zakat* of Islam.

An interesting fact to emerge from the crisis over Bahrain between 1851 and 1855, and one particularly relevant to Saudi Arabia's present claim to the disputed region on the grounds of past occupation, was the Amir Faisal's affirmation of his dependence upon the Sublime Porte. In June 1851, after a visit from a confidential emissary of the Amir, a Shaikh Abdul Aziz, Colonel Hennell reported:

'Of the connexion subsisting between Ameer Fysul and the Ottoman Porte there can, I think, exist no doubt. Sheik Abdool Azeez, while at Koweit, passed himself off to the Sheik of that place as an envoy of Abbas Pasha of Egypt, and he also informed me that messengers from the Viceroy were now present with the Ameer.'[2]

Faisal himself wrote to Hennell's successor, Captain Kemball, on 14 January 1855: 'Being a dependent of the Exalted (Turkish) Government, I hold the confirmation of the Sultan to my continuance

---

[1] [I.O.] Enclos. to Bombay Sec. Letters, Vol. 123, enclos. to Sec. Letter 66 of 1 November 1855, Kemball to Chief Secy., Bombay, 26 May 1855 (No. 1B Sec. Dept.). Italics added.

[2] [I.O.] Enclos. to Bombay Sec. Letters, Vol. 101, enclos. to Sec. Letter 71 of 17 September 1851. Hennell to Chief Secy., Bombay, 24 June 1851 (No. 205 Sec. Dept.).

The Wahhabi Period, 1800–1869

in authority over all the Arabs.'¹ The admission is important, for it was made in the context of exchanges between Faisal and Kemball over the Amir's claims to authority over Bahrain and Trucial Oman, following the Wahhabi expedition to Buraimi in 1853. Faisal had written to Kemball in September 1854, affecting not to understand why the British Government were opposed to his invading Bahrain, since, he said, 'an understanding has long existed between me and the British Government regarding my dependencies extending from Oman to Koweit over which you should exercise no control nor should you interfere in any way in their affairs'.²

Kemball firmly disabused the Amir of the notion that any such understanding had ever existed.

'With . . . reference to your Highness's claim to supremacy over the maritime states of Oman it is my duty to declare plainly that the British Government can recognize no authority between itself and their respective chiefs whom it has always regarded as independent and with whom it has contracted treaties and engagements of upwards of 30 years' standing.'³

Faisal's reply to this was his letter, already cited, of 14 January 1855, in which he sought to lend weight to his claims to authority over Trucial Oman by invoking his position as an Ottoman dependant. Claiming again that an agreement existed between the British and the Al Sa'ud, 'of 100 years' duration', for the maintenance of peace at sea, he went on to assert that the energies of his *naib* at Buraimi were constantly directed towards restraining the tribes of the interior from molesting those on the coast. When quarrels arose among them, Faisal declared, 'there was none could check them and restore order and goodwill among them, except the Lieutenant in charge of Oman, whose office is among the things pleasing to God and his Prophet, as also to the Sultan of the Faithful—may God strengthen the faith by his means!'⁴

It would seem, then, that when Faisal seized Buraimi in 1853 he was a dependant of the Porte, and that his continued occupation of the oasis after that date was in his capacity as Ottoman *qaim-maqam*,

---

[1] [I.O.] Enclos. to Bombay Sec. Letters, Vol. 123, enclos. to Sec. Letter 66 of 1 November 1855, Faisal to Kemball, 24 Rabi' II, 1271/14 January 1855.
[2] [I.O.] Enclos. to Bombay Sec. Letters, Vol. 121, enclos. to Sec. Letter 12 of 31 January 1855, Faisal to Kemball, 6 Muharram 1271/29 September 1854.
[3] Kemball to Faisal, 18 October 1854, in preceding collection.
[4] [I.O.] Enclos. to Bombay Sec. Letters, Vol. 123, enclos. to Sec. Letter 66 of 1 November 1855, Faisal to Kemball, 24 Rabi' II, 1271/14 January 1855.

The Wahhabi Period, 1800-1869

or governor, of Najd.[1] It is arguable, therefore, that the final Wahhabi occupation of Buraimi from 1853 onwards was, ultimately, an Ottoman occupation, and that any sovereign rights that may have accrued to the Al Sa'ud from that occupation lapsed with the dissolution of the Ottoman Empire.[2]

The final Wahhabi occupation of Buraimi, which lasted from 1853 until 1869, was made possible by a number of circumstances. First, and perhaps most important, was the stabilizing of the power of Faisal ibn Turki after 1855. His principal rival in Arabia, Muhammad ibn Aun, Sharif of Mecca, died in 1858, and he himself had overcome any remaining opposition from the tribes of Najd and Hasa by what one authority has described as 'his merciless severity'.[3] A second factor was the deposition from power in 1855 of Sa'id ibn Tahnun of Abu Dhabi, hitherto the most steadfast opponent of the Wahhabis in south-eastern Arabia. A year later Shaikh Sa'id was killed in a family quarrel of the type that has disfigured the history of the Al Bu Falah for a century and a half. Saiyid Sa'id ibn Sultan, the greatest of the Al Bu Sa'id rulers of Muscat, also died in 1856. Five years later the Sultanate was divided between his sons; Saiyid Thuwaini succeeded to Muscat and Oman, Saiyid Majid to Zanzibar and the East African ports. The effects upon Oman were profound. Henceforth the country was forced to rely less upon the wealth that the enterprise of the Al Bu Sa'id had brought it through their overseas trade and possessions, and more upon its own resources. To the Al Bu Sa'id Sultans the loss of Zanzibar meant the closing of an

---

[1] A letter from the *vali* of Baghdad to the British Consul-General in the city in 1861 refers to 'Fysul Beg, the Kaimmakam of Nejd' (see [I.O.] Enclos. to Bombay Sec. Letters, Vol. 146, enclos. to Sec. Letter 2 of 12 February 1862, Ahmed Tewfiq Pasha to A. B. Kemball, 25 Jumada I, 1278/29 November 1861). Faisal himself spoke of his treaties with the Sultan Abdul Mejid in a letter to the Resident in the Gulf in 1859 (see [I.O.] Enclos. to Bombay Sec. Letters, Vol. 142, enclos. to Sec. Letter 13 of 27 March 1860, Faisal to Capt. F. Jones, 7 Rabi' II, 1276/3 November 1859).

[2] Perhaps this is why in the *Saudi Memorial* the authors scrupulously avoid all reference to the dependence of successive Wahhabi Amirs upon the Porte. Thus, using Lorimer's *Gazetteer* as a source (I, 1112-14), they describe (Vol. I, Chapter IV, para. 200) Faisal's correspondence with Kemball in 1855, but omit all the references in Lorimer to Faisal's avowal of his Ottoman status. Indeed, the number of omissions in the historical section of the *Memorial* is one of its more remarkable features. (See below, Chapter VII.)

[3] Lorimer, *Gazetteer of P. Gulf*, I, 1109.

The Wahhabi Period, 1800–1869

era in which they had neglected the internal affairs of Oman for adventures abroad and had become estranged from many of the inland tribes. The road back was not to be easy, especially as the Al Bu Sa'id continued to be distracted by intra-dynastic struggles for power of the kind common to all the states of Arabia at the time.

'... The people of the districts in the interior of Oman and at the seats of the Bedouin tribes,' the Amir Faisal had written to Kemball in January 1855, 'are more powerful than, and have the command over, the inhabitants of the coast, and could not be restrained from preying upon and slaughtering them, but that I maintain a Lieutenant with a force in Oman, who holds them back from the people on the coast. These last are well assured of his protection; otherwise, were they abandoned to their fate they could not subsist.'[1]

Faisal's lieutenant in Oman at the time was Ahmad al-Sudairi, whom Abdullah ibn Faisal had left in charge of the garrison at Buraimi in 1853. In the spring of 1855, not long after Kemball had received the above letter from Faisal, Ahmad al-Sudairi seized the opportunity offered by disturbances in the Trucial Shaikhdom of Sharjah to attack the settlement of Himriyah on the coast, with the object of converting it into a Wahhabi base. The attempt failed, partly because of the help given the defenders of Himriyah by a contingent of Al Bu Shamis from Buraimi. When Kemball arrived off Himriyah in June, on his annual tour of the Gulf, he found the Al Bu Shamis chief, Fadhil ibn Muhammad, waiting for him. Shaikh Fadhil wanted to know whether the British Government would organize a confederation of the tribes of Trucial Oman to drive the Wahhabis from Buraimi. The Na'im, it appeared, did not greatly appreciate Ahmad al-Sudairi's presence in the oasis or his methods of promoting the welfare of the tribes of Trucial Oman. Kemball, however, had no choice but to tell the Na'imi chieftain that, although his government sympathized with any tribe that had lost its independence to the Wahhabis, their policy remained one of non-interference in tribal politics in the interior of Arabia.[2]

The Na'im were relieved of the presence of Ahmad al-Sudairi in the later eighteen-fifties, but it is doubtful whether they were any more fortunate in getting as his successor his son, Turki. Turki's

[1] [I.O.] Enclos. to Bombay Sec. Letters, Vol. 123, enclos. to Sec. Letter 66 of 1 November 1855, Faisal to Kemball, 24 Rabi' II 1271/14 January 1855.
[2] [I.O.] Bombay Pol. Proc., Range 395, Vol. 27, Consuln. 14 of 22 August 1855, voucher 5820, Kemball to Pol. Secy., Bombay, 6 June 1855 (No. 2A Pol. Dept.).

The Wahhabi Period, 1800-1869

first move was to strengthen the Wahhabi position in the oasis by constructing a new fort, the Qasr al-Sudairi, in the open ground to the south of Buraimi village. For the next few years little is heard of him, and it is possible that he was fully occupied in maintaining himself at Buraimi. Early in 1865 a revolt broke out in Oman against the Sultan Thuwaini, led by Saiyid Azzan ibn Qais, a member of the collateral branch of the Al Bu Sa'id, whose family had been dispossessed of the hereditary governorship of Sauhar by the late Sultan Sa'id in 1851. The Amir Faisal immediately took advantage of the situation and sent envoys to Muscat to demand four times the annual amount of *zakat* agreed upon in 1853. To lend weight to the demand Turki al-Sudairi dispatched a force from Buraimi to ravage eastern Oman, where it plundered the coastal town of Sur and murdered a British Indian subject. Cowed by the attack, Thuwaini paid Faisal's envoys $M.T. 16,000. The British authorities in India now advised him to take a stand against the Wahhabis, and to end their menaces once and for all by driving their garrison from Buraimi. Thuwaini agreed to act and towards the close of 1865 he assembled a general levy of the tribes of Oman at Sauhar. Annoyed by this show of spirit, and especially by the British Government's encouragement, the Wahhabis raided a town on the Batinah Coast, where they concentrated on terrorizing the British Indian inhabitants, driving a number of them into the sea where one was drowned. Colonel Lewis Pelly, the Resident in the Gulf, sent a demand to Riyadh for compensation for the murders and robberies, and accompanied it with a threat of punitive action against the Wahhabi ports on the Hasa coast if compensation were not forthcoming within a certain time. The demand arrived as the Amir Faisal lay dying, in December 1865, and the reply did not reach Pelly in time to prevent him from carrying out an ineffectual naval bombardment of Dammam in January 1866. Meanwhile, the Sultan Thuwaini had also died, murdered by his son, Salim, at the instigation of the Wahhabis and with the help of a Wahhabi accomplice.[1]

Thuwaini's murder was designed to place in power in Oman someone, like Salim, more subservient to the wishes of Riyadh. Colonel Pelly was afterwards told by Abu Isa, who was W. G. Pal-

---

[1] Lorimer, *Gazetteer of P. Gulf*, I, 474–6 and [I.O.] Collections to Political Despatches to India, Vol. 85, Colln. to Desp. 61 of 22 August 1866, Pelly to Chief Secy., Bombay, 14 March 1866 (No. 17 Pol. Dept.). The accomplice's name was Saif ibn Sulaiman al-Bishari.

The Wahhabi Period, 1800–1869

grave's companion on his journey to Riyadh in 1863, that Abdullah ibn Faisal, who had now succeeded his father as Amir, had had knowledge of the murder plot well in advance.[1] Abdullah himself asserted to Pelly in January 1866: 'As regards Muscat, you as well as others know that they are our subjects, and has [sic] given tribute (zakat) to our ancestors for years past.'[2] He was willing, however, to be accommodating, and in April 1866 he sent a mission to Bushire to discuss the recent attacks upon Oman. Shaikh Muhammad ibn Abdullah ibn Manah, the leader, told Pelly in the course of the discussions that Abdullah considered himself an Ottoman subject.[3] In fact, even as Shaikh Muhammad was telling Pelly this, another Wahhabi mission was at Baghdad, offering the Amir's submission to the Porte, and asking for protection against any further British naval operations on the Hasa coast.[4] At the close of the discussions at Bushire Shaikh Muhammad offered to give Pelly a written undertaking, on behalf of the Amir, that attacks such as those recently made upon the Sultanate of Muscat would not recur, and he offered, also, to extend the guarantee to cover states like Bahrain and the Trucial Shaikhdoms, in treaty relations with the British Government. Pelly accepted the offer and the undertaking was written out and signed on 21 April. It read:

'I, Mahomed bin Abdullah bin Maneh, am certain on the following points:

'I am authorized by Imaum Abdullah bin Fysul to request the Sahib, the Resident in the Persian Gulf, to become the medium of friendship between Imaum Abdullah bin Fysul and the British Government.

'*Secondly*.—I assure the Resident in the Persian Gulf on the part of Imaum Abdullah bin Fysul that he will not oppose or injure British subjects residing in territories under the authority of Abdullah bin Fysul, and

'*Thirdly*.—I assure the Resident in the Persian Gulf on the part of Imaum Abdullah bin Fysul that he will not injure or attack the territories of the Arab tribes in alliance with the British Government,

---

[1] [I.O.] India Foreign Proceedings (Political), Range 437, Vol. 68, August 1866, no. 174, Pelly to Pol. Secy., Bombay, 9 July 1866 (No. 80).
[2] [I.O.] India For. Proc. (Pol.), Range 437, Vol. 67, January 1866, no. 63, Abdullah ibn Faisal to Pelly, 10 Ramadhan 1282/28 January 1866.
[3] [I.O.] Collns. to Pol. Desp. to India, Vol. 85, Colln. to Desp. 61 of 22 August 1866, Pelly to Chief Secy., Bombay, 23 April 1866 (No. 42 Pol. Dept.).
[4] [I.O.] Collns. to Pol. Desp. to India, Vol. 88, Colln. to Desp. 37 of 28 February 1867, A. B. Kemball (Consul-General) to Lord Lyons (H.B.M. Ambass. at Constantinople), Baghdad, 18 April 1866 (No. 15).

The Wahhabi Period, 1800-1869

specially on the Kingdom of Muscat, further than in receiving the zukat that has been customary of old.'[1] It might be observed here, with reference to what has been said previously about the nature of the *zakat* paid to the Wahhabi Amirs in the nineteenth century,[2] that the *zakat* mentioned in the declaration obviously carried with it no implication of political overlordship or territorial sovereignty on the part of Abdullah ibn Faisal. If it had, Pelly would never have agreed to its continued payment, seeing that for nearly fifty years his government had upheld the independence of the littoral states of Eastern Arabia against a number of pretenders to their sovereignty—Wahhabis, Egyptians, Persians and Turks. What is more, as Abdullah ibn Faisal was, by admission, an Ottoman subject, any acknowledgement of his overlordship over the littoral states would have been tantamount to a recognition of Ottoman suzerainty over them. Pelly's sole reason for agreeing to the continued payment of *zakat* from these states to Abdullah was the same as that which had prompted Colonel Hennell in 1851 to advocate its payment by the Shaikh of Bahrain, viz., that it conduced to the peace of the Arabian shore.[3]

The parricide, Salim ibn Thuwaini, reigned in Oman for only two years. From the moment of his accession he had been at the mercy of two opposing groups which sought to dominate him—the Wah-

[1] C. U. Aitchison, *A Collection of Treaties, Engagements and Sanads relating to India and Neighbouring Countries*, 3rd edn., 11 vols., Calcutta, 1892, X, 116. The original instrument was forwarded by Pelly to Bombay with his dispatch of 23 April 1866 (see above, note 3, p. 84).

[2] See above, pp. 77-79.

[3] The authors of the *Saudi Memorial* are greatly exercised by the mention of *zakat* in the declaration of 1866, because it clashes with their theory that the payment of *zakat* is an acknowledgement of political sovereignty (see below, pp. 239-40 and Appendix B). They find a way out of their dilemma by asserting that the *zakat* of the 1866 declaration was not 'true Islamic *zakah*' but 'political tribute, pure and simple', and that it was, in fact, called by other names at the time—*qanun, kharaj*, etc. (See *Memorial*, I, Chapter IV, paras. 195 and 217, and II, Appendix B, Part 2.) The question of the nature of 'true Islamic *zakah*' aside, might it not be presumed that the payment of 'political tribute, pure and simple' is an acknowledgement of political subjection? In this case, as remarked above, Pelly would hardly have agreed to the inclusion of the clause on *zakat* in the declaration. The point is not worth labouring: Abdullah ibn Faisal himself called the payments '*zakat*' in his letter to Pelly of 28 January 1866 (above, p. 84) and his envoy wrote the word into the declaration of 21 April 1866.

The Wahhabi Period, 1800–1869

habis at Buraimi and the Ibadi *mutawwa'*s.[1] *Mutawwa'* literally means 'one who obeys or submits'. As a class, the *mutawwa'*s of Oman were the most fiery and intolerant adherents of Ibadiya. They were led by Sa'id ibn Khalfan al-Khalili, and they derived their main material support from the *tamimah* of the powerful Al Hirth tribe of the Sharqiyah, Salih ibn Ali, and from Saiyid Azzan ibn Qais of Rastaq, the head of the cadet branch of the Al Bu Sa'id. The ultimate goal of the coalition was the overthrow of the main Al Bu Sa'id line and the inauguration of a strict religious régime in Oman. In October 1868 Salim was ousted from power by Azzan ibn Qais, who not long afterwards would appear to have been elected Imam of Oman by his immediate followers, although there is no indication that the election received the necessary ratification by the tribes. For the first few months of his reign the *mutawwa'*s were very much in the forefront, and their energies were directed largely towards persecuting the many foreigners, and especially Indians, who dwelt at Muscat and other ports for trade. By the spring of 1869, however, Azzan had largely shaken himself loose from their grip and was asserting his mastery over Oman.

Salim ibn Thuwaini was then on the Trucial Coast, trying to gather support for an attempted overthrow of Azzan. In April the Wahhabi *naib* at Buraimi, Turki al-Sudairi, journeyed to Sharjah to see if he could rally the Trucial Shaikhs to Salim's cause. He told the Assistant Political Resident, Captain A. Cotton Way, whom he met at Sharjah, that he had no definite orders from the Amir Abdullah to help Salim, but presumably the Amir would not be distressed by Azzan's overthrow. On 7 April al-Sudairi was shot dead at Sharjah in an affray with the Shaikh's retainers. Way, who was then at Dubai, returned to Sharjah to inquire into the killing, and he was told that al-Sudairi had been shot after he had taken the Shaikh prisoner by treachery, in an endeavour to force him to lend support to Salim, and had killed one of the Shaikh's retainers who had tried to rescue him.[2]

---

[1] The authors of the *Saudi Memorial* state in Vol. I, Chapter IV, para. 216, that the British Government were reluctant to recognize Salim as Sultan. Two paragraphs later they refer to him as 'the chosen instrument of the British'. In view of the circumstances in which he came to power, one might properly ask whose 'chosen instrument' he was.

[2] [I.O.] Secret Letters, Various, Vol. 15 (1869), Way to Pelly, 15 April 1869. The version of this event given in the *Saudi Memorial* (I, Chapter IV, para. 224) runs as follows:

The Wahhabi Period, 1800–1869

Al-Sudairi's death gave the Na'im of Buraimi the opening that they had long awaited. 'The Naeem tribe', runs a report from Muscat in July 1869, 'complained bitterly of oppression suffered at the hands of Sidayree, the late Wahabee Lieutenant, resolved in their minds how they could free themselves from the Wahabee yoke, and resorted to the expedient of inviting Azan to take possession of Beraymee. Azan and Khulelee [Sa'id ibn Khalfan al-Khalili] not being the men to allow the grass to grow under their feet, the offer of the Naeem was accepted.'[1]

Azzan marched on the oasis in June, and on the 18th of that month he forced the surrender of the Wahhabi garrison in the forts. His own account of the event, as given afterwards to the Resident in the Gulf, runs:

'... We have returned to Muscat—Praise be to the Sublime—in the best of health, after forcing the Buraimi town in a battle which lasted for four days, some of the enemy having been killed, and some of their fortresses having been destroyed by the action of a cannon; and when they were hard pressed, and saw that they had no power [left] to offer resistance, they submitted reluctantly and asked for security for themselves, and for what they wanted to keep of their livestock of horses and camels, [which] we granted in grace, and under no compulsion. On this they camped [for a while], and then they decamped, and moved on towards the north.

'God has thus relieved his people from the aggressive Wahhabis. He drove them out "in shame and feeling low". We found the people living in those parts under the worst conditions from what they had to suffer of their despicable tyranny and high-handed cruelty. And we returned to these all that those had robbed or confiscated of their stock and property. And their eyes were gladdened with the removal of [their] misfortune, and they praised their Lord, for He is the Almighty who possesses [all], and they settled down in their own land in peace.'[2]

Abdullah ibn Faisal was not prepared, at first, to accept the loss

'Turki al-Sudairi, the Amir of Buraimi, went to Sharjah in April to help adjust dynastic difficulties there. A fight broke out in the town during the course of which Turki was shot and killed. Those who did the deed were filled with remorse, for their impulsive act deprived the region of a leader who had worked untiringly over the years for the welfare of the people.'

[1] [I.O.] Sec. Letters, Various, Vol. 15, Lieut.-Col. H. Disbrowe (Pol. Agent at Muscat) to Pelly, 16 July 1869.

[2] [I.O.] Sec. Letters, Various, Vol. 15, Azzan ibn Qais to Pelly, Jumada I, 1286/August 1869. See also, *U.K. Memorial*, I, 77.

The Wahhabi Period, 1800-1869

of Buraimi. At the beginning of 1870 he was reported to be assembling a force in Hasa to retake the oasis, and in February Azzan ibn Qais went to Buraimi to confer with Shaikh Zaid ibn Khalifah, the ruler of Abu Dhabi, on its defence. On 1 May he wrote to Major Way, now Political Agent at Muscat: 'Sheikh Zaeed of Abuthabi has arrived and sworn friendship and promised to oppose Wahabis. Mahomed [ibn] Ali Naeem [has] sworn allegiance and promised [that the] Littoral Chiefs should visit me at Sohar. Shan't visit [Trucial] coast, but shall return to Sohar when arrangements [are] finished for protection of Beraymi.'[1] The threatened attack by Abdullah never materialized, the Amir fearing to attempt the crossing of the Dhafrah against the opposition of Zaid ibn Khalifah, especially as the region was in the grip of a drought which made water and forage scarce.[2] Before long Abdullah was to be fully occupied in coping with a rebellion raised against him by his brother Sa'ud.[3]

Rebellion also broke out against Azzan ibn Qais in Oman in the latter half of 1870. Saiyid Turki ibn Sa'id, a son of the great Saiyid Sa'id ibn Sultan, landed on the Oman coast from Bandar Abbas in Persia, where he had been in exile, in September 1870, and made for Buraimi at the invitation of the Na'im.[4] They had apparently become disenchanted with the rule of Azzan ibn Qais, particularly as he had insisted upon stationing a garrison of his own men in the main fort, the Qasr al-Khandaq. Their kinsman, the Shaikh of Ajman, had told Colonel Pelly, the Political Resident, the previous year that the Na'im, 'being somewhat implicated in the death of the Wahabee Lieutenant [al-Sudairi], joined Syud Azan for fear of the Imaum [Abdullah ibn Faisal]'.[5] Now that the danger from the Wahhabis was past, the Na'im were prepared to challenge Azzan. The Political Agent at Muscat reported in October 1870:

'Shortly after Syud Toorkee arrived at Bereymee Sheik Zaeed, the Chief of Aboothabee, who is under compact with Syud Azan to protect the western frontier, and who had been summoned to render

[1] [I.O.] *Précis of Nejd Affairs*, p. 35, Azzan ibn Qais to Way, 1 March 1870. The letter is contained in a telegram from Way to Bombay.
[2] Loc. cit., Pelly to Pol. Secy., Bombay, 21 March 1870.
[3] Sa'ud had visited Oman in February 1870 to seek help from Azzan ibn Qais. He accompanied him to Buraimi to meet Zaid ibn Khalifah, and afterwards returned to Najd.
[4] Badger, *Imams and Seyyids*, p. cxvii.
[5] [I.O.] India For. Proc. (Pol.), Range 438, Vol. 9, February 1870, no. 275, Pelly to Pol. Secy., Bombay, 17 September 1869 (No. 167).

The Wahhabi Period, 1800–1869

assistance to the Bereymee garrison, arrived, and the Chiefs of Debai, Hejman [Ajman], and Ras-ool-Khyma came from the Arab littoral to assist Syud Toorkee. Several engagements were fought without any apparent success on either side, each party having held his position.'[1]

Turki broke off the engagement at Buraimi early in October and moved south into the Dhahirah. Azzan met him with a hastily assembled force of tribal levies at Dhank, and was badly defeated. Retiring to the Batinah, with Turki in pursuit, he took refuge in Matrah, on the coast just north of Muscat. There Turki caught up with him in January 1871 and slew him.

Abdullah ibn Faisal also fell from power in Najd at the same time. Defeated and driven out by his brother, Sa'ud, Abdullah fled northwards into Jabal Shammar at the close of 1870, and from there, early in 1871, he appealed to the Turkish authorities in the *vilayet* of Baghdad to help him recover his position as Amir of Najd. Midhat Pasha, the vigorous *vali* of Baghdad, promptly appointed Abdullah Ottoman *qaim-maqam* of Najd, and in the spring of 1871 he dispatched an expedition to Hasa to take possession of that province in the name of the Ottoman Sultan. The Turks could make no headway, however, against Sa'ud in Najd, and Abdullah soon deserted them to carry on a running fight alone against his brother for the next four years. At the time of the Turkish landing in Hasa a small party of Wahhabis arrived at Buraimi, led by a certain Mahbub ibn Jauhar, formerly the confidential secretary of the late Faisal ibn Turki. Whether he came as the representative of Sa'ud, as was given out at the time, or of Abdullah, whose agent he was reported to be in 1873, is not certain. His arrival, however, gave Zaid ibn Khalifah of Abu Dhabi a pretext for prevailing upon the Na'im to hand over the Qasr al-Khandaq, which they had reoccupied on the defeat and death of Azzan ibn Qais. The Residency Agent at Sharjah reported in May 1871:

'The news from Beraymee is that Sheikh Zayid bin Khalifa and Ameer Mahboob, Imaum Saood's Deputy, on arrival at Beraymee, demanded the castle from the Naeem. The Naeem would not surrender. Sheikh Zayed tried artifice and succeeded in effecting dissension among the garrison, and at last they made over the castle to Ameer Mahboob without the consent of the Chief of the Naeem.

[1] [I.O.] India For. Proc. (Pol.), Range 438, Vol. 11, December 1870, no. 714, Major Way to Pol. Secy., Bombay, 28 October 1870 (No. 525).

The Wahhabi Period, 1800–1869

Ameer Mahboob, after taking possession of the castle of Beraymee, wrote to the Sheikhs of Oman, asking them for provisions and requesting their allegiance and that they should call on him. The Sheikhs between Debaye and Ras-ul-Khyma would not consent to this. It is probable that differences will arise between the Sheikhs and Ameer Mahboob.'[1]

How long Mahbub remained at Buraimi is not known. Certainly he was gone by 1873,[2] but in all likelihood he had been forced to leave long before that date. Fifty years were to pass before a Saudi agent again made an appearance at Buraimi.

[1] [I.O.] India For. Proc. (Pol.), Vol. 760, September 1871, no. 45, Haji Abdur Rahman to Resident, 16 Safar 1288/7 May 1871.
[2] See *Saudi Memorial*, I, Chapter IV, para. 240.

CHAPTER III

The Ascendancy of Zaid ibn Khalifah, 1871-1909

A general eclipse of Wahhabi power in Eastern Arabia followed the occupation of Hasa by the Turks in 1871. The Turks were to remain in control of that province for the next forty years, during which time the Al Saʻud were to suffer defeat, and eventually dispossession from their homeland of Najd, by the pro-Turkish dynasty of Ibn Rashid of Jabal Shammar in northern Arabia. The politics of Eastern Arabia, south of Hasa, came to be dominated in these years by the figure of Zaid ibn Khalifah ibn Shakhbut, the Al Bu Falah ruler of Abu Dhabi. Zaid, who had succeeded to the chieftainship on the deposition of his cousin, Saʻid ibn Tahnun, in 1855, had become the most powerful of the Trucial Shaikhs by the early eighteen-seventies. His rise to power had been helped by the death in 1866, at an advanced age, of the great chief of the Qawasim of Sharjah and Ras al-Khaima, Sultan ibn Saqr, who for fifty years previously had strenuously contested the paramountcy of the Trucial Coast with the Al Bu Falah. By the last decade of the century Zaid ibn Khalifah had extended his authority over the greater part of the hinterland of Trucial Oman, and even into the Dhahirah province of Oman, where his influence exceeded that of the Al Bu Saʻid Sultan, who consequently entrusted him with the care of his interests there. Indeed, the only serious challenge that Zaid had to contend with in these years came from the Al Thani Shaikh of Qatar, who endeavoured, in the eighteen-seventies and eighteen-eighties, both on his own account and in his role as an Ottoman vassal, to take possession of Khaur al-Udaid.

At the time that he invested Abdullah ibn Faisal with the rank of Ottoman *qaim-maqam* of Najd, Midhat Pasha had let it be known that he took a most comprehensive view of the limits of the *sanjaq* of Najd, considering them to embrace not only that province and Hasa

The Ascendancy of Zaid ibn Khalifah, 1871-1909

but Bahrain, Qatar, Trucial Oman and the Sultanate of Muscat as well. The claim was promptly rejected by the British Government in a protest to the Porte, which in turn dissociated itself from the pretensions advanced by its ambitious *vali*. Nevertheless, in July 1871, the Turkish flag was raised at Dauhah, on the east coast of Qatar, by Shaikh Jasim, son of the aged ruler of Dauhah, Muhammad ibn Thani, after he had been visited by a deputation from Midhat Pasha.

To the south of Dauhah, at Khaur al-Udaid, was a colony of the Qubaisat section of the Bani Yas who had again defected from Abu Dhabi in 1869. Early in 1871, following complaints from Zaid ibn Khalifah that the existence of the colony was a threat to Abu Dhabi's prosperity, the Resident in the Gulf, Colonel Pelly, made careful inquiries into the status of Khaur al-Udaid. He later reported to his government:

'Being uncertain whether Adeyd [Udaid] did *bona fide* belong to Aboothabee, and being desirous further of ascertaining whether the Chief's apprehensions were well founded, I requested Major Smith [the Assistant Resident], on his recent visit to the Arab Coast, to give attention to these questions. Major Smith arrived at the opinion that Adeyd did belong to Aboothabee, and that the Chief's township was seriously injured in its trade, etc., by the new settlement. Further, that persistence in the maintenance of the settlement would sooner or later lead to collision by sea. For the moment I begged the Aboothabee Chief to refrain from action by sea, and prosecuted my own enquiries from numerous independent sources at various points of the Gulf. The information I collected was wholly to the effect that Adeyd belonged to Aboothabee, while the Guttur [Qatar] Chief, whose territories are on one side coterminous with the district of Adeyd, ignored all connexion with it. Under these circumstances, I addressed a letter to the persons settling at Adeyd, cautioning them that if they choose to settle within the territories of the Aboothabee Chief, they should conform to his rule.'[1]

The Qubaisat, however, were far from willing to return meekly to Shaikh Zaid's control, and the arrival of the Turks at Dauhah and the acknowledgement of Ottoman suzerainty by Shaikh Jasim ibn Muhammad Al Thani provided them with an opportunity to make good their claim to independence. When the Assistant Political Resident, Major Sidney Smith, called at Khaur al-Udaid towards the

---

[1] [I.O.] India For. Proc. (Pol.), Vol. 763, March 1872, no. 369, Pelly to Pol. Secy., Bombay, 11 March 1871.

The Ascendancy of Zaid ibn Khalifah, 1871-1909

end of July, the leader of the Qubaisat, Buti ibn Khadim, not only informed him that he refused to return to Zaid ibn Khalifah's jurisdiction but he also defined the area over which he claimed independent control: '*viz.*, from Ras-ul-Hala, midway to Wakra in Guttur [Qatar], continuously along the southern coast through Adeyd to a point abreast of the island of Seir Beniyas. He further claims the Isles of Dalma and other islets within that circuit, hitherto unquestionably belonging to Aboothabee.'[1] Such a claim, as Smith observed dryly, was 'a modest request for some half of Aboothabee territory'.[2] At the time of preferring it Buti ibn Khadim made pointed reference to the fact that his tribesmen had been offered a Turkish flag, but had so far declined it.[3]

The immediate interest of the British authorities in the Gulf in Khaur al-Udaid was in the possibility of its becoming a refuge for pirates. As matters stood, there was no authority to whom representations could be made were any maritime irregularities to be committed by its inhabitants. An interest of longer range lay in seeing that Ottoman authority should spread no further, even in a nebulous form, along the Arabian littoral of the Gulf, for the extension of Ottoman rule would substitute the ineffective control of Turkish officials over the maritime tribes for the direct surveillance hitherto exercised by the Political Resident. On the other hand, the Resident was not prepared to suspend the operation of the Trucial System to allow the Shaikh of Abu Dhabi to proceed against the seceders at Khaur al-Udaid with naval means, unless that place actually became a piratical haunt. Applications by Zaid ibn Khalifah in 1873 and 1874 to be permitted to attack the settlement from the sea were refused. In 1876-7, however, a number of piracies were committed from Khaur al-Udaid, mainly by Murrah tribesmen from the interior. In May 1877 the Government of India directed the Resident to try to effect a reconciliation between the seceders and Shaikh Zaid. If this failed, he was to use force to bring them under Zaid's control.

The efforts at reconciliation were unsuccessful, largely because the Turks had lately tightened their hold on Qatar. Jasim Al Thani had been appointed *qaim-maqam* of Dauhah in 1876, and the Qubaisat were counting upon Turkish support. At the close of 1877 the Resi-

[1] [I.O.] India For. Proc. (Pol.), Vol. 763, March 1872, no. 374, Smith to Pelly, 21 July 1871 (No. 26).
[2] Ibid.
[3] [I.O.] India For. Proc. (Pol.), Vol. 763, March 1872, no. 373, Pelly to Pol. Secy., Bombay, 31 July 1871.

The Ascendancy of Zaid ibn Khalifah, 1871–1909

dent proceeded to Khaur la-Udaid with one of the cruisers of the Gulf squadron to assist Zaid against the Qubaisat. They did not wait for the blow to fall but fled to Dauhah, after dismantling their houses and filling in the wells. For the next year or two they remained in the vicinity of Dauhah, during which time Jasim Al Thani tried to bring them under his authority. He failed, and in 1880 they came to terms with Zaid ibn Khalifah and returned to Abu Dhabi, where their former property was restored to them.

The sojourn of the Qubaisat at Udaid and at Dauhah started a festering quarrel between the Al Thani and the Al Bu Falah which has endured to the present day. Jasim Al Thani had hoped, by bringing the Qubaisat under his authority, to lay claim to Khaur al-Udaid. His irritation at their return to Abu Dhabi expressed itself in a series of pecuniary claims against their leader, Buti ibn Khadim, and when these were ignored Shaikh Jasim sent a raiding party into Abu Dhabi territory in December 1881. Four years later, having still obtained no satisfaction from the Qubaisat, and in retaliation for a raid on Qatar carried out by Manasir subject to Zaid ibn Khalifah, he sent Bani Hajir and Murrah tribesmen to plunder Abu Dhabi territory. On both occasions Jasim made a feint as if to seize Khaur al-Udaid, only to be warned by the Political Resident that Udaid belonged to Abu Dhabi. A third reminder was given him in 1886, when he tried to make use of his connexion with the Turks to occupy Udaid.

Open warfare broke out between Qatar and Abu Dhabi in 1888, after Manasir of the Al Bu Sha'ar section had raided up to the walls of Dauhah. Jasim retaliated in March by striking at the Liwa Oasis. Further raids on Qatar by Abu Dhabi tribesmen led him finally to make a savage descent upon Liwa in January 1889. In his train, reported the Residency Agent at Sharjah, rode Ibn Rashid's governor of Riyadh and a son of the late Wahhabi Amir, Faisal ibn Turki.

'... Jasim, accompanied by Abdul Rahman Bin Feysal, and Ibn Sabhan the Deputy of Ibn Rasheed in the districts of Riadth, and taking a large army with him has arrived at Elzafrah [al-Dhafrah] and Leevah [Liwa], which lie within the territories of the Chief of Aboothabee; ... they massacred the inhabitants and cut down date trees; ... their messengers had arrived at Baraimee and interviewed Mohamed-Bin-Ali, the head of the Na'aim tribe, and ... Ibn Rasheed will send some soldiers to Jasim's aid. It is reported that the Chief of Aboothabee is at a loss what to do as regards the approaching warfare, as he fears the advent of Ibn Rashid, and it is

The Ascendancy of Zaid ibn Khalifah, 1871–1909

thought that Jasim would not have ventured to come down so far, without the assistance of Ibn Rashid.'[1]

Fratricide and intestine jealousies had by this time brought the Al Sa'ud to a low pass. Sa'ud ibn Faisal, on his death in January 1875, had been succeeded by his brother, Abdullah, the former Amir. Abdullah was deposed by his family in 1887, and Riyadh was occupied shortly afterwards by the forces of the ruler of Jabal Shammar, the Amir Muhammad ibn Rashid. Abdur Rahman ibn Faisal, who rode to the sack of Liwa with Jasim Al Thani, was the fourth son of the great Faisal, and the father of Abdul Aziz, the future King of Saudi Arabia. Two years later, together with other members of the Al Sa'ud, he was to be driven from Najd altogether by Ibn Rashid, to become a refugee and a wanderer.

Ibn Rashid's support of Jasim Al Thani did not last long. When Zaid ibn Khalifah called out the Awamir, Al Bu Shamis, Bani Qitab and Dhawahir to aid the Bani Yas and Manasir in avenging the attack on Liwa, Jasim found that he had to face them alone. Prudently, he retired on Qatar.[2] Raids and counter-raids by both sides went on for another two years, when they gave way to an uneasy peace.

In November 1875, six years after the end of the Wahhabi occupations of Buraimi, Colonel S. B. Miles, the Political Agent at Muscat, visited the oasis. He travelled with the permission of the Sultan, Turki ibn Sa'id, by way of the Batinah Coast and the Wadi al-Jizzi. He found on his arrival that the fort built by Turki al-Sudairi had been destroyed by Azzan ibn Qais in 1870, and that the Qasr al-Khandaq was now in the possession of the Na'im.

'They occupy el-Bereymi proper and Su'areh [Sa'ara] and their possession of the fort enables them to overawe the whole of the settlement. Since the time of Seyyid 'Azan they have been practically uninterfered with by the Muscat Government, but of course owe allegiance to the present Sultan. The Na'im are at feud with the Beni Yas who occupy part of el-Bereymi and their hostility is interrupted only by occasional truces; collisions frequently occurring

[1] *U.K. Memorial*, II, Annex B, no. 22, Officiating Agent, Sharjah, to Res. 18 January 1889 (No. 8).
[2] See *U.K. Memorial*, II, Annex B, nos. 21 and 23, Res. Agent, Sharjah, to Res., 13 January and 19 February 1889.

The Ascendancy of Zaid ibn Khalifah, 1871–1909

between them. Of the two sections of the Na'im one inhabits more particularly el-Jow and Bereymi, the other el-Dhahireh. They are of the more orthodox or Sunni persuasion unlike the generality of 'Omanis who are Ibadhiya. The chief Sheikh of the tribe is Mohammed-bin-'Ali-bin Hamud, who lives at Dhank, his representative at el-Bereymi being his son, Salim. The principal Hinawi tribe at el-Bereymi is the Beni Yas who formerly gained so much notoriety by their piratical exploits. The Chief of this tribe is Sheikh Zaid-bin-Khalifah, a man of strong character, and perhaps the sole individual possessing any real personal power and authority. He resides at Abuthabi and there are four smaller Sheikhs subordinate to him residing at el-Bereymi. This tribe takes the lead on the Hinawi side in all dissensions between the Hinawis and Ghafiris at el-Bereymi, and during Seyyid 'Azan's reign held the predominant position here. The Beni Yas occupy the villages of Jemi [Jimi], Katareh [Qattarah], Heyli [Hili], and the Wady Mes'udi at el-Bereymi, and are said to have formerly out-numbered the Na'im but this state of affairs has become reversed of late.'[1]

In the years following Miles's visit the balance of power in the oasis swung in favour of the Bani Yas. A revolt of the Dhawahir against Al Bu Falah rule was suppressed in 1887–8, and in 1891, with the aid of the Shaikh of Dubai, Zaid ibn Khalifah captured the principal Dhahiri village of al-Ain. A fort erected by him there still stands today, an inscription on its base recording the year, 1897, in which it was built. In the same year Zaid appropriated, or re-possessed, the settlement of Jahili and began a new Bani Yas colony in the Wadi Mas'udi.[2] With the occupation of al-Ain all five Dhahiri villages in the oasis—al-Ain, Jimi, Hili, Qattarah and Mu'tiridh—were now under Al Bu Falah control. The paramount shaikh of the Dhawahir, Ahmad ibn Muhammad ibn Hilal of Jimi, became Zaid's *wali* in the oasis, exercising a general power of superintendence over the headmen of the other villages and acting as his agent in dealings with the other tribes of the Buraimi region. Inevitably, under such an arrangement, the *tamimah* of the Na'im suffered a decline in importance. Sultan ibn Muhammad Al Hamuda, the head of the Al Bu Khuraiban of Buraimi village, who had become *tamimah* on the death of his father, Muhammad ibn Ali of Dhank, was reduced,

---

[1] 'On the Route between Sohar and el-Bereymi in Oman', *Journ. As. Soc. Bengal*, XLVI (1877), 52.
[2] Lorimer, *Gazetteer of P. Gulf*, I, 771.

The Ascendancy of Zaid ibn Khalifah, 1871-1909

in effect, to the status of a vassal of Zaid ibn Khalifah. He eventually grew to accept the relationship, partly as a result of Zaid's taking to wife one of his daughters but more particularly because Zaid consistently supported his authority over the other elements of the Na'im in the Dhahirah and at the western end of the Wadi al-Jizzi.

The workings of this relationship, and the extent of Zaid's influence within and beyond the Buraimi Oasis are illustrated by two local collections of letters from this period, one from the archives of the Ruler of Abu Dhabi printed in the *United Kingdom Memorial* of 1955, the other preserved in the family of Ahmad ibn Hilal. The latter, which came to light after 1955, range in date from the last decade of the nineteenth century to the nineteen-thirties.[1] The bulk of the letters in both collections deal with the adjustment of tribal disputes: most are from Zaid ibn Khalifah to Ahmad ibn Hilal, but there are a number from other shaikhs.

In June 1895, when war threatened between the Na'im of Buraimi and the Awamir, Sultan ibn Muhammad, the *tamimah* of the Na'im, wrote to Ahmad ibn Hilal: 'I would inform you that we have received a declaration of war today from the Awamir. We could not do anything against them, because our interests and yours are one. ... Whatever you decide please let us know because they (the Awamir) are with you.'[2] Again, in 1903, when fighting broke out between the Shaikh of Sharjah and his dependant, the headman of Fujairah, on the coast of the Gulf of Oman, some of the Al Bu Shamis dwelling at the western end of the Wadi al-Jizzi, who were subject to Sultan ibn Muhammad, joined in the quarrel and tried to persuade other tribes to do the same. Zaid sent orders to Ahmad ibn Hilal in April that the Al Bu Shamis were to be forced to return and made to respect Sultan ibn Muhammad's authority. 'They interfered with the Bani Ka'b and other tribes of "the son", Shaikh Sultan bin Muhammad. It is better that Sultan bin Muhammad should show his mind to them and threaten them and not allow them to go (to the coast). ... As you are aware our interests and those of Shaikh Sultan are one, in good times and in adversity.'[3] The following

---

[1] The collection, which is referred to in the following pages as the 'Dhawahir Collection', contains more than 200 letters, most of them relating to the period 1890–1910.
[2] *U.K. Memorial*, II, Annex J, no. 1, Sultan ibn Muhammad to Ahmad ibn Hilal, Dhu'l-Hijjah 1312.
[3] *U.K. Memorial*, II, Annex F, no. 6, Zaid to Ahmad ibn Hilal, 5 Muharram 1321.

month Zaid issued a general interdiction to the tribes of the hinterland between Buraimi and Fujairah against participating in the quarrel, and he told Ahmad ibn Hilal to do his best to compose it.

'We would inform you that the letter we are sending you for the Bani Qitab, the Bani Ka'ab, the Ghafalah and the Khawatir should be shown to "the son" Shaikh Sultan ibn Muhammad. If God wills that you should proceed towards and meet with "the son" Shaikh Saqr ibn Khalid [of Sharjah], you are to bring before you all those for whom you have letters and tell each of these separately and directly that you are sent by us to "the son" Shaikh Saqr to make peace between him and Hamad ibn Abdullah of Fujairah. . . .'[1]

A year later, when the *tamimah* of the Na'im was having difficulties with the Baduin Bani Qitab, who dwell in the hinterland of the Shaikhdom of Sharjah, he appealed through Ahmad ibn Hilal to Zaid for help: 'We have been depending on him for all matters since long ago.'[2] Zaid sent his son Khalifah to Buraimi with instructions to settle matters to Sultan ibn Muhammad's satisfaction. '. . . We, in our relations to him, shall not be overtaken in our attitude towards God by the blame of any blamer. He is dependent on God and on us in good and its opposite.'[3] More serious trouble with the Baduin Bani Qitab developed in 1905, when they erected a fort at the head of the Wadi Hatta, which connects Dubai on the Trucial Coast with the Batinah Coast, and began molesting passing caravans. They also took control of a nearby village, Masfut, subject to Sultan ibn Muhammad. He again appealed to Zaid in May 1905. 'God may witness', he told Ahmad ibn Hilal, 'that we are relying on God and on him in all matters, trifling or important, for, as you know, we are [to him] like an article in the hand of its maker.'[4] A meeting of the Trucial Shaikhs was held at Dubai in September, when it was decided that the Bani Qitab should dismantle the fort in the Wadi Hatta and return Masfut to the *tamimah* of the Na'im.

Almost immediately fresh trouble broke out with the Bani Qitab, begun this time by the settled branch of the tribe at Aflaj Bani Qitab, a group of settlements in the Dhahirah. They quarrelled with and

---

[1] [Dhawahir Colln.] Zaid to Ahmad ibn Hilal, 29 Safar 1321.

[2] [Dhawahir Colln.] Sultan ibn Muhammad to Ahmad ibn Hilal, 14 Muharram 1322/March 1904.

[3] [Dhawahir Colln.] Zaid to Khalifah ibn Zaid and Ahmad ibn Hilal, 14 Rajab 1322/September 1904.

[4] [Dhawahir Colln.] Sultan ibn Muhammad to Ahmad ibn Hilal, 22 Rabi' II, 1323.

The Ascendancy of Zaid ibn Khalifah, 1871-1909

then attacked their vassals, the Baluchis of the nearby village of Mazim.[1] The Baluchis called upon Zaid ibn Khalifah for help, and he tried, but without success, to prevent the Baduin Bani Qitab from reinforcing their kinsmen. Mazim continued to hold out against their combined attack, and in February 1906, after stating that he intended to exact blood-money for the Baluchis slain, Zaid collected his forces to march against the Bani Qitab. They, in turn, applied to Shaikh Rashid ibn Ahmad of Umm al-Qaiwain for help, but further hostilities were averted by the convening of a meeting of the Trucial Shaikhs at Dubai in April. There a settlement was reached and an agreement drawn up, formally recognizing the spheres of tribal influence of the Shaikhs of Abu Dhabi and Umm al-Qaiwain. The Bani Qitab, the Ghafalah and the Bani Ka'ab were assigned to Shaikh Rashid ibn Ahmad, while Sultan ibn Muhammad of Buraimi and Muhammad ibn Sulaiman, the paramount shaikh of the Bani Ghafir of Dariz, in the Dhahirah, were recognized as dependants of Shaikh Zaid.[2] Zaid later wrote to Ahmad ibn Hilal at Buraimi to see to it that the Bani Qitab made restitution to the Baluchis, in accordance with the decision of the conference. 'Coming to you is Muhammad Baluchi. It is requested that you explain to him the particulars of the properties of your Arabs who have been robbed by the Bani Qitab, important or trifling, that he may claim them. Please do not delay him because we have despatched him for the stolen property of the Arabs which is with the Bani Qitab.'[3]

Zaid's influence in the Dhahirah, as indicated by his tutelary relationship to the Bani Ghafir, or Miyayihah,[4] was such that tribal leaders from distant parts of inner Oman sought his intercession. In the spring of 1899 the *tamimah* of the Ifar, a tribe living at the edge of the Oman steppes, appealed to Zaid to prevent the Manasir from attacking his tribe in retaliation for an Ifari raid into the Dhafrah. Zaid replied in May: 'The Manasir intend to attack the 'Afar, but we have stopped them, and asked them to wait until the 25th of the month. Would you come to us on the receipt of this

---

[1] The Baluchis of the Dhahirah doubtless originated in Baluchistan, but they have been so long settled in the Dhahirah that they are now classed as an Omani tribe. They have no direct connexion with the Baluchis living on the Batinah Coast or elsewhere in Oman.
[2] Lorimer, *Gazetteer of P. Gulf*, I, 753-4.
[3] [Dhawahir Colln.] Letter dated 11 Rabi' I, 1324/April 1906.
[4] This tribe, which originally gave its name to the Ghafiri faction in Omani politics, was subsequently so inconstant in its adherence to that faction as to earn for itself the name of 'the waverers', or *Miyayihah*.

The Ascendancy of Zaid ibn Khalifah, 1871-1909

letter and before the end of this period so that we may settle this trouble before anything happens.'¹ The Manasir undertook not to raid the Ifar, but two years later they broke their pledge, much to Zaid's displeasure. 'We have received news', he wrote to Ahmad ibn Hilal in September 1901, 'that the Manasir, Al Bu Sha'ar, are raiding the Ifar. On receipt of this letter you are to send a special messenger to the Ifar to warn them, lest our honour be affected in this respect.'² In 1904, while staying at Buraimi, Zaid forced the Bani Qitab to pay blood-money for two inhabitants of Ibri whom they had killed.³ Again, in September 1906, after Shaikh Sultan ibn Rashid al-Ya'aqubi of Ibri and Shaikh Muhammad ibn Sulaiman of the Miyayihah had complained of trouble from the sedentary Bani Qitab, he ordered Ahmad ibn Hilal to look into the matter and, if necessary, to call upon the *tamimah* of the Na'im for help.

'We also wish to inform you, and we emphasize this, that if a fight takes place between the people of the South and Bani Qatab of the South you should draw the attention of "the Son" Shaikh Sultan bin Muhammad bin Ali to the obligations he has to us and we have to him so that they may move in support of the Shaikhs Sultan bin Rashid and Muhammad bin Sulaiman. This is in accordance with the terms between us and "the son", Shaikh Sultan bin Muhammad. This is to be known to you.'⁴

Ahmad ibn Hilal replied a month later:

'As regards your information in respect of the dear "son" Shaikh Sultan ibn Muhammad ibn Ali, that he is as we expect him to be and more is well known to us. We are very definite about it and we maintain no suspicions or doubt in this respect. As you know, what we expect from him we do not expect from anyone else. He is to us, as God knows and witnesses, as one of my own children.'⁵

For much of the period under review Shaikh Zaid also watched over the interests of the Sultan of Muscat on the inner side of the

---

¹ *U.K. Memorial*, II, Annex I, no. 3, Zaid to Munakhir ibn Abdullah [Ifari *tamimah*], 11 Muharram 1317.
² [Dhawahir Colln.] Zaid to Ahmad ibn Hilal, 29 Jumadi II,1319.
³ Lorimer, *Gazetteer of P. Gulf*, I, 772.
⁴ *U.K. Memorial*, II, Annex F, no. 3, Zaid to Ahmad ibn Hilal, 18 Rajab 1324.
⁵ [Dhawahir Colln.] Ahmad ibn Hilal to Zaid, 2 Ramadhan 1324. In view of the relationship between the *tamimah* of the Na'im and Zaid ibn Khalifah it is odd to find the authors of the *Saudi Memorial* writing of this period:

The Ascendancy of Zaid ibn Khalifah, 1871-1909

Hajar Mountains and in the Dhahirah. The arrangement seems to have been similar to that originally made by Azzan ibn Qais after the eviction of the Wahhabis from Buraimi, and it was rendered all the more necessary by the decline in power of the Na'im. The tribe as a whole had stood by the Sultan in tribal revolts which had broken out in 1890 and 1895, but the second of the rebellions had revealed that the *tamimah* lacked the power to act effectively as the Sultan's representative in this quarter. In 1896, therefore, the Sultan Faisal ibn Turki, who had succeeded his father in 1888, entered into compact with Zaid ibn Khalifah by which Zaid was to receive a *farizah*, or annual allowance, of $M.T. 3,000 for maintaining peace and security in the Sultan's northern frontier districts.[1] The Na'im still continued, however, to receive a regular subsidy from the Sultan.

In discharging the obligation that he had assumed, Shaikh Zaid worked in close co-operation with the Sultan's *wali* at Sauhar, Sulaiman ibn Suwailim. In 1899 he was called upon to use his influence with the tribes of the Dhahirah to bring them to settle some differences which they had with the Sultan. Zaid acted through Ahmad ibn Hilal, to whom he wrote in April of that year:

'We are sending you some letters from us to Sayyid Faisal [the Sultan] and the Wali Sulaiman bin Suwailim. . . . If they intend to reach a settlement of the problems between them and the people of the Dhahirah and they want a fair mediation, so much the better. Take what part you see fit according to your experience. Try to reduce the opportunism of the people of the Dhahirah; let them be satisfied with what Sayyid Faisal would give them of his own accord. You know the people of the Dhahirah are likely to take advantage of a situation if they have the chance. However, if the Sayyid seeks the enmity of the Dhahirah the whole matter should be reconsidered. Look into this: it is for you to decide.'[2]

In 1902 the Al Bu Shamis of the Buraimi region, dissatisfied at not having received their regular allowances from the Sultan, raided the Batinah Coast. Zaid undertook to bring them to heel. 'We should

---

'When the people of Nu'aim were in difficulty during a period of Saudi eclipse, it was not to Abu Dhabi or to Muscat that they referred.' (I, Chapter IV, para 257.) 'In the oasis itself and its immediate vicinity, the tribe of Nu'aim remained the dominant local group, and its leaders regarded themselves as in some sense officiating there on behalf of the House of Sa'ud pending the restoration of its direct authority.' (I, Chapter VI, para. 62.)

[1] Lorimer, *Gazetteer of P. Gulf*, I, 747.
[2] *U.K. Memorial*, II, Annex F, no. 6, letter dated 12 Dhu'l-Hijjah 1316.

inform you', he wrote to Ahmad ibn Hilal in September, 'that we have told the shaikhs of the Al Bu Shamis to return the property which their men looted from the Batinah. We also told them to prevent their people from attacking the Batinah. We promised to favour them as regards their financial help from the Sayyid. We should like to explain to the Sayyid and the Wali Sulaiman bin Suwailim (the need) to continue helping the Al Bu Shamis, as they are relying upon God and ourselves. This must be so unless the Sayyid Faisal bin Turki releases us from our responsibility regarding them. Were this so, well and good.'[1]

The Al Bu Shamis again raided the outskirts of Sauhar in the summer of 1905, in company with the Maqabil, who live in the vicinity of the Wadi al-Jizzi. Shaikh Zaid intervened in July, sending his son Khalifah and Ahmad ibn Hilal to compel the Al Bu Shamis to withdraw. His orders to Ahmad ibn Hilal ran:

'In case the trouble caused by the Maqabil and the Shawamis of Saif ibn Sultan in the settlements of Sauhar is still going on, your "brother" Khalifah is to proceed there by our orders to mediate between them. What we inform you of and request you to do is to accompany the son Khalifah in this respect. Also it is required that efforts be made to receive all our dues from those concerned.'[2]

This last must have referred to the *farizah* paid to Zaid by the Sultan, for in September the assistant *wali* at Sauhar wrote to Ahmad ibn Hilal: 'We should like you to know that the "father" the Wali Sulaiman bin Suwailim has ordered us to send 2,000 dollars which is the usual payment for Shaikh Zaid. We hope that we will arrive soon at your place. We will tell you what we have to say verbally.'[3]

Captain P. Z. (later Sir Percy) Cox travelled to Buraimi and the Dhahirah from the Trucial Coast in 1902, when he was Political Agent at Muscat. Zaid ibn Khalifah, as Cox later recalled, 'insisted that I should travel as his guest as far as Ibri, after which I was to become the responsibility of the Ruler of Muscat'.[4] On his journey Cox found that 'Sheikh Zaeed's influence was much stronger than that of the Sultan of Muscat throughout the Dhahireh district of Oman; and was as far as one could judge almost invariably exercised

---

[1] *U.K. Memorial*, II, Annex F, no. 6, Zaid to Ahmad ibn Hilal, 17 Jumada II, 1320/September 1902.
[2] [Dhawahir Colln.] Zaid to Ahmad ibn Hilal, 11 Jumada I, 1323.
[3] *U.K. Memorial*, II, Annex F, no. 7, Yusuf ibn Sa'id al-Hajari to Ahmad ibn Hilal, 4 Rajab 1323.
[4] 'Some Excursions in Oman', *Geog. Journ.*, LXVI, 200.

The Ascendancy of Zaid ibn Khalifah, 1871–1909

in the interests of the general peace'.[1] Three years later, when he was Officiating Resident in the Gulf, Cox visited Buraimi again. As before, he travelled under the protection of Zaid ibn Khalifah, who wrote to Ahmad ibn Hilal before Cox left for the interior in December 1905: 'On the 6th H.E. the Political Resident arrived here. We had some discussions with him. Probably his intention is to travel to the Jaw area [Buraimi] *via* Ras al Khaimah. It is asked from God and from you that, on his arrival, you go to meet him. Perhaps he will wish to go to the Batinah and Sohar. If so, you, with those whom you choose from our people, should accompany him to those parts. We hope you will not fail us.'[2]

Cox reached Buraimi from Ras al-Khaima at the close of the month, and later gave the following account of the oasis:

'We entered Baraimi on this occasion from the north-west, through the recently formed Bani Yas colony called Mas'udi, started by the eldest son of the Shaikh of Abu Dhabi, and made our camp at the village of Jimi, that being the settlement nearest the centre of the Oasis and convenient as a point for fixing its position. When one speaks of "Baraimi", one means not the village of that name but the whole oasis, composed of ten separate villages situated roughly in a circle about six miles in diameter. Baraimi village, being the original settlement, has given its name to the whole. It is the head-quarters of the Naim tribe, the original owners of the oasis, and possesses the usual square fort of sun-dried brick with a tower at each angle. . . . The water supply is from numerous fulug or underground aqueducts coming in from the hills to the east, and one or two also from Jabal Hafit. Light though it is, the soil is evidently most prolific, and it was calculated that the oasis supported not less than 60,000 date palms besides all the fruit and vegetables to be found in the region. . . . Trade is partly with Sohar, on the coast to the eastward, but mainly nowadays with Sharja and Dibai, which latter is now a port of call for the British India Company's steamers. Baraimi boasts no bazaar properly so called; local trade is done almost entirely by barter at an

---

[1] *U.K. Memorial*, II, Annex B, no. 25, Cox to For. Secy., Govt. of India, 18 January 1904 (No. 176). Cf. *Saudi Memorial*, I, Chapter IV, para. 297: 'In the whole hinterland stretching from Abu Dhabi to beyond 'Ibri there was no political official representing either Abu Dhabi or Muscat, and no signs whatsoever of political authority held by them.' Although this statement is said to be derived from Cox's article in the *Geographical Journal*, it has, in fact, no counterpart in that article.

[2] *U.K. Memorial*, I, 36, Zaid to Ahmad ibn Hilal, 10 Shawwal 1323.

open-air market which is carried on in the Khidama quarter of Baraimi village. Here the Shaikhs of the Naim, though not now the most powerful tribe in the oasis, still enjoy a special position by virtue of their past history; but the real power in the neighbourhood is the Shaikh of Abu Dhabi, whose material possessions and consequent influence in the oasis are yearly increasing.'[1]

Abdul Aziz, the son of Abdur Rahman ibn Faisal Al Sa'ud, returned from exile in Kuwait in 1901, and in January 1902 he drove the Rashidi garrison from Riyadh. His father then declared himself Amir of Najd, but the real power rested from the first with Abdul Aziz, afterwards better known as Ibn Sa'ud. In the summer of 1905 Ibn Sa'ud journeyed to the base of the Qatar peninsula, where he camped at the wells of al-Uraiq, near Salwah. There he was visited by the aged Shaikh Jasim Al Thani, but Jasim's brother Ahmad sent him a warning that any attempt on his part to cross the border of Qatar would be opposed by the joint forces of Qatar and Abu Dhabi. From al-Uraiq Ibn Sa'ud sent letters to the Trucial Shaikhs, informing them of his arrival and adding that he hoped to visit them the following spring. According to Lorimer, 'these communications were received with dismay by the Hināwi Shaikhs of Abu Dhabi and Dibai, who foresaw a great diminution to their own prestige as a result of the intrusion of the Wahhābis, and with corresponding relation [elation?] by the other or Ghāfiri Shaikhs, who were longing for deliverance from the twenty years' hegemony of Abu Dhabi.'[2]

The Ghafiri shaikhs in question were the Rulers of Sharjah and Ajman. Zaid ibn Khalifah journeyed to Muscat in November 1905 to consult with the Sultan on what might be done to oppose Ibn Sa'ud, and the following month the Sultan paid a visit to Abu Dhabi, where the two rulers had a meeting with the Political Resident, Major Cox. Cox sent a warning to Ibn Sa'ud, through the medium of the Shaikh of Kuwait, that any interference by him in the affairs

---

[1] 'Some Excursions in Oman', *Geog. Journ.*, LXVI, 207. The American missionary, Samuel Zwemer, reported after a visit to Buraimi in 1901 that the Na'im still followed the Wahhabi practice of Islam. 'Although no longer under foreign rule, Bereimi is still a Wahabi centre, but the people are very friendly, and have put off the austere garment of Arab Puritanism, although retaining its ritual in their mosques.' ('Three Journeys in Northern Oman' *Geog. Journ.*, XIX, 62.)
[2] *Gazetteer of P. Gulf*, I, 746–7.

of Trucial Oman would not be welcomed by the British Government. Ibn Saʻud replied in February 1906, through Shaikh Mubarak of Kuwait:

'Your Excellency knows from beforehand that the people of Oman have been our correspondents from the day that we were in Koweit and it is true that we have sent to them letters and correspondence... but by God it was not intentional (with any ulterior motive?), and we did not mention in it any affairs in which we saw any harm but these may have been something which we were not careful over. God forbid that there should be harm in it!'[1]

Ibn Saʻud made no further move after this in the direction of Trucial Oman, lacking, as he did, the resources for any enterprise beyond the borders of Najd. Moreover, he was anxious not to antagonize the British authorities in the Gulf at this stage. He had made overtures for the establishment of friendly relations in 1902, and again in 1904, when a Turkish occupation of the Qasim, to the west of Najd, was threatened. On neither occasion were the overtures successful. He made a more serious approach in 1906, following the Turkish occupation of the Qasim the previous year. His father, the Amir Abdur Rahman, was afterwards appointed Ottoman *qaim-maqam* of Najd, but Ibn Saʻud's ambition was to expel the Turks from both the Qasim and Hasa. If he should succeed in recovering Hasa, there was a chance that he might be counter-attacked by the Turks from the sea. With a view to securing himself against such a possibility, Ibn Saʻud approached the Political Resident three times in 1906—once through a personal emissary, once through the Shaikh of Qatar, and finally through Shaikh Mubarak of Kuwait—with a request to be permitted to subscribe to the Trucial System. He was willing, if his request were granted, to accept a British political agent and to enter into engagements similar to those which bound the Trucial Shaikhs, relative to piracy, the slave trade, maritime warfare, the non-alienation of territory, and British control of their foreign affairs. Largely because such an arrangement would embarrass British relations with the Porte, but also because Ibn Saʻud was in no position to enter into undertakings regarding his neighbours, or even himself, his proposals were rejected.

*

[1] *U.K. Memorial*, II, Annex D, no. 1, Capt. S. G. Knox (Pol. Agent, Kuwait) to Cox, 25 February 1906, transmitting text of Ibn Saʻud's letter to Shaikh Mubarak.

The Ascendancy of Zaid ibn Khalifah, 1871–1909

Until the day of his death in 1909 Zaid ibn Khalifah retained his great authority over Trucial and northern Oman. The absolute nature of his jurisdiction from the Dhafrah to the Dhahirah has been indicated in the foregoing pages, and it was not seriously challenged in the last thirty years of his reign, notwithstanding the Shaikh of Qatar's attacks on Liwa in the eighteen-eighties and the return to power of the Al Sa'ud in Najd at the turn of the century. No Al Bu Falah ruler before him, nor, for that matter, any other Trucial Shaikh, had exercised such power in Eastern Arabia. The reason for this did not lie in the character and ability of Zaid ibn Khalifah alone, or in the particular circumstances of the time, such as the absence of a strong Wahhabi power in Najd. Abu Dhabi had always been the leading territorial power among the Trucial Shaikhdoms. Ras al-Khaima, Sharjah and Dubai were essentially maritime states, their resources lying in their ships and in the men who sailed them. The passing of the great piratical era, of the slave trade, and, with the coming of European competition, of the carrying trade, had brought them almost to ruin. It was they who had possessed the great *baghlahs* of 500–1,000 tons and the deep-water seamen, who sailed every autumn, with the north-east monsoon, for India, Africa and the Red Sea, to bring back cloth and sugar and slaves and coffee and the plunder of a thousand raids. By the last quarter of the nineteenth century all that was left to the principal maritime shaikhdoms was the pearl fishery.

Abu Dhabi had never possessed many large sea-going vessels, but it had a multitude of small fishing boats, and by mid-century there were more Abu Dhabi craft and fishermen on the pearl banks of the lower Gulf than there were from any of the other shaikhdoms. Only a small proportion of the fishing crews was made up of professional fishermen. The great majority were Baduin from the Dhafrah and the hinterland behind Abu Dhabi. They were the real foundation of the strength of the Al Bu Falah, so that while the maritime power of the Qawasim waned in the second half of the nineteenth century, the military power of the Al Bu Falah remained unaffected. It reached its peak in the reign of Zaid ibn Khalifah, and although it was to fall away thereafter, it still remained superior to that of the other Trucial Shaikhs.

CHAPTER IV

Frontier Negotiations and Saudi Ambitions, 1909–1949

Le sandjak ottoman de Nedjd, dont la limite septentrionale est indiquée par la ligne de démarcation définie à l'article 7 de cette convention, se termine vers le sud au golfe faisant face à l'île de Zahnounié, qui appartient audit sandjak. Une ligne partant du fond extrême dudit golfe ira directement au sud jusqu'au Ruba'-al-Khali et séparera le Nedjd de la presqu'île d'El-Katr [Qatar]. Les limites du Nedjd sont indiquées par une ligne bleue sur la carte annexée à la présente convention. Le Gouvernement Impérial ottoman ayant renoncé à toutes ses réclamations concernant la presqu'île d'El-Katr, il est entendu entre les deux Gouvernements que ladite presqu'île sera, comme par le passé, gouvernée par le cheikh Djassim-bin-Sani [Jasim Al Thani] et par ses successeurs.

Anglo-Turkish Convention of 29 July 1913, Article 11[1]

In the summer of 1911 the British and Ottoman Governments entered into what was to prove a protracted series of negotiations on a number of outstanding questions between them. These were mainly concerned with the construction of the Baghdad Railway and its possible extension to the head of the Persian Gulf. In the course of the negotiations the two governments decided to define formally their respective spheres of influence in the Gulf region, and the Convention of 29 July 1913 was the result. It was concerned mainly with Kuwait and Qatar. The former was declared in Article 1 to be an autonomous *qaza* (administrative unit) of the Ottoman Empire, and its boundaries were fixed in Articles 5 and 7. In Article 11 the Porte renounced all claims upon Qatar, and, in effect, declared the furthest limits of Ottoman jurisdiction in Eastern Arabia to be the eastern boundary of the *sanjaq* of Najd. This was defined as a line beginning on the Gulf coast to the west of Qatar, opposite Zakh-

[1] G. P. Gooch and Harold Temperley (eds.), *British Documents on the Origins of the War, 1898–1914*, Vol. X, London, 1938, pp. 190–4.

nuniyah Island, and running due south to the Rub' al-Khali. Its course took it roughly down the middle of the Jafurah Desert. It became known, in time, as the 'Blue Line'.

Even as the convention was being negotiated events were taking place in Eastern Arabia which promised to complicate its eventual application. In May 1913 the young Amir Ibn Sa'ud, operating from Najd, drove the Turkish garrison and administration from Hasa and announced that henceforth he would rule the province directly. 'And we have now-a-days conquered the country of our fathers and grandfathers (viz.), El Hasa and El Qatif, as well as their dependencies', he wrote to the Political Resident in the Gulf, Sir Percy Cox, on 13 June. '. . . In view of my friendly feelings I desire to be on the same terms with you as existed between you and my ancestors and (I desire that these terms) should exist between you and me after them (my ancestors).'[1] Ibn Sa'ud also alluded to the undertaking given by the Amir Abdullah in 1866 not to injure or attack the littoral states in alliance with the British Government,[2] adding, 'I desire to establish the same in the same manner as it existed between you and my ancestors and this (fact) has prompted me to make this reference.' Cox did not reply to this letter until 11 September, when he wrote:

'. . . I have my Government's authority to assure you that, provided you undertake on your part to abstain from all action calculated to disturb the *status quo*, or to create unrest among Arab principalities whose rulers are in relations with the British Government, including the principality of Qatar, the independence of which under the government of the late Sheikh Jasim and his successors of the Bin Thani has been recently recognized by the British and Turkish Governments, the British Government will continue to maintain the friendly relations which have been sustained in the past.'[3]

Ibn Sa'ud's eviction of the Turks from Hasa aroused some apprehension in the Trucial Shaikhdoms. 'The Sheikhs of Abu Dhabi and Dibai', it was reported from the Trucial Coast in the summer of 1913,

---

[1] *U.K. Memorial*, II, Annex D, no. 2, Ibn Sa'ud to Cox, 8 Rajab 1331.
[2] He actually referred to a 'treaty belonging to the time of my grandfather Faysal'. As no such undertaking had ever been given by Faisal, and as he died a few months before his successor Abdullah gave the undertaking of April 1866, there seems little doubt that Ibn Sa'ud was referring to this document. (See, e.g., H. St. J. B. Philby, *Arabian Jubilee*, London, 1952, p. 34.)
[3] [F.O.] 371/1820, file 22076, Cox to Ibn Sa'ud, 11 September 1913.

Frontier Negotiations and Saudi Ambitions, 1909–1949

'who belong to the same tribe have been in consultation. The former has obtained, and holds, a position of supremacy in Baraimi and the vicinity since the Wahabis left. He feels certain that Bin Saud's activities will now be turned in that direction, and fearing this, he has decided with [the] Sheikh of Dibai to call out their Bedouin followers in the Sabkhat and Matti and take the initiative against him.'[1]

Oman was at this time in turmoil, with many of the tribes in revolt against the Sultan. The white *mutawwa'* banners had been unfurled in inner Oman and in the Sharqiyah, where the *tamimah* of the Bani Riyam of the Jabal Akhdhar, the foremost of the Ghafiri tribal leaders, and the *tamimah* of the Al Hirth, the leader of the Hinawi faction, had united to elect an Imam of the Ibadiya, Salim ibn Rashid al-Kharusi, in May 1913.[2] Ibn Sa'ud, however, was too busy consolidating his hold on Hasa in the next few months to take advantage of the political upheaval to the south-east.

It had been agreed at the time of the signing of the Anglo-Turkish Convention of 29 July that as soon as ratifications had been exchanged the Turkish garrison would be withdrawn from Qatar. In October 1913 the Foreign Office suggested to the India Office:

'Sir Percy Cox should be instructed to explain to Ibn Saud, who doubtless will be able to appreciate the communication, that effect will naturally be given to our agreement with Turkey within a short time of its ratification, and that His Majesty's Government expect ratification to take place before the end of the year.'[3]

Ratification, it was added, 'is dependent upon the conclusion of negotiations between the Ottoman Government and the Baghdad Railway Company. . . . Pending the conclusion of such negotiations, the Anglo-Turkish Agreements cannot be operative.'[4] The instructions were sent to India on 4 November: 'Cox should inform Bin Saud, if he raises the question, that effect will be given to the Anglo-Turkish agreement within a short time of its ratification. . . .'[5] Ibn Sa'ud, however, had shown little interest in the convention after he

---
[1] *U.K. Memorial*, II, Annex B, no. 30, Govt. of India to Secy. of State, 2 August 1913.
[2] For the revival of the Imamate, see J. B. Kelly, 'Sultanate and Imamate in Oman', *Chatham House Memoranda*, London, 1959.
[3] [F.O.] 371/1820, file 22076, F.O. to I.O., 31 October 1913.
[4] Ibid.
[5] [F.O.] 371/1820, file 22076, Secy. of State to Viceroy, 4 November 1913.

had been informed of its existence in Cox's letter of 11 September, being more concerned in the latter half of 1913 with putting his relations with the Porte on a regular basis.[1]

On 15 December 1913 he showed the British Political Agents from Kuwait and Bahrain, at a meeting at Uqair, the draft of an agreement between him and the Porte.[2] The following April he wrote to the Political Agent at Bahrain:

'I have further to inform you that on the 11th of the current month I will reach to the direction of Jubail; and this time I received information from the Turkish plenipotentiary who has come from Constantinople directly and his name is Bin Bahi [Bin-bashi?] Saiyid Omar Fauzi Beq Mardini, formerly vali at Basra, now vali of Suria'a [Syria?]. He has with him some messages and letters and intends to settle between myself and themselves. He has arrived at Basra and apparently will come to Kuwait or might have come already. He is bound to see me and I will meet him very soon at the direction of Kuwait, if God decrees so.'[3]

Ibn Sa'ud's negotiations with the Porte culminated in an agreement, signed on 15 May 1914, by which he recognized Ottoman suzerainty over Najd and Hasa. By the second article of the agreement Ibn Sa'ud accepted appointment as Ottoman *vali* of Najd for his lifetime, after which the office was to be held by his sons and grandsons. (His forefathers were referred to as 'previous *valis*'.) In the fourth article Ibn Sa'ud recognized the Ottoman Government's right to station troops at such ports as Qatif and Uqair. In the seventh article he agreed to use the Turkish flag, and in the ninth he undertook not to 'interfere with or correspond about foreign affairs and international treaties, or to grant concessions to foreigners'.[4] Confirmation of Ibn Sa'ud's appointment as Ottoman *vali* of Najd was given by the Turkish Ambassador in London in a Note to the Foreign Office on 9 July 1914. It stated:

'Un firman Impérial nomme Ibni Suoud Gouverneur-Général et Commandant de Nedjd;

---

[1] There are grounds for believing that he had earlier succeeded his father as Ottoman *qaim-maqam* of Najd.

[2] [F.O.] 371/2123, file 6117, Maj. A. P. Trevor (Pol. Agent, Bahrain) to Pol. Res., 20 December 1913.

[3] [F.O.] 371/2124, Ibn Sa'ud to Trevor, 6 Jumada I, 1332/2 April 1914.

[4] [F.O.] 371/2769, reprinted in *U.K. Memorial*, II, Annex A, no. 8. The original instrument was found in the Turkish archives at Basra on its occupation by British troops after the outbreak of war in 1914. The Muslim date is 4 Rajab 1332.

Frontier Negotiations and Saudi Ambitions, 1909–1949

'Ibni Suoud n'aura pas le droit de conclure des conventions ou contracter des engagements avec les Puissances Etrangères;
'Il aura en tous points respecter les traités entre l'Empire Ottoman et les autres Etats.'[1]

The Convention of 29 July 1913, establishing the Blue Line as the eastern frontier of the *sanjaq* of Najd, was never ratified by the Porte. Negotiations for a settlement of the differences between the British and Ottoman Governments dragged on through 1913 and 1914 without reaching a satisfactory conclusion. The period originally allowed for the ratification of the 1913 Convention, viz., three months, was renewed several times, but ratification had not taken place when war broke out between Britain and the Ottoman Empire on 31 October 1914. The Porte, however, had obviously accepted the Blue Line as the valid frontier of its dominions in Eastern Arabia, because on 9 March 1914 it concluded a second frontier convention, defining the limits of Ottoman jurisdiction in south-western Arabia, which contained an express reference to the Blue Line. This convention was ratified by the Ottoman Government on 5 June 1914. The reference to the Blue Line was contained in Article 3 of the convention, which stated that, beginning in the south-west,

'... la frontière des territoires ottomans suivra une ligne droite qui ira du Lekemet-ul-Choub [Lakmat al-Shu'ub] vers le nord-est au désert de Ruba-al-Khali avec une inclinaison de 45°. Cette ligne rejoindra dans le Ruba-al-Khali, sur le parallèle 20°, la ligne droite et directe vers le sud qui part d'un point sur la rive méridionale du golfe d'Oudjeir [Uqair] et qui sépare le territoire ottoman du sandjak de Nedjd du territoire d'El Katr, en conformité de l'article 11 de la Convention anglo-ottomane du 29 juillet, 1913, relatif au Golfe Persique et aux territoires environnants.

'La première des deux lignes est indiquée en violet et la seconde en bleu sur la carte spéciale ci-jointe.'[2]

Ratification of the 1914 Convention took place a few weeks after Ibn Sa'ud had concluded his treaty with the Porte. He was legally bound, therefore, to abide by it and to observe the Blue Line, which was given legal effect by the 1914 Convention, as the eastern frontier of the *sanjaq* of Najd, over which he ruled as Ottoman *vali*. It was, in fact, no hardship for him to do so, since the Blue Line corre-

[1] [F.O.] 371/2124, Hakki Pasha to F.O., 9 July 1914, reprinted in *U.K. Memorial*, II, Annex D, no. 40.
[2] Gooch and Temperley, *Documents on the Origins of the War*, X, 341.

Frontier Negotiations and Saudi Ambitions, 1909–1949

sponded with the limits of his effective authority in the east. He had himself, in his letter to Cox on 13 June 1913, described his ancestral territories, other than Najd, as 'El Hasa and El Qatif, as well as their dependencies', and no member of his dynasty had wielded any power east of the Jafurah for nearly half a century.[1]

The outbreak of war in the autumn of 1914 did not materially affect Ibn Sa'ud's position in Eastern Arabia. Throughout the war he was principally concerned with reducing the power of his rival to the northwards, Ibn Rashid, who was the Turks' most active supporter in Arabia. Ibn Sa'ud was assisted in this undertaking by a monthly subsidy from the British Government of £5,000. He was, however, looking for something more from the war than the defeat of Ibn Rashid. According to Philby, he was 'above all genuinely concerned of the necessity of the British alliance as the only secure safeguard of the interests of his country and people both now and hereafter'.[2] In other words, Ibn Sa'ud wanted recognition of his independence. He achieved this to some extent in a treaty concluded by him with Sir Percy Cox on the island of Tarut, opposite Qatif, on 26 December 1915. Article I of the treaty stated:

'The British Government do acknowledge and admit that Najd, Al Hassa, Qatif and Jubail, and their dependencies and territories, which will be discussed and determined hereafter, and their ports on the shores of the Persian Gulf are the countries of Bin Sa'ud and of his fathers before him, and do hereby recognize the said Bin Sa'ud as the Independent Ruler thereof. . . .'[3]

In return, Ibn Sa'ud undertook, as the Trucial Shaikhs had earlier undertaken, not to enter into relations with foreign powers or to alienate any portion of his territories without the consent of the British Government. The offer that he had originally made to Cox in 1913 to renew the undertaking given by Abdullah ibn Faisal in

[1] The authors of the *Saudi Memorial* of 1955 argue (I, Chapter V, para. 19) that Ibn Sa'ud was not bound by the 1914 Convention because he had already succeeded to Ottoman sovereignty in Eastern Arabia by expelling the Turks from Hasa. 'By 1914 he alone had competence to deal with the areas through which the Blue Line passed, unless in some way Turkey was authorized to act on his behalf.' It is difficult to see how this argument can be sustained, since by the agreement of 15 May 1914 Ibn Sa'ud recognized both Ottoman sovereignty over Najd and Hasa and the Porte's right alone to make treaties concerning these territories.
[2] *Arabian Jubilee*, p. 54.
[3] C. U. Aitchison, *A Collection of Treaties, Engagements and Sanads relating to India and Neighbouring Countries*, 5th edn., 14 vols., Calcutta, 1929–33, XI, 207–8.

Frontier Negotiations and Saudi Ambitions, 1909–1949

1866 was taken up and embodied in the sixth article of the treaty: 'Bin Sa'ud undertakes, as his fathers did before him, to refrain from all aggression on or interference with the territories of Kuwait, Bahrein and of the Shaikhs of Qatar and the Oman Coast, who are under the protection of the British Government, and who have treaty relations with the said Government; and the limits of their territories shall be hereafter determined.'[1]

At the close of the war the Sultanate of Najd emerged as a successor state of the Ottoman Empire. Its frontier with the new state of Iraq was defined in a protocol to the Treaty of Muhammarah on 2 December 1922,[2] and that with Kuwait in the Convention of Uqair of the same date. The eastern frontier of the Sultanate was not defined. There is little doubt, however, that both Ibn Sa'ud and Cox, who conducted the negotiations at Uqair, understood it to be the Blue Line of the Anglo-Turkish Conventions. That this was so has been denied in recent years by the Saudi Government, and it may be of use, therefore, to see what the position was, in law and in fact, at the time that the agreements of Muhammarah and Uqair were concluded.

Up to the conclusion of the Convention of Uqair the frontiers of Kuwait had been those laid down in the Convention of 1913, and they could not be altered except by agreement between the Ottoman and British Governments. By negotiating his frontier with Kuwait with the British Government, Ibn Sa'ud both signified his acceptance of this principle and acknowledged his legal status as a successor of the Ottoman Empire. As a successor to Turkish sovereignty in Najd and Hasa he succeeded in international law to the treaty obligations of the Porte with respect to the frontiers of these districts. 'Succession takes place', said Oppenheim, 'with regard to such international rights and duties of the predecessor as are locally connected with the part of the territory ceded or broken off.'[3] The Blue Line was given legal validity as the eastern frontier of the Ottoman *sanjaq* of Najd in Article 3 of the Anglo-Turkish Convention of 9 March 1914, ratified on 5 June of that year. It created an international obligation, locally connected with Najd and Hasa, to which Ibn Sa'ud later

---
[1] Ibid. Unlike the 1866 Declaration, the treaty contained no reference to the collection of *zakat* in these principalities, presumably because none had been collected by the Al Sa'ud for nearly fifty years.
[2] The Treaty of Muhammarah itself was signed on 5 May 1922, but agreement on the Iraq-Najd frontier was not reached until the following December.
[3] L. F. L. Oppenheim, *International Law*, 8th edn., edited by H. Lauterpacht, London, 1955, p. 159, cited in *U.K. Memorial*, I, 124.

succeeded. 'Parmi les traités d'ordre territorial,' one authoritative writer on international law has stated recently, 'on cite souvent, à titre d'exemple, les traités réglant les frontières. La doctrine est unanime à considérer que de pareil traités engagent le nouveau souverain du territoire.'[1] Ibn Sa'ud, in the preamble to the Anglo-Saudi Treaty of 26 December 1915, described himself, and was accorded recognition in Article 1 of the treaty, as 'Ruler of Najd, Al Hassa, Qatif and Jubail, and the towns and ports belonging to them'. Finally, the Blue Line was mentioned in the negotiations at Uqair in 1922 without drawing from him any sign that he did not regard it as his eastern boundary. In fact, there is nothing to show that he was unaware at that time, or afterwards, of his obligations to respect it.

In the years after 1922 Ibn Sa'ud's energies were absorbed in overthrowing the Sharifian dynasty in the Hijaz and in trying to force a revision of his frontiers with Iraq and Kuwait. His chosen instrument for both undertakings was the *Ikhwan*, the more warlike of the Baduin tribesmen whom he had banded together in settlements, or *hijras*, and infused with a fanatical loyalty to himself and to the Wahhabi cause. Colonel H. R. P. Dickson, who served for many years as a British political officer in Eastern Arabia, wrote of their proceedings in the nineteen-twenties:

'For a brief period only during Arab history have women been treated in any other way than with chivalry and consideration; this was in 1925 and the following years, when the fanatical 'Ikhwan, evolved of Bin Saud's genius for furthering his political ends, were at the height of their power, and were raiding the Iraq, Kuwait and trans-Jordan tribes, and cutting up scattered detachments of the Muntafiq and Khazail shepherd tribes in the southern desert. In these attacks the 'Ikhwan unpardonably butchered numbers of women and children. In mitigation of their offence it may be said that most of the women and children were shot down when the 'Ikhwan fired their first heavy volleys into the camps, preparatory to charging home, as was their wont, with the sword and dagger.'[2]

[1] E. J. S. Castren, *Recueil des Cours de l'Académie de Droit International*, LXXVIII (1951), 437, cited in *U.K. Memorial*, loc. cit. The principle is endorsed by the great majority of writers on international law. (For examples, see *U.K. Memorial*, loc. cit.)
[2] *The Arab of the Desert*, London, 1949, pp. 347-8.

Frontier Negotiations and Saudi Ambitions, 1909–1949

It was largely due to the Ikhwan that Mecca fell to Ibn Sa'ud towards the close of 1925. Madinah and Jeddah were taken the following year, and Ibn Sa'ud soon afterwards proclaimed himself King of the Hijaz. His efforts to obtain a revision of his frontiers with Iraq and Kuwait, however, were unavailing, despite the several savage raids made upon their border tribes by the Ikhwan.[1]

The first signs of a revived Saudi interest in the area east of the Jafurah, after a lapse of over half a century, were manifested in 1925. Widespread fighting had broken out in Trucial Oman in 1920 between the Awamir, the Al Bu Shamis and the Duru' on the one side, and the Manasir and Bani Yas on the other. At one stage in the fighting, several tribesmen of the Manasir and of the Mazari' section of the Bani Yas made their way to Hasa to seek aid from Ibn Sa'ud's governor there, the Amir Abdullah ibn Jiluwi. Presents were exchanged and Ibn Jiluwi agreed to receive the tribesmen under his protection. A truce was later brought about by Shaikh Hamdan ibn Zaid, the Ruler of Abu Dhabi, who had succeeded his brother, Tahnun, in 1912. The Mazari' returned home to Liwa but some of the Manasir remained in Hasa. Fighting broke out again in 1922, when Shaikh Hamdan was murdered by his brother, Sultan, and it continued until 1925. During this time the chiefs of the Awamir, Al Bu Shamis and Duru', taking a leaf out of their opponents' book, journeyed to Hasa and sought Ibn Jiluwi's protection. The upshot was that in the spring of 1925 Ibn Jiluwi dispatched a strong force of Al Murrah to raid the Bani Yas and Manasir in Abu Dhabi territory, where they made off with some 150 camels.

In the wake of the raid a Saudi agent, Su'ayyid Al Arafa,[2] accompanied by Shaikh Hamad ibn Salim Al Rakkadh of the Awamir and a Duru' shaikh, arrived at Abu Dhabi. They told the Ruler, Shaikh Sultan ibn Zaid, that Ibn Sa'ud had taken the Awamir, the

---

[1] For an account of these raids, see Sir John Glubb, *War in the Desert*, London, 1960, Chapters III–XI. Glubb was then serving as an administrative officer with the tribes on the Iraq-Najd border. After three raids by Ikhwan of the Mutair and Harab tribes in December 1924, he relates (p. 136), 'Along the whole length of the Nejed frontier from Basra to near Nejef the shattered and terrified remains of the Iraq shepherd tribes arrived back in panic and confusion on the banks of the Euphrates. In these three heavy inroads, several hundred Iraqis had been massacred, and many thousands of sheep had been looted, not to mention donkeys, tents, clothing, food, utensils and money. It was a devastating blow.'

[2] He is called 'Su'ayyid Al Faisal' in the *Saudi Memorial* (see Vol. I, Chapter IV, para. 342).

Duru' and the Al Bu Shamis under his protection, and that Su'ayyid Al Arafa had been sent to collect *zakat* from them. Despite Sultan ibn Zaid's refusal to recognize the arrangement, Su'ayyid Al Arafa went on to Buraimi. There he was entertained by Ahmad ibn Hilal of Jimi village, the paramount shaikh of the Dhawahir and Sultan ibn Zaid's *wali* in the oasis. At Hamasa, Su'ayyid Al Arafa collected *zakat*, at the rate of $M.T. 1 per camel and one sheep in forty, from a few Awamir, Duru' and Baduin Al Bu Shamis who were visiting the village. He collected nothing from any of the settled inhabitants of the oasis, Na'im or Dhawahir, or from any other Baduin. During his stay Su'ayyid Al Arafa apprehended a fugitive criminal from Hasa and hanged him publicly at Buraimi, much to the disgust of the inhabitants.[1]

While the Saudi agent's visit aroused resentment in Trucial Oman it also provided the Ibadi Imam of Oman and his chief supporters with an excuse for attempting to extend their power northwards from Oman proper into the Dhahirah. The Imam elected in 1913, Salim al-Kharusi, had been assassinated in 1920. His successor, also chosen by the *tamimahs* of the Al Hirth and the Bani Riyam, was Muhammad ibn Abdullah al-Khalili of the Bani Ruwaihah.[2] He was described a few years later by the commander of the Sultan of Muscat's levies, Captain G. J. Eccles of the Indian Army, as 'merely a puppet in the hands of Shaikh 'Isa bin Salih of the Hirth'.[3] Eccles made his observation while on a journey into the interior of Oman in the autumn of 1925, when he accompanied a survey party of the D'Arcy Exploration Company. The whole of the Dhahirah, he found, had been disturbed by Su'ayyid Al Arafa's visit to Buraimi, and the *tamimah* of the Hirth had not been slow to turn the situation to advantage.

'Shaikh 'Isa, alarmed at threats of Wahhabi invasion, determined to advance into the Dhahirah, and bring by force or persuasion all the tribes of that district, both Ghafiri and Hinawi, up to and

[1] Cf. *Saudi Memorial*, loc. cit.: 'During his stay in Buraimi, he carried out the regular collection of *zakah* from the inhabitants of the oasis and the Bedouin tribes in the vicinity. A criminal condemned to death was executed in the public market place of Buraimi Town.' For the arguments of the *Memorial*'s authors on the significance of this *zakat*-collecting at Buraimi, and for the inconsistencies in those arguments, see below, pp. 240–1.

[2] He was a member of the family of Sa'id ibn Khalfan al-Khalili, who had been a leading supporter of Azzan ibn Qais.

[3] 'The Sultanate of Muscat and 'Oman,' *Journal of the Central Asian Society*, XIV (1927), 23.

Frontier Negotiations and Saudi Ambitions, 1909-1949

including the Biraimi oasis, into his confederacy. All went well at first. Dariz, 'Ibri and Dhank submitted, but a severe attack of dropsy and a quarrel with one of his most powerful allied tribes caused him to break up the expedition and hurry back to 'Oman. This ignominious retreat so humiliated the Imam under whose banner the tribes had been united that he offered to resign the Imamate, but was persuaded to carry on by the leading Shaikhs.'[1]

Before the Imam and Isa ibn Salih began their retreat they had a meeting at Qabil, to the south of Buraimi, with two nephews of the Shaikh of Dubai, who had been sent by their uncle to discuss the possibility of concerted action, should Ibn Sa'ud make any further move towards Oman. Sulaiman Baruni, a Tripolitanian exile living at Qabil, described the meeting in the Cairo newspaper *Ash Shora* on 29 October 1925:

'In Muharram 1344 [July-August 1925] there called here at Qabil a deputation headed by Shaikh Sa'id and Suhail bin Bati. They presented to Shaikh Isa bin Salih ... a letter from their uncle Shaikh Sa'id bin Maktum, Chief of Dubai, who wrote in conjunction with Shaikh Sultan bin Zaid, the Chief of Abu Dhabi, strengthening the cord of union and laying down the course of joint action in case anybody attacked the country from either the sea or the land. Similar deputations were received from al-Dhahirah and the Shaikh of Ja'alan.'

Isa ibn Salih himself wrote to the Residency Agent at Sharjah at the beginning of November:

'As regards your enquiry whether Ibn Jiluwi asked us to pay *zakat* I am quite amazed at it. Verily, Ibn Sa'ud knows from whom to demand it. The Shaikhs of Bani Yas came to us and we received and entertained them with honour fit for their position and friendship. Thanks to God that the whole nation is with us. If God decrees that Ibn Sa'ud is tempted to march against us our adherence is to

---

[1] Cf. the rather puzzling account of these events, drawn from the same source (Eccles, loc. cit.), given in the *Saudi Memorial* (I, Chapter IV, para. 343):

'The activity of the official Saudi party under Su'ayyid Al Faisal in Buraimi, not being thoroughly understood, caused some apprehension in the Imamate of Oman.... A more realistic appraisal of the situation at close range, however, induced the Imam to check his progress. He was aware that the people of al-Dhahirah were not Ibadhites and that they considered themselves Saudi subjects, so that the only way in which they might be attached to the Imamate was by compulsion.... The Imam, coming to see that his wisest policy would be to cultivate friendship with the Saudi State, abandoned the expedition and withdrew to his capital.'

God. You should not give ear to nonsensical talk. . . . God willing, we, the Amirs of Ja'alan and Shaikh Mansur, all will act united against whoever intends evil to us.'

In December the D'Arcy Exploration Company survey party was at Mahadhah, the chief town of the Bani Ka'ab at the western end of the Wadi al-Jizzi. There they received an invitation from the shaikhs of the Na'im at Buraimi to visit the oasis, but lack of time prevented them from accepting it. Shaikh Salim ibn Dhiyan, the chief of the Bani Ka'ab, told Captain Eccles that he was highly annoyed with the Na'imi shaikhs, who had, it seems, sent to Ibn Jiluwi for help when the Imam and Isa ibn Salih began their advance into the Dhahirah. 'His grandfather', Eccles discovered, '. . . had been taken prisoner by the Wahhabis and led in chains to Dara'-iyyah, where he was kept for seven years, so that Salim had no love for them.'[1] Even stronger sentiments were voiced by the Na'imi chief of Dhank in a letter to the Sultan of Muscat a few months later. The chief, Hamad ibn Ahmad al-Yahyayi, was particularly disgusted with the chief of the Baduin Al Bu Shamis for seeking aid from the Saudis in his fight with the Bani Yas and Manasir, and for allowing a Saudi *amil*, or tax-collector, to visit the Buraimi region. 'And lo,' he lamented, 'how a person enjoying honour becomes a procurer for his own wife. But alas, men have become extinct from the centre of the Arabs.'

Ibn Jiluwi was considerably put out by the clamour caused by Su'ayyid Al Arafa's visit to Buraimi. He wrote to Shaikh Sa'id ibn Maktum of Dubai in November 1925, assuring him that he had nothing to fear from him, and blaming Sultan ibn Zaid of Abu Dhabi for causing the clamour.

'We have now heard that our brother Sultan bin Zaid has sent you a messenger warning you that Said [Su'ayyid Al Arafa?] has made for your side with 400 men, riding dromedaries, that he is digging wells and that we are following in his footsteps, but that you have rejected this information and you have not yielded to the least suspicion. . . . This proves that you repudiate lies told about Bin Sa'ud and you punish liars. . . . Our brother Sultan is mad; he does not know that we are stronger than he in men and materials: the lies

---

[1] 'The Sultanate of Muscat', *Journ. Central Asian Soc.*, XIV, 36–37. Cf. *Saudi Memorial*, I, Chapter III, para. 94: 'Bani Ka'b . . . have a long history of co-operation with the ruling family of Saudi Arabia. . . .' See also below, p. 232.

Frontier Negotiations and Saudi Ambitions, 1909-1949

carried to him by the Bedouin excite him; but lies that excite men do not yield any fruit. However, sooner or later our power shall prevail upon him and others.'[1]

The implied threat could have been taken as an indication of Ibn Sa'ud's ultimate intentions towards Oman, which Sir Percy Cox, who was in a position to know, described two years later as follows:

'Practically he [Ibn Sa'ud] thinks that he is justified, in principle, in regaining any territory that his forefathers had a century ago, whether as territory or as a "sphere of influence". 'Oman was in their sphere of influence. Bereimi itself was actually in Wahhabi hands, and that accounts for the fact that even now a large section of the population are Wahhabi in principle. . . . I have little doubt but that in the course of time he will seek to extend his authority over the interior of 'Oman.'[2]

It was presumably in execution of this policy that a second Saudi *amil* was dispatched to visit the Buraimi Oasis in the spring of 1926. The *amil*, Muhammad ibn Mansur, collected *zakat* from some Awamir, Duru' and Baduin Al Bu Shamis in the vicinity of the oasis, but like Su'ayyid Al Arafa he got none from the settled inhabitants. That same year Sultan ibn Zaid of Abu Dhabi was murdered by his brother, Saqr. Sultan's sons, Shakhbut and Hazza', who were spending the summer at Buraimi, took refuge with Ahmad ibn Hilal, fearing that Saqr might seek them out and slay them. Later they made for Hasa, where the Amir Ibn Jiluwi gave them protection. Saqr ibn Zaid, in an effort to persuade Ibn Jiluwi not to help the refugees to avenge their father's death, sent him substantial presents, and he also agreed to allow the Amir's agents to collect *zakat* in Buraimi and its environs the following spring.

The Saudi *amils* came in the spring of 1927 and they were still at Buraimi in May when Bertram Thomas, then *wazir* to the Sultan of Muscat, arrived in the vicinity of the oasis in the course of a tour of the Sultanate. He had written in advance to the shaikhs of the Na'im to say that he was coming and that he wished to visit them. When he reached the western end of the Wadi al-Jizzi he received a letter from the shaikhs, urging him to forgo his visit.

'Your letter brought by the hands of Shaikhs Ali and Hamdan is understood. The Wali (Abu Sandan) was not present in the place

[1] *U.K. Memorial*, II, Annex B, no. 41, Abdullah ibn Jiluwi to Sa'id ibn Maktum, 19 Jumada I, 1344/27 November 1925.
[2] *Journ. Central Asian Soc.*, XIV, 40.

Frontier Negotiations and Saudi Ambitions, 1909–1949

... but on his return he saw it and does not agree to it. ... You suddenly wrote to us about this proposal. We did not know of it. These places are reckoned to be in the hands of God and in our hands. This is a disturbance from you. These places are within the territory of Ibn Sa'ud. It is better and safe for you to return. We fear the opening of the hole of trouble. He who knows things is not to be made knowing. He who gave you this privilege is not frank with you. These places belong to Al Hamuda and after them they belong to Ibn Sa'ud. This is all that is to be said. Salaams. Dated 13th Dhu'l Qa'ada [1345].'[1]

The shaikhs, Muhammad and Saqr ibn Sultan Al Hamuda, were both young and had recently succeeded their father. They were very much under the thumb of his slave, the 'wali' Abu Sandan. It was he and not they, Thomas discovered afterwards, who was so opposed to his visit. 'And so, when the phantom had passed, and a year later I was to meet the authors of the solemn letter, there was a good deal of merriment displayed.'[2]

Ibn Jiluwi's *amils* again collected *zakat* from Baduin tribesmen in the vicinity of Buraimi in the spring of 1928, and possibly also in 1929. After that the visits ceased. The ultimate significance of this *zakat*-collecting was assessed by Bertram Thomas at the time.

'The principle of "No Taxation without Representation", the notion that if you pay rates you ought to get Police and Drains for it —these are Western conceptions. In the primitive societies of the Peninsula, a man does not have to worry his head about what positive benefits he will receive in lieu of his payments. There are none. Payment is ordained by religious law: the Ruler has a Divine Right to a tenth of all the increase—*zakat* or tithe. It is the application of "Render unto Caesar the things that are Caesar's". Nor do any hair-splitting polemics decide who Caesar is. This is done by Caesar himself. In a fatalistically and realistically minded society, the test is whether the exactor has power to exact or something worse. If so, then the will of God has declared itself. In the tribal consciousness another's capacity to bring pressure through neighbouring tribes, by the simple device of ensuring or denying the fruits of raiding, is a strong determinant in the payment of *zakat* and of much other action. It is an insurance premium, and by no means signifies

---

[1] *Alarms and Excursions in Arabia*, London, 1931, p. 174.
[2] *Alarms and Excursions*, p. 175.

Frontier Negotiations and Saudi Ambitions, 1909-1949

a voluntary or lasting acknowledgement of sovereignty, though lip service may be paid at the moment.'[1]

Zakat was also collected by Saudi *amils* in the Dhafrah in these years. The first collection was made in the spring of 1926, and others were made every spring up to 1930. The *amils* confined themselves, in the main, to taking camel-*zakat* from those Manasir and Mazari' tribesmen who had sought Ibn Jiluwi's protection during the tribal fighting of the early nineteen-twenties. In 1928 *amils* penetrated to the Liwa Oasis where they took camel-*zakat* from some of the Manasir, mainly of the Al Bu Mundhir section, whose shaikh, Qirran ibn Mani', had by this time taken up residence in Hasa,[2] and from a few Mazari'. The *amils* came again in 1929, when they tried, without success, to collect *zakat* from the other camel-owning Bani Yas sections like the Hawamil and Maharibah. The *amils*, Muhammad ibn Mansur, Sa'id al-Sahali and Muhammad al-Sahali, did not attempt to collect date-*zakat* from either the Manasir or the Bani Yas. When Muhammad al-Sahali arrived again in the spring of 1930, the Hawamil, who were growing tired of the Saudis' efforts to intimidate them, gave him and his party a sound beating. The Ruler of Abu Dhabi protested to Ibn Jiluwi against the harassment of his subjects, and the Amir gave up sending *amils* to Liwa or trying to extract camel-*zakat* from the Baduin Bani Yas. What attempts were made in succeeding years to collect *zakat* in the Dhafrah were directed almost wholly towards the Manasir, and more particularly towards the Al Bu Mundhir section.[3]

Ibn Sa'ud's relations with the British Government were placed on a new footing in 1927 with the conclusion of the Treaty of Jeddah on 20 May of that year. The new treaty was a recognition of the great changes that had taken place in Ibn Sa'ud's position and power since the conclusion of the treaty of December 1915. He had overrun Jabal Shammar in 1921, conquered the Hijaz in 1925, and forced the Asir to submit in 1926. The Treaty of Jeddah took note of these conquests by according him the title of 'King of the Hejaz and of Nejd and its Dependencies'.[4] The restrictions placed upon the conduct of his

[1] *Alarms and Excursions*, pp. 174-5.
[2] See above, p. 40.
[3] For Saudi tax-collecting in the Dhafrah in the nineteen-thirties and nineteen-forties, see below, pp. 238-9.
[4] Cmd. 2951 (1927), Treaty Series No. 25.

foreign relations and other activities by the treaty of 1915 were removed, and the 'complete and absolute independence' of his dominions was recognized by the British Government. Ibn Sa'ud undertook, however, to continue to respect the territorial integrity of the states of Eastern Arabia under British protection. Article VI of the Treaty of Jeddah read:

'His Majesty, the King of the Hejaz and of Nejd and its Dependencies, undertakes to maintain friendly and peaceful relations with the territories of Kuwait and Bahrain and with the Shaikhs of Qatar and the Oman Coast who are in special treaty relations with His Britannic Majesty's Government.'[1]

No mention was made in the treaty of the frontiers of the new kingdom, but there is no reason to believe that Ibn Sa'ud regarded his territories in Eastern Arabia as extending anywhere to the east of the Jafurah Desert. It might be noted that, in an authoritative history of Najd published in 1927, *Najd al-Hadith wa Mulhaqatahu* ('The New Najd and its Dependencies'), by Amin al-Raihani, the eastern boundary of the kingdom was shown as beginning at Dauhat al-Salwah and running south through the Jafurah, approximately along the course of the Blue Line of 1913.[2]

In 1932, following the formal annexation of Jabal Shammar, Ibn Sa'ud changed the name of his kingdom to 'Saudi Arabia'. The following year he granted a petroleum concession to the Standard Oil Company of California. According to a royal proclamation of 14 July 1933, the concessionary area was to be 'the eastern portion of our Saudi Arab Kingdom, within its frontiers . . .'[3]. As these frontiers were not specified the United States Government in the next few months made inquiries about the actual limits of the concession, first of the Turkish Government and later of the British Government. On 24 April 1934 the United States Embassy in London was informed by the Foreign Office that the eastern frontier of the kingdom of Saudi Arabia was the Blue Line of the Anglo-Turkish Conventions of 1913–14, and that Ibn Sa'ud had succeeded to Turkish sovereignty to the west and north-west of that line.[4] The United States Government were satisfied with the statement and did not raise the matter again.

[1] Ibid.
[2] The work was republished in Beirut in 1951 under the title, *Tarikh Najd wa Mulhaqatihi*.
[3] *Umm al-Qura* (Mecca), 17 Rabi' I, 1352.
[4] [F.O.] E 2481/279/91, G. W. Rendel to Millard, 24 April 1934, in *U.K. Memorial*, II, Annex D, no. 3.

Frontier Negotiations and Saudi Ambitions, 1909-1949

On 28 April 1934 the British Minister at Jeddah informed the Saudi Government of the contents of the communication to the United States Embassy in London.[1] The reaction of the acting Saudi Foreign Minister, Fuad Bey Hamza, was to protest that in view of the considerable changes that had taken place in the position of Saudi Arabia since the conclusion of the 1913–14 Conventions, his government could not regard the Blue Line 'as actually constituting the correct line of their frontier with the neighbouring territories in the East and South of Arabia'.[2] This was the first official intimation that the British Government had had that Ibn Sa'ud did not regard the Blue Line as his eastern frontier, and their reaction to it was equally strong. Fuad Bey Hamza was informed on 15 June that the legal position established by the Anglo-Turkish Conventions had not been modified by subsequent events, that Saudi Arabia was bound to respect that position, and that the increase that had taken place in the power of Ibn Sa'ud had no bearing upon the validity of the Blue Line.[3]

Undeterred by this rebuff, Fuad Bey Hamza re-stated his original argument in a lengthy Note on 20 June. The Ottoman Government, he said, did not possess the right in 1913–14 to determine the destinies of the countries of the Arabian peninsula, because Ottoman authority in Eastern Arabia had ceased entirely in 1913 when Ibn Sa'ud recovered possession of his ancestral territories. The British Government, by the treaty of 1915, had recognized Ibn Sa'ud as the independent ruler of Najd, Hasa, Qatif and Jubail and their dependencies, which were to be determined thereafter. It might be deduced from this, he continued, that the British Government themselves had acknowledged Ibn Sa'ud's right to his ancestral territories and to authority over the tribes inhabiting them. These territories were easily discernible from those of neighbouring rulers. In the case of Qatar, '... the confines (frontiers) of Qatar are the confines (frontiers) of the inhabited towns and villages ...'.[4] As for the rest of Eastern Arabia: 'All the tribes living between the coastal towns of Qatar and

---

[1] [F.O.] E 3167/279/91, Sir A. Ryan to Fuad Bey Hamza, 28 April 1934, in *U.K. Memorial*, II, Annex D, no. 4.
[2] [F.O.] E 3651/279/91, Fuad Bey Hamza to Ryan, 13 May 1934, in *U.K. Memorial*, II, Annex D, no. 5.
[3] [F.O.] E 4341/279/91, Ryan to Fuad Bey Hamza, 15 June 1934, in *U.K. Memorial*, II, Annex D, no. 6.
[4] [F.O.] E 4451/279/91, Fuad Bey Hamza to Ryan, 20 June 1934, in *U.K. Memorial*, II, Annex D, no. 7.

Frontier Negotiations and Saudi Ambitions, 1909–1949

the coast of Oman and the Hadhremaut belong to the Saudi Arab Kingdom, are entirely submissive to the laws of the country, pay Zakât, and are obedient to the calls of the Government in time of war (Jihâd) etc.'[1]

These were very large claims and plainly called for detailed examination. Fuad Bey Hamza was invited to London in September 1934, and a series of preliminary meetings was held at the Foreign Office to enable each side to state its position more fully. The meetings were not very fruitful, largely because Fuad Bey Hamza had not been supplied with definite instructions by his government. He did indicate, however, that Ibn Sa'ud intended to argue that the territories of tribes long under his rule should be included in his dominions. Fuad Bey Hamza made particular mention, in this connexion, of the Murrah and Manasir tribes. He was told in reply that while the Murrah might be regarded as subjects of Ibn Sa'ud, the Manasir were mostly dependent upon the Shaikh of Abu Dhabi.[2] As nothing more was heard of Ibn Sa'ud's intentions in the months following these exchanges, the Saudi Government were asked at the beginning of 1935 for a definite statement of his claims. The request was renewed in March, and on 3 April 1935 Fuad Bey Hamza handed the British Minister at Jeddah a memorandum setting forth a proposed frontier of Saudi Arabia with Qatar, the Trucial Shaikhdoms, the Sultanate of Muscat and Oman, and the eastern Aden Protectorates.

The boundary with Qatar started on the west coast of the peninsula, about 15 miles from the head of the Dauhat al-Salwah, ran eastwards for about five miles, then south-eastwards to strike the east coast about seven miles north of Khaur al-Udaid. The line placed both Jabal Nakhsh, at the western foot of the peninsula, and Khaur al-Udaid, at its eastern foot, in Saudi territory. The proposed frontier with the Trucial Shaikhdoms began at a point about 16 miles south of Khaur al-Udaid, ran southwards for about 10 miles, then east-south-east in a curve until it met longitude 56° E. at its junction with latitude 22° N. From there it ran down longitude 56° E. to its junction with latitude 19° N., then turned south-westwards until it reached longitude 52° E. at its junction with latitude 17° N., and followed latitude 17° N. as far as the Violet Line of 1914.[3] According

---

[1] Ibid.
[2] [F.O.] E 5908/2429/25, Record of Second Meeting, 20 September 1934, and E 5997/2429/25, Record of Fifth Meeting, 24 September 1934, in *U.K. Memorial*, II, Annex D, no. 8.   [3] See Map 2 at end.

Frontier Negotiations and Saudi Ambitions, 1909–1949

to the memorandum, the proposed frontier ran 'parallel to the lands known as Majann, Sabakhat-Matti, and Kufat al-Liwa, leaving the lands belonging to Kufat al-Liwa to the Arab Amirates and those to the west to the Saudi Arab Kingdom'.[1]

A settlement at this stage seemed possible, in the form of a frontier somewhere between the Blue Line of 1913 and the 'Red Line', as it came to be known, of the Saudi Government's claim. There appeared to be a genuine Saudi interest east of the Blue Line in that there were two Saudi Ikhwan *hijras*, or settlements, Sikak and Anbak, to the east of that line, at the base of the Qatar peninsula (see Map 1). It was not unreasonable, also, that the Saudi Government should want access to the line of coast between the Blue Line and the head of the Dauhat al-Salwah. On 9 April 1935 the British Minister at Jeddah, Sir Andrew Ryan, handed the Saudi Government an aide-mémoire proposing a frontier (the 'Green Line') running from the head of the Dauhat al-Salwah south-eastwards to a point about 5 miles north-east of Sikak, and then almost due south to latitude 20° N., eventually joining the Violet Line at a point to be agreed upon.[2] This left the *hijras* of Sikak and Anbak in Saudi territory.

Discussions on the basis of these two lines were opened in London in June 1935. In a memorandum of 2 July Fuad Bey Hamza stated that his government found the Green Line unacceptable. They could not retreat from the frontier claimed in their memorandum of 3 April 1935, which, he said, had been drawn up 'after the most careful investigation into the actual situation at the present moment', and which was a minimum statement of Ibn Sa'ud's claims.

'... The Government of His Majesty King Abdul Aziz did not adopt the wide principle which was the basis of her relations with the tribes of the desert which had declared their allegiance and submission to His Majesty the King, such as the tribes of Da'kiyeh—*viz*. Almanaheel, Al Kotheir and Almohrah—and most of the tribes of Almonaseer, Aldoroo', Al'awamir and Bani Ghafir and others, but were content to mention the natural boundaries which were at the same time generally recognised by the tribes on whose members and lands His Majesty's Government has exercised direct influence for a long period, during which their ordinary members and their Sheikhs

[1] [F.O.] E 2700/77/91, Memo. by Fuad Bey Hamza to Sir A. Ryan, 3 April 1935, in *U.K. Memorial*, II, Annex D, no. 9.
[2] [F.O.] E 3783/77/91, Aide-mémoire from Sir A. Ryan to Saudi Govt., 9 April 1935, in *U.K. Memorial*, II, Annex D, no. 10. The line is not shown in Map 2 at end.

were actually in His Majesty's service and His Majesty's regular army.'[1]

Asked to define the *diyar* of tribes considered to be directly subject to Ibn Sa'ud, Fuad Bey Hamza produced a list of 161 wells running northwards from the Rub' al-Khali towards the Gulf coast, all of which, he said, lay in the *dirah* of the Murrah.[2] Two of the northernmost wells, Bunaiyan and Sufuq, had been excluded from Saudi territory by the Green Line. Fuad Bey Hamza also said that Mijan and the Sabkhat Matti were shared by the Murrah and the Manasir.[3] Finally, he pointed out that Khaur al-Udaid had been excluded from Saudi territory by the Green Line, although Ibn Sa'ud possessed 'an established and irrefutable right' to it. The *khaur* had been used in the past as a landing-place for merchandise destined for Hasa, and it was now desired to develop it commercially.[4]

From Fuad Bey Hamza's submissions it was evident that Ibn Sa'ud took an exaggerated view of the extent of his authority in Eastern Arabia. Not only did he claim the allegiance of the Murrah and the Manasir, but he claimed also that of the Manahil, most of whom dwelt in the Hadhramaut, the Al Kathir of the same region (presumably the Al Rashid branch, which roamed the Rub' al-Khali), the Duru' of the Oman steppes, the Bani Ghafir, or Miyayihah, of the Dhahirah, and the Awamir, the settled branches of which dwelt in the Hadhramaut and Oman, the nomadic elements in the eastern sands, the Dhafrah, and the fringe of the Oman steppes. The claim to the loyalty to the Duru' and the Awamir presumably arose from their seeking Ibn Jiluwi's protection a decade earlier. Ibn Sa'ud's resolve not to include their *diyar* within his claims was due less to his forbearance, as alleged by Fuad Bey Hamza, than to the fact, as Fuad Bey Hamza himself implicitly admitted, that the actual situation in these areas did not justify their inclusion.

The whole notion that the frontiers could be defined on the basis of tribal *diyar* alone was strongly challenged by G. W. Rendel, the leader of the British delegation. While he agreed that certain areas in Eastern Arabia were frequented, predominantly or exclusively, by

---

[1] [F.O.] E 4111/77/91, Fuad Bey Hamza to G. W. Rendel, 2 July 1935, in *U.K. Memorial*, II, Annex D, no. 12.
[2] [F.O.] E 4314/77/91, Statement by Fuad Bey Hamza, 8 July 1935, in *U.K. Memorial*, II, Annex D, no. 13.
[3] Fuad Bey Hamza to Rendel, 2 July 1935.
[4] [F.O.] E 3944/77/91, Record of First Meeting, 24 June 1935, in *U.K. Memorial*, II, Annex D, no. 11 (i).

Frontier Negotiations and Saudi Ambitions, 1909–1949

tribes owing allegiance to one ruler or another, most of the areas involved in the current discussions were deserts, over which several tribes wandered, whose allegiances were uncertain or shifting. A territorial frontier based only on tribal considerations, therefore, would be impracticable. Rendel went on:

'... There was no question of attempting to establish a sharply defined frontier in the ordinary European sense with frontier posts and a close frontier control. It was, however, necessary ... to set some definite limit beyond which territorial sovereignty could not be exercised, even if such territorial sovereignty were not in fact exercised up to that limit. This would not prevent the tribes wandering freely from one territory to another, and no doubt suitable arrangements could eventually be made regarding their taxation, etc., as had been done in the case of the tribes which migrated between Saudi Arabia, Transjordan, Syria and Iraq.'[1]

Rendel conceded that a larger slice of the Rub' al-Khali might be allotted to Saudi Arabia than had been allowed by the Green Line, but he ruled out any concession to Saudi claims in the vicinity of the Qatar peninsula. Bunaiyan Well, at the northern edge of the Rub' al-Khali, was in Abu Dhabi territory; Jabal Nakhsh was geographically part of Qatar; and Khaur al-Udaid had long been recognized as belonging to Abu Dhabi.[2]

The London discussions terminated in July 1935 on an understanding by the British delegation that they would make a further study of the tribal situation in the areas east of the Blue Line to which Saudi Arabia laid claim. Investigations made in the latter half of 1935 showed that the *dirah* of the Al Murrah was, in fact, more extensive than had previously been believed. It stretched from the southern tip of the Sabkhat Matti south-eastwards for a considerable distance into the Rub' al-Khali. It was decided, therefore, without withdrawing the basic objection to defining frontiers on the grounds of tribal lands and loyalties alone, to make some accommodation to Saudi Arabia's claims, especially in the Rub' al-Khali. On 25 November 1935 Sir Andrew Ryan handed Fuad Bey Hamza at Riyadh a memorandum proposing a frontier radically more favourable to Saudi Arabia than the Green Line had been. It began at the head of the Dauhat al-Salwah and ran south-eastwards, skirting the southern tip of the Sabkhat Matti, and eastwards along the northern edge of

[1] [F.O.] E 3944/77/91, Record of First Meeting, 24 June 1935, in *U.K. Memorial*, II, Annex D, no. 11 (i).   [2] Ibid.

Frontier Negotiations and Saudi Ambitions, 1909–1949

the Rub' al-Khali to the junction of longitude 55° E. with latitude 22° 30' N. From there it ran south down longitude 55° E. to its junction with latitude 20° N., then turned approximately south-westwards to run in a straight line to the junction of longitude 52° E. with latitude 19° N., and thence in a straight line to meet the Violet Line at its intersection with latitude 18° N.[1]

The 'Riyadh Line', as it came to be called, differed from the Saudi Red Line of the previous April principally in that it assigned more of the lower half of Qatar to that shaikhdom, retained Khaur al-Udaid in Abu Dhabi territory, and reduced Ibn Sa'ud's claims upon Oman and the eastern Aden Protectorate. It conceded to Saudi Arabia Bunaiyan Well, which was used prodominantly by the Murrah, but retained for Abu Dhabi Sufuq Well, which lay on the route from Abu Dhabi to Qatar and was much closer to the coast than had previously been supposed. Ryan told Ibn Sa'ud that the Riyadh Line represented the furthest possible concession that his government could make. Ibn Sa'ud rejected it within 24 hours, maintaining his claim to Jabal Nakhsh and Khaur al-Udaid.

No further discussions on the frontier were held until March 1937, when Rendel visited Jeddah to talk to the Saudi Foreign Minister, Shaikh Yusuf Yasin. Their conversations revolved mainly around Jabal Nakhsh and Khaur al-Udaid. Rendel pointed out that Khaur al-Udaid had been recognized as Abu Dhabi territory as far back as the eighteen-seventies. Saudi Arabia's claim to it on the grounds put forward by Fuad Bey Hamza, viz., that it was intended to develop it commercially, would not hold water as the *khaur* was practically useless as a harbour. Possession of its foreshore, on the other hand, was essential to Abu Dhabi as affording a land link with the adjoining Shaikhdom of Qatar. Rendel also pointed out, with respect to the area south and east of Khaur al-Udaid, that the Saudi Government, in their memorandum of 3 April 1935, had agreed that the Sabkhat Matti and the line of wells described as the Qufat al-Liwa lay in Abu Dhabi territory. The northernmost of these wells was Sufuq, which F. F. Hunter's map of Arabia, which had been used in the discussions to date, placed too far to the southwards. Shaikh Yusuf Yasin promptly

---

[1] See Map 2 at end, and *Saudi Memorial*, I, Chapter V, para. 38. The *Memorial* states incorrectly that the line passed through the junction of longitude 53° E with latitude 19° N.

Frontier Negotiations and Saudi Ambitions, 1909–1949

declared that Sufuq Well belonged to the Murrah. Rendel protested that this kind of progressive claim for the *dirah* of the Murrah could not be accepted. 'If the Saudi Government always claimed as a Murra well the next well beyond the last well we had conceded, there would be no reason why they should not eventually claim Muscat town.'[1]

Following Rendel's visit, the British Minister at Jeddah, Sir Reader Bullard, wrote to Shaikh Yusuf Yasin on 27 March to say that Sufuq Well had definitely been located as lying 12 miles from the Gulf coast, due south of Ras Asqhaila.[2] Later in the year it was reported that the Californian Arabian Standard Oil Company, which held the Saudi concession, were exploring in the vicinity of Salwah. On 4 December Bullard drew the attention of the Amir Faisal, now Saudi Foreign Minister, to these reports, and to prevent misunderstandings from arising he reminded the Amir of the course of the Riyadh Line. The British Government, he added, were willing to re-open negotiations on the frontier on the basis of that line, which had now been modified slightly in Saudi Arabia's favour, following the ascertaining of the exact location of Sufuq Well.[3] Faisal's reply to this was to lay the blame for the failure to reach agreement upon a frontier upon the British Government. So long as they insisted, he said, upon regarding the Riyadh Line as an acceptable frontier, a settlement of the question would be very difficult.[4] For all practical purposes—there were some informal conversations on the subject in 1938—this marked the end of negotiations on the frontier for a decade to come.

Of late years the Saudi Government have found their frontier claim of 3 April 1935, the Red Line, to be something of an embarrassment, because it did not take in areas which they now claim as theirs, notably, the Dhafrah, the Sabkhat Matti, the Liwa Oasis, and the Buraimi Oasis. In fact, the Red Line, at its nearest point, did not come within 100 miles of Buraimi. As a result, the Saudi Government have been at pains in the last decade to explain away their 1935

---

[1] [F.O.] E 2124/258/91, Record of Discussion between Rendel and Yusuf Yasin, 19 March 1937, in *U.K. Memorial*, II, Annex D, no. 14.
[2] [F.O.] E 2124/258/91, Bullard to Yusuf Yasin, 27 March 1937, in *U.K. Memorial*, II, Annex D, no. 16.
[3] [F.O.] 7572/258/91, Bullard to Faisal, 4 December 1937, in *U.K. Memorial*, II, Annex D, no. 17.
[4] [F.O.] E 439/150/91, Faisal to Bullard, 16 Shawwal 1356/19 December 1937, in *U.K. Memorial*, II, Annex D, no. 18.

claim, and even to disown it completely. In the *Saudi Memorial* of 1955, for example, the authors state: '... The description was framed in general terms, suggesting the areas through which the boundary might pass rather than the precise location of the line.'[1] There is nothing in Fuad Bey Hamza's memorandum of 3 April 1935, or in the subsequent exchanges, to justify such an assertion. The *Memorial*'s authors, however, do not rest content with this but attempt to reduce the disparity between the Saudi Government's 1935 and 1949 lines by implying, wrongfully, that the 1935 claim included the Liwa Oasis. Fuad Bey Hamza, it may be recalled, proposed in his memorandum that the frontier should run *'parallel* to the lands known as Majann, Sabakhat Matti, and Kufat al-Liwa, leaving the lands belonging to Kufat al-Liwa to the Arab Amirates'.[2] The authors of the *Saudi Memorial* render this as: 'It [the frontier] then runs to the south and southeast *through* the territories known as al-Majann, Sabkhat Matti, and Kaffat al-Liwa. . . .'[3] Maps I and II accompanying the *Memorial* show the Red Line as passing to the *north* of Liwa, so as to attach it to Saudi Arabia, despite Fuad Bey Hamza's explicit disclaimer.

Another dubious argument is advanced in the *Saudi Memorial* with respect to Sufuq Well. The authors state that until March 1937 Sufuq was assumed to lie some 75 kilometres from the coast, 'and on this assumption it was conceded by the British to lie to the Saudi side of the Ryan [Riyadh] Line of 1935'.[4] They go on to say that when the true position of Sufuq was ascertained the British Government, though reluctant to admit that it lay in Saudi territory, stated, by means of Sir Reader Bullard's letter of 4 December 1937, that the modification had been accepted.

The argument is not sustained by the facts of the case. Sufuq was not specifically mentioned in the original Saudi claim of 3 April 1935. Although Fuad Bey Hamza in his letter of 2 July 1935 to Rendel claimed Sufuq as a well belonging to the Murrah, Rendel in his conversation with Yusuf Yasin on 19 March 1937 refused to recognize the claim. Bullard's letter of 27 March 1937, describing the correct location of Sufuq, certainly did not concede it to lie in Saudi territory. His letter of 4 December 1937, while stating that an adjustment had been made in the Riyadh Line in favour of Saudi Arabia as a result of the discovery of the correct location of Sufuq, did not

---

[1] Vol. I, Chapter V, para. 31.   [2] See above, p. 125. Italics added.
[3] Loc. cit. Italics added.   [4] Vol. I, Chapter V, para. 44.

Frontier Negotiations and Saudi Ambitions, 1909-1949

specify on which side of the line it lay. Indeed, any suggestion that it was considered to be in Saudi territory is given the lie by the *Saudi Memorial* itself, Maps I and II of which show Sufuq to the *north* of the Riyadh Line, that is to say, in Abu Dhabi territory. Moreover, these same maps show the Red Line proposed by Saudi Arabia as running to the *south* of Sufuq, again leaving it in Abu Dhabi territory.[1]

Before leaving the subject of the 1934-7 frontier negotiations it might be worth while to draw attention to the fact that the Saudi claim of 1935 was based almost wholly upon the *diyar* of tribes and their loyalty, real or imagined, to Ibn Sa'ud. No elaborate arguments about the collection of *zakat* and its significance, such as were to be advanced in support of the 1949 claim, were brought forward between 1934 and 1937. Sporadic collections of *zakat*, as has been seen, had been made by Saudi *amils* in the Dhafrah and in the vicinity of Buraimi before 1935, yet no claim was made to these areas. It might well be deduced from this that the collection of *zakat* was not considered at that time to confer any rights of political or territorial sovereignty.

The occasional visits of Ibn Sa'ud's *amils* to the Dhafrah after 1926 and to Buraimi between 1925 and 1929 did not seem to have any effect upon the authority of the local rulers. Jurisdiction over the coast and islands between Khaur al-Udaid and Abu Dhabi continued to be exercised by the Al Bu Falah Ruler through a *wali* or *amir* resident on Dalma Island. The *wali* was assisted by a *muzakki*, or *zakat*-collector, and his prime duties were to maintain order and collect customs dues and pearling taxes. Pearling in the waters off Qatar and the Trucial Coast is free to all, but the shaikhs usually collect a pearling tax from their own subjects. The Residency Agent at Sharjah reported in 1906:

'Dalma island is thickly populated during diving seasons, being visited by the natives of Katr [Qatar], Bahrein, Lingah and the towns on the Arab Coast, who are dealing in pearls and miscellaneous goods. They pay the Chief of Abu Dhabi a tax (at the rate of) 40 or 30 $ for every merchant and 10 or 6 $ for every petty pearl dealer (Tawwash) whose capital amounts to Rs 1000/- more or less.'[2]

---
[1] See *Saudi Memorial*, Vol. II.
[2] *U.K. Memorial*, II, Annex G, no. 2, memo. dated 4 September 1906.

Frontier Negotiations and Saudi Ambitions, 1909–1949

Thirty years later the Residency Agent reported:

'Dalmah Island is inhabited by some of the Qubaisat, Mazari', Maharibah and Muraikhat tribes of Abu Dhabi.[1] The Shaikh has a customs Mudir named Abdul-Ghani bin Ali who lives in Dalmah. At the opening of the pearl season, the Shaikh sends two of his men, Ali bin Muhammad and Abbas bin Abdullah to Dalmah in order to recover his Taraz (diving tax) where they remain until the end of the season and then return to Abu Dhabi.'[2]

Customs duties on Dalma were levied at the rate of $2\frac{1}{2}$ per cent on all imports except pearls. The Ruler of Abu Dhabi also controlled fishing off the coast up to Khaur al-Udaid by the issue of fishing licences. His control extended only to fishing done from the shore, by casting or by setting nets across the mouths of creeks, for *hayyal*, or deep-sea fishing, is free to all. Disputes arising out of fishing and pearling were settled by the 'Diving Court', or *Salifat al-Ghaus*, which, for some years past, has been located at Abu Dhabi town. Its juridical competence is recognized by all who go fishing from the coast, whether Bani Yas or Manasir. The Shaikh of Abu Dhabi was responsible both for the recovery and disposal of wrecks along the coast, and, under the Treaty of Maritime Peace in Perpetuity, for any breaches of the maritime truce committed by those who frequented the coast.

Al Bu Falah authority over the Dhafrah in this century has normally been wielded by an *amir* or *wali* appointed by the Ruler. Usually, he is assisted by a *muzakki*. Several of the *walis* have been members of the ruling family.[3] His normal place of residence is Mariyah, in the Liwa Oasis, and his authority extends to the Batin, Bitanah, Qufa, Saruq, Ramlat al-Hamra and Bainunah. He is responsible for the keeping of order among the tribesmen, the adjustment of disputes, and the collection of *zakat* for the Ruler. A letter of appointment of a new *muzakki* by the present Ruler, Shakhbut ibn Sultan, in November 1936 reads: 'To all the people of Liwa who may see it: The bearer, Humaid bin Dahnan, is an agent for us and on our behalf to collect the *zakat* due to us with you. Anyone who refuses him refuses us. This should be known

---

[1] The Muraikhat are not an Abu Dhabi tribe. Those on Dalma in 1937 probably came from Bahrain.

[2] *U.K. Memorial*, II, Annex G, no. 1, Res. Agent to Pol. Agent, Bahrain, 24 February 1937.

[3] For a list of the *walis* of Liwa since the reign of Zaid ibn Khalifah (1855–1909), see *U.K. Memorial*, II, Annex E, no. 4.

Frontier Negotiations and Saudi Ambitions, 1909-1949

to you.'[1] The *zakat* is collected on dates, at the rate of 10 per cent on anything over and above a minimum amount (*nisab*), normally about 700 kilogrammes, or two-thirds of a ton.

The administration of the Abu Dhabi villages in the Buraimi Oasis remained unchanged after the death of Zaid ibn Khalifah. Ahmad ibn Hilal, the principal Dhahiri shaikh and *wali* of Jimi, continued to exercise control over the other Abu Dhabi villages on behalf of successive Al Bu Falah Rulers—Tahnun ibn Zaid (1909-12), Hamdan ibn Zaid (1912-1922), Sultan ibn Zaid (1922-6), Saqr ibn Zaid (1926-8), and Shakhbut ibn Sultan, who has ruled since 1928. The *tamimah* of the Na'im, Sultan ibn Muhammad Al Hamuda of Buraimi village, whose authority had been greatly eclipsed during the lifetime of Zaid ibn Khalifah, attained more prominence after 1909. He shared responsibility with the Ruler of Abu Dhabi for the care of the Sultan of Muscat's interests in the oasis and its vicinity, and he received, in return, half of the *farizah*, or annual allowance, originally paid in full by the Sultan to Zaid ibn Khalifah. He still stood, however, in a semi-dependent relationship to Zaid's successors and received subsidies from them, as may be seen from this letter to him from Hamdan ibn Zaid in August 1917: 'You have written in respect of the *zakat*. Please note that we have written to [our] brother, Shaikh Sultan ibn Zaid, in respect of what we have allotted to you.'[2] The *zakat* in question was collected on dates in the Dhahiri villages. A share was customarily allotted to the *tamimah* of the Na'im, while other shares went to the shaikhs of the Dhawahir. Thus, Hamdan ibn Zaid, in a letter to Ahmad ibn Hilal in July 1921, writes: 'You have written about Sultan bin Muhammad al-Darmaki [of Qattarah] and the Zakat. Please know, God save you, that is originally allotted for (feeding) the horses. We have written to Shaikh Sultan bin Rashid to give him one hundred jurabs.'[3]

The close connexion of the Al Bu Falah with the Na'im continued after Sultan ibn Muhammad's death in the early nineteen-twenties. His sons, Saqr and Muhammad, the new *tamimahs*, are referred to in this fashion in a letter from Shaikh Sultan ibn Zaid to Ahmad ibn Hilal in November 1925: 'We have received a letter from our "sons",

---

[1] *U.K. Memorial*, I, 68, letter dated 20 Ramadhan 1355. For a reference to Humaid ibn Dahnan from another source, see below, p. 220.

[2] [Dhawahir Colln.] Hamdan ibn Zaid to Sultan ibn Muhammad, 8 Dhu'l-Qa'dah 1355.

[3] *U.K. Memorial*, II, Annex J, no. 1, letter dated 8 Dhu'l-Qa'dah 1339. A *jurab* is between 70 and 80 lb.

the sons of Sultan bin Muhammad. . . . As you know, we and the sons of Sultan bin Muhammad are one party. Whatever harms them, harms us, and we will never agree to this.'[1] Sultan ibn Zaid, who assassinated his brother Hamdan in 1922, ruled only four years before he, too, lost his life to a brother's ambition. The manner of his death was reported by the Residency Agent at Sharjah in August 1926 as follows:

'On the 1st day of Muharram (12-7-1926) Shaikh Sultan bin Zaid sent his family and his sons Shakhboot and Hazza' to Baraimi, his summer resort: Shaikh Khalifah and Muhammad bin Zaid also went there with their families. There remained in Abu Dhabi Shaikh Sultan bin Zaid and his son named Khalid, and Shaikh Saqar bin Zaid, with his sons Dhiab, Rashid and Zaid. On the night of the 24th Muharram (4-8-1926) Shaikh Sultan bin Zaid invited his brother Shaikh Saqar to supper. The latter on his arrival at his brother's residence fired on his brother who died there and then. The murdered Shaikh's son Khalid seeing this ran away. Khalid was chased and wounded with a dagger in three places in his body but he managed to reach his uncles, Chiefs of the Qubiyat tribe. Shaikh Saqar bin Zaid after the burial of Shaikh Sultan bin Zaid, took Khalid from his uncles saying he wanted to cure his wounds; it is however said that Khalid will die.

'Shaikh Saqar bin Zaid also sent his son Dhiab in company with 30 men to Baraimi with a false letter purporting to be from Shaikh Sultan bin Zaid: addressed to his sons Shakhboot and Hazza' asking them to come back to Abu Dhabi for some urgent business. He had instructed the men to kill the two boys as soon as they would reach a distance beyond Baraimi.

'Information received from Baraimi shows that Shakhboot and Hazza' have received the news of their father's murder and have taken refuge with Shaikh Ahmad bin Hilal-al-Dhahiri and that the Abu Dhabi subjects who reside in Baraimi have recognised Shaikh Saqar bin Zaid through his son.'[2]

Shaikhs Shakhbut and Hazza', as related earlier, sought refuge for a time with Ibn Jiluwi in Hasa. In 1928 Saqr ibn Zaid was murdered and Shakhbut was appointed Ruler by the other members of the Al Bu Falah.

[1] [Dhawahir Colln.] Sultan ibn Zaid to Ahmad ibn Hilal, 26 Rabi' II, 1344.
[2] *U.K. Memorial*, II, Annex B, no. 33, Res. Agent to Pol. Res., 13 August 1926.

Frontier Negotiations and Saudi Ambitions, 1909-1949

Ahmad ibn Hilal died in 1936, after serving Shakhbut as Abu Dhabi *wali* at Buraimi for eight years. Ali ibn Ghanim replaced him as *wali* of Jimi, but he did not possess the same influence as had the old Dhahiri chieftain. Instead, the *wali* of al-Ain, Ibrahim ibn Othman, was vested by Shakhbut with a general power of superintendence over the *walis* of the other Abu Dhabi villages. He died in 1946 and Shakhbut's brother, Zaid, became the Abu Dhabi *wali* in the oasis, a post which he has held to the present day. The power of the *tamimah* of the Naʻim, Saqr ibn Sultan, which had increased in the decade following the death of Ahmad ibn Hilal, was again reduced after 1946 by the influence of Zaid ibn Sultan, who showed himself to be of much the same mettle as his grandfather, the great Zaid. Wilfred Thesiger's first impression of him, at a meeting at Buraimi in 1948, was:

'He was a powerfully built man of about thirty with a brown beard. He had a strong, intelligent face, with steady observant eyes, and his manner was quiet but masterful. He was dressed, very simply, in a beige-coloured shirt of Omani cloth, and a waistcoat which he wore unbuttoned. He was distinguished from his companions by his black head-rope, and the way in which he wore his head-cloth, falling about his shoulders instead of twisted round his head in the local manner. He wore a dagger and cartridge-belt; his rifle lay on the sand beside him.

'I had been looking forward to meeting him, for he had a great reputation among the Bedu. They liked him for his easy informal ways and his friendliness, and they respected his force of character, his shrewdness, and his physical strength. They said admiringly, "Zayid is a Bedu. He knows about camels, can ride like one of us, can shoot, and knows how to fight." '[1]

Shaikh Zaid governed the Abu Dhabi villages from Muwaiqiʻ, where he resided after 1946. It was his responsibility to collect the *zakat* on the dates grown in al-Ain, Hili, Jimi and Qattarah. The rate was the same as that at Liwa, although the *nisab* was smaller. No *zakat* was collected at Muwaiqiʻ, where the palms were all owned by the Al Bu Falah. Zaid also collected water-taxes from all users, other than members of the ruling family, of the *aflaj*, or underground conduits, which carried water to the oasis. In the collection of taxes he was assisted by a *muzakki* and *arifs* (collectors of water-taxes), and in the administration of justice by a *qadi*. Every winter he spent much

[1] *Arabian Sands*, p. 250.

of his time in the Khatam, the neighbouring desert, where the Baduin all acknowledged his authority.

Al Bu Sa'id authority in the Buraimi Oasis and its vicinity was exercised much less directly and forcefully than that of the Al Bu Falah in these years. Since their accession in the eighteenth century the Al Bu Sa'id Sultans had ruled Oman by a dual administration: through *walis* appointed and paid by them, and through the *tamimahs* of the more important tribes, who discharged the functions of *walis* and, in return, were subsidized by the reigning Sultan. In the Buraimi region the Sultan's representative, the *tamimah* of the Na'im, suffered, as has been seen, fluctuations in importance and authority in the years between the death of Zaid ibn Khalifah and the appointment of Zaid ibn Sultan as Al Bu Falah *wali* at Buraimi in 1946. One consequence of this was that the Sultan, for most of this period, preferred to rely for his control of the region upon his *wali* at Sauhar, Mudhaffar ibn Sulaiman, son of the *wali* Sulaiman ibn Suwailim who died in 1907.

The *wali* Mudhaffar accompanied the D'Arcy Exploration Company's geological survey party into the interior of Oman in 1925, and he was described by Captain Eccles as having inherited 'much of the character of his father—is forceful, active, much liked by the Arabs'.[1] Mudhaffar gave a demonstration of his authority at the end of the expedition, after he had been informed that the Bani Jabir had raided the Baduin Al Bu Shamis, whose centre is at al-Sunainah, to the south of Buraimi. Summoning the *tamimahs* of both tribes to Sauhar, he made the Bani Jabir make restitution to the Al Bu Shamis. The latter's *tamimah*, Muhammad ibn Salimin ibn Rahmah, afterwards wrote to the Sultan:

'We have to inform you that as soon as we arrived at Sohar the Wali Mudhaffer conveyed the message to Beni Jabir and after hardship and difficulty they had paid 300 rials in cash and have written a document for 100 until an expiry of one month. We thank God by your existence the matter has been settled. We have approached to what you have instructed us and the matter is now for your disposal and Salaam.'[2]

[1] 'The Sultanate of Muscat', *Journ. Central Asian Soc.*, XIV, 29.
[2] *U.K. Memorial*, I, 38, Muhammad ibn Salimin to Saiyid Taimur ibn Faisal, 20 Rajab 1344/February 1926. Letter from the Muscat archives.

Frontier Negotiations and Saudi Ambitions, 1909-1949

From the early nineteen-twenties until 1939 the joint *tamimahs* of the Na'im were the brothers Muhammad and Saqr ibn Sultan. Muhammad, the elder of the two, died at the end of January 1939, after which Saqr ruled alone as *tamimah*. Shortly after his brother's death he wrote to the Sultan, assuring him of his continued loyalty. 'The understanding between you and him [his brother] is confirmed by us, as it was in the time of our fathers. . . .'[1] A few months afterwards Saqr visited Muscat to affirm his allegiance in person, and to complain that the subsidy normally paid to him through the *wali* Mudhaffar was in arrears. The Sultan evidently referred him back to the *wali*, for he wrote on his return to Buraimi:

'We wish to write to Your Honour concerning our salary, which is by your favour. On our return from the capital we called on your servant the Wali Mudhaffar. . . . He alleges that he has been deducting the salary since the days of the brother Muhammad bin Sultan. . . . He should not do things like this. The decision lies with God and Your Honour. You are the Giver and will not permit such a thing. . . .'[2]

Mudhaffar ibn Sulaiman's object in withholding the subsidy would appear to have been to induce Saqr to compose a quarrel in which he was engaged with Rashid ibn Hamad, chief of the settled Al Bu Shamis of Hamasa. He also endeavoured to persuade the chiefs of other tribes in the vicinity of Buraimi to bring pressure to bear upon Saqr. One of these chiefs, Ubaid ibn Juma' of the Bani Ka'ab, wrote to the Sultan in May 1939: 'We have received a letter from the Wali Mudhaffar bin Sulaiman, on the subject of the quarrels between Shaikhs Saqr bin Sultan and Rashid bin Hamad, and it seems to us that these matters will not be disposed of unless they appear before you. It is best and nearest for settling the matters, and you are the justice.'[3] Ubaid ibn Juma' was right: the quarrel was not settled until the Sultan summoned Saqr and Rashid to Muscat in the spring of 1940. Rashid afterwards wrote to the Sultan, on his return to Buraimi: 'You told us about your servant, Shaikh Saqr bin Sultan al Hamud, and we have no objection to what you will arrange between us and Shaikh Saqr bin Sultan. If he agrees to what you are

---

[1] *U.K. Memorial*, II, Annex F, no. 8, Saqr ibn Sultan to Saiyid Sa'id ibn Taimur, 6 Safar 1358/28 March 1939. Letter from the Muscat archives.

[2] *U.K. Memorial*, II, Annex F, no. 8, Saqr to Saiyid Sa'id ibn Taimur, 18 Rajab 1358/September 1939. Letter from the Muscat archives.

[3] *U.K. Memorial*, I, 39, Ubaid ibn Juma' to Saiyid Sa'id ibn Taimur, 7 Rabi' II, 1358. Letter from the Muscat archives.

going to tell him, and order him, we . . . accept what you tell us, and your order to us will be valid.'[1]

Normally, however, the Sultan did not intervene personally in the administration of the region but left it in the hands of the *wali* at Sauhar and his Minister of the Interior, Saiyid Ahmad ibn Ibrahim, the grand-nephew of Azzan ibn Qais. Thus, in 1942, when the Awamir raided the vicinity of Buraimi and made off with some camels, the *wali* went there to investigate. He took with him letters from Saiyid Ahmad, calling upon all the chiefs of the region to help bring the thieves to justice. The camels were recovered through the agency of Muhammad ibn Salimin of the Baduin Al Bu Shamis, who prevailed upon the Amiri chiefs to meet the *wali*. All the shaikhs—Saqr ibn Sultan, Rashid ibn Hamad, Muhammad ibn Salimin and Ubaid ibn Juma'—afterwards wrote to Saiyid Ahmad to impress upon him that they had helped to settle the affair ('You have asked us to help the Wali. We have accepted your call in obedience to His Majesty the King (Sultan).')[2]

In 1937 the Sultan, Saiyid Sa'id ibn Taimur, granted an oil concession for Muscat, Oman and Dhufar to Petroleum Concessions Ltd., a subsidiary of the Iraq Petroleum Company. The following year he informed the shaikhs of Buraimi and the upper Dhahirah that a survey of the region would probably be made in the coming winter months. Saqr ibn Sultan replied in November 1938:

'There is no news to give you from this country of yours—for Your Honour—but what is good and pleasant. Your Majestic letter which came by the hand of your servant, Ali bin Mudhaffar [son of the *wali* Mudhaffar] has been received, and we noted its contents—especially regarding the arrival of the engineers mentioned in it. God willing, we will obey your orders and give them every good consideration. There is no opposition to your order. The agreement which we reached when we last parted stands with us and we have no opposition. This place is yours.'[3]

Muhammad ibn Salimin of al-Sunainah wrote the same day: 'Your

---

[1] *U.K. Memorial*, I, 40, Rashid ibn Hamad to Saiyid Sa'id ibn Taimur, 4 Rabi' I, 1359/April 1940. Letter from the Muscat archives.
[2] See *U.K. Memorial*, II, Annex F, no. 8, Ubaid ibn Juma' and Rashid ibn Hamad to Saiyid Ahmad, 3–13 Dhu'l-Qa'dah 1361. The letters of Saqr ibn Sultan and Muhammad ibn Salimin, both dated Dhu'l-Qa'dah 1361/November 1942, are also in this collection. All are from the Muscat archives.
[3] *U.K. Memorial*, I, 39, Saqr to Saiyid Sa'id ibn Taimur, 13 Ramadhan 1357. Letter from the Muscat archives.

Frontier Negotiations and Saudi Ambitions, 1909–1949

kind letter which has honoured the position of your servant has reached me and your slave has understood its meaning. We are happy to obey your orders and to do what you want. We are under the orders of the Wali and his companions. It is our duty to do our best for them.'[1] Saqr ibn Sultan journeyed to Muscat before the surveying party set out, and he and Mudhaffar ibn Sulaiman accompanied it to Buraimi, travelling by way of Ibri, Yanqul and Dhank.

Oil exploration in Oman and Trucial Oman, suspended in the war years, was resumed after 1945. By the beginning of 1948 Petroleum Concessions Ltd., having surveyed the Buraimi region on the Abu Dhabi side, wanted to explore the Muscat side. The Na'imi shaikhs put up a show of resistance, for reasons that Thesiger, who was in the area at the time, explains: 'Each sheikh, excited by avarice, was noisily asserting his independence; while each of his tribesmen fancied that he could get better terms for himself by refusing to acknowledge any authority other than his own.'[2] Thesiger also heard that the shaikhs were denying that they owed any allegiance to the Sultan.

'Recently Saiyid Sa'id, Sultan of Muscat, pressed his claims to overlordship in the Buraimi area but the sheikhs and tribesmen concerned clamorously rejected them. Well aware that these claims were occasioned by the growing search for oil, these tribes, who are of the Ghafari faction, determined to prevent all further exploration of their territories by Europeans.'[3]

Opposition to oil exploration and opposition to the Sultan, however, did not necessarily go hand in hand. For instance, in February 1948 the chief of the Khawatir branch of the Na'im at Hafit, Ahmad ibn Muhammad al-Salf, wrote to the Sultan:

'Regarding the matter of the Christians: they have joined Zaid [ibn Sultan] and sent to the tribes asking them to come and see them. We did not go to them, and we refused them admission to our territory. The country is yours and the matter is in the hands of God and in your hands. Please ask the Head of State [i.e. the Political Resident] to prevent (these people) from entering our territory. We have no alliance except yours. The above mentioned territory is the territory of the Na'imi. All of it is prohibited to them. We will not allow them to come near us without your order.'[4]

[1] *U.K. Memorial*, II, Annex K, no. 3. [2] *Arabian Sands*, p. 254.
[3] 'Desert Borderlands of Oman', *Geog. Journ.*, CXVI, 140.
[4] *U.K. Memorial*, I, 41, Ahmad al-Salf to Saiyid Sa'id ibn Taimur, 14 Rabi' II, 1367/February 1948. The letter, from the Muscat archives, is wrongly dated '1364' in the *Memorial*.

Frontier Negotiations and Saudi Ambitions, 1909–1949

In the summer of 1948 a representative of Petroleum Concessions Ltd., Richard Bird, went to Muscat to obtain permission from the Sultan to examine Muscat territory around Buraimi and to bring motor transport through the Wadi al-Jizzi. The Sultan wrote to the shaikhs, recommending Bird to them, and stating that he would handle any dealings with the oil company in the future. Bird travelled to Buraimi via the Wadi al-Jizzi at the end of June, accompanied by Saiyid Ahmad ibn Ibrahim. On 11 July 1948 (23 Sha'ban 1367) the shaikhs entered into a formal agreement, in the presence of Saiyid Ahmad, confirming Saqr ibn Sultan in his position as *tamimah* of the Na'im and the Sultan's representative, and binding themselves to communicate with the Sultan only through him. The agreement, which was signed by Saqr ibn Sultan, Rashid ibn Hamad, Muhammad ibn Salimin, Ahmad ibn Muhammad al-Salf, and Ubaid ibn Juma' among others, read:

'All agreed in the presence of Sayid'Ahmad bin 'Ibrāhim, the Director of Internal Affairs, to entrust their affairs to Saqr bin Sultān, and to delegate him in all political and economical matters. They will undertake to support him, and agree with him in every matter of common interest. He will represent them, and it is his responsibility to take care of their interests. . . . He is their representative in communicating with His Majesty, God save him, in all requests and matters issuing from His Majesty. They all agree to delegate the aforementioned Shaikh to His Majesty in every request, whether in the matter of materials, and there will be no opposition from them. Shaikh Saqr has recognized that he is absolutely accredited to His Majesty and is responsible on behalf of the aforementioned Shaikhs, so that there will be no concealment.'[1]

All the signatory shaikhs wrote letters confirming their allegiance to the Sultan, and they later affirmed their allegiance in person at Muscat.[2]

During the period under review the only signs of Saudi activity in the disputed areas were the occasional *zakat*-collecting expeditions described earlier. The Saudi Government did not maintain a frontier post anywhere beyond Salwah, they had no permanent officials to the east of the Jafurah, and they carried out no administrative acts,

---
[1] *U.K. Memorial*, I, 43.
[2] For these letters, see *U.K. Memorial*, I, 41–43.

Frontier Negotiations and Saudi Ambitions, 1909-1949

apart from some *zakat*-collecting, in the western areas or the Buraimi region. Nor did they protest against acts of jurisdiction carried out in these areas by the Shaikh of Abu Dhabi or the Sultan of Muscat. In 1936 Shaikh Shakhbut granted an oil concession to Petroleum Concessions Ltd. for the whole of the shaikhdom up to the Qatar peninsula. Although negotiations were then going on for the delimitation of Saudi Arabia's frontiers in this region, the Saudi Government made no protest against the grant of the concession. In 1945 a United States Army survey unit mapped the coast from Qatar to Sharjah, after securing permission to do so from the Trucial Shaikhs through the British Government. No permission was sought from the Saudi Government, nor was any protest made by them about the survey. The surveying of the coast from Khaur al-Udaid to Khaur Kantur (twenty miles south-west of Abu Dhabi) by the Royal Navy in 1947 also passed without comment. In that same year, Petroleum Concessions Ltd. resumed exploratory operations in Abu Dhabi territory. During the winter of 1947-8 they set up camps at Mirfa and Ruwais from which they surveyed the coast up to Khaur al-Udaid to a depth of twenty-eight miles. The Saudi Government raised no objections to these operations, nor did the surveying parties anywhere encounter any evidence of Saudi administration. Eighteen months later the Saudi Government claimed that the whole of the area had been Saudi since the eighteenth century.

CHAPTER V

The Development of the Frontier Dispute, 1949–1954

It would appear to have been the resumption of oil prospecting by Petroleum Concessions Ltd. in the Trucial Shaikhdoms and Oman, and, in particular, their surveying of the Buraimi region in 1947–8, that re-awakened Ibn Sa'ud's interest in the region to the east of the Jafurah after the lapse of more than a decade. Early in 1949 survey parties of the Arabian-American Oil Company began to penetrate the coastal region to the east of Qatar. They erected beacons on Ras al-Hazra, a headland between Khaur al-Udaid and the Sabkhat Matti, and on Ghaghah Island nearby. In March a party in four vehicles left Qasr al-Salwah, the Saudi border post at the western foot of Qatar, and travelled eastwards along the coast towards Abu Dhabi. On 3 April it was sighted at a point to the east of Abu Dhabi town. Later that month another ARAMCO party set up camp on the coast near Ghaghah Island. On 18 April the Ruler of Abu Dhabi, Shaikh Shakhbut ibn Sultan, complained to the Political Officer, Trucial Oman, about these violations of his territory.

The Political Officer, P. D. Stobart, went to investigate, in company with Shakhbut's brother, Hazza'. They found an ARAMCO camp at Ain Baiwa, two and a half miles south of Ras al-Sila', and another camp, with an air-strip, twelve miles south of Khaur al-Duwaihin. In this camp were a Saudi official and twenty armed Saudi guards, who stated that they were there on the orders of the Amir Sa'ud ibn Jiluwi, Governor of Hasa. One of the ARAMCO surveyors admitted that he knew, from the Company's map from which he was working, that he was in Abu Dhabi territory. On 22 April Stobart handed the leader of the ARAMCO party a written protest, advising

The Development of the Frontier Dispute, 1949–1954

him that the Shaikh of Abu Dhabi would regard his party's presence 'at points North of Sufuq as an incursion, particularly as the Company have Saudi Soldiers with them', and asking him to withdraw without delay.[1] Four days later the Saudi Government protested to the British Embassy at Jeddah against Stobart's action, asserting that the ARAMCO party had camped within Saudi territory, as was borne out by the presence in the area of tribes owing allegiance to Saudi Arabia. The British Government replied on 11 May, rejecting the Saudi protest and lodging a counter-protest against the Saudi Government's violation of Abu Dhabi sovereignty. If there was any doubt about territorial rights in the area, it could be removed by discussions between the two governments. The Saudi Government agreed to open discussions, but they stipulated that the starting-point for them should be the conquest of Hasa by Ibn Sa'ud in 1913. They further maintained that delimitation of the frontier should be based upon the evidence of the Baduin tribes inhabiting the region, and that the criteria for the determination of sovereignty should be the effective levying of *zakat* and the existence of grazing rights.

There had been a calculated air about all of the Saudi Government's moves so far. They seemed to be confident that they could make out a strong claim to the sovereignty of the region in question, provided that negotiations took place on their terms. These were not terms considered by the British Government to be appropriate to a proper treatment of the frontier issue, and on 17 June they informed the Saudi Government that they did not regard the stipulations laid down by that government as constituting, of themselves, a satisfactory basis for the delimitation of frontiers. 'There is a wide difference between the extreme limits of a tribe's wanderings and the territory within which it may be predominant.'[2] Recent developments in Eastern Arabia, the British Government felt, particularly those connected with the discovery and exploitation of oil and increased governmental administration, made the demarcation of the frontier desirable. There was no question, however, of restricting the movements of tribes which normally wandered across the region under discussion. 'The frontier would serve to mark the limits of concessions granted by either party and the limits of their Governmental

[1] *U.K. Memorial*, I, 93.
[2] [F.O.] E 8082/1052/25, Aide-mémoire to H.M. King Abdul Aziz ibn Sa'ud, 17 June 1949, in *U.K. Memorial*, II, Annex D, no. 24.

The Development of the Frontier Dispute, 1949–1954

suzerainty; it need not have any other effect on the inhabitants of Arabia.'[1]

No indication had yet been given by the Saudi Government of the extent of their territorial claims, and none was given up to the time that negotiations began at Riyadh on 30 August. Pressed to state these claims precisely, the Saudi Government came forward on 14 October with the following statement:[2]

'After detailed study of the tribal areas and of the facts, the Saudi Arabian Government consider that the frontiers between Saudi Arabia and Qatar are as follows:

'(a) The frontier between Qatar and the Saudi Arabian Kingdom starts from a point at the coast of Dohat Salwa at 24° 56′ North (point A).

'(b) From point (A) the line runs due East until it intersects longitude 51° 00′ East (point B).

'(c) The frontier runs in a straight line from point B until it reaches the sea coast at latitude 24° 48′ North (point C), leaving Amirah to the Saudi Arabian Kingdom.

'The Saudi Arabian Government consider that the frontier line between Saudi Arabia and Abu Dhabi starts from a point on the Persian Gulf between Bandar Al Mirfa and Bandar Al Maghira two kilometres east of Bandar al Mirfa (point A). From this point the boundary runs in a straight line to the South West until it reaches latitude 23° 56′ North (point B). From there it runs due east till it intersects longitude 54° 00′ East (point C) and from that intersection it runs in a straight line as far as latitude 24° 25′ North and longitude 55° 36′ East (point D).

'The Saudi Arabian Government consider that these frontiers correspond with reality, having regard to their authority and the authority of Abu Dhabi and relying on the fact that the lands thereby allocated to Saudi Arabia are inhabited by tribes owing allegiance to the Saudi Arabian Kingdom: the Bani Hajir, the Manasir, the Awamir, the Al Murrah, the Dawasir and other tribes.

'As regards what lies to the South and East of the position 24° 25′ North and longitude 55° 36′ East, this is under the authority of Sheikhdoms which are not in treaty relations with the British Government. Therefore, the frontier between the Saudi Arabian

---

[1] Ibid.
[2] See Map 2 at end.

The Development of the Frontier Dispute, 1949–1954

Kingdom and these Sheikhdoms will be agreed between the Saudi Arabian Government and the Sheikhdoms in question.'[1]

This new frontier did not even remotely correspond with the Red Line of 1935, and it appeared to have no justifiable foundation whatever. It may be recalled that the map accompanying Amin Raihani's *The New Najd and its Dependencies*, published in 1927, the year of the Treaty of Jeddah, showed the eastern frontier of Ibn Sa'ud's kingdom as beginning at the Dauhat al-Salwah and running due south to the Rub' al-Khali, approximately along the course of the Blue Line of 1913. In the Treaty of Jeddah itself, the description of his dominions given by Ibn Sa'ud in no way corresponded with the territory he was now claiming. Fuad Bey Hamza, in his book, *The Country of Saudi Arabia*, published by the Saudi Government Press in 1937,[2] described the administration of 'Najd and its Dependencies' without making the slightest suggestion that the term included the areas now being claimed. On the contrary, he stated that the eastern frontier of Saudi Arabia lay 'along the coast of the Persian Gulf between Ras al-Qaliyah in the north and the Qatar peninsula in the south'.[3] ARAMCO, in a special report in 1948 on oil concessions in the Middle East, published a map which showed the eastern boundary of Saudi Arabia as beginning at the Dauhat al-Salwah and following a course not very different from the boundary which was to be claimed by the Shaikh of Abu Dhabi in 1952. The map prescribed officially for use in Saudi Arabian schools after 1945 showed the eastern boundary of the country as beginning at Dauhat al-Salwah, running south to the Rub' al-Khali, then eastwards along the northern rim of the great desert to the borders of Oman, and finally southwards and south-westwards towards the Aden Protectorates.[4]

---

[1] [F.O.] E 13024/1081/25, Note from Saudi Govt., dated 22 Dhu'l-Qa'dah 1368/14 October 1949, in *U.K. Memorial*, II, Annex D, no. 26. There seems to have been some confusion about the direction that the frontier with Abu Dhabi should take after leaving point 'A' on the coast east of Mirfa. In their note to the British Government of 14 October 1949, the Saudi Government stated that the line should run *south-west*; yet in the version of the same note reproduced in the *Saudi Memorial* (I, Chapter V, para. 56, and II, Annex 26) the line is made to run *south-east*, and is so portrayed in Maps I and II accompanying the *Memorial*. This could be merely an error, but it could also represent a modification of the claim between 1949 and 1955 in Saudi Arabia's favour.

[2] *Umm al-Qura*, Jeddah.
[3] *Country of Saudi Arabia*, pp. 242–3.
[4] This map was withdrawn from circulation and disappeared from view after the formulation of the 1949 claim. For it, and the other maps mentioned,

The Development of the Frontier Dispute, 1949–1954

If put into effect the new frontier would detach a strip of territory, twenty-five miles broad, from the Shaikhdom of Qatar. Its implications for Abu Dhabi were less straightforward. Presumably, by starting on the coast two kilometres east of Mirfa, it was designed to imply that the whole coastline westwards to Khaur al-Udaid and the entire hinterland behind the coast would go to Saudi Arabia. In other words, with the exception of the enclave from Khaur al-Udaid to Khaur al-Dhuwaihin, the new frontier assigned to Saudi Arabia areas that the Saudi Government in 1935 had explicitly or implicitly admitted to lie inside the Shaikhdom of Abu Dhabi, viz., the Mijan, Sabkhat Matti, Bainunah, Dhafrah and the Liwa Oasis. The implications of the frontier's terminating in a point (24° 25′ N., 55° 36′ E.) were rather more obscure. By ending to the north-west of the Buraimi Oasis the frontier cut across the main track leading from Abu Dhabi to the oasis.[1] One presumes that, if it had ever become a fact, travellers from Abu Dhabi could have reached Buraimi by making a detour around the end of the line. The significance of this terminal point, however, was to become apparent later. Its immediate purpose seemed to be to challenge the rights of the Shaikh of Abu Dhabi and the Sultan of Muscat in the oasis without actually claiming it for Saudi Arabia. Moreover, by asserting that the territory to the south of the terminal point was under the authority of shaikhdoms not in treaty relations with the British Government, the Saudi Government were plainly seeking to deprive the British Government of any *locus standi* in negotiations that might be entered into to determine the frontier beyond that point.

The British response to the new claim was to reject it as totally unrealistic. In a Note of 30 November 1949 they informed the Saudi Government that as Saudi Arabia was now claiming territory which she had acknowledged in 1935 to lie in Trucial Oman, Britain was left with no option but to stand upon her legal rights under the Anglo-Turkish Conventions of 1913–14. The Note continued:

'If the Saudi Arabian Government are relying on historical arguments in their present statement of claims, His Majesty's Government feel bound to state that brief interludes of temporary conquest in areas in question can in no circumstances be taken to

---

see *U.K. Memorial*, III. It might be added that, at the sitting of the Buraimi Arbitration Tribunal at Geneva in 1955, the Agent for Saudi Arabia, Abdur Rahman Azzam, said that the frontier of Hasa was at Salwah.

[1] See Map III of the *Saudi Memorial*.

The Development of the Frontier Dispute, 1949–1954

give the Saudi Arabian Government any appearance of authority after this interval. Moreover the brief period in which Saudi authority was exercised by force was followed by a declaration by the Amir Abdulla in 1866 that, beyond collecting tribute established by ancient custom, he would not in future interfere with Arab principalities in alliance with His Majesty's Government in the United Kingdom. This declaration, the text of which is enclosed, shows clearly that the Amir Abdulla did not contend that the collection of tribute affected the independent status of these principalities. The spirit of this declaration was moreover re-affirmed in Article 6 of the Treaty of Jedda.'[1]

The Saudi Government's contention that the territory to the south and east of the terminal point of the proposed frontier was controlled by independent shaikhdoms, and that, therefore, the British Government had no say in the delimitation of the frontier here, was inadmissible on two grounds. Immediately to the south of the terminal point lay the Buraimi Oasis, and here the Shaikh of Abu Dhabi, the conduct of whose foreign relations was the responsibility of the British Government, had claims. In the second place, the Sultan of Muscat claimed jurisdiction over the area to the south of Buraimi, and he had asked the British Government to represent him in the negotiations.[2]

In replying to these arguments on 10 December, the Saudi Government ignored the discrepancy between their 1935 and 1949 claims. They refused to accept the Blue Line as a basis for negotiations, and they declared that their new claim was based upon 'the right of lawful possession, reinforced by the continued exercise of sovereignty and influence'. They could find no such document as the Amir Abdullah's declaration of 1866 in their archives, but in any case such a document, if it existed, would only confirm the Amir's jurisdiction with respect to the collection of *zakat* from the tribes in the areas in question. 'As for the reference . . . to Bureimi,' they concluded, 'the position is that Bureimi, and the lands of Imam Khalili and their dependencies, are populated by Saudi Arabian tribes, and are not under the jurisdiction of the Sultan of Maskat, not under the Shaikh of Abu Dhabi; nor is there any treaty between it [*sic*] and the British Government. . . .'[3]

[1] [F.O.] E 14598/1081/25, Note to Saudi Govt., 30 November 1949, in *U.K. Memorial*, II, Annex D, no. 27.
[2] Ibid.
[3] [F.O.] 15073/1081/25, Note from Saudi Govt., 19 Safar 1369/10 December 1949, in *U.K. Memorial*, II, Annex D, no. 28.

The Development of the Frontier Dispute, 1949–1954

The absurdity of this last assertion aside—it is scarcely conceivable that the fiercely individualistic Ibadi tribes of inner Oman would regard themselves as Saudi subjects—its effect was to enlarge the original Saudi claim of 14 October. At that time they had merely claimed that Buraimi and the areas to the south and east of it were independent. Now they were, in effect, saying that they were Saudi lands. A similar technique was used with regard to the Dhafrah in the next few months. In April 1950 the British Government complained, on behalf of the Shaikh of Abu Dhabi, against the visit of a Saudi *zakat*-collecting party under Muhammad ibn Mansur to the Liwa Oasis, where they had assaulted and robbed a subject of the Shaikh. The Saudi Government rejected the complaint on the grounds that Ibn Mansur had not been trespassing but had merely been visiting places and tribes from which *zakat* had been collected since the conquest of Hasa by Ibn Sa'ud in 1913. The only new element, in the Saudi Government's view, that had been introduced into a situation of long standing was the attempt by the Shaikh of Abu Dhabi to dissuade the Manasir of Liwa from paying *zakat* to Saudi collectors. In view of this, the Saudi Government wanted to know 'the real historical bases of the claims' of the Shaikh of Abu Dhabi to 'regions which belong to Bedawin who have been, for a long time, subject to the rule of the Saoud family, and have been paying Zakat to their representatives continuously'.[1]

To this the British replied on 25 July 1950 that it was not the Shaikh of Abu Dhabi, who was in possession of these areas, who had to prove his title to them, but the Saudi Government. At the time that the Anglo-Turkish Conventions of 1913–14 established the Blue Line as the furthest limits of Turkish sovereignty in Eastern Arabia, Ibn Sa'ud had been a Turkish subject and he was, therefore, bound by those conventions. He could not afterwards base a claim to areas east of that line on events before 1913–14, but he would have to prove that he had acquired title since then. The collection of *zakat* from tribes in these areas did not, of itself, constitute adequate proof in international law of sovereign rights. The movements of nomadic tribes were irregular, their loyalties flexible. They paid taxes to various overlords at one time or another, usually for motives of prudence or expediency. The Saudi Government had suggested that a thorough investigation be made to determine accurately the

---

[1] [F.O.] ES 1081/65/70, Note from Saudi Govt., 24 Rajab 1369/11 May 1950, in *U.K. Memorial*, II, Annex D, no. 29.

The Development of the Frontier Dispute, 1949–1954

loyalties of the tribes inhabiting the areas in dispute. The British Government agreed that a joint technical commission might be set up for this purpose, but certain conditions would have to be observed if it was to function properly. These were:

'(a) . . . That pending and during the Commission's investigations both sides will abstain from any measures of pressure or inducement on persons or tribes who may be called upon to give evidence before the Commission.

'(b) . . . That the Commission should be empowered to discuss, as part of their general investigation, the situation in regard to Bureimi and the areas claimed by the Sultan of Muscat.

'(c) . . . [That] the Saudi Arabian Government are prepared to furnish detailed evidence in support of the claims east of the Blue and Violet lines of the Anglo-Turkish Conventions of 1913 and 1914 which they have put forward.'[1]

If the commission proved ineffective, then the frontier dispute might by submitted to arbitration by an independent body.[2]

Although the Saudis refused to accept the argument regarding the legal position established by the 1913–14 Conventions—they denied, for example, the existence of the 1914 treaty between Ibn Sa'ud and the Porte—they were prepared, in general, to accept the conditions concerning the proposed joint frontier commission. In a memorandum of 22 September 1950 they agreed that there should be no pressure or irregular influence exerted by either party upon the work of the commission, and that the *status quo ante* October 1949 should be respected. Although they continued to assert that Buraimi did not lie within Abu Dhabi territory, nor the adjacent areas in Muscat territory, and that, consequently, the British Government had no legal standing in these areas, they were willing that the frontier commission should be empowered to examine the situation in Buraimi and its vicinity. They refused to supply detailed proof in advance of their right to territory east of the Blue and Violet Lines. '. . . Proofs are to be demanded only from him who claims ownership of what is not in his possession.'[3]

Exchanges continued between the two governments until the early

---

[1] [F.O.] ES 1081/59, Aide-mémoire to Saudi Govt., 25 July 1950, in *U.K. Memorial*, II, Annex D, no. 30.
[2] Ibid.
[3] [F.O.] ES 1081/74, Memo. from Saudi Govt., 22 September 1950, in *U.K. Memorial*, II, Annex D, no. 31.

The Development of the Frontier Dispute, 1949–1954

months of 1951 over the functions of the frontier commission. The British explained on 10 January 1951 that they had not intended that Saudi Arabia should be required to supply detailed evidence in support of her claims before the commission convened, but only that she should furnish such evidence during the commission's investigations. The Saudis insisted on 7 February 1951, as they had previously, that there should be reciprocity in this matter. They also agreed, as they had not done specifically in their Note of 22 September 1950, that pending and during the commission's work no pressure or inducements should be brought to bear upon persons or tribes in the disputed areas.[1] By April 1951 both governments were agreed that the commission should begin work the following autumn.

At this point the British Government invited the Amir Faisal, the Saudi Foreign Minister, to London for discussions on the maritime frontiers of Saudi Arabia with Kuwait and Bahrain. The discussions took place in August 1951, and they touched only lightly upon the question of the territorial frontiers. Faisal suggested that a round-table conference of the various parties might be held, to see whether a settlement could be reached. The British agreed, and arrangements were then made for the curtailment of activities by the parties to the dispute in the areas concerned in the interval before the conference convened. Faisal at first wanted all activities in the disputed areas suspended until a decision on their sovereignty had been reached. In particular, he insisted upon the withdrawal of the Trucial Oman Levies, a British-officered local force under the control of the Political Resident in the Gulf, which had been raised in 1950 to maintain internal security in the Trucial Shaikhdoms. In the British view, the suspension of all activities in areas which, before the Saudi claim of 1949, had not been in dispute was unreasonable. Nevertheless, they accepted the more extensive definition of the disputed areas put forward by Faisal. The agreed résumé of the discussions, drawn up by Faisal at the end of the London meetings, stated:

'It was agreed by both parties that, until the conclusion of the conference to be held in the coming winter, the movements and activities of representatives of the oil companies on both sides and also movements and activities of the Trucial Oman Levies would be restricted to areas outside that which will be the subject of discussion

---

[1] For the communications of 10 January and 7 February 1951, see *U.K. Memorial*, II, Annex D, nos. 32 and 33.

The Development of the Frontier Dispute, 1949–1954

at the Conference. This was agreed by both parties without prejudice to their rights in the areas which will be under discussion.'[1] The résumé further stated that the purpose of the conference would be to study what territory belonged to Ibn Sa'ud and what to the other rulers concerned, in order to arrive at a just delineation of their frontiers. The idea of a joint frontier commission had not been abandoned: provision was made for the setting-up of a commission to collect information on both the territories and the tribes involved.[2]

Despite their specific undertakings of 22 September 1950 and 7 February 1951 not to disturb the *status quo ante* 1949 in the disputed areas, pending the investigations of a frontier commission, the Saudis deliberately engaged, in 1950 and 1951, in activities designed to influence the findings of such a commission. This is clear from some of the documents printed as annexes to the *Saudi Memorial* of 1955, designed to illustrate the affection in which Saudi Arabia is held by the tribes of Oman. According to one of them (Annex 53), a letter from Muhammad ibn Salimin, chief of the Baduin Al Bu Shamis of al-Sunainah, to the south of Buraimi, to the Amir Faisal, he visited Riyadh in the latter half of 1950 and talked with Faisal about oil prospecting by British companies in Oman. In the letter, which was written after that meeting, he says, 'The people of Oman are followers of the Arabian Reformation. They wish to have the rule of the King in Oman and to have him install a deputy in Oman.' Another letter, Annex 49, from Rashid ibn Sa'id, the Baluchi chief of Araiqi, a town near Ibri in the Dhahirah, to Shaikh Yusuf Yasin, deputy Saudi Foreign Minister, dated 15 Shawwal 1370/20 July 1951, reads in part: 'We have sent our son, Sa'id ibn Rashid, and his group. They met Shaikh Fuad Hamzah and reached an agreement with him. We and the tribes which are with us will follow King Ibn Sa'ud. We request a Saudi flag.' Sa'id ibn Rashid, the Baluchi chieftain's son, had also visited Saudi Arabia the previous year, when he met Ibn Sa'ud. The nature of the agreement that he concluded with Fuad Bey Hamza in the summer of 1951 is not explained in the *Saudi Memorial*.

Another visitor to Saudi Arabia that summer was Rashid ibn Hamad, chief of the settled Al Bu Shamis of Hamasa village in the Buraimi Oasis. Annex 48 of the *Memorial*, a letter from him to Ibn

---

[1] [F.O.] ES 1053/18, Agreed final text of Amir Faisal's résumé, in *U.K. Memorial*, II, Annex D, no. 35.   [2] Ibid.

The Development of the Frontier Dispute, 1949–1954

Sa'ud, dated 14 June 1951, states that while in Hasa he had a conversation with a Saudi official, Abdullah ibn Ali Al Mahmud. 'He warned us', Rashid ibn Hamad told Ibn Sa'ud, 'of the schemes of the imperialistic foreigners and the mischief-making Arabs, who are acting in accordance with the demands of the foreigner.'[1] The letter continues: 'He asked us to visit Your Majesty as he asked the other Amirs of the tribes of Oman, explaining the truth to them. We are now, God willing, going back home and waiting for that happy day in which your reign will be proclaimed. We, our towns and our lands belong to you.' A month later, on his return to Hamasa, Rashid ibn Hamad wrote cheerfully to the Sultan, Sa'id ibn Taimur:

'No news but good news. My master, we are intending to visit Sharjah to condole with them regarding Sultan bin Saqr (late Ruler of Sharjah) etc. Here is our messenger your servant 'Omar bin 'Omair, proceeding to you regarding the regular payment which you have been kind enough to grant us. This is a year and half's (arrears). Please pay him.'[2]

Ubaid ibn Juma', chief of the Bani Ka'ab of the Mahadhah tract, according to Annex 54 of the *Saudi Memorial*, also signified his devotion to the Saudi cause in a letter to Ibn Jiluwi, saying: 'We are your subjects and our territories are yours.'

The letters, and others like them in the *Saudi Memorial* from Omani tribal leaders (Annexes 50–52), are interesting on more than one count. They all reveal, one assumes inadvertently, that Saudi rule in the Buraimi region, even in prospect, was a new phenomenon. Yet it was later to be argued by the authors of the *Saudi Memorial* that Saudi authority in the region had been continuous since 1800.[3] Again, three of the writers now expressing their desire to be ruled by Ibn Sa'ud, viz., Rashid ibn Hamad, Muhammad ibn Salimin and Ubaid ibn Juma', had only three years earlier solemnly re-affirmed, in person and in writing, their allegiance to the Sultan of Muscat. It is difficult, therefore, to accept the impression conveyed by the *Memorial*'s authors that the letters were completely unsolicited. Still less is one able to accept the implication, which both the text of the *Memorial* and the way in which the letters are introduced are

---

[1] The text in the *Saudi Memorial* (I, Chapter V, para. 83) makes out that it was Rashid ibn Hamad who warned Ibn Sa'ud of the 'schemes'.

[2] U.K. *Memorial*, II, Annex K, no. 3, Rashid ibn Hamad to Saiyid Sa'id ibn Taimur, 20 Jumada II, 1370/7 July 1951. Letter from the Muscat archives.

[3] See, for example, Vol. I, Chapter VI, para. 21.

The Development of the Frontier Dispute, 1949–1954

designed to convey, that the exchanges took place after the round-table conference proposed by the Amir Faisal had been held.[1]

The round-table conference opened at Dammam, on the Gulf coast of Saudi Arabia, on 28 January 1952. The Saudi delegation was led by the Amir Faisal and included Shaikh Yusuf Yasin, deputy Foreign Minister, the Amir Sa'ud ibn Jiluwi, Governor of Hasa, and Shaikh Hafiz Wahba, Saudi Ambassador in London. The British delegation was led by the Political Resident in the Gulf, Sir Rupert Hay, who was accompanied by the Ruler of Qatar, Shaikh Ali ibn Abdullah Al Thani, and the Ruler of Abu Dhabi, Shaikh Shakhbut ibn Sultan. The frontiers of Saudi Arabia with Qatar and Abu Dhabi were discussed by the principal delegates in seven plenary sessions, and by their deputies in five informal sessions. At the second plenary session, on 29 January, after consultation with the Shaikh of Qatar, Sir Rupert Hay put forward as the boundary claimed by the Shaikh a line beginning at Ghar al-Buraid on the Dauhat al-Salwah and running eastwards through three named points to Hazm Sauda Nathil, and thence through Aqlat Manasir to a point on the western shore of Khaur al-Udaid.[2] Such a frontier would retain for Qatar the strip of territory, roughly twenty-five miles deep, across the base of the peninsula, which had been included in the 1949 Saudi claim. At the third plenary session Hay put forward as the boundary claimed by the Shaikh of Abu Dhabi a line beginning at Hazm Sauda Nathil and running on a straight course to the southernmost tip of the Sabkhat Matti. From there the line ran approximately south-eastwards to al-Quraini, then roughly east-north-east to Umm al-Zamul.[3] The southern boundary so formed, it was later explained, included within Abu Dhabi territory the district known as Kidan, to the south of Liwa, to which it was more closely allied, topographically, than to the heavy sands of the Rub' al-Khali. Further east, the great sand dunes of the Ramlat ibn Su'aidan formed a natural boundary as far as Umm al-Zamul.

The grounds upon which the Shaikh of Abu Dhabi based his claim were explained at the fourth plenary session. They were:

---

[1] Mention of the letters in the text is reserved until after the conference has been described, and they are introduced with the statement (I, Chapter V, para. 83): 'For some time prior to the spring of 1952, the Saudi Arabian Government kept receiving reports from Buraimi and its neighboring areas about the increased interest being taken in that region by the British and persons acting on their behalf.'

[2] See Map 2 at end.   [3] See Map 2 at end.

The Development of the Frontier Dispute, 1949-1954

i. that the area to the east and south of Hazm Sauda Nathil, including the Aqal and Mijan, although admittedly barren, was frequented when grazing was available by the Qubaisat, Maharibah, Hawamil and Mazari' sections of the Bani Yas, an Abu Dhabi tribe. Camel routes from Abu Dhabi to Qatar ran through this area;

ii. that the coast from Khaur al-Udaid was recognized by those who frequented it as belonging to the Shaikh of Abu Dhabi; that anyone who wished to fish from the coast with nets had to obtain a licence from him to do so (for instance, a member of the Rumaithat section of the Bani Yas had leased such fishing rights from the Shaikh for the coast from Khaur al-Udaid to Ras al-Hamra for an annual fee of Rs 350 since 1945-46); and that no Saudi fishermen were to be found on this coast;

iii. that the British Government had, over a long period of time and on specific occasions, recognized the Shaikh of Abu Dhabi's title to Khaur al-Udaid;

iv. that the Dhafrah was inhabited principally by two tribes, the Bani Yas and the Manasir, of which the former were the more numerous and settled. Those Bani Yas who owned palms in the Liwa Oasis spent half the year there and the other half on the coast or at Abu Dhabi. The Manasir were a primarily nomadic tribe. Several of them owned palms in Liwa and spent part of the year there. For the remainder of the year they grazed their herds in the Dhafrah. The Bani Yas were an Abu Dhabi tribe, and the Manasir were also followers of the Shaikh of Abu Dhabi. They had fought for him in his recent war with Dubai and many of them had been killed in the fighting;

v. that the Bani Yas and the Manasir adhered to the Maliki school of Islamic law, not the Hanbali school followed in Saudi Arabia, a fact which underlined their connexion with Abu Dhabi; and

vi. that Lorimer's *Gazetteer of the Persian Gulf* described the Dhafrah in 1908 as being part of Trucial Oman and as falling within the political sphere of the Shaikh of Abu Dhabi.[1]

Most of these submissions were challenged by the Amir Faisal at the fifth plenary session on 2 February, and they were argued over exhaustively in the series of informal sessions that followed. Faisal denied that the Bani Yas used the Aqal and Mijan for grazing, and asserted that only Saudi tribes, like the Murrah, Manasir and Bani

[1] [F.O.] ES 1081/63, Record of Fourth Meeting at Dammam, 31 January 1952, in *U.K. Memorial*, II, Annex D, no. 36.

The Development of the Frontier Dispute, 1949–1954

Hajir, subject to the Governor of Hasa, went there for that purpose. If any Bani Yas passed through the area they also submitted to the Governor's authority. He refused to accept that the existence of fishing rights and the issue of fishing licences by the Shaikh of Abu Dhabi could be adduced as proof of Abu Dhabi sovereignty over the coast from Khaur al-Udaid eastwards. At the London Conference in August 1951, he said, it had been agreed that fishing and pearling were free to all and did not imply rights of sovereignty. 'It could also be proved', he added, 'that the Saudi authorities exercise jurisdiction along the above mentioned coasts.'[1]

Contrary to what Faisal said, it had not been agreed at London that fishing and pearling did not imply rights of sovereignty. Faisal had asked for the exclusion of fishing and pearling rights as criteria for determining the sovereignty of the islands in dispute between Saudi Arabia and Kuwait and Bahrain, because the Saudis were not a maritime people and they could not, therefore, produce evidence of customary use of the islands and shoals comparable with that which Kuwait and Bahrain could produce. His request was refused for this very reason, and the only agreement reached, which was the one to which Faisal referred, was that embodied in Article IV of the agreed résumé, viz., 'that the final decision as regards sovereignty over the island [sic] and shoals in question will not affect their customary usage for pearling, fishing, navigation and other purposes by the nationals of either party.'[2] Faisal's second assertion, viz., that jurisdiction was exercised over the coast by Saudi Arabia, remains unsubstantiated to this day.[3]

Faisal also denied at the session of 2 February that the British Government's recognition of the Shaikh of Abu Dhabi's title to Khaur al-Udaid could serve to transfer sovereignty to him. This, however, had not been the point made by the British delegation. The first recognition of Abu Dhabi's authority over the *khaur* in the eighteen-seventies had come about as a result of its being used as a refuge for pirates. Later recognitions were accorded because no one

---

[1] Loc. cit., Record of Fifth Meeting at Dammam, 2 February 1952.
[2] [F.O.] ES 1053/18, Agreed Final Résumé, August 1951, in *U.K. Memorial*, II, Annex D, no. 35.
[3] No evidence of such jurisdiction had been produced by the Saudi Government before 1952, and none was produced in the *Memorial* of 1955. At Dammam, all that was offered in support of the claim to the coast was an off-hand remark by Yusuf Yasin, at the first informal session on 3 February, that Saudi Arabia 'might possibly wish to build a port'.

155

else could prove title to the place, and because the Turks and the Shaikh of Qatar endeavoured, at various times, to occupy it. Saudi Arabia did not put forward a formal claim to its sovereignty until 1935. If, as Faisal seemed to be saying, the earlier recognitions had been made with the object of thwarting Saudi Arabia's later ambitions, then he was crediting the British Government with remarkable foresight.

The positive arguments put forward by the Saudi delegation in support of the 1949 claim were concerned largely with the Dhafrah and the western areas in general. Faisal stated on 2 February that the Dhafrah was the *dirah* of the Manasir and that any other tribes found there were interlopers. The Bani Yas in the Dhafrah did not outnumber the Manasir, nor were they all Abu Dhabi subjects. The Mazari' section owed loyalty to Saudi Arabia. The Manasir, he went on, were a Saudi tribe, and the British Government had admitted this in a letter from the British Minister at Jeddah on 20 April 1942, concerning the Anglo-Saudi agreement of that year on Kuwait.[1] It was pointed out to Faisal that the letter referred to tribes in the vicinity of Kuwait, and that it did not actually admit the Manasir in that area to be a Saudi tribe. Faisal made no attempt to explain during the conference, nor did any other member of his delegation, why the Manasir of the disputed areas had fought for the Al Bu Falah in the Dubai-Abu Dhabi war of 1945–8. He laid considerable emphasis, however, upon the *zakat* collected by Saudi Arabia from the Manasir and others in these areas. The *zakat* collected by the Shaikh of Abu Dhabi on dates at Liwa, he said, was not the *zakat* prescribed by the *Shari'ah* but merely gifts from Bani Yas tribesmen. 'The real zakat is that collected by the Saudi Government in Dhafara.'[2] Shaikh Yusuf Yasin went even further at the fourth informal session on 5 February and asserted, 'The Saudi Arabian Government took zakat on livestock only and no zakat is ever taken on growing crops.'[3]

Both of these suggestions are quite untenable. In Trucial Oman it is the general practice to levy *zakat* on crops rather than on camels. There is nothing in the *Shari'ah* to support the view that more

---

[1] See [F.O.] E 3760/1430/25, F. H. W. Stonehewer-Bird to Yusuf Yasin, 20 April 1942, in *U.K. Memorial*, II, Annex D, no. 37.

[2] [F.O.] ES 1081/63, Record of Fifth Meeting at Dammam, 2 February 1952, in *U.K. Memorial*, II, Annex D, no. 36.

[3] Loc. cit., Minutes of Fourth Informal Meeting, 5 February 1952.

The Development of the Frontier Dispute, 1949–1954

significance attaches to camel-*zakat* than to crop-*zakat*.[1] Yusuf Yasin's assertion is demonstrably untrue. Ibn Sa'ud's own proclamation of 20 Safar 1344/9 September 1925 on *zakat*, which is reproduced in the *Saudi Memorial* of 1955,[2] states: '*The zakah on the produce of the earth*. The *zakah* shall (be paid) on all grains and on all fruits which are measured and stored, such as dates. . . .' Faisal was on much firmer ground in dismissing as irrelevant the argument that the adherence of the Bani Yas and the Manasir to the Maliki rather than to the Hanbali school of Islamic law was significant. With less justification he dismissed the evidence quoted from Lorimer's *Gazetteer* that the Dhafrah was an appurtenance of Abu Dhabi with the remark that 'Lorimer was no more than a British official and his statements cannot contradict facts, and therefore cannot be accepted.'[3]

In general, the Saudi approach to the frontier question at Dammam was a negative one. Faisal and his delegation confined themselves mainly to disputing the bases of the claims put forward by the Rulers of Qatar and Abu Dhabi, and they brought forward no valid reason why the Saudi claim of 1949 should have been immeasurably greater than that of 1935. What they did do, however, was to try to argue that Fuad Bey Hamza had put forward the Red Line of 3 April 1935 without instructions from Ibn Sa'ud, and that it did not represent the King's views.[4] The assertion is flatly contradicted by the diplomatic correspondence of the time. Sir Andrew Ryan, when he presented the British proposal of 25 November 1935 (the Riyadh Line), discussed the Saudi claim with Ibn Sa'ud without his disavowing it. On 19 and 21 March 1937 G. W. Rendel and Sir Reader Bullard discussed the two frontier proposals with Ibn Sa'ud without receiving so much as a hint from him that he disowned the Red Line. Following these conversations Yusuf Yasin wrote to Bullard: 'During the conversation His Majesty did not think of giving up the claim concerning

---

[1] Even the *Saudi Memorial* of 1955 bears this out. In an opinion by a Muslim jurist printed in Volume II, Appendix B, it is stated: 'The *zakah* (Property Tax) is divided into four classes: (1) The *zakah* on field grains and fruits. Its payment is in kind.'

[2] Vol. II, Appendix B.

[3] [F.O.] ES 1081/63, Record of Fifth Meeting at Dammam, 2 February 1952, in *U.K. Memorial*, II, Annex D, no. 36. Apparently Faisal's view of Lorimer's unreliability was not shared later by the compilers of the *Saudi Memorial*, who ransacked the pages of the *Gazetteer* for references favourable to the Saudi case. (See below, Chapter VII.)

[4] See [F.O.] ES 1081/63, Minutes of Second Informal Meeting, 3 February 1952, in *U.K. Memorial*, II, Annex D, no. 36.

the frontiers put forward by the Government of His Majesty.'[1] On 19 December 1937 Faisal wrote to Bullard: 'Whenever an opportunity presented itself my Government has explained the essential reasons which compelled them to adhere to the frontier which they had explained in the note which was communicated to Sir Andrew Ryan by the Deputy (Minister) for Foreign Affairs on 29/12/1353 (April 3rd 1935).'[2]

A further suggestion made at Dammam by Yusuf Yasin was that the frontier regarded by Ibn Saʻud as the correct one had been agreed upon in correspondence between the Amir Faisal ibn Turki and the British Government at some time between 1860 and 1870, and in a letter from Abdullah ibn Faisal to the British Government after 1880.[3] No correspondence of this nature has been produced to this day by the Saudi Government and no trace of it can be found in the British archives. The only exchange of correspondence between 1860 and 1870 remotely connected with the subject was Abdullah's undertaking of 1866. No communication was held with him on the subject after 1880, when he was hardly in a position to discuss frontiers, with the Turks in occupation of Hasa and the Ibn Rashid in the process of dispossessing him of Najd itself.

The last session of the Dammam Conference was held on 14 February 1952. Sir Rupert Hay made a final offer to continue discussions on the basis of the Saudi Red Line of 1935, if Ibn Saʻud saw fit to modify that line so as to exclude Khaur al-Udaid from his claim. The Amir Faisal, after saying again that the Red Line did not represent the King's views, agreed to lay the proposal before him and to obtain his instructions. The conference then adjourned, on the understanding that the restrictions agreed upon at London the previous August on the movements of the oil companies and the Trucial Oman Levies should remain in force. It was never reconvened.

The lesson that the Saudi Government would seem to have drawn from the Dammam Conference was that there was little chance of achieving their territorial ambitions by means of negotiation, and

[1] [F.O.] E 2123/92/25, Yusuf Yasin to Bullard, 11 Muharram 1356/23 March 1937, in *U.K. Memorial*, II, Annex D, no. 15.
[2] [F.O.] E 439/150/91, Faisal to Bullard, 16 Shawwal 1356/19 December 1937, in *U.K. Memorial*, II, Annex D, no. 18.
[3] [F.O.] ES 1081/63, Minutes of Third Informal Meeting, 3 February 1952, in *U.K. Memorial*, II, Annex D, no. 36.

The Development of the Frontier Dispute, 1949–1954

that new tactics must be adopted. On 29 March 1952 they protested that a visit by the Political Officer, Trucial Oman, to the Buraimi Oasis earlier that month was a violation of the London Agreement. The protest stated:

'... The Saudi Arabian Government does not recognize the authority or influence of the Sultan of Muscat or trucial Sheikhs over the area of Bureimi and provinces beyond it and outside the coast of Oman.... The Saudi Arabian Government has been obliged to inform the Amirs of Bureimi, who acknowledge allegiance to King Ibn Saud and his sovereignty over them, that it shall never be possible to recognize any sovereignty over them by the Sheikhs of the Oman coast.'[1]

It was an unwarranted protest. The restrictions imposed at London in August 1951 did not apply to the activities of British officials in the course of their normal administrative duties. On the contrary, the continuation of such administrative duties, whether in the disputed or in the undisputed areas, had been expressly reserved at the London Conference, and had been accepted by the Amir Faisal himself.[2]

The Saudi Government's next move was to dispatch, in July 1952, a party in two vehicles to the Petroleum Concessions Ltd. camp at Tarif, on the coast to the west of Abu Dhabi town and east of Mirfa. As Tarif had been recognized by the Saudis in their 1949 claim as lying in undisputed Abu Dhabi territory, their action was a deliberate violation of the shaikhdom's sovereignty. That same month Rashid ibn Hamad, the Al Bu Shamis chief of Hamasa, left the Buraimi Oasis for Saudi Arabia. Four weeks later, on 31 August, he returned to the oasis, accompanied by the Saudi Amir, Turki ibn Abdullah ibn Utaishan, formerly governor of Ras Tanura, and forty *fidawis*, or armed retainers, in four vehicles. In order to reach Buraimi the force had had to cross undisputed Abu Dhabi territory, as the only feasible motor route from the west in those days ran near the coast.[3] On arrival, Turki ibn Utaishan and his party established themselves in Hamasa, placing part of the oasis, for the first time in over eighty years, under Saudi occupation.

Turki brought with him letters from Sa'ud ibn Jiluwi, Governor of

[1] [F.O.] EA 1084/31, G. C. Pelham (H.B.M. Ambass. at Jeddah) to F.O., 31 March 1952, in *U.K. Memorial*, II, Annex D, no. 38.
[2] [F.O.] EA 1084/31, F.O. to Pelham, 7 April 1952, in *U.K. Memorial*, II, Annex D, no. 39.
[3] See, for example, Map III of the *Saudi Memorial*, which makes this fact quite clear.

The Development of the Frontier Dispute, 1949-1954

Hasa, addressed to all the principal shaikhs of the Buraimi region. A typical letter ran:

'In view of the repeated request made by our *Tawarif* [brethren] in 'Omān and the arrival of Rāshid bin Hamad al-Shamsi for himself, and in behalf of them, for the appointment by us of a representative in their country, we have appointed our servant Turki bin 'Abdullah bin Ataishan, and have supplied him with the necessary instruction, which he should observe. We have full trust in him. As you are one of our *tarifa*, and belonging to us, your help cannot be spared. You will see from him by the will of God, what will please you.'[1]

Among the recipients of the letters were Muhammad ibn Salimin of the Baduin Al Bu Shamis, Rashid ibn Sa'id of the Baluchis of Araiqi, and Ubaid ibn Juma' of the Bani Ka'ab, all of whom, as has been seen, had previously been in communication with the Saudi Government. Other recipients were Saqr ibn Sultan of Buraimi, the *tamimah* of the Na'im, Salim ibn Rakkadh and Salim ibn Hamm, the chiefs of the Baduin division of the Awamir, and the Na'imi shaikhs of Wasit (in the Wadi al-Jizzi), Dhank, Hafit and Qabil.

Saqr ibn Sultan reacted sharply to the Saudi incursion. He wrote to the Sultan at the beginning of September:

'We should like to inform you about the arrival of the Najdi in Hamāsah on the tenth of this month [Dhu'l-Hijjah 1371/August-September 1952], accompanied by Rāshid bin Hamād, and his brother Muhammad. Their arrival at Hamāsah has upset us. We have played no part in this, Your Excellency. We have not extended a hand to any except yourself. I am bound to the understanding and association that is between us. . . . If you wish this place, you must show reaction as quickly as possible to what is necessary to expel them from this country, and for the affairs has [*sic*] reached a crisis. . . .'[2]

[1] *U.K. Memorial*, I, 104–5.
Rashid ibn Hamad travelled to Saudi Arabia on a certificate of identity, issued to him by the Political Officer, Trucial Oman, which described him, with his concurrence, as a subject of Muscat and Oman. Three months before he left he had written to Saiyid Ahmad ibn Ibrahim, the Muscat Minister of the Interior:
'News from these diyar is calm. . . . Omar bin Omair is coming to you, please pay him what is due to us. . . . Added below [is] receipt for Rs 455/– the payment accumulated at the treasury up to the end of April 1952 (22 Sha'ban 1371).'
(*U.K. Memorial*, II, Annex K, no. 3. Letter from the Muscat archives.)

[2] *U.K. Memorial*, I, 44, letter dated 16 Dhu'l-Hijjah 1371; from the Muscat archives.

The Development of the Frontier Dispute, 1949–1954

The Sultan immediately sent sixty men and some vehicles through the Wadi al-Jizzi to reinforce Saqr, and he ordered a general levy of the tribes of Oman to assemble at Sauhar. The Ibadi Imam, Muhammad ibn Abdullah al-Khalili, similarly ordered the tribes under his influence to gather at Dariz, on the inner side of the Hajar Mountains, and he warned the tribal leaders against having anything to do with the Saudis. To the Sultan he wrote asking to be told what further measures should be taken. By early October 8,000 men were under arms at Sauhar and another 800 were gathered at Dariz. In the meantime, following representations from Shaikh Shakhbut of Abu Dhabi, the Political Resident in the Gulf had moved a detachment of the Trucial Oman Levies to al-Ain, one of the Abu Dhabi villages at Buraimi, to support Shaikh Zaid ibn Sultan. He had also ordered R.A.F. aircraft from the airfield at Sharjah to make flights over Hamasa to drop messages of encouragement from the Sultan to his supporters there. Shakhbut himself sent a force of Manasir to Markhiyah, in the Bainunah, to watch for any further Saudi moves from Hasa.

On 14 September the British *chargé d'affaires* at Jeddah protested to the Saudi Government against the introduction of Turki ibn Utaishan and his *fidawis* into Buraimi, and demanded their immediate withdrawal. A second protest was made to Ibn Sa'ud in person at Riyadh the following day. The Saudi reply, delivered on 17 September, denied that any contravention of the London Agreement had taken place. 'The Saudi Government has never at any time regarded it as possible that Buraimi should be a subject for negotiation between it and the British Government.' The reply stated further: 'The relationship and connections of Buraimi with His Majesty himself and his fathers and ancestors before him were and still are continuous.' Saudi Arabia had agreed 'only once' to Buraimi's being included in the proposed frontier commission's terms of reference, and then only after she had denied that the rulers of Muscat and Abu Dhabi had any interest in the oasis and surrounding areas. No mention had been made of Buraimi in the discussions at London in August 1951, and none had been made at Dammam. Saudi Arabia had learned 'for the first time' on 15 September, when the British *chargé d'affaires* had delivered his protest at Riyadh, that the Sultan of Muscat claimed part of Buraimi.

It was all very cool, and highly questionable. The Saudis had agreed unambiguously on 22 September 1950 that the projected

The Development of the Frontier Dispute, 1949–1954

frontier commission should be empowered 'to discuss the real state of affairs in Buraimi and in the other areas, on condition that neither party interferes with the situation'.[1] They repeated this assurance on 7 February 1951: 'the places which the investigations of the Committee shall deal with shall include Buraimi and the area which is claimed by the Sultan of Muscat'.[2] The Amir Faisal had suggested at the London Conference that the Sultan be represented at the forthcoming round-table conference of rulers and parties concerned in the frontier dispute. Obviously there was no point in making such a suggestion if the Sultan were not involved in the dispute; and the only portions of his territory affected by the 1949 Saudi claim were Buraimi and the areas to the south and east of it.[3] The fact that Buraimi was not discussed at Dammam is of no significance. It could as easily be argued that the conference was convened to discuss the claim put forward by Saudi Arabia in 1949, and that Buraimi was not specifically included in that claim. At that time, it will be recalled, the Saudi Government had been content to assert that the areas to the south and east of the terminal point of the frontier claimed were under the control of independent shaikhdoms. Later they were to contend that these areas were inhabited by Saudi tribes, and that the rulers of Abu Dhabi and Muscat had no rights in them; but the first occasion on which they put forward a formal claim to Buraimi and the areas beyond it was after the Dammam Conference, viz., in their protest of 29 March 1952 against the visit of the Political Officer, Trucial Oman, to the oasis.

Not only did the Saudi Government refuse to withdraw Turki from Buraimi but in the first week of October they reinforced him with men and vehicles. An armed clash was clearly in the making, for the Sultan, then on his way to Sauhar to join his tribesmen, was bent on driving the Saudis from Buraimi by force. The Imam had gone even further and declared a *jihad* against them. If Turki were driven out, then Ibn Sa'ud might feel it necessary to his honour to avenge the defeat, and a tribal war of serious proportions might break out in Eastern Arabia. For the moment, however, the Saudis were primarily

---

[1] See above, p. 149.
[2] See above, p. 150.
[3] A similar conclusion can be drawn from the aide-mémoire presented to Faisal by the British delegation at London on the subject of the place of tribal loyalties in determining sovereignty. It referred to tribes professing allegiance 'to His Highness the Sultan of Muscat or to any chief owing allegiance to His Highness'. (See *U.K. Memorial*, II, Annex D, no. 34 (v).)

The Development of the Frontier Dispute, 1949-1954

concerned with keeping their illegally acquired foothold in Buraimi, and with averting any humiliating dislodgement of Turki. They pinned their hopes upon the intervention of the United States Ambassador at Jeddah. He suggested that the British should lift the restrictive measures they had imposed and that the Saudis, also, should refrain from provocative acts, that both sides should remain in Buraimi for the time being and maintain their existing positions, and that direct discussions should be renewed between the Saudi and British Governments. With some reluctance the British agreed to ask the Sultan to abandon his projected attack on Turki. He complied with the request, though not without misgiving, in the middle of October. On 26 October a standstill agreement covering the oasis was signed at Jeddah by British and Saudi representatives. Its main provisions were:

i. the parties in Buraimi were to remain in their present positions; they were not to be reinforced, but replacements and supply visits would be permitted;

ii. neither side was to make any threatening move, and R.A.F. flights over Buraimi were to be suspended (these had already ceased as a result of a direct appeal from Ibn Sa'ud to the British Foreign Secretary);

iii. life in the oasis was to revert to normal; no restrictions were to be imposed on normal movement or trade; the passport regulations for the Trucial Shaikhdoms were not to be applied in such a way as to restrict these movements; and both parties were to avoid actions that might prejudice any future decision on the sovereignty of the area;

iv. the right of the local inhabitants to visit the representatives of the parties in the oasis would not be interfered with nor would they be encouraged to do so; all parties were to desist from provocative actions, from propaganda, or from any action which might influence the tribes; and no party was to issue at Buraimi nationality documents not formerly customarily issued.

It was also agreed that negotiations for a solution of the frontier problem should be renewed.

In retrospect, it would seem that the British decision to restrain the Sultan from marching on Buraimi was unwise. Judging from what happened in October 1955, when the Saudi police detachment in the oasis was forced to capitulate, it is reasonable to assume that Turki's removal might have been accomplished in 1952 without much blood-

The Development of the Frontier Dispute, 1949–1954

shed. Ibn Sa'ud would have been hard put to it, if the position that he had gained by force had been lost in the same way, to justify an armed expedition to Buraimi in retaliation. The Sultan lost a great deal by agreeing to the British request. Many of his tribesmen were greatly dissatisfied with the decision to break up the force gathered at Sauhar, and the Sultan suffered a loss of reputation as a result. If he had retaken Buraimi he might not have been exposed, as he was to be for the next three years, to a sustained campaign of subversion by the Saudis in the Dhahirah and elsewhere in Oman. His later troubles, in particular the rebellion of 1957, might never have come about if he had made a show of strength in 1952. It is possible, too, that the British Government might have avoided some of the difficulties and embarrassments that they were to suffer over the Buraimi question. As it was, by the time that the Standstill Agreement was concluded Turki ibn Utaishan had performed a good part of the task for which he had been sent to Buraimi, viz., the fabrication of evidence to substantiate his government's assertions that the oasis and its neighbourhood were populated by Saudi tribes.

From the time of his arrival Turki had been disbursing large sums of money to tribal leaders and awarding free trips to Riyadh to several of them. At his headquarters at Hamasa he distributed free meals and other gifts to all comers. Those who accepted his hospitality were required to sign a visitors' book, in which they recorded the name of their tribe, its tribal area, their place of residence, and their desire to become subjects of Ibn Sa'ud. Those who wished to go to Saudi Arabia to work were issued with permits headed 'Working Permit for Saudi Subjects'. On 15 September Turki obtained the signatures of twenty-eight tribal leaders and others to a declaration, later reproduced in the *Saudi Memorial* of 1955,[1] to the following effect: '. . . We all affirm that the land is our land, and we have expressed loyalty to our lord His Majesty the great King. Our affairs are in his hands, and he may command us as he wishes, for he is the guardian of our affairs.' Among the signatories were Rashid ibn Hamad, Muhammad ibn Salimin, Ahmad al-Salf (the Na'imi chief of Hafit), and Ubaid ibn Juma'. All of them had signed the declaration of allegiance to the Sultan in 1948, and Ahmad al-Salf had written to Saiyid Ahmad ibn Ibrahim in July 1951, when the

[1] Vol. II, Annex 59.

The Development of the Frontier Dispute, 1949–1954

Saudis were communicating with the chiefs of the region, 'We do not wish to have dealings with any except the Sultan. For the *diyar* are yours and the men also.'[1]

Other signatories were Salim ibn Rakkadh of the Awamir, Muhammad ibn Ali ibn Awwad of the Baduin Al Bu Khuraiban of Hafit, and Matar ibn Salim of the Al Bu Shamis of Dhank. Only one of the twenty-eight signatories, Rashid ibn Hamad, dwelt in the Buraimi Oasis. None of the shaikhs of the Dhawahir signed the statement. The most important absentee, however, was Saqr ibn Sultan. Despite threats from some of the tribal leaders, Saqr refused to have anything to do with Turki. Without his signature, the declaration was practically worthless, for the principal signatories had agreed in 1948 'to entrust their affairs to Saqr bin Sultān, and to delegate him in all political and economical matters'.[2] Nor would the signature of Salim ibn Rakkadh bind the majority of the Awamir, for they no longer recognized him as *tamimah*. On the day after he signed the declaration, his successor as *tamimah*, Salim ibn Hamm, and the principal shaikhs of the Awamir gave a written pledge of allegiance to Zaid ibn Sultan and the Al Bu Falah.[3]

Turki ibn Utaishan secured several more so-called 'declarations of loyalty' from tribesmen in and around Buraimi in the weeks preceding the conclusion of the Standstill Agreement. Annexes 60–66 of the *Saudi Memorial* are testimony to his industry. He even extended his attention to the Bani Qitab, the principal Baduin tribe of the Shaikhdom of Sharjah, some of whose members readily swore allegiance to Ibn Sa'ud in return for the promise of a trip to Saudi Arabia.[4] Taken in conjunction with an effort made by his government during the negotiations for the Standstill Agreement to increase the area of the agreement's application, Turki's wooing of the Bani Qitab indicated that Saudi ambitions stretched well past the Buraimi Oasis. The Bani Qitab shaikhs left on their trip to Riyadh on 27 November, a month after the signing of the Standstill Agreement. If it had been known at the time that this journey was a reward for the giving of a declaration of allegiance to Saudi Arabia, Turki might have been charged with a breach of the agreement. As it was, a protest was lodged with the Saudi Government, to little effect,

[1] *U.K. Memorial*, II, Annex K, no. 3, Ahmad al-Salf to Saiyid Ahmad, 20 Shawwal 1370/25 July 1951. Letter from the Muscat archives.
[2] See above, p. 140.
[3] See *U.K. Memorial*, II, Annex J, no. 2.
[4] See *Saudi Memorial*, II, Annex 63.

The Development of the Frontier Dispute, 1949–1954

against his interference with a tribe subject to the Shaikh of Sharjah.

On 22 November the British Government recommended to the Saudi Government that as the area of disagreement on the frontier question was so great, the question should be submitted to arbitration. The Saudi reply to this on 6 December was to insist that Buraimi be treated separately from the frontier problem as a whole. '... The area of Buraimi and its vicinity is a part of the Saudi Arabian Kingdom, and ... the people who live in that area and its vicinity bear allegiance to His Majesty....' Historically, the reply continued, Buraimi was Saudi territory and its status was not a question susceptible of arbitration. It was simply a matter of confirming the loyalty of the inhabitants of the region to Saudi Arabia, and this could be done, as the Saudi Government had suggested in the negotiations leading to the Standstill Agreement, by means of a plebiscite. Were any differences to arise over particular sections of the frontier in this region, arbitration might be considered as a means of resolving such differences. After the Buraimi frontier question had been settled, Saudi Arabia would be prepared to proceed to the demarcation of her frontiers with Qatar and Abu Dhabi. The principles upon which such demarcation should be based had been decided at the London and Dammam Conferences. Arbitration might possibly have a use here if any disagreement were to arise. Finally, the Saudi Government could not entertain any complaints against Turki ibn Utaishan, such as had been addressed to them by the British Government. '... The Saudi Arabian Government has not been bound by anything that restricts its authority in the Buraimi Oasis. Ibn Utaishan is implementing the authority of His Majesty the King in the Buraimi Oasis and its vicinity.'

The Saudi Government's motives in endeavouring to separate Buraimi from the general frontier question were fairly transparent. If the thesis that Buraimi and nearby districts were populated by tribes connected with Saudi Arabia could be sustained—and Turki ibn Utaishan had been sent to forge such a connexion—Buraimi might be retained, and considerations of equity might work to secure for Saudi Arabia part, at least, of the intervening territory between the oasis and Hasa. More tempting still, a salient would have been established in Oman from which Saudi rule might eventually be extended over inner Oman and over whatever oil deposits that area might be found to contain. Already, Turki's initial successes were

The Development of the Frontier Dispute, 1949–1954

inspiring the Saudi Government with marked confidence. '... All the people of Oman', they had declared in their Note of 6 December, 'bear allegiance and obedience to His Majesty King Abdul Aziz Al Sa'ud, the motive for which being their Arab national feelings, and also a higher and more supreme feeling, and that is a religious loyalty.' It was a boast that would have surprised the more ardent of the Ibadiya, more particularly as most of them had never heard of Arab nationalism. By placing so much emphasis on the alleged longstanding Saudi character of Buraimi, and by insisting that the subject of the western frontier with Abu Dhabi be treated separately, the Saudis were, in effect, admitting that their claim to the western areas was ill-grounded and opportunist.

On 5 January 1953 the British Government informed the Saudi Government that they could not agree to Buraimi's being treated in isolation from the general frontier question. Apart from the circumstance that Saudi Arabia had earlier agreed to the inclusion of the oasis in the area to be examined by a frontier commission, the Standstill Agreement recognized that it was in dispute by stating: 'It is the intention of all parties to avoid any movement prejudicial to a final decision on the sovereignty of the area.' Turki ibn Utaishan's activities were subject to the Standstill Agreement, and the Saudi Government could not reject complaints against him simply by asserting that Buraimi was Saudi territory. The argument had no effect upon the Saudis. They continued to reject charges against Turki with the same reply, and not once did they seek to prove satisfactorily that he was not guilty of the infractions of the Standstill Agreement with which he was charged.

In this, however, they were not entirely consistent. Their numerous, and for the most part frivolous, complaints about the actions of British representatives in the Buraimi area were made on the basis of the Standstill Agreement and not, as might have been expected if they really believed that Buraimi was theirs, on the grounds that their sovereign rights were being infringed. A particular source of irritation was the visits of the Political Officer, Trucial Oman, to the oasis. Such visits had been taking place regularly for years, and they were excluded, along with other normal activities, from the restrictions imposed at the London Conference and confirmed at Dammam. The Saudis chose to ignore this fact, countering every accusation of irregular behaviour levelled against Turki with an accusation of similar kind against the Political Officer or other British officials.

The Development of the Frontier Dispute, 1949–1954

They also ignored the fact that the Standstill Agreement provided for the restoration of normal life at Buraimi, and that the visits of British political officers to the oasis were a normal part of their administrative duties. What was abnormal in the situation was the presence of Turki and his *fidawis* in the oasis. The Saudi Government's ultimate object, of course, was to establish the principle of parity at Buraimi, to place themselves in a position of equality there with the Shaikh of Abu Dhabi and the Sultan. That Saudi Arabia had not had any presence in the oasis before Turki was forcibly introduced was conveniently ignored.

In the pursuit of this policy the Saudis dispatched a *zakat*-collecting party to the Buraimi region in March 1953. The party, consisting of thirty-eight armed men, was led by Muhammad ibn Mansur, who had in the past led tax-collecting parties to Liwa and to al-Aqaila in the Bainunah. Travelling in four vehicles, the party arrived on 12 March at Tarif, in undisputed Abu Dhabi territory, where it was halted by the Trucial Oman Levies detachment stationed there. After threatening to fire on the detachment, the Saudis withdrew and made their way to Buraimi through disputed territory. From Buraimi Ibn Mansur visited al-Sunainah, home of the Baduin Al Bu Shamis, to collect *zakat*, and he even went as far south as Safa Well, twenty miles further on, to try to collect *zakat* from the Duru' and Awamir encamped there. He was offering *ikramiyah* of Rs 200 in exchange for *zakat* of Rs 100, but the tribesmen refused to take advantage of the bargain. When an explanation of Ibn Mansur's activities was demanded of the Saudi Government they replied that he was carrying out 'his mission of *zakat* collection which the Saudi Government have been in the habit of levying from their subjects in that area. . . . The execution by these men of their duty cannot be considered a violation of the Standstill Agreement which does not provide for the prohibition of such a proceeding, but actually provides for the maintenance of the Status Quo.'

Despite what the Saudi Government said, both Ibn Mansur's activities and his use of Buraimi as a base were breaches of the Standstill Agreement, viz., of its provisions regarding reinforcements and actions calculated to influence the tribes. Moreover, *zakat*-collecting by Saudi agents at al-Sunainah and Safa Well formed no part of the *status quo ante* 1952. The expeditions of 1925–9 apart, no Saudi *amil* had visited the Buraimi region in this century, and the Saudi Government were not able to produce any evidence in 1953,

The Development of the Frontier Dispute, 1949–1954

or in their *Memorial* to the arbitration tribunal in 1955, that any such visits had taken place or that *zakat* had been collected, even in 1925–9, from al-Sunainah or districts to the south of it.

Ibn Mansur's incursion, Turki ibn Utaishan's continued subornation of the tribes and creation of disturbances in the Buraimi area, and the Saudi Government's rejection of every complaint made against him convinced the British Government that the Saudis had no intention of abiding by the London Agreement on the *status quo* or the Standstill Agreement. Indeed, they seemed to regard the latter agreement as applying only to the British. On 2 April 1953 the British Ambassador at Jeddah handed the Saudi Government a Note, retracing the steps which had been taken since 1949 to reach an amicable settlement of the frontier dispute, and recapitulating the reasons why his government could not agree to the separation of the Buraimi dispute from the frontier question as a whole, or to a plebiscite as a means of determining sovereignty in the oasis and its vicinity. Turki ibn Utaishan had been sent to Buraimi for the purpose of ensuring, by means of bribery and intimidation, that such a plebiscite would produce results favourable to Saudi Arabia. A plebiscite, moreover, would not take into account the historical bases of the contending parties' claims. The course of action pursued by the Saudi Government since 1951 had destroyed the basis of the London Agreement, and their actions subsequent to October 1952 left no room for doubt that they did not intend to abide by the Standstill Agreement. In these circumstances the British Government had no choice but to declare the Standstill Agreement void, and to reserve complete freedom of action, both on their own behalf and on behalf of the rulers under their protection, with respect to the matters covered by the agreement. The Sultan of Muscat similarly reserved his freedom of action. The Note concluded by repeating the earlier offer to submit the whole frontier dispute to impartial arbitration.

To curb Turki's activities and to prevent further Saudi forays into Abu Dhabi or Muscat territory, additional detachments of the Trucial Oman Levies and of the forces of Muscat and Abu Dhabi were shortly afterwards moved into Buraimi and into the western areas. A blockade was imposed upon Turki's force in Hamasa, which was maintained thereafter from the Buraimi side by Saqr ibn Sultan. The *bona fide* inhabitants of Hamasa were permitted to obtain provisions from outside for their normal needs.

The British Note of 2 April was accompanied by a letter of the same date from the Prime Minister to Ibn Sa'ud, in which Mr. Churchill expressed his government's intention to honour their obligations to the Gulf states with which they were in treaty relationship.

'If in so doing they grieve another valued friend that is a matter for great regret but it cannot be a reason for inaction. What would the friendship of Great Britain be worth if she abandoned the weaker of her friends for the sake of the stronger?

'We shall stand up for what we believe to be right. Your Majesty will undoubtedly do the same and neither of us shall think worse of the other for it. If neither of us can convince the other, is it beyond the power of statesmanship to find means of reconciling our views with justice and honour?'[1]

To this Ibn Sa'ud replied on 20 April that he wished to see a return to the situation created by the London Agreement and the Standstill Agreement. He was willing to consider arbitration as a means of settling the dispute, but he wished it to be combined with his government's earlier proposals for a plebiscite.

Negotiations were re-opened shortly after this exchange to work out the basis of an arbitration agreement. Progress was extremely slow. In order to restore normality to the situation at Buraimi and to safeguard the chances of an impartial arbitration, the British proposed that all forces introduced into the oasis should be withdrawn, and that a supervisory committee be set up to ensure that no further interference took place. This was a twofold concession, for the British had consistently maintained that Saudi Arabia had no right to place forces in the oasis, and because mutual withdrawal went a long way towards meeting the Saudis' demand for parity. The Saudis, however, refused to withdraw Turki, and it can only be concluded, from his subsequent behaviour, that their refusal was prompted by calculations similar to those which made them insist, in the negotiations, upon a plebiscite as an essential part of the arbitration agreement. They also attempted to widen the scope of the arbitration so as to take in Abu Dhabi and Muscat territory not included in their 1949 claim. Apart from the fact that this territory was not the British Government's to bargain with, the Saudi demand might well have led the Sultan to reject arbitration completely. He had been restrained only with difficulty from using force in October 1952, and he was greatly reluctant to submit the question of the sovereignty of his part

[1] *Saudi Memorial*, II, Annex 85.

The Development of the Frontier Dispute, 1949–1954

of Buraimi to arbitration, having little faith in the Saudis' readiness to abide by the terms of an impartial arbitration. Subsequent events were to justify his scepticism to the hilt.

Agreement was reached between the British and Saudi negotiators in October 1953 on an interim régime for Buraimi and the other disputed areas, based upon a mutual withdrawal of forces and the maintenance of a small police force in the oasis by both sides to keep order during the period of arbitration. Discussions began in London in December 1953 on the terms of the arbitration agreement itself, and they went on there and at Jeddah until the following July. There were two main issues on which the two sides differed: one was the definition of the areas whose sovereignty was to be determined by arbitration; the other concerned the activities to be permitted in these areas during the arbitration. The Saudis wanted the territories of the Na'im, Dhawahir, Al Bu Shamis, Bani Ka'ab and Bani Qitab included within the scope of arbitration, as well as the lands of 'any other tribes whose territories may be so situated in relation to the territories of the tribes named as to require their being taken into account in defining a continuous frontier'. Some sections of these tribes, it was claimed, were Saudi in allegiance. In addition, the Saudis wanted the extent of their claims in the Buraimi region defined as the area embraced by a circle, having its centre in the oasis and a radius of fifty kilometres.

These demands amounted, in sum, to an extension of their 1949 claim. The Bani Ka'ab dwelt in the Mahadhah tract, at the western end of the Wadi al-Jizzi. Some of the Al Bu Shamis dwelt in the wadi itself. The *dirah* of the Baduin Bani Qitab was in the Shaikhdom of Sharjah, while the settled branch lived in the Dhahirah. A circle of the kind demanded by the Saudi Government would have taken in territory beyond the terminal point of their 1949 line. Eventually, the demand was whittled down to a circle of twenty-five kilometres' radius, i.e. from the centre of the oasis to the terminal point.

So far as the interim régime in the disputed areas was concerned, the Saudis wanted the removal of forces controlled by the British and by the Shaikh of Abu Dhabi and the cessation of all oil company activities. For their part, the British could not see why oil companies which had acquired their interest in the disputed areas before Saudi Arabia ever put forward a claim to them should have to suspend

The Development of the Frontier Dispute, 1949–1954

their operations. A compromise was found in the device of a neutral zone, separating the areas in which the companies holding the concessions for Trucial Oman and Saudi Arabia respectively could operate.[1] In the neutral zone itself no operations were to be permitted. The British Government were willing to withdraw the five Trucial Oman Levies posts which had been established in the disputed areas on condition that, on the conclusion of the arbitration agreement, Turki ibn Utaishan and his *fidawis* were withdrawn from Buraimi to Saudi Arabia. This was agreed to.

The arbitration agreement was signed at Jeddah on 30 July 1954 and it came into force on that day. Its main provisions may be summarized as follows:[2]

An independent and impartial tribunal was to decide:

(*a*) the location of the common frontier between Saudi Arabia and Abu Dhabi within the line claimed by the former in 1949 and that put forward on behalf of the latter in 1952; and

(*b*) sovereignty in the area comprised within a circle, having its centre in Buraimi village and whose circumference passed through the junction of latitude 24° 25′ N. and longitude 55° 36′ E., i.e. through the terminal point of Saudi Arabia's 1949 claim.

The tribunal was to consist of five members: Saudi Arabia and Britain would each nominate a member, and the other three members, one of whom would act as president of the tribunal, would be chosen by agreement from persons not nationals of either party. In conducting its proceedings and in formulating its award the tribunal was to have due regard to all relevant considerations of law, fact and equity, brought to its attention by the parties concerned or disclosed by its own investigations. In particular, it was to take into account, in so far as they were relevant:

(*a*) historical facts relating to the rights of the rulers concerned and their forefathers;

(*b*) the traditional loyalties of the inhabitants of the areas concerned;

(*c*) the tribal organization and way of life of these inhabitants;

(*d*) the exercise of jurisdiction and other activities in the area; and

(*e*) any other considerations brought to its attention by either party.

[1] See below, p. 174.
[2] Cmd. 9272, Treaty Series No. 65 (1954). The agreement is reprinted in full, together with the accompanying exchange of letters, in Appendix A, below.

The Development of the Frontier Dispute, 1949–1954

Within six months of a date to be fixed by the president of the tribunal the parties were to present simultaneously to the tribunal memorials setting out their submissions on the territories and frontiers in dispute. Afterwards, each party would have the right to submit, within a further period of six months, a reply to the memorial presented by the other. On the conclusion of these written proceedings the tribunal would hear oral arguments by the parties, or, with their consent, it could dispense with such arguments. The tribunal would have the right to call witnesses, conduct inquiries, and visit the areas in dispute. Its award would be final, binding upon the governments concerned, and without appeal.

Accompanying the agreement was an exchange of letters, laying down the conditions that were to be observed in the disputed areas during the arbitration. The more important were:

i. Turki ibn Utaishan and his party were to withdraw from the Buraimi Zone (i.e. the circle defined in the arbitration agreement) to undisputed Saudi territory; the Trucial Oman Levies, other armed forces and officials, introduced into the Zone and other disputed areas after August 1952, were to be withdrawn to undisputed territory in the Trucial States; and local armed forces were to be disbanded;

ii. a small police force, to which each side would contribute up to fifteen men, was to be stationed in tents in the Buraimi Zone, at a mutually agreeable place not inside the villages. Its task would be to maintain peace and good order among the tribes, and it was not to interfere in the internal affairs, administration or politics of any tribe. It was to take action only in the event of an outbreak of disorder, provided that the commanders of the two detachments were in agreement;

iii. neither side was to introduce additional officials or forces into the Buraimi Zone or the other disputed areas, although government officials engaged in the arbitration or persons attending on the tribunal were not so excluded; both parties were to refrain from action which would prejudice a just and impartial arbitration; and the tribunal would have the power to supervise the observance of these conditions, to adjudicate on matters arising therefrom, and to issue such orders and take such action as it saw fit in this respect; and

iv. there were to be no oil operations in the Buraimi Zone during the period of arbitration. Oil operations would be permitted in the area between the 1949 Saudi line and the 1952 Abu Dhabi line, on condition that both sides observed a neutral zone in which no

The Development of the Frontier Dispute, 1949–1954

operations would be allowed. This zone was bounded on the north by latitude 23° 15′ N., on the south by latitude 23° 00′ N., on the west by longitude 51° 35′ E., and on the east by a straight line drawn from the eastern terminus of the 1949 Saudi line to the eastern terminus of the 1952 Abu Dhabi line. Roughly speaking, Petroleum Development (Trucial Coast) Ltd. and D'Arcy Exploration Ltd. could operate to the north of the zone, the Arabian-American Oil Company to the south.[1]

Turki ibn Utaishan and his *fidawis* withdrew from the Buraimi Oasis on 13 August 1954. They were replaced by a fifteen-man Saudi police detachment, which set up camp in open ground at some distance from the villages. A fifteen-man detachment of the Trucial Oman Levies under a British officer also moved into the oasis, and encamped not far from the Saudi police post. The British member of the arbitration tribunal was named in August and the remaining members at the end of December. They were:

Dr. Charles de Visscher (Belgium), a former judge of the International Court of Justice, president;

Sir Reader Bullard (Britain), a retired member of the British Foreign Service who had been Minister to Saudi Arabia, 1936–9;

Shaikh Yusuf Yasin, Deputy Foreign Minister of Saudi Arabia;

Dr. Ernesto de Dihigo (Cuba); and

Mr. Mahmud Hassan (Pakistan).

[1] For the exact definition of these areas, see below, Appendix A.

CHAPTER VI

The Interim Régime in the Disputed Areas, 1954–1955

ii. The police force . . . shall not interfere in any way in the internal affairs, administration or politics of any tribe. . . .
iv. Neither side shall introduce additional officials or forces into the Buraimi zone or into the other disputed areas; both parties undertake to refrain from action which would prejudice the holding of a just and impartial arbitration. . . .
Exchange of Notes between the British and Saudi Governments, 30 July 1954[1]

Before he left Hamasa in the second week of August 1954 Turki ibn Utaishan set up a clandestine organization to carry on the work of subversion in which he had been engaged since 1952. It was headed by Rashid ibn Hamad, the Al Bu Shamis chief of Hamasa, and Muhammad Salih Abdul Karim al-Ajami, a Persian merchant of Hamasa who had been one of Turki's principal lieutenants. Abdullah ibn Nami, the commander of the newly arrived Saudi police detachment, was to be the medium of communication with Hasa, and the sums required for subornation were to be transmitted through him. Liaison between him and Rashid ibn Hamad and Muhammad Salih was to be maintained by the 'clerk' to the police detachment, Abdullah al-Quraishi. This individual, though ostensibly subordinate to Abdullah ibn Nami, was in reality his political superior, and was in actual control of the detachment's activities. Directing the whole operation from Dammam was the Governor of Hasa, the Amir Sa'ud ibn Jiluwi. When the police detachment was forced out of the oasis in October 1955, after the collapse of the arbitration proceedings, its records, comprising some several hundred wireless signals, letters, and other documents, were captured. They have been drawn upon to a considerable extent for

[1] Cmd. 9272, Treaty Series No. 65 (1954), p. 16.

The Interim Régime in the Disputed Areas, 1954–1955

the account that follows of the interim régime in the disputed areas from August 1954 to October 1955.[1]

Within a week of his arrival in the oasis Abdullah ibn Nami was well on his way to achieving what Turki had failed to accomplish during his two years' occupation of Hamasa, viz., the defection to Saudi Arabia of the *tamimah* of the Na'im, Saqr ibn Sultan. '. . . No one has tried to win him over and persuade him so far', Ibn Nami signalled to the Amir Ibn Jiluwi on 20 August.

'. . . We learn from him that his monthly expenditure, being salaries for his soldiers, and other expenses, amounts to Rupees 1,360. It is a small sum if we take into consideration his inducement to our side, especially during the present circumstances. I beg, therefore, that this amount be allocated to him as a monthly salary and paid to him in a secret way. On the other hand, it would be better if Your Highness recommends the payment of a bigger sum to this man, because his demonstration on our side would be of a great help to us.'[2]

Ibn Jiluwi sanctioned the arrangement, after he had obtained the approval of King Sa'ud, who had succeeded to the throne on the old king's death in November 1953.

'My Lord H.M. the King is prepared to help him, but under the agreement between us and the British you cannot involve yourself in such a matter. Saqr, therefore, has to choose a person he trusts, either in Dubai or in Bahrain, to whom what shall be allocated for him shall be handed. You may inform him that His Majesty has ordered to be paid him Rs 10,000, and after that Rs 3,000 will be allocated for him monthly. . . . You must be extremely careful not to write him a signed letter.'[3]

A short time afterwards Turki ibn Utaishan wrote from Hasa to his agent at Hamasa, Muhammad Salih:

---

[1] Many of the documents quoted here were published in the press in 1956, but the documents as a whole have not been systematically studied and collated until now. They are referred to in the present work as the 'Saudi Documents', and are classified according to their original serial numbers. Letters and wireless signals from Dammam to the police detachment at Buraimi were numbered in a single series for each Muslim year. Letters and signals from the detachment to Dammam were numbered in one series from the detachment's arrival in the oasis in August 1954 until the end of A.H. 1374 (19 August 1955), and in a new series from the beginning of A.H. 1375 (20 August 1955) onwards.

[2] [Saudi Documents] Out-signal no. 21, dated 20 Dhu'l-Hijjah 1373/21 August 1954.

[3] [Saudi Documents] In-signal no. 7127, Ibn Jiluwi to Ibn Nami, n.d. August 1954?).

The Interim Régime in the Disputed Areas, 1954–1955

'You will receive through "the Affectionate" a sum of Rs 63,000, out of which Rs 13,000 you are to pay in person to Shaikh Saqr bin Sultan without letting anybody know about it. . . . In future, a sum of Rs 3,000 will be paid to him monthly. As for the balance, you have to pay out of it, as we have previously told you, to Shaikh Rashid bin Hamad the fixed amount, being Rs 37,000, and the balance being Rs. 13,000 you are to distribute it as we have previously instructed you.'[1]

The bribe to Saqr ibn Sultan was increased early in October. 'Inform Shaikh Saqr', Ibn Jiluwi ordered Ibn Nami on the 6th of that month, 'that a further monthly allowance of Rs 2,000 has been allocated to him in addition to Rs 3,000, making the total Rs 5,000. . . . Payment to him should be made through Muhammad Salih al-Ajami and you should have no connexion with any payment made; *for the agreement does not allow this*.'[2]

Later that month the British Government brought to the Saudi Government's notice the fact that the police detachment under Ibn Nami numbered nineteen men, four in excess of the number permitted by the arbitration agreement. Among them was a doctor who had been with Turki's party. No satisfaction was obtained from the Saudi Government on this or on any other occasion when similar complaints were addressed to them, and the Saudi police detachment continued to exceed the number permitted by the arbitration agreement for the whole time that it was stationed in the oasis. In rejecting the British complaint in October, the Saudis put forward a counter-complaint against the arrest, at Mahadhah, at the western end of the Wadi al-Jizzi, of seven Bani Ka'ab tribesmen on their way to Saudi Arabia. The men had been issued with travel documents, describing them as Saudi subjects, by Ubaid ibn Juma', the former chief of the Bani Ka'ab. Ubaid ibn Juma' had been one of the earliest and most fervent adherents of Turki ibn Utaishan, and at his instigation he had begun molesting convoys travelling through the Wadi al-Jizzi in the early months of 1953. Action was taken against him by British forces in May 1953, at the request of the Sultan of Muscat, and he was subsequently deposed and replaced as chief by his nephew, Abdullah ibn Salim. Ubaid then defected completely to the Saudi cause, taking up residence with some of his followers at Hamasa, where he busied

---

[1] [Saudi Documents] In-letter (unnumbered), dated 5 Muharram 1374/ 3 September 1954.
[2] [Saudi Documents] In-signal no. 801, dated 8 Safar 1374. Italics added.

The Interim Régime in the Disputed Areas, 1954–1955

himself on Turki's behalf with intrigues to win over other tribesmen with Saudi money. His issuing of travel documents for Saudi Arabia to tribesmen living outside the disputed areas was illegal, and the tribesmen had been arrested at Mahadhah, which lay outside the Buraimi Zone, by their chief, Abdullah ibn Salim.

The Saudi protest against the arrest of the Bani Ka'ab tribesmen, and the suggestion that they were Saudi subjects, had not been made idly. Since 1950, as has been seen, the Saudis had been making determined efforts to infiltrate the Oman. If they could demonstrate that areas beyond Buraimi were under the control of allegedly Saudi tribes, this fact could hardly fail to influence the arbitration tribunal. If a sufficiently revolutionary situation could be created in these areas, then the whole process of arbitration might be aborted in its early stages. On 24 October 1954 Abdullah ibn Nami informed the Amir Ibn Jiluwi that Rashid ibn Hamad and Ubaid ibn Juma' had a plan to incite the tribes of the Wadi al-Jizzi, and particularly the Al Bu Shamis elements living there, to revolt against the Sultan. 'The best way, subject to your approval,' the Saudi police commander advised, 'is to supply them with some arms and ammunition in a secret way.'[1] The suggestion was adopted: '. . . The places mentioned lie outside the agreement between us and the British,' Ibn Jiluwi replied on 27 October, '. . . but His Majesty My Lord agrees to your proposal to give them arms and money to defend themselves. Advise us of the means by which we can deliver the supplies in extreme secrecy.'[2] Ibn Nami suggested that the best means was to send the arms by camel to the south of the Buraimi Zone, or to ship them by launch, concealed in barrels of paraffin, and land them clandestinely at Dubai, or nearby.[3] Ibn Jiluwi preferred the latter route, and on 8 November he signalled Ibn Nami: 'Inform Ubaid bin Juma' and Rashid bin Hamad to send secretly and immediately some reliable persons to Hamad bin Futaim at Dubai to receive from him 60 rifles with their necessary ammunition—30 rifles for each.'[4]

By December 1954 the plot had been enlarged to bring in the Maqabil and four other tribes in the Wadi al-Jizzi. More arms were

---
[1] [Saudi Documents] Out-signal no. 158, dated 26 Safar 1374. The Al Bu Shamis elements in question were, more correctly, Shawamis, a tribe related to but not identical with the Al Bu Shamis of Buraimi.
[2] [Saudi Documents] In-signal (unnumbered), dated 29 Safar 1374.
[3] [Saudi Documents] Out-signal no. 171, dated 30 [sic] Safar 1374/27–28 October 1954. Safar, the second month of the Islamic year, has only 29 days.
[4] [Saudi Documents] In-signal no. 1590, dated 12 Rabi' I, 1374.

The Interim Régime in the Disputed Areas, 1954–1955

needed for the uprising and they were forthcoming. 'In reply to [your signal] 240 *re* arms,' Ibn Jiluwi informed Ibn Nami on 19 December, 'arrangements for despatching 300 rifles with 100 rounds apiece are being prepared. . . .'[1] A month later he signalled: 'Regarding the arms. . . . They are now at Dubai.'[2] On 22 January 1955 the arms were smuggled out of Dubai, loaded on camels. Two days later they were intercepted and seized to the north of the Buraimi Zone by Salim ibn Hamm, the *tamimah* of the Awamir. Others, however, sent across the desert from Hasa, got through. On 4 February 1955 Ibn Nami signalled Ibn Jiluwi: '. . . Rashid bin Hamad and Ubaid bin Juma' have received their shares of the arms in full. We hope, Inshallah, nobody will come to know about it.'[3]

A scale of bribes for the tribes of the Wadi al-Jizzi was suggested by Ibn Nami to his superior at the beginning of February. It totalled Rs 14,700 *per mensem* and included Rs 4,000 for the Maqabil, Rs. 4,000 for the Al Bu Shamis, and Rs 1,500 for the Bani Hasan. 'I am in favour of this arrangement,' Ibn Nami added, 'lest any of the people of Wadi al-Jizzi should get envious of the other, and lest the British and their lackeys should discover our activities, and in order that the people of Wadi al-Jizzi may constitute a local force on the spot, which receives its orders from God and from you, if this plan is adopted.'[4] Ibn Jiluwi replied on 6 February: 'We approve the monthly allowances you have allotted to the Maqabil and their followers as mentioned by you with effect from Rajab 1374 [February–March 1955]. The amount will be despatched to you by the plane.'[5] The aircraft, which the Saudi Government had by this time been permitted by the arbitration tribunal to use to supply their police detachment at Buraimi,[6] arrived in the second week of February with the money aboard and a letter from Ibn Jiluwi. 'Forwarded to you with Nasir al-Hudhaili is the sum of Rs 81,895, being wages of the people for the month of Rajab. This sum includes Rs 15,000 as allocations to the people of Wadi al-Jizzi.'[7]

[1] [Saudi Documents] In-signal no. 2313, dated 23 Rabi' II, 1374.
[2] [Saudi Documents] In-signal no. 2991, dated 27 Jumada I, 1374/21 January 1955.
[3] [Saudi Documents] Out-signal no. 377, dated 11 Jumada II, 1374.
[4] [Saudi Documents] Out-signal no. 378, dated 11 Jumada II, 1374/4 February 1955.
[5] [Saudi Documents] In-signal no. 3363, dated 13 Jumada II, 1374.
[6] See below, p. 184.
[7] [Saudi Documents] In-letter no. 3377, Ibn Jiluwi to Ibn Nami, 15 Jumada II, 1374/8 February 1955.

The Interim Régime in the Disputed Areas, 1954–1955

One further element in the plot remained to be settled—the assassination of Abdullah ibn Salim, chief of the Bani Ka'ab. On 9 February 1955 Ibn Jiluwi signalled Ibn Nami at Buraimi:

'In reply to your [signal] 379 referring to the assassination of Abdullah bin Salim and his companions: tell the people mentioned that we have no orders to give them in this matter, and that we have no objection if they wish to avenge their shaikhs who were killed nor do we forbid them to take this course. So do not give them any orders or dissuade them. Be careful about this. God keep you. This is by order of His Majesty.'[1]

Abdullah ibn Salim, however, was not assassinated, and, in the end, the plot to rouse the tribes of the Wadi al-Jizzi against the Sultan came to nothing.

Another effort by the Saudis in the closing months of 1954 to sabotage the arbitration was their attempt to effect a *coup d'état* in Abu Dhabi itself. Two sons of a former ruler of Abu Dhabi, Dhiyab ibn Saqr and Zaid ibn Saqr, who had for some time been living in exile at Dubai, travelled to Saudi Arabia shortly after Turki ibn Utaishan's withdrawal from Buraimi, and were entertained in Hasa by Ibn Jiluwi. They returned to Dubai not long afterwards with a considerable sum of money—at least Rs 100,000—and made contact with a tribesman of the Al Bu Mundhir section of the Manasir, Muhammad ibn Haufan, with the object of inducing him to join them in a plot to overthrow Shaikh Shakhbut. Ibn Haufan's task would be to recruit tribesmen from among the Bani Yas, the Manasir, the Awamir and other tribes. Money and arms, he was told, in whatever quantities were required, would be forthcoming. Ibn Haufan told Shakhbut and his brother Hazza' of the plot, and it never materialized. Hazza' and Zaid ibn Sultan recounted these events to the arbitration tribunal at its sitting at Geneva in September 1955. Significantly enough, counsel for Saudi Arabia did not seek to disprove the story, and Shaikh Hazza' was not even cross-examined about it.[2]

The main Saudi effort at subversion in 1954 and 1955, however, was directed to the Buraimi Oasis and the areas to the south of it.

[1] [Saudi Documents] In-signal no. 3364, dated 16 Jumada II, 1374. The authors of the *Saudi Memorial* were later to claim the allegiance of Abdullah ibn Salim for Saudi Arabia on the basis of a declaration made by him in October 1952. (See below, p. 232.)

[2] Dhiyab and Zaid ibn Saqr also contributed a joint statement to the *Saudi Memorial* (see Vol. II, Annex 93).

The Interim Régime in the Disputed Areas, 1954–1955

Money poured into the Saudi police post at Buraimi in large sums in the closing months of 1954. 'Inshallah, you will, as I have already instructed you, receive from Bin Futaim [at Dubai] a sum of Rs 58,260 every month and distribute it as we have already told you about', wrote Turki ibn Utaishan to Muhammad Salih at Hamasa on 24 September.[1] 'We are sending you Rs 50,000 to be a reserve fund for spending in our interest,' Ibn Jiluwi informed Ibn Nami on 6 December, 'but it is not possible for you to spend it directly but through Rashid bin Hamad or Muhammad Salih ... because the agreement does not allow this.'[2] A fortnight later a much larger sum was sent to Buraimi with the doctor attached to the police post. 'In accordance with Your Highness' order No. 2357 dated 25.iv.1374 [21 December 1954], we received the sum of Rs 177,450 which you have forwarded with the doctor', Ibn Nami signalled Ibn Jiluwi on 22 December.[3] The same doctor was in the habit of making frequent visits to Hamasa, contrary to the arbitration agreement. When complaints were addressed to the Saudi Government about these visits they were rejected with the remark that the British apparently wished to interfere with the doctor's humanitarian work of caring for the sick.

Outside the oasis a sustained campaign was conducted to bring within the Saudi orbit tribes from areas far removed from those subject to arbitration. Some of the tribal leaders had been won over earlier, both before and during Turki ibn Utaishan's sojourn in the oasis, and they were employed as agents for the enticement of others. The most prominent of them was Sa'id ibn Rashid, son of the Shaikh of the Baluchis of Araiqi in the Dhahirah, who had thrown in his lot with the Saudis as early as 1950. In 1951 he visited Saudi Arabia and received 6,000 riyals. He visited Saudi Arabia again in 1952 and 1953–4. On 4 January 1955 Ibn Nami received instructions from Ibn Jiluwi to give Sa'id ibn Rashid a regular allowance: 'Pay monthly salary to Sa'id bin Rashid al-Baluchi at the rate of Rs 1,000 and the four Baluchis shaikhs at the rate of Rs 100 each and inform us of their names.'[4]

Rashid ibn Hamad of Hamasa was also one of the chief agents for the subversion of the tribes of the Dhahirah. In November 1954 he

---

[1] [Saudi Documents] In-letter (unnumbered), dated 26 Muharram 1374.
[2] [Saudi Documents] In-signal no. 2124, dated 13 Rabi' II, 1374.
[3] [Saudi Documents] Out-signal no. 276, dated 26 Rabi' II, 1374.
[4] [Saudi Documents] In-signal no. 2668, dated 10 Jumada I, 1374.

The Interim Régime in the Disputed Areas, 1954–1955

suggested to Ibn Nami that he might be able to win over the inhabitants of Ibri and the shaikhs of the Duru', whose *dirah* lies in the central Oman steppes. Ibn Jiluwi approved. 'Reference your report in respect of the Duru' activities,' he signalled Ibn Nami on 26 November, 'make the necessary arrangements to help the people concerned and to win over the Duru' if possible.'[1] Ibn Nami replied the next day: '... We will do our best to entice Al Duru'.'[2] On 1 December Ibn Jiluwi ordered him to send an emissary to the Duru' and to the shaikhs of the Bani Kalban and Al Ya'aqib, the principal tribes of Ibri, 'to ask them on our behalf their attitude towards the Government of My Lord, H.M. the King ....'.[3] *Sharhas*, or cash presents, were to be given to the shaikhs to help them to make up their minds, but it was to be impressed upon them that the receipt of further largesse would depend upon their proving their loyalty by deeds—such as the expulsion of the Muscat garrison and *wali* from Ibri.

'Tell Rashid bin Hamad to inform Hamad bin Saif [of the Bani Kalban] that ... it is not possible for us to stop their presents and salaries yesterday and proceed to allow them today unless they prove their loyalty, sincerity and faithfulness by cutting their relations with Zaid and Saiyid Sa'id bin Taimur, and by expelling those whom they have admitted in their country.'[4]

The subversion of the Duru' was to be carried out by Ahmad ibn Hamad al-Yahyayi, one of the Al Bu Shamis shaikhs of Dhank and an adherent of Muhammad ibn Salimin, chief of the Baduin Al Bu Shamis, and by Tuwairish ibn Hamudah, of the Ifar, a small tribe of the Oman steppes. Tuwairish, whom Thesiger describes as a 'notorious outlaw',[5] performed several services for the Saudis in 1954 and 1955. In January 1955, for example, he successfully guided an arms caravan to Buraimi by a route south of Liwa. His success with the Duru' was less complete. In February 1955 he brought Humaid ibn Ali ibn Hashilah, shaikh of the Labat section of the Duru', to Dhank, where Muhammad al-Yahyayi persuaded him to

---

[1] [Saudi Documents] In-signal no. 1938, dated 30 Rabi' I, 1374.
[2] [Saudi Documents] Out-signal no. 221, dated 1 Rabi' II, 1374. It is an interesting exchange in view of the fact that the Saudi Government had been claiming for years that the Duru' were a Saudi tribe.
[3] [Saudi Documents] In-signal no. 1994, dated 5 Rabi' II, 1374.
[4] [Saudi Documents] In-signal no. 2920, Ibn Jiluwi to Ibn Nami, n.d. (December 1954?).
[5] 'Desert Borderlands of Oman', *Geog. Journ.*, CXVI, 163, n. 12.

The Interim Régime in the Disputed Areas, 1954–1955

sign a declaration of allegiance to Saudi Arabia.¹ Shortly afterwards Ibn Jiluwi signalled Ibn Nami: '... Concerning al-Yahyayi, inform Rashid bin Hamad to thank him on behalf of my Lord, H.M. the King, and on behalf of ourselves for his activities and sincerity....'² Ali ibn Hilal, the *tamimah* of the Duru', and Muhammad ibn Sa'id ibn Tinah, the previous *tamimah*, were much more difficult to persuade. 'Your servant suggests giving Rs 2,000 to the Duru' shaikhs, Muhammad bin Sa'id al-Tinah and Humaid,' Ibn Nami advised his superior on 23 March 1955, 'owing to the fact that the Saiyid [of Muscat] is sending messages to these shaikhs.'³ The Sultan's messages evidently were more effective, for the Saudis succeeded only in suborning Humaid ibn Ali and a minor shaikh.⁴ They had no success at all with the Bani Kalban and Al Ya'aqib shaikhs of Ibri. Tuwairish al-Ifari, however, cheerfully gave a statement of allegiance of questionable value and relevance.⁵

Early in December 1954 the Saudi Government informed the British Government that they wished to bring in replacements for their police detachment at Buraimi by air. The British agreed to the flight on condition that the aircraft landed outside the Buraimi Zone, at Kahil, where a landing-strip already existed. The Saudis agreed to the condition and then proceeded to disregard it altogether. On 21 December their aircraft took off from Dammam, was cleared for Kahil by the air traffic control centre at Bahrain, and flew straight to Buraimi, landing in the oasis. The pilot, when asked by the commander of the British police detachment why he had done so, said that his Saudi guide had led him directly to Buraimi without attempting to locate the landing-strip at Kahil. Later, at Jeddah, the pilot

---

¹ See *Saudi Memorial*, II, Annex 104.
² [Saudi Documents] In-signal no. 3598, dated 24 Jumada II, 1374/17 February 1955.
³ [Saudi Documents] Out-signal no. 513, dated 29 Rajab 1374.
⁴ See below, p. 186.
⁵ The statement, dated February 1955, is reprinted in the *Saudi Memorial* (II, Annex 115). The authors of the *Memorial* describe Tuwairish (I, Chapter III, para. 69) as 'the chief of the 'Ifar' and 'a Saudi notable'. He is not the chief of the Ifar: the chief is Muhammad ibn Khila. The Ifar normally dwell a long way from the areas which were subject to arbitration in 1955. At the time of making his statement Tuwairish was in receipt of Saudi money. (See, e.g., [Saudi Documents] Out-signal no. 593, Ibn Nami to Ibn Jiluwi, 30 [*sic*] Sha'ban 1374/23 April 1955: 'Payments made by us, *vide* enclosed statement, Rs. 21,130.8: Paid to Tuwairish al-Ifari, Rs 500 and Rs 200. . . .')

The Interim Régime in the Disputed Areas, 1954–1955

said that he had been told to land at Kahil but had lost his bearings, and, as the guide also was confused, he had put the aircraft down on the only landing-strip visible, which happened to be in the oasis. The incident was far from being as simple as this. The landing-strip in the oasis had not 'happened' to be there: it had been prepared by the Saudi police detachment before the aircraft's arrival. Ibn Nami, the detachment's commander, waited beside it for the aircraft's arrival while his British counterpart waited at Kahil. As the following signal from Ibn Nami to Ibn Jiluwi on 23 December makes clear, a deliberate deception had been practised:

'The open signal was only made as a cover so far as the British were concerned. It was the best means to convince them that the plane was instructed by the Government to land at Kahil but, in error, and due to the ignorance of the pilot about this airfield, he landed at the oasis. Later on, there was gossip that in spite of the attempt of the British to stop the Government from using this airfield, the plane landed there against their will. . . .'[1]

The incident had more than scored a propaganda point: it had shown the Saudis how the supply of arms and money to Buraimi might be stepped up with little risk of detection. On 23 January 1955 the arbitration tribunal met for the first time at Nice. The British Government were not represented at the meeting, which they understood was being convened solely for administrative purposes. Instead, Shaikh Yusuf Yasin, the Saudi member, acting as a Saudi Government official and not as an arbitrator, brought forward a number of complaints against the British Government, including one that his government did not enjoy equal facility of access to Buraimi. Without having the British side of the case before it the tribunal reached a number of decisions, among which was this one: '. . . The two parties should effect an arrangement whereby each should be entitled to make to Buraimi, by land or air, the same number of visits, not exceeding five per month after notification in each case to the other party.' Subsequent events make it quite clear that Yusuf Yasin was cynically using the tribunal and its powers to facilitate the work of subversion being carried on at Buraimi by his government. The tribunal did not know at the time, nor was it to find out until the following September, when Yusuf Yasin himself admitted it, that he was the minister in the Saudi Government in charge of activities at Buraimi.[2]

---

[1] [Saudi Document] Out-signal no. 283, dated 27 Rabi' II, 1374.
[2] See below, p. 203.

The Interim Régime in the Disputed Areas, 1954–1955

The acquisition of the right of access to Buraimi by air enabled the Saudis to intensify their campaign to set up the new Imam of the Ibadiya as *de facto* ruler of inner Oman in opposition to the Sultan. The old Imam, Muhammad ibn Abdullah al-Khalili, had died in May 1954, and the office of Imam had been assumed by a shaikh of little reputation and less consequence, Ghalib ibn Ali of the Bani Hina. The crucial element in his attainment of the office was the support given him by Sulaiman ibn Himyar al-Nabhani, the *tamimah* of the Bani Riyam of the Jabal Akhdhar, and by Salih ibn Isa, the *tamimah* of the Al Hirth of the Sharqiyah and the son of Isa ibn Salih, who had been the old Imam's chief supporter in the nineteen-twenties.[1] Talib ibn Ali, the new Imam's brother and a much more forceful personality, tried to force the Duruʻ in the summer of 1954 to acknowledge his brother's election by sending a force to seize the tribe's date gardens at Ibri. But the Duruʻ, with the help of a detachment of the Muscat Levies, the Sultan's army, drove Talib's men from Ibri in September, and two months later the Sultan appointed a *wali* to the town.

At the time that he was trying to coerce the Duruʻ Talib ibn Ali was also in touch with the Saudis, a fact that no doubt stiffened the Duruʻ chiefs in their resistance to the Saudis' efforts to seduce them. The old Imam al-Khalili had regarded the Saudis with dislike and distrust, but his successor had no scruples about cultivating their friendship for the gains it could bring. From the Saudi viewpoint, helping Ghalib and Talib was tantamount to extending Saudi influence into inner Oman. The real power behind Ghalib, however, was Sulaiman ibn Himyar, and it was to him as much as towards Ghalib that the Saudis directed their efforts in 1955. Sulaiman had long aspired to dominate the politics of the Oman, and he had asked Thesiger in 1950 to find out whether the Political Resident in the Gulf would agree to recognize him as independent Amir of the Jabal Akhdhar, with a status similar to that of the Trucial Shaikhs.[2]

---

[1] See above, p. 116. The circumstances of Ghalib's election to the Imamate are obscure. When Thesiger was travelling in the Oman in 1948–9 he was told that the Imam al-Khalili's successor would probably be the son of the previous Imam, Salim ibn Rashid al-Kharusi, who died in 1920. (See 'Desert Borderlands of Oman', *Geog. Journ.*, CXVI, 162, n. 6.) It has also been said both that the old Imam, on his death-bed, named Ghalib as his successor, and that he did so under pressure from Sulaiman ibn Himyar and Salih ibn Isa. There is no record of Ghalib's election having received the necessary ratification by the tribes.

[2] *Arabian Sands*, p. 305.

The Interim Régime in the Disputed Areas, 1954–1955

Sulaiman had been in contact with the Saudis since 1951, at least, and he had been one of the recipients of the letters from Ibn Jiluwi brought by Turki ibn Utaishan on his arrival at Buraimi in 1952. Gifts of money had followed later, and they were increased after the stationing of the Saudi police detachment at Buraimi. For instance, on 30 December 1954 Ibn Jiluwi instructed Ibn Nami: '... Regarding Sulaiman bin Himyar: Pay him Rs 30,000 from the amount you have in hand and we shall remit you a similar amount....'[1] The money, presumably, was in part a reward for Sulaiman's having induced Huwaishil ibn Ali, shaikh of the southern section of the Duru', to give a declaration of allegiance to Saudi Arabia.[2]

On 4 January 1955 Ibn Jiluwi signalled Ibn Nami: 'Send immediately Rs 30,000 to Imam Ghalib that he may help by it the Wahibah tribe and others as he sees fit.'[3] Late the following month an Egyptian officer, Lieutenant-Colonel Ali Khashabah, was flown into Buraimi on the Saudi supply aircraft and sent on his way to the Imam. He returned from the Oman on 27 March. Ibn Nami signalled to Ibn Jiluwi:

'Today, 3 Sha'ban 1374, Lieut.-Col. Ali Khashabah, the delegate of Gamal Abdul Nasser to the Interior of Oman, arrived at Hamasa, accompanied by Hamad bin Rashid al-Hajari and Harith bin Musallim al-Umairi. They are in possession of letters from the Imam and Sulaiman bin Himyar addressed to us, and Rashid bin Hamad requested the despatch of the Lieut.-Col. by the Saudi aircraft.'[4]

The Egyptian officer was flown out on the aircraft which came in on 9 April. Presumably his visit had been prompted by motives similar to those behind the Saudis' activities in Oman. As Ibn Jiluwi put it succinctly, in a message to Ibn Nami at this time, 'We have no purpose from this except to work for the unity of the Muslims, and to expel the Imperialists from the Muslims' lands....'[5] Considering

---

[1] [Saudi Documents] In-signal no. 2564, dated 5 Jumada I, 1374.
[2] The declaration, dated 29 November 1954, is reproduced as Annex 137 of the *Saudi Memorial*. It is witnessed by Sulaiman. Huwaishil ibn Ali was also rewarded. 'Payments made by us,' Ibn Nami reported to Ibn Jiluwi on 23 April 1955, '*vide* enclosed statement, Rs 21,130.8: ... Paid to Huwaishil al-Duru', Rs 1,000' ([Saudi Documents] Out-signal no. 593, dated 30 [*sic*] Sha'ban 1374).
[3] [Saudi Documents] In-signal no. 2669, dated 10 Jumada I, 1374.
[4] [Saudi Documents] Out-signal no. 521.
[5] [Saudi Documents] In-signal no. 4515, dated 6 Sha'ban 1374/30 March 1955.

The Interim Régime in the Disputed Areas, 1954–1955

that the Saudi Government were at this time busily endeavouring to turn Oman into a Saudi satrapy, one might reasonably ask who the 'imperialists' really were.

As September 1955 had been fixed by the arbitration tribunal as the date for the submission by both parties of their memorials, the Saudi Government made a particular effort from March 1955 onwards to collect material to bolster their case. Rs 156,960 had been sent to Ibn Nami in February, Rs 50,000 as a reserve fund, the rest for distribution in the coming month or to replace money already paid out. The list of instructions contained such entries as:

'Rs 48,545 to be given to Shaikh Rashid bin Hamad al-Shamsi for payment from his part;
'Rs 5,000 allocated to Shaikh Saqr bin Sultan;
'Rs 15,000 allocations of the Shaikhs of the people of Wadi al-Jizzi and their followers. It should be handed to Shaikh Ubaid bin Juma'.'[1]

Saqr ibn Sultan's salary was raised in March: 'Pay immediately to Muhammad Salih', Ibn Jiluwi ordered Ibn Nami on 22 March, 'a sum of Rs 2,000 and ask him to give it to Saqr bin Sultan as being an addition to his salary. Treat his salary as at Rs 7,000 with effect from this month. Inform Saqr to this effect. Emphasize to Muhammad Salih to treat this question as most secret.'[2] Ibn Nami acknowledged the receipt of Rs 84,750 in April, 'including a sum of Rs 655 being allowances for the last batch of refugees'.[3]

Much of the money was to be used to facilitate the manufacture of evidence for the *Saudi Memorial*. On 8 April 1955 Ibn Jiluwi's son, Abdul Aziz—who was apparently acting for his father in his absence —told Ibn Nami to obtain statements from the shaikhs in receipt of subsidies to the effect that they were Saudi subjects. Among those named were Saqr ibn Sultan, Rashid ibn Hamad, Muhammad ibn Salimin, Salim ibn Rakkadh, Sa'id ibn Rashid al-Baluchi, and Dhiban ibn Ali al-Rubayyi', one of the chiefs of Aflaj Bani Qitab in the Dhahirah.[4] Ibn Nami was also to try to obtain similar statements

---

[1] [Saudi Documents] In-letter no. 3377, Ibn Jiluwi to Ibn Nami, 15 Jumada II, 1374/8 February 1955.
[2] [Saudi Documents] In-signal no. 4259, dated 28 Rajab 1374.
[3] [Saudi Documents] Out-signal no. 595, dated 29 Sha'ban 1374/22 April 1955. The Saudi Government were later to assert that the huge sums of money being sent to Buraimi at this time were for the relief of tribesmen who had sought their protection.
[4] [Saudi Documents] In-signal no. 4687, dated 15 Sha'ban 1374.

The Interim Régime in the Disputed Areas, 1954-1955

from the shaikhs of the Dhawahir.[1] To help him in the preparation of the statements Abdul Aziz ibn Jiluwi sent the tax-collector Muhammad ibn Mansur to Buraimi the next day on the supply aircraft. With him went a certain Abdul Latif, who had been a member of Turki ibn Utaishan's party. This was only one of the increasingly irregular uses to which the Saudi Government were putting the supply aircraft, uses which had not been envisaged by the arbitration tribunal when it made its ruling the previous January. On 19 March, for example, a number of tribesmen from the Buraimi area had been flown to Saudi Arabia, five of whom returned in the aircraft of 9 April. Two of the five, Sa'id ibn Mubarak, a shaikh of the Al Bu Rahmah section of the Manasir, and Ali Aba al-Rus, an Amiri tribesman, had made statements at Dammam, useful to the Saudi case, on the day before their departure. The statements later appeared in the *Saudi Memorial*.[2] At Buraimi on 9 April Muhammad ibn Mansur and Ibn Nami obtained statements from Saqr ibn Sultan, Rashid ibn Hamad, Sa'id ibn Rashid al-Baluchi, Salim ibn Rakkadh, Muhammad ibn Salimin and Dhiban ibn Ali al-Rubayyi', among others.[3] Some were later replaced by new statements obtained the following June. All eventually found their way into the *Saudi Memorial*.[4]

Ibn Nami's success with the Dhawahir was more limited. Through the agency of Rashid ibn Hamad he obtained statements from four minor shaikhs and a Dhahiri tribesman.[5] Two of the shaikhs, Sa'id and Muhammad ibn Sultan al-Darmaki, were the sons of the former headman of Qattarah village. On Turki ibn Utaishan's arrival in 1952 the two youths (one was 16 years of age, the other about 18) began frequenting his headquarters, and they were sent on a trip to Saudi Arabia. On their return they hoisted a Saudi flag on their house at Qattarah and began calling themselves Saudi subjects. Shaikh Zaid ibn Sultan, the Al Bu Falah governor in the oasis, ordered them to quit Qattarah and never to return. They went to Hamasa where Rashid ibn Hamad put them on the Saudi payroll. The other two shaikhs, Shabib and Sa'id ibn Muhammad al-Hilal of

---

[1] [Saudi Documents] In-letter no. 4703, dated 15 Sha'ban 1374.

[2] See Vol. II, Annexes 99 and 102. Photographs of Sa'id ibn Mubarak, Ali Aba al-Rus, and Muhammad ibn Abdullah al-Najadi of al-Ain village, taken at Dammam, are also in the *Memorial*.

[3] [Saudi Documents] Out-signal no. 560, Ibn Nami to Ibn Jiluwi, 16 Sha'ban 1374/9 April 1955.

[4] For further details of these statements and of the manner in which they were procured, see below, pp. 225-7.

[5] See *Saudi Memorial*, II, Annexes 128-30.

The Interim Régime in the Disputed Areas, 1954–1955

Jimi village, were the grandsons of Ahmad ibn Hilal, who for the forty years preceding his death in 1936 had been the Abu Dhabi *wali* in the oasis. They had begun accepting presents from Turki in 1953, but they did not receive regular allowances from the Saudis until the end of 1954. In March 1955 they moved from Jimi to Hamasa after Rashid ibn Hamad had threatened to cut off their allowances if they did not do so.[1]

The principal shaikhs of the Dhawahir, Sultan ibn Surur and Mani' ibn Muhammad of Mu'tiridh, rebuffed both Ibn Nami's and Rashid ibn Hamad's approaches. The authors of the *Saudi Memorial* were later to imply that the shaikhs had been prevented from giving statements of loyalty to Saudi Arabia by Zaid ibn Sultan and the British authorities in Trucial Oman. 'In 1955 the chiefs of Al Sarur, along with other notables of the Dhawahir, were forced by Zayid, a brother of the Ruler of Abu Dhabi, to go to Sharjah, where attempts were made to secure from them declarations of allegiance to Abu Dhabi.'[2] The truth of the matter is rather different. Sultan ibn Surur and Mani' ibn Muhammad testified before the arbitration tribunal in September 1955 that they had received gifts of Rs 950 each the previous January from one of Turki ibn Utaishan's former adherents. In March they had gone to Sharjah to give the Political Agent there information about the Buraimi area. He had given them presents of Rs 1,000 and Rs 600 respectively, as payment for their services. Counsel for Saudi Arabia made no suggestion before the tribunal that the money had been given for any improper purpose, such as the securing of declarations of allegiance. He could hardly have done so, seeing that the two shaikhs had given declarations of this nature to the Ruler of Abu Dhabi a year previously, on 17–18 March 1954.[3]

Sultan ibn Surur and Mani' ibn Muhammad further told the arbitration tribunal that, on their return to Buraimi, Rashid ibn Hamad had approached them with an offer of truly lavish proportions to come over to the Saudi side—a *lakh* of rupees (Rs 100,000) each *per mensem* and generous compensation for any property of theirs that might be confiscated as a consequence of their defection. The shaikhs reported the offer to Shaikh Zaid, much to the con-

[1] Cf. *Saudi Memorial*, I, Chapter III, para. 80: 'Because of their loyalty to Saudi Arabia, Shabib and Sa'id have been compelled to seek refuge in Hamasa. . . .' For the allowances given to the brothers Al Hilal and Al Darmaki, see below, p. 228.   [2] *Saudi Memorial*, I, Chapter III, para. 81.
[3] They are reprinted in *U.K. Memorial*, II, Annex L, no. 1.

The Interim Régime in the Disputed Areas, 1954–1955

sternation of Ibn Nami. 'I report to Your Excellency', he signalled Ibn Jiluwi at the beginning of April, 'that Rashid ibn Hamad has written to us that the amount sent to the Shaikhs of the Dhawahir has been brought to the knowledge of Zaid who has asked for information from them which they have given.'[1] In an attempt to cover up the blunder Rashid ibn Hamad concocted a story, which he incorporated in a letter to Ibn Nami, to the effect that the shaikhs were called to Dubai by the Political Agent, where pressure was put upon them to acknowledge Shaikh Shakhbut as their ruler: they refused to do so, whereupon the Political Agent gave them money and sent them away. It hardly needs remarking that the tale credits the Political Agent with a poor business sense. Rashid ibn Hamad's letter is reproduced in the *Saudi Memorial* and provides the basis for the authors' story.[2]

There seems to have been some apprehension on the part of the Saudi Government at this time that their clandestine activities might be discovered, for at the close of April Shaikh Yusuf Yasin warned Ibn Jiluwi to take even greater care in his communications with the Saudi police commander at Buraimi.

'You remember, Your Excellency, that I have already informed you during my stay with you at Dammam of His Majesty's desires as follows:

'1. Changing the code which is held by Bin Nami once every month. The new code should be forwarded by air mail.

'2. Bin Nami should not disclose the names of informers in ordinary or cypher signals. He should say instead: "We learn from our informer. . . ." He can give you the name of the informer by air mail, if necessary.

'3. All local news and arrangements at that district should be reported by mail and not by signals.

'I hope that you have already forwarded the necessary instructions to comply with His Majesty's order by last [Saturday's] plane because I noticed that the names of the informers are still mentioned in the signals sent by Bin Nami.'[3]

[1] [Saudi Documents] Out-signal no. 553, dated Sha'ban 1374/March–April 1955.   [2] See Vol. II, Annex 127, dated 16 May 1955.
[3] [Saudi Documents] In-signal no. 5498, Ibn Jiluwi to Ibn Nami, 23 Ramadhan 1374/15 May 1955, enclosing Yusuf Yasin to Ibn Jiluwi, 8 Ramadhan 1374/30 April 1955 (No. 28/5/5/1574).

The Interim Régime in the Disputed Areas, 1954-1955

Acting, perhaps, on the maxim that the best form of defence lies in attack, the Saudi Government, on 2 April, handed the British *chargé d'affaires* at Jeddah a long list of complaints of alleged British infractions of the conditions of arbitration. Most of them referred to the customs post between Kahil and Mahadhah, which had been established by the Sultan of Muscat to prevent the smuggling of arms into the Buraimi region, particularly from Dubai. According to the Saudi Government, the Sultan's officials were interfering with the normal transit of goods and people into the Buraimi Zone. Seeing that many of the persons using the route through Mahadhah were avowed Saudi supporters from Hamasa, it is hardly surprising that an interest was taken in their movements. There had, in fact, been only one incident involving the interruption of goods or people in transit, and that had been caused by a misunderstanding. The Saudi Government's other complaints related to the entry of a British supply vehicle into the Zone without prior notification having been given to the Saudi police commander, to the activities of Shaikh Zaid, and to the import of arms into the Zone by British authorities. Only one of these complaints, that concerning the supply vehicle, had any substance to it, and an apology had already been made for the incident. Shaikh Zaid was perfectly at liberty, under the terms of the arbitration agreement, to continue to administer the Abu Dhabi villages in the Buraimi Oasis. The accusation of arms smuggling was not only without foundation but it was the height of impudence, coming at a time when the Saudis were using the supply aircraft for a large arms build-up in the Buraimi Zone.

On 17 May Abdul Aziz ibn Jiluwi sent the following message to Abdullah ibn Nami at Buraimi:

'You are receiving 20 bags of rice, 1 case cardomom, 1 case tea, inside all of which are concealed 10,000 rounds of ammunition which you are to put into store as usual. You are to inform Muhammad Salih that he is to issue them personally and should tell nobody about them except those he trusts. You are to tell Sa'id bin Rashid al-Baluchi to receive from Muhammad Salih 5,000 rounds which he is to send to his people and have them distributed equally among them. You are also to pay him Rs 20,000, which he is to distribute among his people in the same manner as the rounds. By this money they are to buy more arms. . . . Also Bani Qitab of the Aflaj are to be given, similarly to the Baluchis, 5,000 rounds of ammunition and Rs 20,000 both of which are to be handed over to Dhiban and Ali

The Interim Régime in the Disputed Areas, 1954–1955

ibn Rubayyi' who are to distribute them equally among their people who are to buy arms by the money. . . . We are sending you by the hand of Hamad bin Uwais a sum of Rs 100,000, out of which Rs 40,000 are to be disposed of as we have instructed you above, and the balance Rs 60,000 is to be held by you. . . . Please be careful to note our instructions, and do your best to keep it secret.'[1]

A week later more money and ammunition were flown in by the supply aircraft. 'Forwarded to you with Sa'ad al-Omani', wrote Abdul Aziz to Ibn Nami on 24 May, 'is the sum of Rs 84,850, being the allocation of the people for the month of Shawwal. Twenty sacks of rice concealing 10,000 rounds of ammunition will also reach you with him.'[2]

The purpose of the arms build-up was explained in a letter of the same date from Abdul Aziz ibn Jiluwi to Saqr ibn Sultan. Saqr had written to King Sa'ud, expressing fears that the Saudi position in the Buraimi region was deteriorating, and suggesting that a demonstration of some kind was needed to restore it. The King's reply, according to Ibn Jiluwi, was:

'. . . As long as the matter has reached to this extent we are ready as far as money and arms are concerned. . . . He [Saqr] should immediately go outside Buraimi with the tribes who are loyal to us. . . . He should meet Shaikh Rashid bin Hamad and agree to keep this matter secret, and organize it properly and very accurately together with Bin Nami . . . and make it a red fire.'[3]

Four days later another message arrived from Ibn Jiluwi: 'A signal received from His Majesty reads as follows: "Inform Bin Nami that the matter is now of extreme importance. Accuracy and diligence are essential because, in view of our political situation, we can't make a military demonstration." '[4]

Saqr and the other shaikhs, however, did not seem in any hurry to set the Oman ablaze, so more money and arms were poured in during June. The Amir Ibn Jiluwi, who had by now returned to his duties, wrote to Ibn Nami on 12 June: 'Forwarded to you with Salim bin Jahaman is the sum of Rs 87,050. . . . Ten sacks of rice, one sack of coffee, . . . [etc.] will also reach you with the above-mentioned. Note: the ten sacks of rice conceal 5,000 rounds.'[5] On

---
[1] [Saudi Documents] In-letter no. 5557, dated 25 Ramadhan 1374.
[2] [Saudi Documents] In-letter no. 5738, dated 2 Shawwal 1374.
[3] [Saudi Documents] In-letter no. 5739, dated 2 Shawwal 1374.
[4] [Saudi Documents] In-signal no. 5859, dated 6 Shawwal 1374.
[5] [Saudi Documents] In-letter no. 6196, dated 21 Shawwal 1374.

The Interim Régime in the Disputed Areas, 1954–1955

25 June Ibn Jiluwi informed Ibn Nami that the aircraft the following day would bring in further ammunition and money. 'We have sent to you by the hand of Salim bin Jahaman 20 bags of rice inside which 10,000 rounds are concealed. . . . You will also receive from the above-mentioned a sum of Rs 38,000 in replacement of the amount we have ordered you to pay to Yusuf Ibrahim.'[1] Yusuf Ibrahim was the principal agent for the transmission of arms and money to the Imam Ghalib ibn Ali. On 12 June Ibn Jiluwi had sent to Ibn Nami a letter addressed to the Imam, which was to be delivered by Yusuf Ibrahim. He was also to tell the Imam that a large consignment of arms was on its way to him. '. . . Yusuf Ibrahim . . . should also be instructed to inform the Imam that we have delivered to his messenger Mubarak bin Umair 1,000 rifles, 100,000 rounds of ammunition, 20,000 rupees and 400 baskets of dates.'[2]

On the aircraft of 15 July Rs 150,000 and 10,000 rounds of ammunition, concealed in twenty sacks of rice, were flown into Buraimi.[3] A few days later Ibn Jiluwi informed Ibn Nami: 'The sum of Rs 87,250, being the allocations for the month of al-Hijjah will reach you with Salim bin Jahaman. Nine sacks of rice containing 4,500 rounds will also reach you with the above-mentioned.'[4] On 24 July Ibn Jiluwi signalled Ibn Nami: 'Pay Rs 70,000 to the Imam Ghalib and Rs 30,000 to Sulaiman bin Himyar. If the latter is found away with the Ruler of Muscat then the whole sum should be paid to Imam Ghalib.'[5] Despite all these efforts, the 'red fire' in the Oman failed to catch. The tribes, while interested in what was going on at Buraimi, and being only too happy to accept gifts of arms and money from any source, showed no particular willingness to act as Saudi mercenaries.

Although the British were well aware of the bribery and arms build-up going on in the Buraimi Zone, they had no substantial proof of them to lay before the arbitration tribunal. On the other hand, several overt breaches of the conditions of arbitration had been committed by the Saudis, and these were made the subject of a protest delivered to the Saudi Ambassador in London on 27 May. The

---

[1] [Saudi Documents] In-letter no. 6558, dated 5 Dhu'l-Qa'dah 1374.
[2] [Saudi Documents] In-letter no. 6198, dated 21 Shawwal 1374.
[3] See [Saudi Documents] In-letters nos. 7087 and 7088, Ibn Jiluwi to Ibn Nami, 24 Dhu'l-Qa'dah 1374/14 July 1955.
[4] [Saudi Documents] In-letter no. 7242, dated 29 Dhu'l-Qa'dah 1374/19 July 1955.
[5] [Saudi Documents] In-signal no. 7330, dated 4 Dhu'l-Hijjah 1374.

The Interim Régime in the Disputed Areas, 1954–1955

Note dealt first with the complaints laid by the Saudi Government on 2 April, and then went on to protest against the fact that the Saudi police detachment at Buraimi numbered twenty-one men, including former members of Turki ibn Utaishan's party, against the use of the supply aircraft to fly persons in and out of the Buraimi Zone, in particular, the Saudi officials Muhammad ibn Mansur and Abdul Latif on 9 April, and against the activities of Ibn Nami's so-called 'clerk', Abdullah al-Quraishi.

For three years before his appointment to Buraimi al-Quraishi had been a political officer on the staff of Ibn Jiluwi at Dammam. He was the person actually in charge of the police detachment at Buraimi, and under his direction it was taking on more and more the character of an embryo Saudi administration in the oasis.[1] In February 1955 he had married a girl from Hamasa, and together with another member of the police detachment, who had been a member of Turki's party and who had also married a girl from Hamasa, he went to live in the village, contrary to the conditions laid down in the exchange of notes governing the stationing of the police detachment in the oasis.

At the end of March 1955 al-Quraishi had grown so bold as to attempt to suborn Shaikh Zaid ibn Sultan. Zaid told the arbitration tribunal at Geneva in September 1955 that al-Quraishi had met him on 30 March and told him that the arbitration was certain to go against Abu Dhabi, and that he, Zaid, would be well advised before that time to come to terms with Ibn Jiluwi. If he did so, he would be assured of his position in Buraimi and would receive not only funds from Ibn Jiluwi but also 50 per cent of any profits that might result from the discovery of oil in the area. When al-Quraishi was brought before the tribunal to testify on these matters he admitted that he had been living at Hamasa, contrary to the conditions of arbitration, and that the meeting with Zaid—and subsequent meetings to which reference will be made shortly—had taken place. He insisted, however, that the initiative in arranging the meetings had been taken by Zaid.

---

[1] That al-Quraishi was much more than a clerk is clear from this signal from Ibn Jiluwi to Ibn Nami shortly after the establishment of the police detachment in the oasis:

'This signal is for Abdullah al-Quraishi. Begins: regarding signals you receive from Muhammad bin Turki, they are by our order and it is in order for you to show them to Abdullah bin Nami. All you receive you have to show to him. . . . The reason for not signalling the "brother" Abdullah is [firstly] that we do not like to increase his responsibility, and, secondly, we like him to be away from such matters.' ([Saudi Documents] In-signal no. 454, n.d. (August 1954?).)

The Interim Régime in the Disputed Areas, 1954–1955

The Saudi Government never answered the British charges of 27 May 1955. They did not even reply formally to them. Al-Quraishi told the arbitration tribunal in September that his superiors had never inquired of him whether the charges made against him had any foundation. Obviously, such inquiries would have been superfluous: there was no need for the Saudi Government to investigate a system of bribery which they had themselves initiated and were still conducting. Al-Quraishi took his orders from Ibn Jiluwi, and it was clearly at the latter's direction that he had taken up residence at Hamasa so as to be in a more effective position to conduct his subversive activities.[1]

The manufacture of material for use in the *Saudi Memorial* reached its peak in June. 'Herewith are 4 copies [of a statement]', wrote Ibn Jiluwi to Ibn Nami on the 12th of the month. 'You are to make the Shaikhs sign them in replacement of the previous documents which have been lost.'[2] Ibn Nami replied the next day: 'In accordance with your instruction ... we have taken the statements from the Shaikhs found at the oasis. They are Shaikh Saqr bin Sultan, Ubaid bin Juma', Sa'id al-Baluchi, the sons of Al Darmaki, the sons of Bin Hilal, Hamdan bin Khalfan, ... and Ibn Rakkadh.'[3] The statements, all of them dated 13 June 1955, later appeared in the *Saudi Memorial*.[4] Their authors did not go unrewarded. The list accompanying the sum of Rs 87,050, sent on 12 June, referred to above, contained these entries:

'Rs 6,070 for Shaikh Salim bin Rakkadh, his brother Muhammad, and the Awamir;

'Rs 12,150 for Shaikh Rashid ibn Hamad and his entourage;

'Rs 7,000 for Shaikh Saqr ibn Sultan;

'Rs 1,640 for Shaikh Sa'id bin Rashid al-Baluchi;

'Rs 6,320 for Shaikh Ahmad al-Salf and his people.'[5]

Again, in instructions sent by Turki ibn Utaishan to Rashid ibn Hamad on 13 August 1955 for the disbursement of Rs 53,250 the following items occur:

[1] The somewhat unconvincing excuse was later offered by the Saudi Government that al-Quraishi and the other member of the police detachment who had married a girl from Hamasa had gone to live in the village because they wanted to be with their mothers-in-law.
[2] [Saudi Documents] In-letter no. 6203, dated 21 Shawwal 1374.
[3] [Saudi Documents] Out-signal no. 723, dated 22 Shawwal 1374.
[4] See below, p. 227.
[5] [Saudi Documents] In-letter no. 6196, Ibn Jiluwi to Ibn Nami, 21 Shawwal 1374.

The Interim Régime in the Disputed Areas, 1954–1955

'Rs 12,150 for Rashid bin Hamad and his supporters;
'Rs 6,470 for Ubaid bin Juma' and the Bani Ka'ab;
'Rs 7,660 for the people of Hamasa;
'Rs 6,500 for Salim bin Rakkadh, his brother Muhammad, and the Awamir;
'Rs 1,640 for Sa'id bin Rashid al-Baluchi;
'Rs 1,000 for Ahmad al-Salf.'[1]

In the latter half of June Abdullah ibn Nami made a strenuous effort to obtain all the statements that he could, whether relevant to the arbitration or not. Large numbers of tribesmen from the surrounding districts were then camped in and around the oasis, as was the custom during the height of the summer, and the Saudi police commander was able to persuade several of them to affix their thumbprints to standard declarations of allegiance to Saudi Arabia. Seven of these statements were afterwards printed in the *Saudi Memorial*.[2] Ibn Nami's work was much appreciated at Dammam. 'In reply to your signal no. 797,' Ibn Jiluwi informed him on 22 June, 'we submitted this to His Majesty and his answer is as follows: Regarding what you have received from Bin Nami about the arrival of the tribes in the oasis [and] the good effect that resulted out of that. . . . Inform Bin Nami to do what is required in a confidential way. Pay these people and treat them very well.'[3] Ibn Nami, however, had one or two disappointments. Ahmad al-Salf, chief of the Khawatir branch of the Na'im at Hafit, refused to make a statement, despite the fact that he had regularly taken Saudi money. Ibn Nami made a last-minute attempt in July to win him over. 'The allocation in the name of Al-Salf is Rs 6,320, according to the pay-sheet sent to us by you', he told Ibn Jiluwi on 23 July. '. . . We wish to increase the salary of Al-Salf and also allocate payments to his three sons. . . .'[4] The effort, however, was unavailing.

Much more distressing to Ibn Nami than the obduracy of Ahmad al-Salf was the defection in June of Muhammad ibn Salimin, of al-Sunainah, chief of the Baduin Al Bu Shamis. Only two months earlier, it may be recalled, Muhammad ibn Salimin had given a statement of loyalty on the occasion of Muhammad ibn Mansur's visit to Buraimi.[5] Early in June he re-affirmed his allegiance to the Sultan of

[1] [Saudi Documents] In-letter (unnumbered), dated 24 Dhu'l-Hijjah 1374.
[2] See Vol. II, Annexes 103, 105, 120, 121 and 123–5.
[3] [Saudi Documents] In-signal no. 6981, dated 2 Dhu'l-Qa'dah 1374.
[4] [Saudi Documents] Out-signal no. 873, dated 3 Dhu'l-Hijjah 1374.
[5] See above, p. 188, and *Saudi Memorial*, II, Annex 122.

The Interim Régime in the Disputed Areas, 1954–1955

Muscat, and his example had a noticeable impression upon the other shaikhs of the Buraimi region. 'One cannot tell when the people of Oman are telling lies or speaking the truth', complained Ibn Nami to Ibn Jiluwi on 11 June. 'One day they promise and the next day they turn disloyal.'[1] A fortnight later he was even more unhappy. '... The Shaikhs have made our position critical', he told Ibn Jiluwi. 'Some request financial help, some monthly salaries. We have done our utmost to please them, but they are seizing this opportunity which has resulted from Bin Salimin's behaviour.'[2] Ibn Jiluwi counselled patience and perseverance.

'We are aware of the fact that you are in a sensitive position and that you are confronted with certain difficulties, but you should try to overcome them by your fair judgement and discrimination and leniency towards the people. . . . If you have orders to pay someone convey his payment to him through the authority concerned as usual. Those for whom you do not have orders of payment give them good promises and always speak gently to them. . . . As you know the Government has spent a great deal in order to secure the support of the people and to oppose the threats of the enemy. Please adhere to aforesaid instructions and try to win over the people so that they may keep their loyalty to the Government of His Majesty.'[3]

This letter disposes of the argument put forward by Richard Young, counsel for Saudi Arabia, at the sitting of the arbitration tribunal in September 1955, in defence of the Saudi Government's disbursement of large sums of money in the Buraimi Zone, viz., that the tribes receiving the money were Saudi tribes, who were simply sharing, as they had customarily done in the past, in the bounty distributed by a benevolent government. Another matter raised at that sitting was the increasing use being made of the Saudi supply aircraft from June onwards to fly out people from the Buraimi Zone to Saudi Arabia. Twenty-eight persons were flown out on 26 June, 32 on 15 July, and 60, in two aircraft, on 3 September. Young's explanation of this breach of the conditions of arbitration was that

---

[1] [Saudi Documents] Out-signal no. 689, dated 20 Shawwal 1374.
[2] [Saudi Documents] Out-signal no. 776, dated 9 Dhu'l-Qa'dah 1374/29 June 1955. Five shaikhs of the Na'im (one Al Bu Shamis and four Baduin Al Bu Khuraiban) had accompanied Muhammad ibn Salimin to Muscat, where they testified to having received money from the Saudis. (See *U.K. Memorial*, II, Annex K, no. 2, and below, pp. 224–5.)
[3] [Saudi Documents] In-letter no. 7243, Ibn Jiluwi to Ibn Nami, 29 Dhu'l-Qa'dah 1374/19 July 1955.

The Interim Régime in the Disputed Areas, 1954–1955

all these people had been flown out for medical treatment or to go on the pilgrimage. Presumably it was mere coincidence that some of these people while in Saudi Arabia made or witnessed statements which were later used in the *Saudi Memorial*? A Mansuri shaikh and an Amiri tribesman, as has been seen,[1] made statements at Dammam, after being flown from Buraimi on 19 March. They were flown back to the oasis on 9 April. Seven statements obtained at Hamasa on 13 June and later reprinted in the *Saudi Memorial* were witnessed by four tribesmen, who, according to the *Memorial*, authenticated their signatures before the government registrar at Dammam that same day.[2] It is hardly likely that they could have performed this feat without the aid of the supply aircraft. Similarly, a further seven statements in the *Memorial*, obtained through the instrumentality of Rashid ibn Hamad between 14 and 25 June, were witnessed by four more tribesmen who, the *Memorial* states, authenticated their signatures at Dammam on 28 June.[3]

In any case, even if the tribesmen had been flown out to go on the pilgrimage or to receive medical treatment, the fact remains that these were not the purposes for which the Saudi Government had been granted permission to fly aircraft into the Buraimi Zone. The whole matter is put in its true perspective by the following signal from Ibn Nami to Ibn Jiluwi on 29 June:

'In view of these critical circumstances we cannot obtain the sympathy of all the Shaikhs, except by money, as is the custom. . . . The Darmakis are requesting to travel to perform the pilgrimage, together with ten followers. The time is short. I failed to convince them to wait until I obtain your agreement. Also Sa'id al-Baluchi is requesting to perform the pilgrimage, and so on. This is the habit of the people of Oman who envy each other everything. In fact I am doing my best but none is satisfied without money.'[4]

The nervousness felt by the Saudi Government over the outcome of the arbitration expressed itself also in manœuvres to discredit the British. The general uprising of the tribes planned the previous May, having come to nothing, something else was needed to influence outside opinion in favour of Saudi Arabia. On 8 July a fire broke out at Hamasa which destroyed dozens of houses and left many people in a distressed condition. Hardly were the ashes cold before

---

[1] Above, p. 188.   [2] See Vol. II, Annexes 101, 107, 131–4 and 136.
[3] See Vol. II, Annexes 103, 105, 120, 121 and 123–5.
[4] [Saudi Documents] Out-signal no. 783, dated 9 Dhu'l-Qa'dah 1374.

The Interim Régime in the Disputed Areas, 1954–1955

rumours were being circulated by the Saudi press that the fire had been started by the British. The British Government's action following the fire hardly squares with this accusation. Aid was immediately offered to the fire's victims in the form of food, medical supplies, blankets and clothing. The Saudis, when informed of the offer, said that an agreement would have to be worked out before it could be put into effect, and that they would need time to consider the matter. On 19 July the British *chargé d'affaires* at Jeddah told the Saudi Government that the people of Hamasa could not be made the pawns in a political game and that a motor convoy with relief supplies would be dispatched to Hamasa without delay. When the convoy reached the village it was turned back by Rashid ibn Hamad with the remark that he could not permit the supplies to be unloaded without the permission of the Saudi police commander. The following message from Ibn Jiluwi to Ibn Nami on 21 July leaves little doubt that the Saudis were exploiting the situation at Hamasa for their own ends:

'A signal received from His Majesty reads as follows:

"The answer of the Ministry of Foreign Affairs was that the distribution of these supplies prior to the approval of the Saudi Government would be considered as an indirect abrogation of the Agreement, *vide* Article 4 of the two exchanged letters which states that both parties undertake to stop any actions which might affect impartial and sound arbitration. It is also considered as a breach of Article 2 which says that the police force at Buraimi should not interfere in any way with the internal, administrative and political affairs of any of the tribes. Inform Bin Nami of all this and tell him that the Saudi Government does not approve the entry of these provisions and their distribution because Buraimi land and people are ours *and we have already compensated them for their fire losses.*" '[1]

Counsel for Saudi Arabia told the arbitration tribunal in September that the supplies had been refused by Rashid ibn Hamad because they were unnecessary.

On 25 August 1955 the British Government, having received no reply from the Saudi Government to their Note of 27 May, referred the complaints contained in it, together with several new ones, to the arbitration tribunal for consideration at its forthcoming sitting at

[1] [Saudi Documents] In-signal no. 7268, dated 1 Dhu'l-Hijjah 1374 Italics, added.

The Interim Régime in the Disputed Areas, 1954–1955

Geneva. A copy of the complaints, which referred to the various breaches of the conditions of arbitration committed by Saudi Arabia since August 1954, was sent to the Saudi Government the same day. They hastily put together and laid before the tribunal on 5 September a list of counter-complaints, which until then, it would seem, they had not considered worth making. The submission of the British charges apparently invested them with urgency and importance. It was, as Sir Hartley Shawcross, counsel for the United Kingdom, remarked to the tribunal later, like defending oneself by abusing the police. No attempt was made in the Saudi dossier to answer the British charges, and the dossier itself was incomplete. While purporting to be a full record of the exchanges between the two governments on the matters referred to in the Saudi counter-charges, it in fact left out all the answers made by the British Government over the preceding months. Every charge laid by Saudi Arabia before the tribunal had been made before to the British Government and had been answered. Where infractions of the conditions of arbitration had been found to have occurred, an apology had been tendered.

When the tribunal opened its hearings on 11 September Shaikh Zaid ibn Sultan gave evidence of last-minute attempts by Abdullah al-Quraishi to induce him to desert his brother and declare for Saudi Arabia. On 26 July al-Quraishi had approached him through an emissary, Ali ibn Barak, and offered him a new car that was coming in on the Saudi supply aircraft and the sum of Rs 40,000. The offers were refused by Zaid. On 4 August al-Quraishi himself approached Zaid and endeavoured to win him over with an argument similar to the one he had used the previous March. If Zaid were prepared to throw in his lot with Saudi Arabia, the Saudi Government would reward him with as much as Rs 400,000,000 from the proceeds of any oil found in the disputed areas. Zaid remained unimpressed by the argument. On 26 August, on the eve of his departure for Geneva to give evidence before the tribunal, Zaid was again approached by an agent of al-Quraishi, who said that the Saudi official wanted to present him with three pistols. The offer, with its ambiguous implication, was ignored by Zaid.

At the sitting of 11 September, and at subsequent sittings, the tribunal also heard evidence of Saudi bribery and gun-running, of the plot to overthrow the Ruler of Abu Dhabi, of the circumstances surrounding the fire at Hamasa, of the abuse of the Saudi supply aircraft, and of other violations of the conditions of arbitration. The witnesses who gave evidence were Shaikhs Zaid and Hazza' ibn Sultan, Sultan ibn Surur and Mani' ibn Muhammad of the Dhawahir, and Captain P. H. Clayton, the former commander of the Trucial Oman Levies detachment at Buraimi. On their side, on 13 September, the Saudi Government brought forward Abdullah al-Quraishi to refute the charges brought against him. He denied that he had ever tried to bribe Zaid and said that Zaid, not he, had made the approaches.

The credibility of al-Quraishi's testimony may be tested by an examination of the circumstances in which he appeared to testify before the tribunal. At 5 p.m. on 12 September, the Agent for Saudi Arabia, Abdur Rahman Azzam, told the tribunal that he could not say what witnesses he would be calling, or if al-Quraishi would be among them. Two hours later al-Quraishi arrived in Geneva. Asked by Sir Hartley Shawcross the next day to say when he had first learned that he was to appear before the tribunal, he replied that he had been told on 9 September, one day after he had returned to Saudi Arabia from Buraimi. Asked by Shawcross why he had left Buraimi, al-Quraishi said that he had applied for leave on 5 September to attend to some family affairs. His replies hardly square with the following signal sent by Ibn Jiluwi to Ibn Nami on 7 September:

'Inform your clerk Abdullah al-Quraishi that he should leave by the plane which will arrive at your end tomorrow to meet Yusuf Yasin in Switzerland. He is wanted there to give information about what others might pretend together with some other details concerning this case. This matter should be kept secret. . . .'[1]

Again, when Shawcross asked him when he had first learned that he was being accused of attempting to bribe Shaikh Zaid, al-Quraishi answered that he had never known that he had been so accused until the question was put to him by Shawcross on that day, 13 September. Later, in evidence, he said that he had first learned of the charge on his arrival at Geneva the previous evening, when Shaikh Yusuf Yasin had asked him in astonishment whether he had done the things he was being accused of. Yusuf Yasin's astonishment cannot be taken seriously. Apart from the fact that he was in charge of what al-Quraishi was doing at Buraimi, it would be remarkable if, as Deputy Saudi Foreign Minister, he was not aware that his subordinate's doings had been made the subject of formal complaints by the British Government over the preceding months.

[1] [Saudi Documents] In-signal no. 384, dated 19 Muharram 1375.

The Interim Régime in the Disputed Areas, 1954–1955

Al-Quraishi also admitted that he had discussed his evidence with Yusuf Yasin before giving it. His reply to Shawcross's questions about the campaign of bribery being carried on at Buraimi was that no money had been given to anyone. If this were true, how were the large sums of money sent to Ibn Nami to be accounted for? The Saudi police commander's correspondence with Ibn Jiluwi shows that in seven months alone out of the fourteen that the Saudi police post was maintained in the oasis the following sums of money were sent from Hasa to Buraimi:

Muharram 1374/August–September 1954	Rs 121,260
Rabi' II, 1374/November–December 1954	Rs 227,450
Jumada I, 1374/December 1954–January 1955	Rs 156,960
Ramadhan 1374/April–May 1955	Rs 271,900
Dhu'l-Qa'dah 1374/June–July 1955	Rs 337,250
Safar 1375/September–October 1955	Rs 103,435
Rabi' I, 1375/October–November 1955	Rs 104,035

This makes a total for seven months of Rs 1,322,290. It makes one wonder what the total for the full fourteen months must have been, let alone for the three years since Turki ibn Utaishan's arrival. In addition, between November 1954 and July 1955 at least 1,361 rifles and 183,500 rounds of ammunition were sent from Saudi Arabia to the Buraimi Zone and the Oman. Counsel for Saudi Arabia, as mentioned earlier, explained to the tribunal that the sums of money were normal payments, customarily made to the shaikhs of the Buraimi region. The Saudi Government later called them 'charity' payments. The arms shipments could hardly be labelled 'charity' payments, and Young did not attempt to call them such. Instead, he told the tribunal that no evidence had been submitted that Saudi Arabia had smuggled arms into the disputed areas. Here, as in the case of the monetary payments, Young had obviously not been fully informed by the Saudi Government. A more likely explanation of the purpose of the money and the arms shipments was suggested by Shawcross, viz., to ensure that if the tribunal should visit the disputed areas 'it might hear the multitudes who have sold their tongues acclaiming their Saudi Arabian paymasters'.

As the tribunal's hearings proceeded, it became more and more evident that Shaikh Yusuf Yasin, far from confining himself strictly to his functions as a member of the tribunal, was more concerned with presenting his government's case. He astounded the other

The Interim Régime in the Disputed Areas, 1954–1955

members by sending a Note to the Saudi Agent, Abdur Rahman Azzam, in open tribunal. Al-Quraishi admitted that it was to Yusuf Yasin that he had gone immediately on his arrival at Geneva, and there is little doubt, from what al-Quraishi said later in cross-examination, that Yusuf Yasin had thought it proper to rehearse his evidence with him. At the hearing of 15 September Yusuf Yasin candidly informed the tribunal that he was the minister in the Saudi Government in charge of affairs at Buraimi, and as such he accepted full responsibility for al-Quraishi's conduct.

The following day the British member of the tribunal, Sir Reader Bullard, resigned. He explained in a statement:

'I have been shown by the President a copy of the letter which the United Kingdom delegation sent to him today, and I have in the meantime given very serious consideration to my own personal position as a member of this tribunal. I have always felt uneasy about the position of Sheikh Yusuf Yasin in connexion with these proceedings, but I had not realized until yesterday, when Sheikh Yusuf Yasin openly asserted the fact, that he himself was the Saudi Arabian official in charge of affairs at Buraimi, and that he accepted full responsibility for the conduct of Qureishi. Moreover, in the last few days it has become abundantly clear that Sheikh Yusuf Yasin is, in fact, in effective control of the conduct of the proceedings on behalf of the Saudi Arabian Government, and is representing that Government on this tribunal rather than acting as an impartial arbitrator. . . .

'I have always regarded my own position as one of complete independence of the British Government, and this I know is the position which the British Government desires me to occupy. Indeed, I regard it as essential to any system of arbitration that each member of the arbitration tribunal should feel completely at liberty to give any decision he thinks right, including one against his own Government. I am afraid the position of the tribunal has been hopelessly compromised by the conduct of Sheikh Yusuf Yasin and by other distasteful matters which have come to notice. I do not think that the tribunal is any longer in a position to reach a unanimous or judicial conclusion on the matters before it, and I feel the only step I can take which is consistent with my own independence and honour is to tender my resignation.'[1]

Very shortly afterwards the president, Dr. de Visscher, also

[1] *The Times*, 17 September 1955.

The Interim Régime in the Disputed Areas, 1954–1955

resigned, and his resignation was followed by that of the Cuban member, Dr. Dihigo. On 4 October the Foreign Office issued a statement on the proceedings at Geneva. After listing the various breaches of the arbitration agreement committed by Saudi Arabia, the statement went on: '. . . Finally, confirmation was secured of her Majesty's Government's suspicion that attempts had been made by the Saudis to tamper with the impartiality of the tribunal behind the president's back.'[1] The Saudis were later to allege that Bullard had been ordered to resign by the British Government. The allegation is without foundation: Bullard resigned because he felt unable to continue to work in the conditions described in his statement of resignation, where what he refers to as 'other distasteful matters' may safely be equated with what the Foreign Office afterwards called 'attempts . . . by the Saudis to tamper with the impartiality of the tribunal'.

The breakdown of the arbitration proceedings did not affect the Saudi Government's conduct at Buraimi in the least. The aircraft that took out al-Quraishi brought in as his replacement a certain Aqil, who had been a member of Turki ibn Utaishan's party. He brought more money to continue the work of corruption. 'The Rs 100,000 which were delivered to you by Aqil', Ibn Jiluwi told Ibn Nami, 'should be sent to Imam Ghalib immediately and in the usual way you have been following before. Make sure that the Imam treats this as most secret.'[2] Ibn Nami was now styling himself 'Amir of Buraimi'.[3] Rs 103,435 were sent to him by Ibn Jiluwi on 3 October and a further Rs 104,035 on 21 October.[4] The money had its effect. 'Last night, 15 Safar,' reported Ibn Nami on 4 October, 'removal of Shaikh Sa'id al-Darmaki, together with his family, from al-Qattarah to Hamasa was effected at 8 o'clock. . . . Zaid's dogs are much worried at this step.'[5]

It was a situation that the British Government did not feel inclined

---

[1] *The Times*, 5 October 1955.
[2] [Saudi Documents] In-signal no. 406, n.d.
[3] [Saudi Documents] Out-letter (unnumbered), Ibn Nami to Imam Ghalib ibn Ali, 5 Safar 1375/23 September 1955.
[4] [Saudi Documents] In-letters nos. 1010 and 1496, Ibn Jiluwi to Ibn Nami, 15 Safar and 4 Rabi' I, 1375.
[5] [Saudi Documents] Out-signal no. 101, Ibn Nami to Ibn Jiluwi, 16 Safar 1375.

The Interim Régime in the Disputed Areas, 1954–1955

to allow to continue. On 26 October the British *chargé d'affaires* at Jeddah informed the Saudi Government that, as the chances of a fair and impartial arbitration had been wrecked by Saudi Arabia, the rulers of Muscat and Abu Dhabi had been advised to resume their former control over the Buraimi Oasis, and, in the case of the Shaikh of Abu Dhabi, over the western areas also. The forces of the two rulers, supported by the Trucial Oman Levies, moved into the oasis that same morning and forced the surrender of Ibn Nami and his detachment. Saudi casualties in the action were two men slightly wounded. Ibn Nami and his men not long afterwards left for Saudi Arabia, accompanied by Saqr ibn Sultan, Rashid ibn Hamad, Ubaid ibn Juma', and a number of minor figures who had cast in their fortunes with the Saudis.

The British Prime Minister, Sir Anthony Eden, explained the reasons for his government's decision to the House of Commons later that day.

'The Ruler of Abu Dhabi and the Sultan of Muscat have scrupulously observed the conditions of arbitration which Her Majesty's Government, in good faith, recommended to them. They have had to stand by and watch their subjects being suborned, and the outcome of the arbitration itself being gravely prejudiced in advance. A fair and impartial arbitration is not possible in such circumstances.

'These facts, combined with the conduct of the Saudi Government in relation to the tribunal itself, have led Her Majesty's Government to conclude that the Saudi Arabian Government are no more willing now to reach an equitable solution by arbitration than they were previously by negotiation. Their actions and conduct amount to a repudiation of the Arbitration Agreement, and have made a continuation of the arbitration impossible.

'Her Majesty's Government have, therefore, felt obliged, in the exercise of their duty to protect the legitimate interests of the Ruler of Abu Dhabi and the Sultan of Muscat, to advise them that the attempt to reach a just compromise by means of arbitration has failed.'[1]

Henceforth, Eden continued, the frontier between Saudi Arabia and Abu Dhabi would be regarded as the Riyadh Line, as amended in 1937. No unauthorized crossings of that line by the Saudis, by land or air, would be permitted. He concluded:

[1] Hansard, *Parliamentary Debates*, 5th series, H. of C., Vol. 545 (1955–6), cols. 199–200.

The Interim Régime in the Disputed Areas, 1954–1955

'I hope that in time the Saudi Arabian Government will accept the solution we have had to declare. Her Majesty's Government are ready at all times to discuss with the Saudi Arabian Government any minor rectifications of the line which may seem convenient in the light of local circumstances.'

When he surrendered on 26 October, Ibn Nami had in his possession the sum of Rs 159,598 and 300 Saudi *riyals*. The money was returned to the Saudi Government on 22 November with the comment that it seemed an unusually large sum for the upkeep of fifteen men, and it must be presumed that it was intended for purposes incompatible with the late arbitration. The Saudi Government accepted the money but rejected the accusation. '. . . It is not part of the traditions of the Saudi Arabian Government', they declared, 'to make colonies of nations, whether by force or by buying their loyalties with bribes.'

CHAPTER VII

The Saudi Memorial *of 1955*

From the welter of accusations and recriminations that followed the breakdown of the arbitration proceedings a suggestion emerged that Sir Reader Bullard's resignation had been connected with a desire on the part of the British Government to forestall a decision by the tribunal on the frontier question as a whole. A statement issued by the Saudi delegation to the United Nations on 26 October 1955 said, with reference to the reassertion of Abu Dhabi and Muscat control over the Buraimi Oasis on that day,

'At the moment when the Government of the United Kingdom felt that the tribunal's decision was going to be unfavourable to her she ordered the British representative to resign in order to hinder the work of this international body and forestall any peaceful settlement of the dispute.

'Saudi Arabia firmly believes that the sabotaging of the efforts of the international arbitration tribunal was a deliberate step taken by the Government of the United Kingdom to force the Buraimi issue to an armed conflict and not to settle it by peaceful means.'[1]

It was not made clear in the statement what it was that the tribunal had supposedly been about to rule upon when Bullard resigned, whether, as seemed most likely, it was the charges of Saudi misconduct brought by the British Government, or whether it was the basic issue of sovereignty in the disputed areas. A few weeks later, however, King Sa'ud publicly implied that it was the latter question. In an interview at Bombay on 12 December, while he was on a visit to India, he said:

'Buraimi Oasis is an integral part of the Saudi kingdom. It had been so for over 250 years. In spite of that fact, we accepted arbitration with Great Britain by the amicable intervention of the United

[1] *The Times*, 27 October 1955.

The Saudi Memorial of 1955

States Government. After both sides had submitted their cases to the arbitration commission at Geneva the British Government found that theirs was a losing case and have withdrawn . . . without any notice. At the same time they occupied the area militarily, when according to the arbitration agreement we had only 15 Arab policemen there purely to maintain internal security.'[1]

The suggestion that the British Government had sabotaged the arbitration because they had an unconvincing case gained currency as time went by. The Winter 1956 issue of the *Middle East Journal* reported, in the column entitled 'Developments of the Quarter', the British Government's unilateral declaration of the frontier line with the comment:

'This action was justified, in the eyes of the British, by the belief that prolonged negotiation with Saudi Arabia would only lead to gradual encroachment on the territory of the shaykhdoms under their protection. To the Saudi Arabs, on the other hand, it was evidence of the weakness of Britain's substantive case.'

The most explicit allegations, however, regarding the reasons for Bullard's resignation and the British Government's motives in withdrawing from the arbitration were made in a pamphlet entitled *British Imperialism in Southern Arabia*, which was issued by the Arab Information Centre in New York in November 1958. It stated:

'The British member of the Tribunal knew that the charges [of bribery] had failed to impress the neutral members, and that the expressed readiness of the Saudis to comply with any ruling of the Tribunal had convinced them of Saudi sincerity and of Saudi eagerness to make the arbitration succeed. When the Tribunal met to announce its decision, the British member, Sir Reader Bullard, resigned over the protests of his colleagues and walked out.

'Does this action leave any doubt about its purpose when viewed in the light of the subsequent British-led occupation of the disputed territory and the unilateral declaration of the British 1935–37 boundary line?[2]

'. . . Quotations from the Saudi Memorial . . . proved from British sources the weakness of British claims and supported Saudi Arabia's contentions. When the British saw the record, to which their authorities had contributed so much, laid before the Arbitration Tribunal

---

[1] *The Times*, 13 December 1955.
[2] *British Imperialism in Southern Arabia*, p. 78.

The Saudi Memorial of 1955

in 1955, is it any wonder that they sought an excuse to scuttle the proceedings?'[1] What these various speculations and allegations overlooked was that it was impossible for the tribunal to have ruled on the issue of sovereignty at such an early stage in the arbitration proceedings. The procedure laid down in the agreement of 30 July 1954 provided for the presentation of counter-memorials by both parties within six months of submitting their original memorials. The latter were only submitted at the beginning of September 1955. The speculations also credit the *Saudi Memorial* with being a document of formidable consequence, more or less echoing what St. John Philby had been saying for some time, viz., that Saudi Arabia had 'a cast-iron case in the Buraimi dispute',[2] and that 'the admirable brief prepared by the American advisers of the Saudi Government would have had a very fair chance of acceptance on the basis of law and historical precedent'.[3] Did the *Saudi Memorial*, in fact, merit this judgement? The question seems well worth investigating.

The *Saudi Memorial* of 1955 consists of three volumes: the first contains the text, the second, annexes, appendices and maps, and the third, tax registers from the office of the Governor of Hasa province. As set out in the text, Saudi Arabia's claim to the areas in dispute rests upon a threefold basis:

 i. that the tribes inhabiting these areas bear allegiance to Saudi Arabia;

 ii. that Saudi Arabia possesses historical title to these areas, deriving from past occupation; and

 iii. that Saudi Arabia has regularly collected *zakat* from tribes in these areas, and that this constitutes evidence both of state activity and of the allegiance of the tribes.

The case with respect to the tribes is set out primarily in Chapter III, 'The People and the Tribes', and to a lesser extent in Chapter II, 'The Geographical Setting'. It is supported by several of the annexes in Volume II. The historical case is set out in Chapter IV, 'Historical Background relating to the Disputed Areas, 1765–1955'. The argu-

---

[1] *British Imperialism in Southern Arabia*, p. 76.
[2] *Forty Years in the Wilderness*, London, 1957, p. 239.
[3] The *Sunday Times*, 23 October 1955. For an account of the circumstances surrounding the preparation of the *Saudi Memorial* see Bushrod Howard, Jr., 'Buraimi: A Study in Diplomacy by Default', *The Reporter*, 23 January 1958.

The Saudi Memorial of 1955

ment on *zakat* is developed in Volume II, Appendix B, and at various places in the text, notably in Chapter VI, 'Legal Submissions of Saudi Arabia'. These four chapters, together with Chapter I, 'Introduction', Chapter V, 'The Diplomatic Background, 1911–1954', and Chapter VII, 'Other Considerations', make up the text of the *Memorial*. In the following examination of the *Memorial*, consideration will be given, first, to the arguments concerning the tribes, next, to those on *zakat*-collecting, and, finally, to those concerning the history of the region in dispute.

THE TRIBES

More than a quarter of Chapter III of the *Memorial* (26 out of 94 paragraphs) is taken up with descriptions of tribes which live wholly outside the disputed areas or visit them so infrequently, and in such small numbers, that they cannot be reckoned as *bona fide* inhabitants of these areas. These tribes, which number seven out of the thirteen listed in the *Memorial*, are:

Al Murrah, Rashid, Manahil, Bani Ka'ab, Baluchi, Ifar and Bani Qitab.

The first three are well-known Saudi, or virtually Saudi, tribes, whose *diyar* lie well to the west or south of the disputed region. The Rashid and the Manahil originate in the Hadhramaut, and some of their sections roam the Rub' al-Khali. The *dirah* of the Murrah has its heart in the Rub' al-Khali, as the authors of the *Memorial* themselves admit ('between Longitude 48° E and Longitude 54° E'[1]), and only its edges touch the western areas in dispute in the vicinity of the Qatar peninsula. The Bani Ka'ab, Baluchi and Ifar all dwell in the Sultanate of Muscat, beyond the disputed areas. The nomadic element of the Bani Qitab has its *dirah* principally in the Trucial Shaikhdom of Sharjah, while the settled element resides in the Dhahirah.

It can only be concluded that the authors' purpose in including the Murrah, Rashid and Manahil among the inhabitants of the disputed areas was to give the impression that these recognizably Saudi tribes were of importance in the western areas, whereas, in fact, they are not. The inclusion of the other four tribes would appear to have had another purpose, that of enlarging the area in dispute around

[1] See Vol. I, Chapter III, para. 15.

The Saudi Memorial of 1955

Buraimi so as to bring in tribes whose leaders had been won over to Saudi Arabia by 1955. If all seven tribes are removed from the list of those given in the *Memorial*, one is left with the six which can properly be described as dwelling wholly or largely in the disputed areas. They are:

Manasir, Bani Yas, Mazari', Awamir, Na'im and Dhawahir.

THE MANASIR. Saudi Arabia's case for claiming the sovereignty of the western areas in dispute hinges almost completely upon the contention that the Dhafrah and the other districts to the east of the Sabkhat Matti constitute the *dirah* of the Manasir, and that the Manasir are a Saudi tribe.[1] The authors of the *Memorial* state:

'The Manasir joined the ranks of the House of Sa'ud in the last years of the eighteenth century when Saudi forces first reached the Buraimi region. British records show that by 1865 the Manasir were paying *zakah*, chiefly in kind, estimated to be worth two thousand dollars a year, into the Saudi treasury (Chapter IV, paragraph 211, *infra*). Immediately after King 'Abd al-'Aziz recaptured Hasa in 1913, the Manasir were again rallying under the standard of the House of Sa'ud and regularly paying their taxes. The official tax records of the tribe, and the statements of the leaders of the tribe (Annexes 98, 99 and 100) confirm the allegiance to Saudi Arabia of its members. The statement of the Governor of the Eastern Province of Saudi Arabia (Annex 94) and of his chief tax collectors (Annexes 95, 96 and 97) attest to the regularity with which these taxes have been collected from the Manasir.'[2]

To claim that the Dhafrah and the other western areas are the *dirah* of the Manasir is to ignore the presence in them of the Bani Yas. There are no exclusive *diyar* in the Dhafrah; the area is shared by the Bani Yas and the Manasir, and in the coastal tract the Bani Yas outnumber the Manasir.[3] The statement that the Manasir joined

[1] See *Saudi Memorial*, I, Chapter III, paras. 23 and 25–27. '... They occupy the whole territory east of the *sabkhah* ...' (para. 26). 'Although the *dirah* of the Manasir extends beyond al-Dhafrah to the northeast and the northwest, al-Dhafrah is the tribe's homeland. Al-Dhafrah has much to offer the Manasir, and they enjoy a predominant position there' (para. 27).

[2] *Saudi Memorial*, I, Chapter III, para. 32.

[3] This is not to say that some sections of these tribes do not regard certain areas as being peculiarly theirs. The Al Bu Khail section of the Manasir dwelling at Liwa, for example, regards the district around Tharwaniyah as its *dirah*, while the Al Bu Sha'ar regards the Ramlat al-Hamra and the southern part of the Khatam as its *dirah*.

The Saudi Memorial of 1955

the Al Sa'ud in the late eighteenth century is unsubstantiated by the *Memorial*'s authors. Indeed, apart from two very doubtful historical references which will be alluded to again,[1] they offer no evidence at all of a connexion between the Al Sa'ud and the Manasir in the whole of the nineteenth century. The statement that the Manasir were paying *zakat* of $M.T. 2,000 to the Saudis in 1865 is taken from Colonel Lewis Pelly's account of his journey to Riyadh in that year.[2] There is nothing in this account to show that Pelly was referring to the Manasir of the region now in dispute. Against this paucity, not to say entire lack, of evidence of any affiliation of the Manasir with the Saudis in the last century may be set the many historical references to the alliance subsisting between the Manasir and the Al Bu Falah Shaikhs of Abu Dhabi in that period. The authors' assertions may also be compared with the following statement in an article on Abu Dhabi, by the distinguished Arabist, Dr. George Rentz of ARAMCO, in the new *Encyclopaedia of Islam*: 'Āl Bū Falāh are on friendly terms with many of the beduins of the hinterland, though in recent years *the once firm connections with the Mānāsir* have grown weaker.'[3]

No conclusive evidence is offered in the *Memorial* of the Manasir's 'rallying' to the Al Sa'ud after 1913. The tax registers from the office of the Governor of Hasa, which are reproduced in Volume III of the *Memorial*, do not begin until 1935, and they by no means support the contentions of the authors. The registers and their relevance to the question of sovereignty in the disputed areas will be examined later,[4] but some notice may be taken here of those entries in them, cited in the section on the Manasir, which are said to prove the regularity with which the Saudi Government have collected *zakat* from the Manasir in the disputed areas since 1935.

These entries are listed in paragraph 28 of Chapter III, and they number thirteen. Although described as 'examples', they prove, upon examination of the tax registers, to be the total number of such entries for the Manasir in all the registers. What is more, not all of them are relevant. One entry relates to tax collected from Al Murrah tribesmen at a place in Hasa called al-Jahiliyah, and another to tax collected from some Manasir at the same place.[5] A third entry does

---
[1] Below, p. 247.
[2] *Journey to the Wahabee Capital of Riyadh*, Bombay, 1866, p. 93.
[3] Vol. I, fasciculus 3, p. 166. Italics added.
[4] Below, pp. 237–43.
[5] See *Saudi Memorial*, III, 361–5 and 366–7.

The Saudi Memorial of 1955

not specify the place of collection, but this appears, from the register concerned (A.H. 1361), to lie also in Hasa.[1] Only ten entries, it emerges, are concerned with tax collected in the disputed areas.[2] These show that Saudi *amils* collected taxes from groups of Manasir and other tribesmen at al-Uraiq at the western foot of Qatar or in the Bainunah or western Dhafrah, on four occasions in the sixteen years (1935–51) spanned by the registers. The *amils* also made one collection in the Liwa Oasis in the spring of 1941, and a second at its western end in 1951.[3] It seems a very slender basis upon which to erect a claim that the Manasir have been regularly taxed as Saudi subjects.

The statements of the Governor of Hasa, Sa'ud ibn Jiluwi, and his chief tax-collectors, reproduced in Volume II of the *Memorial*, hardly advance the case. They are couched in the most sweeping terms ('since the conquest of Hasa [1913] . . . tax collectors have been sent to al-Dhafrah and the Rub' al-Khali to collect the *zakah* from all the Bedouins there'), and they are uncorroborated by any documentary evidence, apart from the doubtful evidence of the tax registers. The same may be said of a statement by Ibn Jiluwi, dated May 1955 and reproduced as Annex 109 of the *Memorial*, which is supposed to prove that Saudi Arabia has exercised criminal jurisdiction over the Manasir and other tribes in the disputed areas since 1913. The statement, apparently composed from memory, lists twenty-nine occasions between 1919 and 1950 when Ibn Jiluwi, or his predecessor, is said to have taken punitive action against wrongdoers, mainly for camel-stealing. Nine of the incidents described are undated, and in another six the places at which they are supposed to have occurred are unspecified. Four of the incidents involved Saudi tribes like the Murrah and Bani Hajir, and punishment was inflicted on them in Hasa. Three of the incidents are not remembered among the tribes said to have been involved in them. The versions given of five are inaccurate, and state wrongly that action was taken by Saudi officials. Only seven of the twenty-nine are pertinent to the question

---

[1] See *Saudi Memorial*, III, 194–5.
[2] See *Saudi Memorial*, III, 41–44, 119–20, 121, 178–9, 508–9, 510–11, 592–3, 593–4 and 594–8.
[3] The collections in the Bainunah were made in the spring of 1937, 1940, 1948 and 1951 at al-Aqaila, al-Markhiyah, al-Jahiliyah and Bid' al-Ghainah, all of which lie within a few miles of one another. The collection at the western end of Liwa in 1951 was made at Bid' Nukhairah and Bid' Tarjim, which lie about five miles apart.

213

The Saudi Memorial of 1955

at issue, that is to say, they took place within the disputed areas at specified times. All seven relate to the theft of camels and their restoration by Saudi *amils* on *zakat*-collecting expeditions. The general accuracy and reliability of Ibn Jiluwi's account may be illustrated by the first of the incidents described, a raid by the Manasir, Bani Yas and Awamir on the Rashid in 1921, when 300 camels or more were stolen. According to Ibn Jiluwi, 'These were taken back from them by our representative, Su'ayyid Al Faisal at Muwafaqah, west of Buraimi....' The raid in question had been organized by Shaikh Hazza' ibn Sultan of Abu Dhabi, originally against the Duru'. Finding the Duru' away, the raiders attacked the Rashid in the sands south of Umm al-Zamul, in Saudi territory, taking 300 camels. Su'ayyid Al Faisal came to Abu Dhabi on behalf of Ibn Jiluwi to ask for the return of the camels. They were recovered through the agency of Hazza' ibn Sultan.[1]

The final grounds upon which the *Memorial*'s authors claim the Manasir as a Saudi tribe are 'sworn statements of allegiance' from four leading Mansuri shaikhs.[2] The principal shaikhs of the Manasir are:

Al Bu Mundhir: Qirran ibn Mani';
Al Bu Rahmah: Hamad ibn Mubarak, Sa'id ibn Mubarak, and Nasir ibn Sa'id ibn Suwaid;
Al Bu Sha'ar: Muhammad ibn Khadim and Rashid ibn Khadim;
Al Bu Khail: Amir ibn Mubarak;
Al Bu Hamir: Abdullah ibn Baruk.[3]

The statements produced in the *Saudi Memorial* are from Qirran ibn Mani', Sa'id ibn Mubarak, Nasir ibn Sa'id ibn Suwaid, and a shaikh of the Al Bu Mundhir named Salih ibn Aziz.[4] Qirran ibn Mani''s statement, which, like several others in the *Memorial*, was made before Ibn Jiluwi at Dammam on 13 June 1955, reads:

'... I and my people have been, and still are, subjects of H.M.

[1] A supporting statement in the *Memorial* (II, Annex 116), describing an incident which is said to illustrate Ibn Jiluwi's control over the Manasir, is signed by a man who was three or four years old at the time that the incident took place.
[2] See *Saudi Memorial*, I, Chapter III, para. 35.
[3] See *U.K. Memorial*, II, Annex I, no. 1, and *Saudi Memorial*, loc. cit. The latter source gives Ghanim ibn Juraiw as the chief of the Al Bu Sha'ar section. He is not an active shaikh of the section, having lived in retirement at Dubai for several years.
[4] See Vol. II, Annexes 98–100 and 110.

The Saudi Memorial of 1955

King Saʻud ibn ʻAbd al-ʻAziz, just as we were subjects of his father the late King, may God have mercy upon him, and his forefathers before (him). We pay *zakah* in the form of camels, sheep and goats, dates, and rice, in accordance with the rules of Islamic law, to the tax collectors sent by His Majesty or to his representative in Buraimi, as we used to do before for a long time.'[1]

Qirran ibn Maniʻ, it may be recalled, is the head of that segment (over half) of the Al Bu Mundhir which migrated to Hasa after the tribal fighting of the nineteen-twenties, and which has stayed there, for the most part, ever since. Those members who own palms at Liwa usually visit them in the summer for the date harvest, returning to Hasa afterwards. Qirran ibn Maniʻ himself has lived permanently in Hasa for many years. That his statement applies only to those Al Bu Mundhir domiciled in Hasa, and not to those living in the disputed areas, is clear from the statement itself:

i. the Saudi Government have never claimed—indeed, they have explicitly denied it, both at the Dammam Conference and in the present *Memorial*—that they have collected *zakat* on dates in the disputed areas. They do, however, collect *zakat* on dates in Hasa;

ii. rice is not, and never has been, grown at Liwa or at any other place in the disputed areas. It is, however, grown in Hasa.

The reference to the payment of *zakat* by the Al Bu Mundhir to a Saudi representative at Buraimi is surprising. Nowhere in the text of the *Memorial* do the authors claim that *zakat* has been collected from the Manasir at Buraimi. Furthermore, they assert that the Saudi representative at Buraimi from the early eighteen-seventies until the arrival of Turki ibn Utaishan in 1952 was the *tamimah* of the Naʻim. There is no mention in the *Memorial* of his ever having collected *zakat* from the Manasir, nor has such a practice been heard of in Trucial Oman.

Saʻid ibn Mubarak's statement was made at Dammam on 8 April 1955, the day before he was flown back to Buraimi in the Saudi supply aircraft.[2] It is not, whatever the authors may say in the text, a declaration of allegiance. It deals merely with the payment of *zakat*, and what it has to say is of dubious validity, viz., '. . . Only Al Saʻud has collected the *zakah* from any of us of the Manasir. . . .'[3]

---

[1] *Saudi Memorial*, II, Annex 98.
[2] He had been one of the five tribesmen flown up in the aircraft of 19 March (see above, p. 188).
[3] *Saudi Memorial*, II, Annex 99.

The Saudi Memorial of 1955

Nor is Salih ibn Aziz's statement, dated 6 December 1954, a declaration of allegiance. On the contrary, it is wholly taken up with a description of the theft of some camels in 1919–20. Of the four statements, only that of Nasir ibn Sa'id ibn Suwaid is of relevance, in that it is a declaration of allegiance from a person who is a resident of the disputed region. Ibn Suwaid has made frequent visits to Saudi Arabia in past years, and his statement was made before Ibn Jiluwi at Dammam on the same day as that of Qirran ibn Mani'.[1]

BANI YAS. The Bani Yas provide the authors of the *Memorial* with their principal stumbling-block in their effort to prove that the Dhafrah and the other western areas belong to Saudi Arabia because they are the preserve of the Manasir. The Bani Yas are not only the most numerous and widely distributed inhabitants of the Dhafrah but they are, almost without exception, loyal to the Shaikh of Abu Dhabi. To overcome the obstacle presented by these facts the *Memorial*'s authors have resorted to casuistry. 'The tribe of "Bani Yas"', they say, 'is a fiction, yet the false concept of its existence has become so common that to avoid the use of the name entirely would be pedantic.'[2] This is certainly a novel theory, and one not previously advanced by any authority on Eastern Arabia. The authors continue:

'What support the Ruler of Abu Dhabi has comes from groups sometimes associated with Bani Yas. However, it should not be supposed that the Ruler of Abu Dhabi is the chief of a tribe called Bani Yas, or, for that matter, that most of the people called Bani Yas live within either his real or fancied domains.'[3]

This statement can hardly be meant to be taken seriously. It runs counter to what every reputable authority has had to say about the Bani Yas in the last century and a half. It may be compared, for example, with the following extracts from a work entitled *The Eastern Reaches of al-Hasa Province*, produced by the research division of ARAMCO, under the direction of George Rentz, in January 1950.[4]

'While the seafarers of the tribe of Bani Yas generally consider the Ruler of Abu Dhabi as their lord, they hold Ibn Sa'ud in high esteem as the great ruler; but it should not be understood from this

[1] See *Saudi Memorial*, II, Annex 100.
[2] *Saudi Memorial*, I, Chapter III, para. 36.
[3] *Saudi Memorial*, I, Chapter III, para. 37.
[4] It was issued in both an English and an Arabic version. The extracts here are translated from the Arabic.

The Saudi Memorial of 1955

that they owe their direct loyalty to any other than the Ruler of Abu Dhabi' (p. 19).

'Nevertheless there is no cause to doubt that the Bani Yas of al-Dhafrah, or at least the majority of them, owe allegiance to Al Bu Falah of Abu Dhabi' (p. 53).

The *Memorial*'s authors further endeavour to deprive the Bani Yas of any rights whatever in the Dhafrah or in the region at the foot of the Qatar peninsula.

'In al-Dhafrah groups associated with Bani Yas graze their camels with those of the Manasir, with whom they are on good terms, but it is clearly admitted by these elements that they are in the *dirah* of the Manasir.'[1]

'... In the coastal region between al-Dhafrah and Qatar the Manasir have prior rights recognized by all their neighbors.'[2]

'The northern part of the gravel plateau of al-Majann falls within the *dirah* of the Manasir. To them belong the watering places of Nakkut, Duwaihin, al-Munba'aj with its palm trees, Ba'ja, al-Sil', and others.'[3]

It has been pointed out earlier that there are no exclusive *diyar* in the Dhafrah and that the Bani Yas and the Manasir share control of the region amicably. Nor, as the *Memorial*'s authors imply elsewhere, are the numbers of nomadic Bani Yas very much smaller than those of the Manasir.[4] The figure given for the nomadic Bani Yas in the *United Kingdom Memorial* is 1,700;[5] while the ARAMCO report just cited states that the number of the Manasir 'hardly exceeds 2,000'.[6] The *Saudi Memorial* gives no figures. So far as the claim regarding the coastal region near Qatar is concerned, the following passage from the ARAMCO report is of interest:

'The waters of the Gulf are relatively deep along the coasts of Khaur Duwaihin, Ras al-Hadhra and Ras Mushairab, when compared with other zones close inshore on the southern coast of the Gulf. There are at least seven anchorages, called *banadir* by the Arabs, which lie close to the coast between al-Udaid and Sabkhat Matti.... These *banadir* are used by those Arabs who frequently

---

[1] *Saudi Memorial*, I, Chapter III, para. 38.
[2] *Saudi Memorial*, I, Chapter III, para. 23.
[3] *Saudi Memorial*, I, Chapter III, para. 25.
[4] See Vol. I, Chapter III, para. 38: '... An even smaller number [of Bani Yas] lead the nomadic life of camel-raising Bedouins.'
[5] Vol. I, p. 52.
[6] *Eastern Reaches of al-Hasa*, p. 127.

travel in the Gulf, and by the Badu who have business on the sea or on the islands of the Gulf. Most of those who go to sea are fishermen or pearl divers, the majority of whom belong to the Bani Yas tribe. They come to the *banadir* to get water from the wells near the coast or to pick up Badu travellers.'[1]

These wells must be those—Ba'ja, Duwaihin, etc.—said by the authors of the *Memorial* to belong to the Manasir alone.[2]

Perhaps the most remarkable feature of the section on the Bani Yas in the *Saudi Memorial* is that it virtually denies the tribe any rights in its ancestral home, the Liwa Oasis. Thus:

'The Manasir own most of the date palm groves of al-Jiwa [Liwa], and next to the Manasir the Mazari' of Bani Yas own the most. Other small groups of Bani Yas in al-Jiwa are the Qubaisat, the Hawamil, the Maharibah, and Al Bu Muhair.'[3]

'The fact is that the Manasir own the greatest number of date groves in al-Jiwa, and they are paramount in the western quarter and eastern third of that long, narrow belt of cultivation. . . . These holdings are not untended collections of palm trees visited only at harvest time to collect nature's yearly increase. The trees must be cultivated, and members of the tribe live the year round in the villages of al-Jiwa to do so. These settlements also provide homes for the sick, the aged, and children of the tribe; they remain behind when the stalwarts go back to the range with their herds.'[4]

The statements that the Manasir own all the date groves in the western quarter of Liwa and that they predominate in the eastern third have been taken from articles by Wilfred Thesiger.[5] The *Memorial's* authors choose, however, to regard him as a suspect source ('His later articles have shown more of a tendency than the earlier ones to conform with British official views'[6]), presumably because he states that the Manasir of Liwa owe allegiance to the Al Bu Falah.[7] It would appear that the authors have also made use of

---

[1] *Eastern Reaches*, p. 16.
[2] Ba'ja is described in the ARAMCO report as 'a sheltering place consisting of two huts, which is used by fishermen from the Qubaisat section of the Bani Yas' (p. 19).
[3] *Saudi Memorial*, I, Chapter II, para. 52.
[4] *Saudi Memorial*, I, Chapter III, para. 30.
[5] See 'A Further Journey across the Empty Quarter', *Geog. Journ.*, CXIII, 39; and 'Desert Borderlands of Oman', *Geog. Journ.*, CXVI, 142.
[6] *Saudi Memorial*, I, Chapter III, para. 30.
[7] See 'A Further Journey', *Geog. Journ.*, CXIII, 40, and 'Desert Borderands', *Geog. Journ.*, CXVI, 140.

The Saudi Memorial of 1955

ARAMCO's *Eastern Reaches of al-Hasa*. Presumably this, too, was regarded as a suspect source, for it states:

'The people of al-Jiwa say that the majority of the villagers in al-Jiwa are Bani Yas; but the Manasir, who for the most part prefer the nomad life, undoubtedly own most of the gardens of the region' (p. 52).

'In addition to the gardens of the settled Arabs who tend them, there are other date-palm gardens owned by nomads of the Manasir, who do not cultivate them carefully but visit them only during the harvest season in the summer' (p. 51).

Any suggestion, such as the authors make, that the numbers of Bani Yas at Liwa, with the exception of the Mazari' section, are small compared with those of the Manasir is quite erroneous. The testimony of the ARAMCO report just cited agrees with the tables given in the *United Kingdom Memorial*,[1] which show that the comparative numbers of Manasir and Bani Yas families in Liwa at the time of the date harvest in one representative year, 1955, were 315–420 and 304–335. The comparative numbers of Mazari' and other Bani Yas families in the oasis the preceding year were 151 and 211.[2] Nor is it true, as the *Memorial*'s authors imply, that the Manasir remain behind at Liwa in any numbers during the winter. Eleven of the thirteen permanent settlements in the oasis are occupied by Bani Yas, while the other two are shared by Bani Yas and Manasir.[3]

Finally, the authors of the *Memorial* try to detach the Mazari' from the main body of the Bani Yas and to claim their allegiance for Saudi Arabia. The Mazari', they say, are a separate and distinct tribe, whose members are dispersed through Eastern Arabia and even as far away as the coast of East Africa.

'... The attempt to identify them with Bani Yas has neither a tribal nor a political justification.'[4]

'... The Mazari' [of the disputed areas] ... are a Saudi Arabian group.'[5]

'... The Mazari' ... have repeatedly demonstrated and affirmed their allegiance to Saudi Arabia.'[6]

[1] Vol. II, Annex E, no. 1.
[2] *U.K. Memorial*, I, 53. The *Saudi Memorial* gives no figures, which is rather strange in view of the claim that Liwa has long been Saudi territory.
[3] See above, p. 32.
[4] *Saudi Memorial*, I, Chapter III, para. 57.
[5] *Saudi Memorial*, I, Chapter III, para. 59.
[6] *Saudi Memorial*, I, Chapter VI, para. 32.

The Saudi Memorial of 1955

Little support can be obtained for these propositions from any recognized authority on Eastern Arabia. While the Mazari' who live in the mountains of the northern Trucial States, for example, may be considered a separate group, there is no reason to believe that those in the disputed areas regard themselves, or are regarded by others, as anything but an integral part of the Bani Yas. They are even described in the *Saudi Memorial*, in a passage quoted a little earlier,[1] as the 'Mazari' of Bani Yas', and they are so classified in ARAMCO's *Eastern Reaches of al-Hasa* (p. 53):

'The tax on the date crop [at Liwa] is assessed by an Al Bu Falah representative, Humaid ibn Dahnan, who lives all the year round in Kayyah. He takes one in ten *jirab*. This tax is collected only from the four sections of the Bani Yas who own gardens in al-Jiwa. These are Al Hawamil, Al Mazari', Al Maharibah and Al Qubaisat.'

The allegiance of the Mazari' of the disputed areas to Saudi Arabia is said by the authors to be demonstrated by statements of loyalty from Faris ibn Ghanim, whom they describe as 'the Chief of the Mazari'',[2] and by the regular payment of taxes by the tribe to Saudi *amils*. Faris ibn Ghanim's statements, reprinted in the *Memorial* as Annexes 118–19, are, unfortunately, of no relevance. Not only was he never the chief of the Mazari' but he lived at Dubai, outside the disputed areas, from 1940 until his death in 1957. The joint shaikhs of the Mazari' are Muhammad ibn Sayyah, who lives permanently at Khannur village in the Liwa Oasis, and Sahail ibn Khamis. Neither of them has ever sworn allegiance to Saudi Arabia. Faris ibn Ghanim met his death at the hands of three young Mansuri tribesmen, whose fathers he had put to death after he had taken them prisoner in the Abu Dhabi-Dubai war of 1945–8, when he fought on the side of Dubai. Although this 'Saudi' subject was killed by 'Saudi' Manasir in the vicinity of the Buraimi Oasis, the deed went unremarked by the Saudi Government.

Saudi tax-collecting among the Mazari' is said by the *Memorial*'s authors to be proved by the statements of Ibn Jiluwi and his tax-collectors already referred to, and by entries in the tax registers in Volume III of the *Memorial*. Only three instances of tax-collection among the Mazari' are cited,[3] and two of these prove, on inspection,

---

[1] See above, p. 218.
[2] *Saudi Memorial*, I, Chapter III, para. 61.
[3] See *Saudi Memorial*, III, 30–31, 120–1 and 170–1.

The Saudi Memorial of 1955

to have taken place in Qatar, where the Mazari' sometimes wander in search of pasturage.

THE AWAMIR. 'All of the central group of the 'Awamir', say the authors of the *Memorial*, 'are subjects of Saudi Arabia.'[1] One is tempted to ask how long this has been so, since the authors make no claim to the historical allegiance of the Awamir and the evidence that they present of the tribe's present allegiance is scarcely convincing. It consists of the statements of Ibn Jiluwi and his officials about tax-collecting and the exercise of criminal jurisdiction, used already in connexion with the Manasir, a handful of entries in the tax registers, and declarations of allegiance from tribal leaders.[2] Ibn Jiluwi's statement on criminal jurisdiction contains references to three so-called 'police actions' taken by him against the Awamir for camel-stealing between 1921 and 1946–7. One of the 'police actions' took place in Hasa, and neither in this instance nor in the other two cited, according to both contemporary and current testimony available in Trucial Oman, did Ibn Jiluwi do anything to recover the stolen camels. The tax entries cited by the authors are valueless to demonstrate Saudi jurisdiction over the Awamir in the disputed areas. Nine examples are given, all of which prove, on examination, to relate to taxes collected from individual Amiri tribesmen at three places, al-Bahath, Sa'qah and Shaj'ah, which lie well within Saudi Arabia, far from the disputed areas.[3]

The declarations of allegiance produced are from Ali Aba al-Rus al-Dhu'ayyif and Salim ibn Hamad ibn Rakkadh, described here as the 'chiefs of the group'.[4] The former is also said to have been 'deputed by the provincial government [of Hasa] to carry out policing activities and to collect taxes'.[5] If this were so, then it was a peculiar choice, for Ali Aba al-Rus was a well-known camel thief, and the Amir Ibn Jiluwi himself records in the *Saudi Memorial* that he once 'severely punished' him for camel-stealing.[6] Ali Aba al-Rus is not, and never has been, a chief of the Awamir. He is not even a shaikh, and he is not listed as one, for example, in ARAMCO's *Eastern Reaches of al-Hasa*. His 'statement of allegiance' relates not to political loyalty

[1] Vol. I, Chapter III, para. 65.
[2] See *Saudi Memorial*, I, Chapter III, paras. 62–65.
[3] See *Saudi Memorial*, III, 193, 195, 197, 200, 201, 205–7 and 212.
[4] *Saudi Memorial*, I, Chapter III, para. 65.
[5] *Saudi Memorial*, I, Chapter III, para. 63.
[6] See Vol. II, Annex 109.

but to *zakat*-collecting, and it was made at Dammam on the same day as that of Sa'id ibn Mubarak of the Manasir, 8 April 1955.[1] Like him, Ali Aba al-Rus had been flown up from Buraimi on 19 March and returned on 9 April.

Salim ibn Hamad ibn Rakkadh, the ex-*tamimah* of the Awamir, made his statement at Hamasa on 13 June 1955, and it closely resembles the other statements collected on that day. It was ordered by Ibn Jiluwi on 12 June, as will be seen shortly, and it was paid for through the Saudi police commander at Buraimi.[2] The authors of the *Memorial* do not mention that the Awamir were divided in their loyalties, or that Ibn Rakkadh had been deposed as *tamimah* and replaced by Ibn Hamm in 1947. Ibn Rakkadh's statement is a little odd.[3] After saying that he and his people consider themselves subjects of King Sa'ud, and that 'every one' of them pays *zakat* to Saudi officials, he goes on to claim that their 'forefathers' did so also. Not even the *Memorial*'s authors claim that the Awamir were subjects of the Al Sa'ud in bygone generations or that they paid *zakat* to the Saudis. Perhaps Ibn Rakkadh was carried away by his enthusiasm to do Ibn Jiluwi's bidding, or perhaps he merely put his signature to a standard form of declaration. Whatever the case, he did not go unrewarded. 'Allocate to Salim bin Rakkadh and his brother Muhammad, the Shaikhs of the Awamir,' signalled Ibn Jiluwi to Abdullah ibn Nami at Buraimi on 24 June 1955, 'the sum of Rs 1,000 with effect from Dhu'l-Qa'dah 1374 [June–July 1955].'[4]

THE NA'IM. As set forth in the *Memorial*, Saudi Arabia's claim to the Buraimi Oasis on the grounds of tribal allegiance depends largely upon the contention that the Na'im are loyal subjects of the Al Sa'ud. This contention, in turn, rests almost wholly upon two statements of allegiance, one from Saqr ibn Sultan, the former *tamimah* of the Na'im, the other from Rashid ibn Hamad, the late chief of the Al Bu Shamis of Hamasa. The authors of the *Memorial*, in their

---

[1] See *Saudi Memorial*, II, Annex 102, and cf. Annex 99. A second statement by Ali Aba al-Rus (Annex 108), dated 6 December 1954, relates to a *zakat*-collecting expedition to the Buraimi region, on which he accompanied Su'ayyid Al Faisal, 'about thirty-six or thirty-seven years ago' (see Vol. I, Chapter IV, para. 342).

[2] See above, p. 195, and [Saudi Documents] In-letters no. 6196, Ibn Jiluwi to Ibn Nami, 21 Shawwal 1374/12 June 1955, and (unnumbered), Turki ibn Utaishan to Rashid ibn Hamad, 24 Dhu'l-Hijjah 1374/14 August 1955.

[3] *Saudi Memorial*, II, Annex 101.

[4] [Saudi Documents] In-signal no. 6525, dated 4 Dhu'l-Qa'dah 1374.

The Saudi Memorial of 1955

description of the Na'im,[1] make no reference, as they do in the cases of the Manasir and Awamir, to the administration of justice in the oasis by the Governor of Hasa, nor do they cite any entries in the tax registers to show that Saudi Arabia has collected *zakat* among the Na'im of Buraimi in this century. Yet they print as Annex 93 to the *Memorial* a statement by Zaid and Dhiyab ibn Saqr ibn Zaid, the two exiled members of the Al Bu Falah whom the Saudi Government paid in late 1954 to try to effect a *coup d'état* in Abu Dhabi, which contains this passage:

'We bear witness, as does all the world, that right up to our own time the agents of Al Sa'ud have been coming to Buraimi to collect the *zakah* and preserve law and order. We do not deny this, and God is witness to what we say.'

Nearly three pages of the five devoted to the Na'im are taken up with a list of the principal sections of the tribe, their leading shaikhs, and references to 'documents of allegiance' in which their names occur. Thirty-one sections are listed, 55 shaikhs, and 15 documents of allegiance (Annexes 48, 53, 59, 62, 106, 107, 120–6, 134 and 138 of the *Memorial*). Some three dozen individuals from 16 sections, it would appear, are named in these documents, which range in date from late 1950 to 1955. What the point of this exercise may be it is difficult to say, for the great majority of the persons named dwelt outside the areas subject to arbitration in 1954–5. In fact, the only pertinent documents seem to be those concerning Saqr ibn Sultan of Buraimi village (Annex 107), Rashid ibn Hamad (Annexes 48, 59 and 106), and two other inhabitants of Hamasa (Annex 59).

The other documents all concern shaikhs or tribesmen who dwelt at Hafit, Qabil, Sunainah, Dhank, or other places south of the Buraimi Zone. They fall, roughly speaking, into two categories: those concerning recognized tribal leaders and those concerning tribesmen who, although they are dubbed 'leaders', 'amirs' or 'notables' by the *Memorial*'s authors, are actually persons of little consequence in the region. Such, for example, are the tribesmen who affixed their thumbprints to the documents which appear as Annexes 120, 121, 123–5 and 138. These statements, in which the signatories declare that they are subjects of the Saudi Government, were all made in June 1955, when, it will be recalled, the Saudi police commander at Buraimi was feverishly trying to win over as many tribesmen to the Saudi cause as he could. Annex 125, with which the *Memorial*'s

[1] Vol. I, Chapter III, paras. 70–74.

The Saudi Memorial of 1955

authors associate the name of Rashid ibn Abdullah ibn Zuraiq of Dhank, does not have his name in it anywhere. Its signatories describe themselves as 'Amirs of the tribe of Bani Sa'idah of the tribes of Nu'aim', a group that does not appear in the list given by the *Memorial*'s authors.

The principal shaikhs of the Na'im whose names appear in the first category of documents listed by the authors are:

Ahmad ibn Muhammad al-Salf and Sultan ibn Ali al-Salf of the Khawatir of Hafit;
Humaid ibn Rashid and Muhammad ibn Ali ibn Awwad of the Al Bu Khuraiban of Hafit;
Matar ibn Salim of the Al Bu Shamis of Dhank;
Hamdan ibn Khalfan of the Al Bu Shamis of Wasit; and
Muhammad ibn Salimin ibn Rahmah of al-Sunainah, chief of the Baduin Al Bu Shamis.

In the case of the first three, the only document with which their names are associated is the 'Declaration by Notables of the Buraimi Region', obtained by Turki ibn Utaishan in September 1952, shortly after his arrival at Buraimi, and reproduced as Annex 59 of the *Memorial*. Its legal validity is, to say the least, open to question, since it was not signed by the *tamimah* of the Na'im, whom the shaikhs of the tribe had recognized four years previously, in a written agreement, as their sole representative in all political matters, and since Ahmad ibn Muhammad al-Salf had, in the same agreement, declared his allegiance to the Sultan of Muscat. He and Humaid ibn Rashid, furthermore, re-affirmed their allegiance to the Sultan at Muscat in June 1955.[1] Muhammad ibn Ali ibn Awwad, another signatory of Annex 59, is associated by the *Memorial*'s authors with two other documents, Annexes 62 and 120. Annex 62 is a letter from him to the late King Ibn Sa'ud in September 1952, placing himself and his tribe under Saudi protection. Annex 120 is a statement by two of his tribesmen, dated 14 June 1955, saying that they had deposed him from the chieftainship for disobedience to Saudi Arabia. They had, in reality, done nothing of the kind. What they had done was to take advantage of the absence of Muhammad ibn Awwad in Muscat, where he had gone to re-affirm his allegiance to the Sultan,[2] to set

---

[1] See *U.K. Memorial*, II, Annex K, no. 2. For the 1948 agreement, see above, p. 140.
[2] See *U.K. Memorial*, loc. cit.

The Saudi Memorial of 1955

their thumbprints to the document which now appears as Annex 120.

Hamdan ibn Khalfan, also a signatory of Annex 59, gave a declaration of allegiance to Saudi Arabia on 13 June 1955, which appears as Annex 134. It was dictated, as will be seen shortly, on the orders of the Amir Ibn Jiluwi. Hamdan ibn Khalfan, who at this time was living as a refugee at Hamasa, is regularly named in the lists of recipients of money sent down from Dammam to the Saudi police commander at Buraimi, Abdullah ibn Nami, every month.

Muhammad ibn Salimin, the last of the chiefs in question, was in correspondence with the Amir Faisal late in 1950 (Annex 53), signed Annex 59 in September 1952, and gave a declaration of allegiance to Saudi Arabia on 9 April 1955 (Annex 122). This declaration, as will also be seen shortly, was written on the orders of Ibn Jiluwi. Seven years earlier, Muhammad ibn Salimin, along with other shaikhs of the Na'im, had signed a pledge of allegiance to the Sultan Sa'id ibn Taimur. Two months after giving his declaration of allegiance to the Saudis he testified in Muscat that his loyalty had been bought.[1] It had, indeed. 'Instruct Muhammad Salih', Ibn Jiluwi ordered Ibn Nami on 10 January 1955, 'to pay to Muhammad bin Salimin the balance of his two months' allocations at the monthly rate of Rs 1,000 which included the allocations of the sons of Salimin.'[2] A month later Ibn Jiluwi wrote to Ibn Nami: 'Forwarded to you with Nasir al-Hudhaili is the sum of Rs 81,895 . . .: Rs 1,200, balance of the salary of Shaikh Muhammad bin Salimin bin Rahmah for the months of Rabi' II, Jumada I and Jumada II [December 1954–February 1955].'[3]

Rashid ibn Hamad's name is associated in the *Memorial* with Annex 59, Annex 48, a letter from him to Ibn Sa'ud in June 1951, and Annex 106, a statement of allegiance to Saudi Arabia dated 9 April 1955. The circumstances in which this declaration came to be written are as follows.

On 8 April 1955 Abdul Aziz ibn Jiluwi sent the following message to Ibn Nami at Buraimi:

'Obtain statements from the following to the effect that they are Saudi subjects:

---

[1] See *U.K. Memorial*, II, Annex K, nos. 1 and 2.
[2] [Saudi Documents] In-signal (unnumbered), dated 16 Jumada I, 1374.
[3] [Saudi Documents] In-letter no. 3377, dated 15 Jumada II, 1374/8 February 1955.

The Saudi Memorial of 1955

'Muhammad bin Salimin, Humaid bin Rashid, Salim bin Rakkadh, Rashid bin Hamad, Muhammad bin Hamad, Saqr bin Sultan, Sa'id bin Rashid al-Baluchi, Dhiban and Ali al-Rubayyi', Faris bin Ghanim al-Mazrui.'[1]

The next day, as has been seen, the tax-collector, Muhammad ibn Mansur, flew down from Dammam in the supply aircraft to supervise the making of the statements.[2] That evening Ibn Nami signalled Ibn Jiluwi:

'With reference to your signal order no. 4687, we have managed to obtain the statements of the following persons:

'Saqr bin Sultan, Rashid bin Hamad, Sa'id bin Rashid bin Sa'id al-Baluchi, Dhiban bin Ali bin Rubayyi', for himself and on behalf of his nephew, Ali bin Muhammad bin Rubayyi', Salim and Muhammad, sons of Hamad bin Rakkadh, Humaid bin Rashid al-Na'imi, Muhammad bin Salimin.

'The rest, owing to the absence of the people concerned from the town, we shall send when we obtain them. We have sent for them to come.'[3]

Only three of the statements obtained on 9 April eventually appeared in the *Saudi Memorial*, those of Rashid ibn Hamad, Muhammad ibn Salimin and Dhiban ibn Ali al-Rubayyi'. All, as has been seen, were obtained by bribery.[4]

Rashid ibn Hamad, it will be recalled, had made an explicit declaration of allegiance to the Sultan Sa'id ibn Taimur in 1948, before Saudi Arabia laid claim to Buraimi, and he continued to receive an annual allowance from the Sultan until 1951 at least.[5] From the moment of Turki ibn Utaishan's arrival at Buraimi in 1952 Rashid received a monthly salary of Rs 5,000 from the Saudis, and he acted as their principal local agent for the disbursement of bribes. His name appears on all the monthly lists of recipients of bribes sent down from Dammam to the Saudi police commander at Buraimi

---

[1] [Saudi Documents] In-signal no. 4687, dated 15 Sha'ban 1374. Muhammad ibn Hamad was a shaikh of the Al Bu Shamis of Hamasa. Dhiban and Ali al-Rubayyi' were shaikhs of the settled Bani Qitab in the Dhahirah.

[2] See above, p. 188.

[3] [Saudi Documents] Out-signal no. 560, dated 16 Sha'ban 1374.

[4] For the bribing of Dhiban al-Rubayyi', see above, p. 191 and [Saudi Documents] Out-signal no. 677, Ibn Nami to Ibn Jiluwi, 14 Shawwal 1374/ 5 June 1955: '. . . We have given to the sons of Rabi' and Dhiban and his cousins the sum of Rs 20,000 and 5,000 rounds of ammunition, as instructed by you.'

[5] See above, p. 152.

The Saudi Memorial of 1955

from September 1954 to October 1955.[1] His declaration of allegiance to Saudi Arabia (Annex 107) can scarcely be said to possess any value. The same may be said of the declaration of Saqr ibn Sultan, dated 13 June 1955, and printed as Annex 107 of the *Memorial*. The earlier statement obtained on 9 April was not used for reasons that the following letter from Ibn Jiluwi to Ibn Nami on 12 June 1955 makes clear:

'Herewith are four copies [of a statement]. You are to make the Shaikhs sign them in replacement of the previous documents which have been lost. If there are other shaikhs with you, write statements of this kind which they are to sign. They should be ready for the next mail. Those signed now should be sent by the next mail as we are in need of them.'[2]

Ibn Nami replied on 13 June:

'In accordance with your instruction no. 6203 of 21.x.1374 we have taken the statements from the Shaikhs found at the oasis. They are Shaikh Saqr bin Sultan, Ubaid bin Juma', Sa'id al-Baluchi, the sons of Al Darmaki, the sons of Bin Hilal, Hamdan bin Khalfan, the shepherd of Wadi al-Jizzi who belongs to Hamasa, and Ibn Rakkadh. We will take the necessary action towards the rest of them and we will forward the statements to Your Highness by the next mail.'[3]

All of these statements, which are similar in content, later appeared in the *Saudi Memorial*.[4] The winning-over of Saqr ibn Sultan has been described in the previous chapter. He was given a lump sum of Rs 10,000 in September 1954 and a monthly salary of Rs 3,000. This was raised to Rs 5,000 in October 1954 and, finally, to Rs 7,000 in March 1955.[5] Like Rashid ibn Hamad he had made a solemn vow of loyalty to the Sultan Sa'id ibn Taimur in 1948, and he continued to act as the Sultan's representative in the Buraimi region after that time.

[1] See, for example, [Saudi Documents] In-letters (unnumbered), Turki ibn Utaishan to Muhammad Salih, 26 Muharram 1374/24 September 1954; no. 3377, Ibn Jiluwi to Ibn Nami, 15 Jumada II, 1374/8 February 1955; no. 6196, Ibn Jiluwi to Ibn Nami, 21 Shawwal 1374/12 June 1955; and Out-signal no. 767, Ibn Nami to Ibn Jiluwi, 6 Dhu'l-Qa'dah 1374/26 June 1955: '... I have put the same question included in Your Excellency's [signal] to Rashid bin Hamad, to which he has replied: "The amount paid to me by Muhammad Salih is the amount decided by Amir Turki the night of his departure."'
[2] [Saudi Documents] In-letter no. 6203, dated 21 Shawwal 1374.
[3] [Saudi Documents] Out-signal no. 723, dated 22 Shawwal 1374.
[4] See Vol. II, Annexes 101, 107, 131–4 and 136.
[5] See above, pp. 176–7 and 187.

The Saudi Memorial of 1955

THE DHAWAHIR. According to the authors of the *Memorial*, the loyalty of the Dhawahir to the Al Sa'ud goes back 150 years, and its continuance today is demonstrated by declarations of allegiance from the Dhahiri shaikhs, reprinted in Volume II of the *Memorial*, and by their regular payment of *zakat* to Saudi collectors, to which the shaikhs have testified in writing.[1] The claim to the past loyalty of the Dhawahir proves, on examination, to be based upon two historical references, pertaining to the decade 1800–10.[2] The declarations of allegiance are not from the principal shaikhs of the Dhawahir, Sultan ibn Surur and Mani' ibn Muhammad, but from four youthful and minor shaikhs, Sa'id and Shabib ibn Muhammad Al Hilal of Jimi village, and Sa'id and Muhammad ibn Sultan Al Darmaki of Qattarah.[3] Like so many of the statements of this kind in the *Memorial*, the declarations were bought by the Saudis. For example, in the list accompanying a sum of money sent by Ibn Jiluwi to Ibn Nami on 8 February 1955 appears the following item: 'Rs 1560, Wage of Shaikh Shabib bin Muhammad [Al] Hilal and his companions for the months of Jumada I and Jumada II.'[4] Sa'id and Muhammad ibn Sultan al Darmaki received an allowance of Rs 400 each *per mensem* until August 1955, when it was raised to Rs 800.[5]

The declarations of allegiance are dated 13 June 1955. That of Sa'id and Shabib ibn Muhammad Al Hilal states, as do all the others obtained on that day, that they and their lands are subject to King Sa'ud, 'just as we and our fathers and forefathers were subjects of his father 'Abd al-'Aziz before him'.[6] One can only say that it is a most peculiar statement to come from the grandsons of Ahmad ibn Hilal, who, for forty years, until his death in 1936, was the Abu Dhabi *wali* in the Buraimi Oasis. Even more peculiar, however, are two further statements by Sa'id and Shabib ibn Muhammad Al Hilal and Sa'id and Muhammad ibn Sultan Al Darmaki, reproduced in the *Memorial* as Annexes 128 and 129. They are both dated 23 April 1955 and they

---

[1] See *Saudi Memorial*, I, Chapter III, paras. 75–86.
[2] These will be referred to again below (pp. 247–8).
[3] See *Saudi Memorial*, II, Annexes 131 and 132. For the unsuccessful attempts to get statements from Sultan ibn Surur and Mani' ibn Muhammad, see above, p. 189.
[4] [Saudi Documents] In-letter no. 3377, dated 15 Jumada II, 1374.
[5] See [Saudi Documents] In-letters no. 6196, Ibn Jiluwi to Ibn Nami, 21 Shawwal 1374/12 June 1955, and (unnumbered), Turki ibn Utaishan to Rashid ibn Hamad, 24 Dhu'l-Hijjah 1374/13 August 1955.
[6] *Saudi Memorial*, II, Annex 132.

The Saudi Memorial of 1955

read almost exactly alike. That of Sa'id and Muhammad ibn Sultan Al Darmaki runs:

'We, Sa'id ibn Sultân al-Darmaki and Muhammad ibn Sultân al-Darmaki, testify that, since the decline of the rule of Al Sa'ud, our *zakah* and that of our people in dates and rice have been in our own hands as Shaikhs of the town of al-Qattarah and (the town of) Hili. Since (the decline of) Al Sa'ud we have never paid (the *zakah*) to anyone (else), either Falahi (of Al Bu Falah) or Sa'idi (of Al Bu Sa'id).'[1]

This statement may be compared with the following instructions sent by Abdul Aziz ibn Jiluwi to Ibn Nami on 8 April 1955, i.e., fifteen days earlier:

'Arrange with Shaikh Rashid bin Hamad to obtain statements from the Dhawahir Shaikhs, Sultan bin Surur, his brother Mani' bin Muhammad, the sons of Ahmad Abdullah and his brother Sultan, *Sa'id bin Sultan and his brother Muhammad*, and Rashid al-Daramikah and Muhammad bin Sa'ud bin Arar, to the effect that, since the decline of the rule of Al Sa'ud the *zakat* of dates and rice due from us and from our people is collected by ourselves, we, the Shaikhs of the country. We have never paid it to any other after Al Sa'ud, neither to a Falahi nor to a Sa'idi. Each statement should be separate.'[2]

Even without the evidence of this letter, the statements themselves are sufficient demonstration that they were composed by a foreign hand. Rice is not, and never has been, grown at Buraimi. Nor have the Al Bu Sa'id Sultans ever claimed the right to collect *zakat* from the Dhawahir. It is scarcely conceivable that the Al Darmaki brothers, or the Al Hilal, would have felt it necessary, on their own initiative, to deny a practice that everyone in Buraimi knew had never existed. As for their testimony that the Al Bu Falah have never collected date-*zakat* in the villages of Qattarah and Hili, they must surely have been aware of the fact that their father, Sultan Al Darmaki, used to receive one-third of the *zakat* collected at Qattarah by the Ruler of Abu Dhabi, since on his death in 1949 the allowance was continued to them. In any case, neither they nor the *Memorial's* authors are entirely consistent in their assertions about *zakat*.

---

[1] *Saudi Memorial*, II, Annex 129. The interpolations in brackets are in the original.
[2] [Saudi Documents] In-letter no. 4703, dated 15 Sha'ban 1374. Italics added.

The Saudi Memorial of 1955

Whereas in their statement of 23 April 1955 they say that 'our *zakah* and that of our people in dates and rice have been in our own hands', in their declaration of allegiance to King Sa'ud of 13 June 1955 they say, 'we pay *zakah* on our livestock and palm trees to his representative who is sent to Buraimi. . . . Our forefathers used to pay *zakah* to his representative in Buraimi.'[1] The authors of the *Memorial*, on the other hand, nowhere claim that the Saudis have collected date-*zakat* from the Dhawahir. At one place they even state: 'Dates from Buraimi, other than those necessary for their immediate subsistence, were not of great interest to collectors from Hasa; and insistence on a money equivalent would often have worked hardship on taxpayers not rich in coin.'[2]

The only other evidence offered by the authors to substantiate their contentions regarding the Dhawahir consists of statements by a former headman of Qattarah village and by an inhabitant of al-Ain. The statement of the headman, Rashid ibn Sa'id Al Darmaki, is said to prove his loyalty to Saudi Arabia.[3] Like so many of the statements in the *Memorial*, it fails to live up to its promise. It is undated, it does not mention Saudi Arabia, and it is not even signed by Rashid ibn Sa'id. It might be compared with a statement by him, dated 17 March 1954 pledging allegiance to the Ruler of Abu Dhabi, which is reproduced in the *United Kingdom Memorial*.[4] The other statement in the *Saudi Memorial* is by Muhammad ibn Sa'ud ibn Arar, described as 'the principal chief'[5] of al-Ain. It declares that his *zakat* has been in his own hands and has not been collected by the Al Bu Falah. Muhammad ibn Sa'ud ibn Arar, as has been seen, had been ordered by Ibn Jiluwi on 8 April 1955 to make this statement. He was not the 'principal chief' of al-Ain but a gardener, who was sometimes employed by Shaikh Zaid ibn Sultan as a falconer.

Shaikh Zaid, who for some years has been the most influential figure in the Buraimi Oasis, is mentioned only once in the *Saudi Memorial*. The Al Bu Falah as a whole do not fare much better. Their presence in the oasis is virtually ignored, and their extensive holdings there are dismissed in one sentence in Chapter II, 'The Geographical Setting': 'To the west of al-Mu'taradh is the estate of Al Bu Falah known as al-Muwaiqi'i, consisting of a few relatively

---
[1] *Saudi Memorial*, II, Annexes 129 and 131.
[2] Vol. I, Chapter VI, para. 46.
[3] See *Saudi Memorial*, I, Chapter III, para. 79, and II, Annex 114.
[4] Vol. II, Annex L, no. 1.
[5] *Saudi Memorial*, I, Chapter III, para. 84. See also Vol. II, Annex 130.

The Saudi Memorial of 1955

new buildings and a handful of scattered huts. . . .'[1] This estimate of the Al Bu Falah's position in the oasis hardly accords with the testimony of Miles in 1875, of Cox in 1905, and of Thesiger, who visited Buraimi on three occasions in 1948–9, before Saudi Arabia laid claim to the oasis. Nor is it easy to reconcile it with the statement made in the article on Abu Dhabi in the new *Encyclopaedia of Islam* by George Rentz that 'several villages of al-Buraymī belong to Āl Bū Falāh.'[2]

The remainder of Chapter III, 'The People and the Tribes', is taken up with a description of three tribes, the Baluchis, the Bani Ka'ab and the Bani Qitab, to include whom in the *Memorial* seems to be stretching the terms of reference of the arbitration agreement. The Baluchis live well to the south of the Buraimi Zone: their centre, Araiqi, is some 90 miles from the oasis. The principal settlement of the Bani Ka'ab, Mahadhah, lies outside the zone; and while the eastern part of the zone may be said to fall within their *dirah*, the main area of their distribution is along the western slopes of the Hajar between the Wadi al-Jizzi and Wadi al-Qaur. As a justification for including these tribes, and the Bani Qitab, the *Memorial*'s authors argue that the situation in the Buraimi Zone cannot be properly understood without reference to the areas to the south and east of it, which they classify, together with the zone itself, as 'the whole region in eastern Arabia which has ordinarily been subject to Saudi rule with Buraimi as the provincial capital'.[3] They may not have been uninfluenced, also, by the fact that they were able to produce declarations of allegiance to Saudi Arabia from some of the leaders of these tribes.

The first of these declarations (Annex 136) is from Sa'id ibn Rashid of the Baluchis. It calls for little comment. He had long been in receipt of Saudi subsidies and was most active in their campaign of subversion.[4] His declaration was one of those collected at Hamasa on 13 June 1955 on the orders of Ibn Jiluwi, and it is couched in the terms prescribed by the Governor in his message to Ibn Nami the previous day. The same is true of the declaration of Ubaid ibn Juma' of the Bani Ka'ab (Annex 133).[5] According to the authors of the

---
[1] *Saudi Memorial*, I, Chapter II, para. 73.
[2] Vol. I, fasciculus 3, p. 166.
[3] *Saudi Memorial*, I, Chapter II, para. 74.
[4] See above, pp. 181, 191 and 195.
[5] For Ubaid's activities, see above, pp. 177–80.

The Saudi Memorial *of 1955*

Memorial, the Bani Ka'ab 'have a long history of co-operation with the ruling family of Saudi Arabia . . .'.[1] This is not exactly what the paramount shaikh of the tribe told Captain Eccles in 1925, nor what he told Bertram Thomas in 1927:

'. . . They [the Saudis] took my grandfather away in chains to Najd, where he embraced their strict tenets and became a holy man. Eventually they let him come back, but within a year he had joined the victorious rebels who finally freed this province of their men. Never since then have we of the Bani Ka'ab acknowledged their overlordship.'[2]

The authors also produce a second declaration from Ubaid ibn Juma', dated 5 October 1952, and a declaration of the same date and similar content from Abdullah ibn Salim, who replaced him as paramount chief of the Bani Ka'ab in 1953. Both declarations were obtained by Turki ibn Utaishan after his arrival at Buraimi, and are in the form of letters addressed to the late King Ibn Sa'ud. Abdullah ibn Salim's reads in part: 'My lord, we praise God who has bestowed your reign upon us. This is a blessing from God Most High, for we always wanted God to bestow the reign of the House of Sa'ud upon our land.'[3] At the time, Abdullah ibn Salim was competing for the leadership of the Bani Ka'ab with Ubaid ibn Juma', and in his zeal he even went so far as to attack a Trucial Oman Levies post in the Wadi al-Qaur, outside the disputed areas, while flying a Saudi flag. Once he had won the contest he severed his connexion with the Saudis, much to their annoyance.[4] These circumstances aside, his statement hardly bears out the contention of the *Memorial*'s authors that the land of the Bani Ka'ab 'has ordinarily been subject to Saudi rule'.

By including the Bani Qitab in the *Memorial* the authors would appear to have over-reached themselves. They describe the Baduin branch of the tribe as 'living between the mountains of al-Hajar and the Trucial Coast'.[5] The *dirah* of the Baduin Bani Qitab can be fixed

---

[1] *Saudi Memorial*, I, Chapter III, para. 94.

[2] Thomas, *Alarms and Excursions*, p. 181. For Eccles's account, see above, p. 118. Colonel Miles got the story from the grandfather himself in 1875 (see 'On the Route between Sohar and el-Bereymi in Oman', *Journ. As. Soc. Bengal*, XLVI). All three sources have been used by the authors of the *Memorial* (see Vol. I, Chapter IV, paras. 248, 343 and 347).

[3] *Saudi Memorial*, II, Annex 65. The declaration of Ubaid ibn Juma' appears as Annex 64.

[4] See above, p. 180.

[5] *Saudi Memorial*, I, Chapter III, para. 87.

The Saudi Memorial of 1955

more accurately than that: most of it lies in the Shaikhdom of Sharjah, and while the Ma'aliya section roams today in the vicinity of Buraimi, the only times in the past that the tribe were to be found in the disputed areas in any numbers were when they were raiding the Rashid. To include them in the *Memorial* and to claim their allegiance for Saudi Arabia is to advance a territorial claim to part of the Shaikhdom of Sharjah. The leaders of the Baduin Bani Qitab are Muhammad ibn Ali ibn Huwaidin and Sa'id ibn Huwaidin. A declaration of allegiance from them is printed as Annex 63. From its date, 2 October 1952, it would appear to have been one of those obtained by Turki ibn Utaishan in the autumn of 1952, and like the others it was probably bought. Several of the Bani Qitab were given trips to Saudi Arabia late in 1952, and their leaders were still receiving cash presents in 1955.[1]

Similarly, by producing a declaration of allegiance (Annex 135) from the chief of the settled Bani Qitab of the Dhahirah, Dhiban ibn Ali ibn Rubayyi', the authors have extended Saudi Arabia's territorial claim deeper into the Sultanate of Muscat. Dhiban ibn Ali had been on the Saudi payroll for some time, and his statement, dated 9 April 1955, was written on the orders of Ibn Jiluwi.[2] It is odd that the authors should have printed his statement and not those which had been secured from two of the Na'imi shaikhs of Dhank, a few miles from Aflaj Bani Qitab. The principal resident shaikhs of Dhank are Matar ibn Salim al-Azizi, Hamad ibn Salim al-Wahshi, and Muhammad ibn Ahmad al-Yahyayi. The last-named, it will be remembered, had been involved in the winter of 1954–5 in the attempt to suborn the Duru'. He and his fellow shaikhs at Dhank had been in receipt of regular payments from the Saudis during 1955. For instance, Ibn Nami wrote to Ibn Jiluwi on 22 April of that year: 'I enclose herewith a statement submitted by Shaikh Rashid bin Hamad of payments he has made to various persons: ... Paid to

---

[1] '*Sharhas* [cash presents] for Muhammad bin Saif, Mubarak bin Rashid, and Salim bin Rashid have been paid to Sa'id bin Huwaidan,' Turki ibn Utaishan informed Ibn Nami at Buraimi in a letter of 12 April 1955 ([Saudi Documents] In-signal (unnumbered), dated 24 Sha'ban 1374).

[2] See above, pp. 225–6. See also [Saudi Documents] Out-signal no. 677, Ibn Nami to Ibn Jiluwi, 14 Shawwal 1374/5 June 1955: 'We informed you in our signal no. 668 that we had given to the sons of Rabi' and Dhiban and his cousins the sum of Rs 20,000 and 5,000 rounds of ammunition as instructed by you. Do you still want us to give them more as indicated in your signal no. 6017? We have also given to al-Baluchi the same, as pointed out in our signal no. 666.'

Matar bin Salim, Rs 1,500; paid to Muhammad bin Ahmad al-Yahyayi, Rs 1,500; paid to Hamad bin Salim al-Wahshi, Rs 500....'[1]

The price of allegiance, however, came high. 'I enclose herewith letters from al-Yahyayi', Ibn Nami signalled to Ibn Jiluwi on 9 April 1955.

'He is in fact a good and faithful man, but we understand from the tenor of his letters that he wishes that something official may be allocated for him through Shaikh Rashid bin Hamad. As the prevailing situation makes it necessary for us to apply this system, in compliance with Your Excellency's wishes, we have ordered Shaikh Rashid to give him what suits his position and efforts. . . . The total amount paid him [was] Rs 1,500, but it appears that he is not satisfied with the amount.'[2]

The following July, when Ibn Nami asked the three shaikhs to sign declarations of allegiance to Saudi Arabia, he ran into trouble, as he later explained to Ibn Jiluwi.

'We received a letter from Matar bin Salim al-Azizi, in which he complains and asks to be given similar sums to those granted to Bani Qitab and Al Bu Shamis. We sent him a certificate to be signed by him and al-Yahyayi and al-Wahshi. The said certificate was signed by the other shaikhs but not by him. He refuses to sign it until he is given equal terms to Bani Qitab's and Al Bu Shamis'.'[3]

Presumably the statements of al-Yahyayi and al-Wahshi arrived too late for inclusion in the *Memorial*.

What, in sum, does the evidence produced in the *Saudi Memorial* of the affiliation of the tribes of the disputed areas to Saudi Arabia amount to? It is, as has been seen, of three kinds:

    i. statements by the Governor of Hasa and his subordinates regarding tax-collecting and the exercise of criminal jurisdiction;

    ii. declarations of allegiance from tribal leaders and tribesmen; and

    iii. entries in the tax registers reproduced in Volume III of the *Memorial*.

It would not, perhaps, be thought uncharitable if, in view of his

---

[1] [Saudi Documents] Out-letter no. 591, dated 29 Sha'ban 1374. See also In-signal no. 3598, Ibn Jiluwi to Ibn Nami, 24 Jumada II, 1374/17 February 1955: 'Pay Rashid bin Hamad Rs 1,300 for onward payment to Hamad al-Wahshi as a supplement to the Rs 700 already paid to him, and pay Rashid bin Hamad Rs 2,000 for onward payment to Matar al-Azizi by a secret manner. None should be acquainted with this payment.'

[2] [Saudi Documents] Out-signal no. 557, dated 16 Sha'ban 1374.

[3] [Saudi Documents] Out-signal (unnumbered), Ibn Nami to Ibn Jiluwi, 15 Dhu'l-Qa'dah 1374/5 July 1955.

The Saudi Memorial of 1955

involvement in the campaign of subversion carried on in the Buraimi region in 1954-5, one were to regard Ibn Jiluwi's testimony with scepticism. His statements, moreover, are unsupported by any substantial documentary evidence (the entries in the tax registers hardly qualify as such), and they are marked by irrelevancies and inaccuracies. The declarations of allegiance fall into two categories: those obtained by Turki ibn Utaishan in the autumn of 1952, and those obtained later, mostly in April and June 1955. Little reliance seems to be placed by the *Memorial*'s authors on the first collection. Normally it is invoked only when no later statements apparently were available. The contents of all the 1952 declarations is similar: the signatories simply express their delight at Turki's arrival and at the prospect of the extension of Saudi rule over them. Since most of the signatories came from areas outside those which were later to be made the subject of arbitration, their declarations are valueless.

Many, if not most, of the 1955 declarations are worthless for the same reason. Others can be dismissed because they are not what they are said to be. The only relevant statements in the *Memorial* from tribal leaders and others normally resident in the disputed areas are these:

Manasir: Sa'id ibn Mubarak (Annex 99)
          Nasir ibn Sa'id ibn Suwaid (Annex 100);
Awamir: Ali Aba al-Rus al-Dhu'ayyif (Annex 102)
          Salim ibn Rakkadh (Annex 101);
Na'im: Rashid ibn Hamad (Annex 106)
          Saqr ibn Sultan (Annex 107);
Dhawahir: Sa'id and Shabib ibn Muhammad Al Hilal (Annexes 128 and 132)
          Sa'id and Muhammad ibn Sultan Al Darmaki (Annexes 129 and 131).

All these declarations, with the possible exception of the first three, were obtained by bribery, and their contents dictated by Ibn Jiluwi or one of his subordinates. Neither the statement of Sa'id ibn Mubarak of the Al Bu Rahmah section of the Manasir nor that of Ali Aba al-Rus of the Awamir is a declaration of allegiance. They relate only to *zakat*-collecting and the administration of justice by Saudi officials. Since both men made their statements on 9 April 1955 at Dammam, where, presumably, they had every opportunity to affirm their loyalty in writing to Saudi Arabia, their failure to give explicit declarations of this nature must be taken as evidence that they did not consider themselves Saudi subjects.[1] The statement of Nasir ibn Sa'id ibn Suwaid, another Al Bu Rahmah shaikh, which was made before Ibn Jiluwi at Dammam on 13 June 1955, is, in contrast, an explicit declaration of this kind. Its value as evidence of the adherence of the Manasir as a whole to Saudi Arabia can only be tested by setting it against the declarations of allegiance to the Ruler of Abu Dhabi by Muhammad ibn Khadim, the principal shaikh of the Al Bu Sha'ar section, and Amir ibn Mubarak, the paramount shaikh of the Al Bu Khail, and similar declarations by tribesmen of the Al Bu Rahmah, Al Bu Sha'ar and Al Bu Mundhir sections, printed in the *United Kingdom Memorial*.[2]

The value of the other statements, even if it had not been vitiated by the fact of their having been obtained by bribery, might be tested in the same way. Against the declaration of Ibn Rakkadh, the ex-*tamimah* of the Awamir, might be set that of Ibn Hamm, the present *tamimah* of the bulk of the tribe, made in September 1952 and pledging allegiance to the Ruler of Abu Dhabi. Against the statements of the four minor Dhahiri shaikhs might be set the declarations of allegiance to the Al Bu Falah of the principal shaikhs of the tribe, Sultan ibn Surur and Mani' ibn Muhammad, made in March 1954. As for Saqr ibn Sultan and Rashid ibn Hamad, they had solemnly pledged their allegiance in writing to the Sultan Sa'id ibn Taimur in July 1948. All these declarations, it might be noted, had been given before the arbitration agreement of 30 July 1954 apparently put a premium upon written affirmations of loyalty.

More than anything else, however, the authors of the *Saudi Memorial* have been unable to demonstrate that the overwhelming majority of the Bani Yas, the most numerous tribe inhabiting the western areas, owe loyalty to anyone other than the Ruler of Abu Dhabi. Nor have they been able to prove that the traditional loyalty of the other tribes of the disputed areas is to the Al Sa'ud. It remains to be seen whether the other ground upon which they base their contention that Saudi Arabia has exercised jurisdiction over these areas in this century, viz., the collection of *zakat* in them, has any more substance to it.

*

---

[1] Sa'id ibn Mubarak, in fact, is a close adherent of Shaikh Zaid ibn Sultan.
[2] See Vol. II, Annex I, no. 5.

The Saudi Memorial of 1955

ZAKAT

The arguments of the *Memorial*'s authors with respect to *zakat* and its collection in the disputed areas are set forth at various places in Volume I, Chapter IV, 'Historical Background', and Chapter VI, 'Legal Submissions', and in Volume II, Appendix B. They are designed to prove two things: that Saudi Arabia has regularly and systematically collected *zakat* from the tribes in the disputed areas in this century; and that the *zakat* collected is, in the authors' words, 'true Islamic *zakah*', the payment of which by the tribes is an acknowledgement of Saudi Arabia's position as the territorial sovereign in these areas. In support of the first contention the authors offer the tax registers which constitute Volume III of the *Memorial*, and in support of the second, a legal opinion by a Muslim jurist and opinions of their own.

1. *The Saudi Tax Registers*

The tax registers from the office of the Governor of Hasa which constitute Volume III cover the years A.H. 1354 to 1370, i.e. from A.D. 1935–6 to 1950–1, with the exception of the year A.H. 1357 (1938–9). Though described as the tax registers of the Murrah and the Manasir, they are, in fact, mainly taken up with taxes collected from the former tribe. The authors say of them:

'It should be reiterated that these tax registers are simple records, mere jottings that note, for the sake of formality, what might almost be called facts of public knowledge. They are usually kept by men in whom piety and faith outweigh the exacting procedures of book-keeping. Thus, individuality of style and vagueness of notation are the rule rather than the exception, particularly in the earlier tax registers. The registers should be studied in the context of traditional Bedouin culture which they reflect. Minor inaccuracies in reckoning and nomenclature do not detract from their status as *bona fide* records of an effective exercise of the taxing power in areas where no other Government has been able to act with authority.'[1]

Elsewhere they remark:

'Occasional errors in the figures indicate that not all payments actually made were entered in the registers, but were cleared on the basis of the field notes; while the unfamiliarity of urban clerks with

[1] *Saudi Memorial*, II, Appendix B, 326–7.

The Saudi Memorial of 1955

the Bedouin tribes concerned led to some vagueness and confusion regarding tribal affiliations and places of collection.'[1]

Since tribal affiliations and places of collection form such a vital part of the Saudi Government's case, one might be forgiven for asking what is the point of reproducing, at such length, records marked by 'some vagueness and confusion' on these matters. However, the general contention that the registers are evidence of 'an effective exercise of the taxing power in areas where no other Government has been able to act with authority' is not questioned—because the registers relate almost wholly to undisputed Saudi territory.

It is casually remarked by the *Memorial*'s authors at one point that 'a number of places named do not lie in the disputed areas, but in unchallenged Saudi territory to the north and west'.[2] The fact of the matter is, as the most cursory examination of the registers would show, that over 90 per cent of their pages relate to taxes collected well within Saudi Arabia proper. The total number of pages in the registers is 624. Of these, 380 pages list taxes collected from the Murrah, long recognized as a Saudi tribe, at various places in undisputed Saudi territory. Nearly another 200 pages list taxes collected from Murrah, Manasir and other tribes at such places in undisputed Saudi territory as al-Bahath, Sa'qah, Shaj'ah, al-Thumailah, al-Ba'al, and even Wari'ah, on TAPLINE, in northern Arabia. The authors of the *Memorial* refer in the text to only 109 pages out of the 624 in Volume III.[3] Some of these pages, however, are referred to two or three times, so that the true number of pages cited is 79. Of these 79, 20 again are taken up with taxes collected well within undisputed Saudi territory, and a further five pages do not specify the places of collection. They would appear, however, from the place-names that precede and follow them in the registers concerned, to lie also in undisputed Saudi territory. In the end, one is left with only 54 pages out of the 624, or about 8 per cent of the whole, which are relevant to the issue of Saudi tax-collecting in the disputed areas.

Twenty-eight of these 54 pages, scattered through Volume III, list taxes collected by Saudi *amils* from groups of Murrah, Awamir and Mazari' Bani Yas, mainly at the base of the Qatar peninsula, in the spring of 1936, 1937, 1939–41, 1944 and 1948. Most of the collections were made at the western foot of the peninsula, usually at al-Uraiq,

---

[1] *Saudi Memorial*, I, Chapter VI, para. 42.
[2] Vol. I, Chapter VI, para. 44.
[3] See Vol. I, Chapter III, paras. 28, 60 and 64, and Chapter VI, paras. 43–45.

The Saudi Memorial of 1955

which lies a few miles from the Saudi frontier post at Salwah. Some collections were made in undisputed Qatar territory, notably at al-Huriyah. One collection only was made at the eastern foot of the peninsula, at Uqlat al-Rimth, which lies at the northern end of the frontier claimed by Abu Dhabi in 1952. The remaining 26 relevant pages in the registers list taxes collected from small groups of Manasir, Awamir and Mazari' tribesmen in the Dhafrah, viz., in the Liwa Oasis in the spring of 1941, at its western end in the spring of 1951, and in the western Bainunah, at the group of wells around al-Aqaila, in the spring of 1937, 1940, 1944, 1945, 1948 and 1951.

What the authors of the *Memorial* are arguing, therefore, is:

i. that the collection of *zakat* in the vicinity of Salwah from groups of tribesmen from the disputed areas on seven occasions between 1935 and 1951 is proof of the continual exercise of jurisdiction by Saudi Arabia over the whole area at the base of the Qatar peninsula in this century; and

ii. that the collection of *zakat* from groups of tribesmen twice in the Liwa Oasis and seven times in the Bainunah in the same period is proof of a similar exercise of jurisdiction over the western areas, from Qatar to Buraimi, in this century.

Neither argument can be called very convincing.

As remarked earlier, no tangible evidence is offered in the *Memorial* of the collection of *zakat* in the Buraimi Oasis, apart from the visits of Saudi *amils* to the oasis between 1925 and 1929. The assertions of Saqr ibn Sultan and Rashid ibn Hamad, contained in their declarations of allegiance to Saudi Arabia, that they have regularly paid *zakat* to Saudi collectors in the past, must therefore be treated with scepticism.[1]

2. The Nature of 'Zakat'

The submissions of the *Memorial*'s authors with respect to Islamic *zakat*, which, they say, has been collected by Saudi Arabia in the disputed areas in this century, may be summarized as follows:

i. that the *zakat* is a property tax, enjoined by the Koran, and collected by the Saudi Government in their capacity as a true Islamic government;

---

[1] See *Saudi Memorial*, II, Annexes 106-7. The authors state (I, Chapter VI, para. 43) that Volume III contains entries of tax payments by 'members of the ... Nu'aim'. But these entries, it is clear from the registers concerned, relate to taxes collected in Hasa or Qatar, indicating that the Na'im involved belonged to the northern branch of the tribe, resident in Qatar and Hasa, and not to the southern branch found in and beyond the Buraimi Oasis.

The Saudi Memorial of 1955

ii. that the *zakat* is a tax imposed by the ruler, implying on his part an assertion of temporal sovereignty, and on the part of those who pay it, secular as well as religious allegiance;

iii. that the payment of *zakat* places the taxpayer under the protection of the collector; and

iv. that the *zakat* levied by the precursors of the present régime in Saudi Arabia upon the littoral principalities of Eastern Arabia in the nineteenth century was simply political tribute and not the 'true *zakat*' prescribed by the *Shari'ah*, which is levied in Saudi Arabia today.[1]

Little support can be found for the first three contentions in Islamic law in general, and in the Hanbali rite, which is officially recognized in Saudi Arabia, in particular.[2] The *zakat* of the Koran and the *Shari'ah* is not, strictly speaking, a property tax. More correctly it may be described as an 'alms tax'. Its payment is held to constitute an act of devotion, not an acknowledgement of secular and religious allegiance to a government. Its collection cannot be interpreted as an assertion of temporal sovereignty, even by a 'true Islamic government'. On the contrary, the payment of *zakat* is enjoined upon Muslims as a religious duty, whether the government is a true Islamic government or not.[3] The question of political loyalty, in fact, does not arise, as is illustrated by the fact that, throughout Islamic history, rulers and pretenders have sent forth agents to collect *zakat* in areas far beyond those in which they had established an effective administration. There is no justification in the Hanbali school of Islamic law for the authors' third proposition, viz., that the payment of *zakat* places the taxpayer under the protection of the collector.[4] Their final propositions concerning the *zakat* levied by former Saudi rulers on the littoral states of Eastern Arabia a century ago and the *zakat* collected in Saudi Arabia today are also untenable.[5]

A further argument is offered by the authors on the subject of 'true *zakat*' and its significance to the issue of sovereignty on the basis of a contention put forward by the Saudi delegation to the Dammam conference in 1952.[6] Aware that the *zakat* collected by Saudi Arabia

---

[1] See *Saudi Memorial*, I, Chapter VI, paras. 26 and 37–48, and II, Appendix B.

[2] A detailed examination of the submissions on *zakat* in the *Saudi Memorial* forms Appendix B, below.

[3] See below, Appendix B.   [4] See below, Appendix B.

[5] See above, pp. 76–9, and below, Appendix B.

[6] See above, p. 156, and *Saudi Memorial*, I, 495–6 and 516.

The Saudi Memorial of 1955

in the disputed areas in this century has been taken on livestock only, and never on crops, they argue that only camel-*zakat* is 'true *zakat*', as prescribed by the *Shari'ah*, and that the date-*zakat* collected by the Shaikh of Abu Dhabi at Liwa, for instance, is merely a gift from tribesmen. It is not a valid argument. The Saudi Government's own proclamation on *zakat* of 9 September 1925 (20 Safar 1344), which is reprinted in the *Memorial*, contains the statement: 'The *zakah* shall (be paid) on all grains and on all fruits which are measured and stored, such as dates. . . .'[1] The authors themselves state elsewhere in the *Memorial* that the reason why Saudi *amils* did not collect date-*zakat* in the disputed areas was because of the difficulty of transporting it to Hasa.[2] In yet another place they say: 'Dates from Buraimi . . . were not of great interest to collectors from Hasa; and insistence on a money equivalent would often have worked hardship on taxpayers not rich in coin.'[3] Commendable sentiments, but they did not prevent the Saudi *amils* who visited Buraimi from 1925 to 1929 from taking camel-*zakat* from tribesmen in the vicinity of the oasis in cash. What the authors overlook is that the only Trucial Shaikhdoms in which it is customary for *zakat* to be taken on livestock are Ras al-Khaima, Sharjah and Fujairah. In the first two, it may be added, the shaikhs of major tribes, like the Khawatir and Bani Qitab, have the right to collect *zakat* from their tribesmen wherever they may be, thus showing that its collection has no territorial significance. In the other Trucial Shaikhdoms *zakat* is traditionally taken only on dates. Saudi Arabia has never been able to collect date-*zakat* in the only places in the disputed areas where dates are grown, viz., the Liwa and Buraimi Oases.

Neither from the tax registers nor from their own arguments concerning the nature of *zakat* have the authors been able to show that the sporadic collections of *zakat* from tribesmen in the disputed areas by Saudi Arabia after 1925 have any significance in the determination of sovereignty in these areas. If this *zakat* was, as the authors contend it was, the classical *zakat* of the *Shari'ah*, then its collection cannot be held to constitute an assertion of temporal sovereignty on the part of Saudi Arabia or an acknowledgement of secular and religious allegiance on the part of those who paid it. Conversely, if the tax collected by Saudi Arabia under the name of *zakat* is, as the authors also contend it is, 'a true tax, leviable only by a sovereign and due

[1] Vol. II, Appendix B. [2] See Vol. I, Chapter VI, para. 45.
[3] Vol. I, Chapter VI, para. 46.

The Saudi Memorial of 1955

from the individual subject',[1] then it cannot be classical *zakat*. If it is a normal state tax, the payment of which, in the words of the authors, 'amounts to a recognition of Saudi Arabia as the territorial sovereign',[2] then it would have to be shown that those inhabitants of the disputed areas who have occasionally paid *zakat* to Saudi *amils* understood it as such. Not one iota of evidence to this effect is offered in the three volumes of the *Memorial*.

The true nature of this so-called '*zakat*' is most likely that of payments made by Baduin to a ruler in whose territory they customarily spend part of the year for grazing purposes and whose protection they enjoy for that period. Such is the case with Baduin from Kuwait and Qatar who spend part of the year in Saudi Arabia. Such, too, is the case with those Manasir, Mazari' and other tribesmen from the disputed areas who regularly avail themselves of grazing in Hasa. The Manasir concerned, as has been seen, are mainly from the Al Bu Mundhir section, most of whom have migrated to Saudi Arabia in the last thirty to forty years. The other principal Manasir sections, the Al Bu Rahmah and Al Bu Sha'ar, usually graze their herds in the Ramlat al-Hamra and Khatam. They have rarely been known to pay *zakat* to Saudi *amils*, and then only when their wanderings in search of pasturage took them to the Qatar peninsula and beyond, and brought them within reach of Ibn Jiluwi's collectors. The Mazari' normally graze their herds in the western Bainunah but they sometimes wander as far as the foot of Qatar or to Hasa, where they find it expedient to pay taxes to any Saudi *amils* whom they may encounter. The fact that *zakat* has sometimes been collected from these tribesmen in the Bainunah is of no more significance than the fact that it has been collected at times from tribes of similar nomadic habits within the Qatar peninsula. It simply depended upon where the tribesmen were in the spring, when the Saudi *amils* made their collections, and upon the zeal and energy of the *amils*.

If any further proof is needed that the '*zakat*' collected in the disputed areas by Saudi Arabia was little more than an exaction by a strong neighbour, backed by an implicit threat of force, it may be found in the toleration shown by the Rulers of Kuwait, Qatar and Abu Dhabi towards the visits of Saudi *amils* to their territories in the past forty years. The excuse usually made by the *amils* for crossing into the territories of these rulers was that they were following Saudi

---

[1] *Saudi Memorial*, I, Chapter VI, para. 38.
[2] *Saudi Memorial*, I, Chapter VI, para. 47.

The Saudi Memorial *of 1955*

tribesmen. As often as not, however, they did not scruple to tax any other tribesmen that they came across, whoever their ruler might be. It was no more suggested at the time that the *amils* were not trespassing on non-Saudi territory than it has been of late years, when Saudi *amils* have made collections deep inside Qatar. In 1949, for instance, they collected *zakat* in the Qatar Petroleum Company's camp at Dukhan, and the following year they pursued some Murrah as far north as Zubarah, near the tip of the peninsula. Yet Saudi Arabia has not laid claim, on the basis of these or similar visits, to central and northern Qatar.

THE HISTORY OF THE DISPUTED REGION

In the introduction to the *Memorial* the authors draw particular attention to Chapter IV, 'Historical Background relating to the Disputed Areas, 1765–1955'. '. . . It is based', they say, 'on extensive original research among both Arabic and Western sources, and it corrects many misapprehensions to be found in standard published works by even the best Western writers.' Chief among the 'misapprehensions' corrected by Chapter IV would seem to be that concerning the aggressive and expansionist character of Saudi rule in Arabia in the past century and a half. 'This history', say the authors at one point in the chapter, 'has shown that aggression against Arab neighbors has never been the policy of the Saudi Government, as, God willing, it never will be.'[1] They close the chapter with an equally pious declaration:

'Saudi Arabia in claiming the areas in dispute is seeking no new accession of territory; its claims are based on the fact that these areas and their inhabitants have been Saudi for 150 years and are Saudi today. These people, imbued with a strong sense of inherited loyalty to the House of Sa'ud, look to Saudi Arabia in 1955 as their best hope for Islamic unity, Arab solidarity, and freedom from foreign tutelage.'[2]

It is a measure of the authors' ingenuity that they have been able to rewrite the history of south-eastern Arabia over the past 160 years so as to fit these propositions. For the most part they have relied upon British sources, in particular, J. G. Lorimer's *Gazetteer of the Persian Gulf, 'Omān, and Central Arabia*. To a lesser extent they have

---
[1] *Saudi Memorial*, I, Chapter IV, para. 217.
[2] *Saudi Memorial*, I, Chapter IV, para. 385.

The Saudi Memorial of 1955

drawn upon published and unpublished Arabic sources. While these are used without reservation, the British sources are praised or damned according to whether or not they provide information useful to the Saudi case. Lorimer, in particular, suffers in this respect. He is, for example, cited with approval in paragraph 308 of Chapter IV for stating that the Buraimi Oasis in 1908 lay in territory 'which may be described as Independent 'Omān'; yet only a paragraph earlier he is vilified for saying that the Dhafrah lay within the Shaikhdom of Abu Dhabi. Unreliable though the authors consider him to be, however, they cite him no fewer than 160 times in Chapter IV.

A good half of the 285 pages covered by Chapter IV—which in itself constitutes over half of the text of the *Memorial*—is taken up with accounts of events unconnected with the question of sovereignty in the disputed areas. For example, 24 pages are devoted to panegyrics upon past Saudi rulers, 13 to Anglo-French relations with Muscat during the Revolutionary and Napoleonic Wars, 21 to animadversions upon the characters of various Al Bu Saʻid and Al Bu Falah rulers, and 16 to events in Muscat and Oman in the early years of this century. Over half of the last 47 pages of the chapter, covering the years 1920-55, are given over to the family quarrels of the Al Bu Falah, to oil exploration in south-eastern Arabia before 1939, and, more especially, to the failings of successive Sultans of Muscat. Indeed, so much space is devoted to this last topic that one is led to wonder whether the authors are not less concerned to prove Saudi Arabia's historical title to the disputed areas than to provide an apologia for the overthrow of the established government of the Sultanate. The purpose behind all these digressions is fairly clear: whenever historical evidence to support Saudi Arabia's case is lacking, or when the proper use of available evidence would result in disclosures embarrassing to that case, the reader's attention is to be diverted from the central issue. In general, these diversions take the form of eulogies of the Saudi Amirs or of rancorous attacks upon the rulers of Abu Dhabi and Muscat and the British Government. Towards the Al Saʻud the authors manifest an almost servile reverence, while to the Al Bu Falah, the Al Bu Saʻid and the British they accord only contempt and contumely. The poverty and relative smallness of Abu Dhabi, in contrast to Saudi Arabia, is constantly harped upon, and the doctrine of 'might is right' is propagated with great fervour throughout.

Where the authors stick to the subject they concentrate upon events

The Saudi Memorial of 1955

in and around the Buraimi Oasis, and touch only lightly upon the history of the western areas in dispute. Their principal contentions may be summarized as follows:

i. that after the initial peaceful adherence of the Buraimi Oasis and its adjacent districts to the Saudi state at the close of the eighteenth century the region was administered, except for a few brief intervals, as an integral part of that state until 1873, throughout which time the Saudi Amir enjoyed the loyalty of the tribes of the region; and

ii. that after 1873 neither the Shaikh of Abu Dhabi nor the Sultan of Muscat obtained or held any authority in the disputed areas, the inhabitants of which remained steadfastly loyal to the Al Sa'ud.

For some of their more striking assertions, particularly those concerning the alleged continuance of Saudi authority in the Buraimi region after 1873, the authors cite a work entitled '*Uqud al-Juman fi Ayyam Al Sa'ud fi 'Uman*, or 'The Pearl Necklaces: in the Days of the House of Sa'ud in Oman'. This is described by the authors as:

'... the manuscript history of the Buraimi region ... written by a contemporary scholar resident in one of the shaikhdoms now under British protection. The author, besides drawing upon his own extensive knowledge of the region and making use of unpublished documents and rare Arabic works, has performed a useful service by assembling information derived from current oral tradition.'[1]

It is legitimate to doubt whether an inaccessible manuscript by an anonymous author is acceptable evidence in a controversial question, especially as the testimony it offers, in many instances, is uncorroborated by any other source. None of the 'unpublished documents' or 'rare Arabic works' is cited by name by the *Memorial*'s authors, who were, apparently, the only persons privileged to see this manuscript. As for 'current oral tradition' in the Buraimi region, its reliability is doubtful after the large infusions of Saudi money into the area. All in all, when coupled with the fact that the manuscript was written in 1955, the year of the arbitration, it would seem that the 'necklace' may well be strung with cultured pearls.

It is not proposed in the following pages to examine all the relevant submissions put forward in Chapter IV of the *Memorial*. Several of them have been commented upon already,[2] and the validity of the remainder can usually be determined by consulting the sources from which they are said to be derived. Instead, it has been thought

---
[1] *Saudi Memorial*, II, Appendix D.
[2] See above, Chapters II and III.

The Saudi Memorial of 1955

sufficient, by drawing attention to some of the more debatable passages in the chapter, to indicate its general character.

Writing of the first Wahhabi occupation of Buraimi, the authors state (paragraph 20):

'In 1793 and 1794 Ibrahim ibn Sulaiman ibn 'Ufaisan, one of the high officials of the Saudi State, was active in the Qatar peninsula. The people of Oman now requested the Imam 'Abd al-'Aziz to take their country within the fold of the new Reformation. In response, the Saudi Government sent Ibn 'Ufaisan to be its representative in Oman with headquarters at Buraimi, and he took up his duties as first Saudi Amir there in 1795. His journey overland through al-Dhafrah to his new post is commemorated in the name Jazayir Ibn 'Ufaisan borne by a place in Sabkhat Matti along the route. During his stay in Buraimi, he built the fort called Qasr al-Subarah midway between Buraimi Town and the town of Hamasa.'

The sole authority given for this passage is the mysterious '*Uqud al-Juman* just described. All reputable authorities for the history of south-eastern Arabia agree that the Wahhabis never reached Buraimi before 1800. Ibn Bishr, the historian of the Al Sa'ud, who is cited frequently by the authors, makes no mention of Ibn Ufaisan's having been sent to Buraimi in his account of the year 1795 (A.H. 1209–10). Nor does he refer to the Saudis in connexion with Buraimi in his account of the years 1795–1800.[1]

The circumstances of the Wahhabis' arrival at Buraimi are portrayed more accurately in this passage, concerning the year 1800, from Badger's translation of Salil ibn Raziq's *Imâms and Seyyids of 'Omân* (p. 230):

'Nevertheless 'Abdu-'l-Azïz sent el-Harîk, one of his Nubian slaves, to 'Omân with a force of seven hundred cavalry, and he waged war upon the Benu-Yâs until they submitted to him. He then attacked the Benu-Nâ'îm and Kutb [Qitab] in conjunction with the Benu-Yâs, and reduced them also. Moreover, the ezh-Zhawâhir [Dhawahir] and esh-Shawâmis [Al Bu Shamis] and all the Hadhr of ezh-Zhâhirah [Dhahirah] eventually yielded to him. He took up his residence at Tawwâm [Buraimi], and levied whatever amount of *Zakâh* he chose from the people.'

This same passage from Badger is rendered by the authors of the *Memorial* in paragraph 27:

'At this time the Saudi Government sent Salim ibn Bilal al-Harq

[1] See *Unwan al-Majid fi Tarikh Najd*, I, 102–21.

The Saudi Memorial of 1955

to Buraimi as Amir. The tribes of Nu'aim, the Dhawahir, Bani Qitab, Bani Yas, and others in al-Dhahirah renewed their pledges of allegiance to the Saudi State, and the new Amir collected *zakah* from them.'

It might be added that a paragraph later the authors cite this same page of Badger to show that Wahhabi religious tracts were circulated in Oman in the early nineteenth century.

'One of the most popular of these was a book entitled *The Resolving of Doubts*, in which the founder of the movement himself expounded the principles he advocated. Specific mention is made of the circulation of this book in Oman at this time.'

'Popular' is not, perhaps, the right word. What Badger had to say was: 'The treatise contained a mass of incoherent sentences quite inconsistent with the truth, and no one took any notice of it.'[1]

It may be recalled that in their account of the tribes of the disputed region the *Memorial*'s authors claimed that the Manasir and the Dhawahir had been loyal to the Al Sa'ud for 150 years.[2] The claim is based upon the following passage in Chapter IV of the *Memorial* (paragraph 38), pertaining to the period 1800–10:

'The Saudi representative in Buraimi at this time was Muhammad ibn 'Abdan, a native of Hasa. Among his supporters the tribe of the Dhawahir of Buraimi and the tribe of the Manasir are named; the early adherence of both to the Saudi State is confirmed by this fact.'

This passage is supposedly derived from Badger's *Imâms and Seyyids*, pp. 274–81. These pages are an account of the civil war that raged through Oman after the death of Saiyid Sultan ibn Ahmad in 1804. The claim regarding the Dhawahir is made solely on the basis of this reference on p. 274: 'In consequence of this appeal, Hazzâa, al-Yâsy, came with two hundred auxiliaries of the ezh-Zhawâhir. Bedr-bin-Seif [of Muscat] also wrote to Ibn-'Abdan, el-Wahhâby, en-Nejdy, who brought the same number.'[3] It may as legitimately be deduced from this that the Dhawahir at that time were under the authority of Shaikh Hazza' of the Bani Yas as that they were under the command of the Wahhabis. The Manasir are referred to twice in Badger's *Imâms and Seyyids*, pp. 274–81, once (p. 280), when an Omani leader is described as having been reinforced

---
[1] *Imâms and Seyyids of 'Omân*, loc. cit.
[2] See above, p. 211, and *Saudi Memorial*, I, Chapter III, paras 32 and 77.
[3] The remaining references to the Dhawahir in these pages, viz., pp. 277, 279 and 281, show that they came under the command of various Omani leaders and not under that of the Wahhabis.

by 'a great many of the Wahhâbis, and also of the Benu-Yâs, the followers of Hazzâa, besides contingents from the el-Manâsir'; and again (p. 281), when the same leader is said to have attacked Bait al-Falaj, to the north of Muscat, 'with the ezh-Zhawâhir and the el-Manâsir'. It is equally legitimate to assume here that the Manasir might have accompanied Hazza' of the Bani Yas. Certainly, none of these references prove the 'early adherence . . . to the Saudi State' of the Dhawahir and the Manasir.

Ibn Bishr is used most inaccurately by the *Memorial*'s authors. For example, writing of the years 1811–12 they state (paragraph 56):

'A leading citizen of Hasa 'Abd al-Aziz ibn Ghardaqah, was appointed Amir of Buraimi as Mutlaq's successor. Trouble resulting from improper administration of the collection of *zakah* led to a revolt by some people of Bani Yas against the Saudi government. The rebels attacked and killed Ibn Ghardaqah on his way to Buraimi. In this affair the tribes of Nu'aim and the Dhawahir stood faithfully by the Saudis, enabling them to maintain their position at Buraimi despite the temporary misfortune which had befallen their cause.'

The sources from which this passage is said to be derived are Ibn Bishr, *Tarikh Najd*, I, 154, and the '*Uqud al-Juman*. Ibn Bishr says nothing whatever about 'trouble resulting from improper administration of the collection of *zakah*', and far from stating that the Na'im and Dhawahir 'stood faithfully by the Saudis', he does not even mention them. If these details come solely from the '*Uqud al-Juman* they are not worth taking seriously. Again, in describing the collection of *zakat* during the reign of the Amir Sa'ud ibn Abdul Aziz (1803–14), the *Memorial*'s authors write (paragraph 66):

'Ibn Bishr states specifically that the *zakah* was collected from the region of Oman, where Buraimi was the center for this and other activities of the Government. . . . Ibn Bishr states that the tax receipts delivered to the capital at al-Dir'iyah from Oman and other parts of the realm reached amounts beyond the capacity of any one to determine.'

The source of these statements is given as Ibn Bishr, I, 173. Ibn Bishr, however, makes no mention of Buraimi on this page. What he says is that the Saudi Amir sent out officials 'to collect the *zakat* on camels and sheep and goats from the Baduin of the Arabian peninsula, from beyond the two holy *harams*, Oman, the Yemen, Iraq and Syria, as well as the Baduin of Najd in between'. He adds: 'In addition to this the revenue that came to al-Dar'iyah from al-Qatif,

The Saudi Memorial of 1955

Bahrain, Oman, the Yemen, Tihamah, Hijaz and other places, and the *zakat* on the crops, commodities and gold and silver in Najd, was beyond count and had no limit.' If the authors of the *Memorial* intend, by citing this page of Ibn Bishr, to convey the impression that the collection of *zakat* from Oman a century and a half ago by the Saudi Amir confers upon Saudi Arabia today historical title to that country, or any part of it, then presumably the same would hold true for Syria, Iraq, Bahrain and the Yemen.

Most authorities are agreed that the second Wahhabi occupation of Buraimi began in 1833. This, however, is not good enough for the *Memorial*'s authors, who say in paragraph 104:

'In 1828 delegations composed of representatives of the people of Oman requested the [Saudi] Imam Turki to send them an Amir and a Qadhi to instruct them in the teachings of Islam. Turki appointed 'Umar ibn Muhammad ibn 'Ufaisan as the new Saudi Amir of Buraimi and Shaikh Muhammad ibn 'Abd al-'Aziz al-'Ausaji as the Qadhi. When these officials arrived, the people of the region came thronging in to greet them. It is significant that in this instance the authority of the Saudi State was re-established in Buraimi about two years before its re-establishment in the province of Hasa.... From this time on, Turki continued the practice of previous Saudi Rulers of sending Qadhis to Oman for tours of duty lasting a year or so.'

Ibn Bishr, II, 33 and 63, is cited as the origin of this passage. Ibn Bishr, however, tells a different story. Ibn Ufaisan, he relates, led an armed expedition to Oman in 1828-9 (A.H. 1244), and by July 1829 (Muharram 1245) he was back in Hasa, fighting in Turki's campaign to recapture that province.[1] Ibn Bishr says nothing to indicate that the Wahhabis remained in occupation of Buraimi after 1828-9. On the contrary, he relates that another expedition was dispatched to Oman in 1832-3 (A.H. 1248).[2] His statement (II, 63), cited by the authors, that *qadhis* were sent to Oman pertains to the year 1833-4 (A.H. 1249). The re-establishment claimed by the *Memorial*'s authors, of Wahhabi control over Buraimi, more than 500 miles to the east of Najd, two years before the re-conquest of Hasa, would have been not 'significant' but well-nigh incredible. One further remark might be made about this subject. In paragraph 108 the authors quote Lorimer's *Gazetteer of the Persian Gulf* (I, 688) to the effect that a

[1] *Tarikh Najd*, II, 38.
[2] *Tarikh Najd*, II, 44. It might be remarked that pp. 38 and 44 of Ibn Bishr are cited elsewhere by the authors of the *Memorial*.

The Saudi Memorial of 1955

large number of people in Oman 'sincerely rejoiced at the appearance of the Wahhābis'. It is a pity that the authors did not see fit to quote the rest of the sentence from which this is taken, viz., 'and Rashid-bin-Hamaid of 'Ajmān even applied for the post of Wahhābi vice-regent in the country, but received the chilling reply that the [Saudi] Amir regarded, and would continue to regard, the Saiyid of Masqat and the Shaikh of Sharjah as the two heads of the tribes of 'Omān'.

One of the more remarkable instances of historical re-interpretation in Chapter IV is the authors' account of the recovery of Buraimi by the Wahhabis in 1849, after they had been expelled from the oasis the previous year by a confederation of tribes led by Sa'id ibn Tahnun of Abu Dhabi. Paragraph 173 reads in part:

'Sa'd [ibn Mutlaq, the Wahhabi commander] escaped from the scene of his humiliation to the coast, where the chiefs and the people combined their forces to assist him in redeeming the lost position. So strong was the alliance supporting Sa'd that Sa'id ibn Tahnun saw the hopelessness of trying to maintain himself in Buraimi. Without a battle he agreed to the conclusion of peace in February 1849, by the terms of which "the Brymee (Buraimi) forts were restored to Syud bin Mootluk (Sa'd ibn Mutlaq), all that had passed was to be buried in oblivion, and all parties were to return to the *status quo ante bellum*".'

The quotation in the latter part of this passage is taken from *Bombay Selections XXIV*, p. 491, which is cited by the authors as their principal authority for the passage as a whole. *Bombay Selections XXIV*, p. 491, reads:

'He [Sa'id ibn Tahnun] fought and shamefully discomfited a considerable Nujdee [Najdi] force that was sent to annihilate him; he forced the proud and not unskilful Syud bin Mootluk to flee for protection to Sharjah; he showed himself ready to confront the combined forces of the Nujdee, Joasmee, Debaye, and Ejman Chiefs; he experienced but one reverse, and that but a slight one; when, finding he was not likely to receive the succours promised by the Muskat Government, he gave ear to the voice of a mediator, who had been sent by the Sherreeff of Mecca to conciliate the contending parties.'

By omitting all mention of the intervention of the Sharif of Mecca, the authors, like Sa'ad ibn Mutlaq, avoid the humiliation of admitting that the Wahhabis were incapable of recovering Buraimi by their own efforts. They also avoid the embarrassment of revealing that the Wahhabi Amir at this time was a dependant of the Sharif of Mecca.[1]

[1] See above, p. 73.

The Saudi Memorial of 1955

Indeed, scrupulous care is taken by the authors throughout the *Memorial* to omit any reference to the fact that past Saudi Amirs were Ottoman vassals, even though the Amirs themselves never hesitated to avow it.

The character of the various Wahhabi occupations of Buraimi is obscured or misrepresented by the *Memorial*'s authors by methods similar to those already indicated. For example, in paragraph 192, dealing with the career of Ahmad al-Sudairi, the Wahhabi commander at Buraimi after 1853, they quote the first half of a sentence from Lorimer's *Gazetteer* (I, 1114) to the effect that al-Sudairi 'appeared to be exerting himself to restrain the Shaikhs of Trucial 'Omān from mutual aggressions and to curb the license of the Bedouins'. The rest of the sentence reads: 'but in 1855 his activities took a mischievous turn, and it was found that he was scheming to obtain possession of the seaboard village of Hamrīyah'. Lorimer also relates on another page (I, 726), cited by the authors elsewhere:[1]

'In this project he [al-Sudairi] was opposed by the Na'im of Baraimi, one of whose chiefs, Fādhil-bin-Muhammad, had an interview with Captain Kemball [the Political Resident] at the coast in 1855, and suggested that British influence should be brought to bear for the expulsion of the Wahhābis....'[2]

It is essential to the authors' case that no hint should be allowed to drop that the Na'im were other than unswervingly loyal to the Al Sa'ud at all times. Their pursuit of this policy leads them to make some curious, and even ludicrous, remarks. Thus, in dealing with the expulsion of the Wahhabis from Buraimi in 1839, they studiously refrain from mentioning that the Na'im took the lead in effecting that expulsion, and remark instead: 'If they [the Na'im] could not be ruled by the House of Sa'ud, they preferred to rule themselves.'[3]

Even more unreal is their account of the ousting of the Wahhabis from Buraimi by Azzan ibn Qais in 1869. In an effort to diminish the fact that the Na'im called upon Azzan to end the Wahhabi occupation, they write (paragraph 225): 'One or two momentarily discontented chiefs may have approached 'Azzan, but the generality of the tribe remained loyal to the Saudi cause.' No evidence whatever is offered for this statement, which runs counter to all available information on the subject. Lorimer, the authors' most frequently

---

[1] *Saudi Memorial*, I, Chapter IV, para. 198.
[2] For this episode, see above, p. 82.
[3] *Saudi Memorial*, I, Chapt. IV, para. 139.

The Saudi Memorial of 1955

cited authority, states: 'After the murder of the Wahhābi agent in 'Omān, the Na'īm tribe of Baraimi, who had suffered much from his tyranny, were inclined to shake off the Wahhābi yoke altogether and applied to 'Azzān for his assistance.'[1] The authors also try to make out that the Na'im were opposed to Azzan's eventual successor, Turki ibn Sa'id, of the main Al Bu Sa'id line. In paragraph 229 they write: 'Turki ibn Sa'id returned to Oman and attempted to take Buraimi in September 1870. By this time Nu'aim had regained possession of all the forts in the oasis except one. Turki's siege was a complete failure.' The sources cited for these statements are Badger, *Imâms and Seyyids*, p. cxvii, and a report from the *Foreign Proceedings* of the Government of India for December 1870. What Badger actually wrote was this:

'... [Turki] crossed over stealthily to Bunder-Fakkan, *where he was met by a deputation from the Benu-Na'îm*, who for some time past had been in arms against 'Azzân-bin-Kais. Marching inland in September, by el-Fujairah and Wâdi-Hâm, he was reinforced by the Benu-Kutb and several of the el-Ya'arubah tribes, *and then joined the Benu-Na'îm at el-Bereimy*, all the forts of which, with the exception of the main one, were in their hands.'[2]

The report from *India Foreign Proceedings* is the same as that used in the account of these events given in the present work.[3] It makes clear that the main fort at Buraimi in September 1870 was in the hands of a garrison left behind by Azzan ibn Qais, and that Saiyid Turki and the Na'im were trying, in concert, to take it.

Five years after these events took place, it may be recalled, Colonel S. B. Miles visited Buraimi and reported of the Na'im: 'Since the time of Seyyid 'Azan, they have been practically uninterfered with by the Muscat Government, but of course owe allegiance to the present Sultan.'[4] Extracts from Miles's report are quoted by the *Memorial*'s authors in paragraph 248, with the comment: 'The information set forth by him on what he saw with his own eyes is naturally much more reliable than what he gathered by hearsay.' This does not apply, however, to what he had to say about the Na'im.

'The statement that Nu'aim of course owned allegiance to the

---

[1] *Gazetteer of P. Gulf*, I, 484. For other evidence on this episode, see above, p. 87.
[2] Badger, loc. cit. Italics added.
[3] See above, p. 89.   [4] See above, p. 95.

The Saudi Memorial of 1955

Sultan of Muscat, a mere assertion unsupported by any evidence, is what might be expected from a British official long in close association with the Sultan himself. The tribe, in fact, owned allegiance then, as it does now, to the House of Sa'ud.'

After 1870 the authors of the *Memorial* have little to offer in the way of evidence in support of Saudi Arabia's claim to historical title to the areas in dispute. As a consequence, they occupy themselves to a considerable extent with matters largely or wholly irrelevant to the issue of sovereignty. Where their arguments are relevant they are directed towards negative ends, viz.,

to show that neither the Shaikh of Abu Dhabi nor the Sultan of Muscat acquired or held any authority in the Buraimi Oasis after 1870;

to disprove the Shaikh of Abu Dhabi's title to Khaur al-Udaid; and

to deny him any historical rights to the western areas in dispute.

Little need be said of the authors' submissions with respect to the first of these propositions. They consist of passages such as this:

'Mahbub ibn Jauhar remained in Buraimi as the Saudi Amir until 1873, when disturbances in Najd made his withdrawal necessary. Before leaving, he worked out arrangements with the loyal chiefs of Nu'aim whereby they were deputed to officiate on behalf of the Saudi regime.'[1]

This assertion is made solely on the basis of the obscure '*Uqud al-Juman*. It cannot be checked, for the whereabouts of this 'manuscript history . . . by a contemporary scholar' is not disclosed by the *Memorial*'s authors. They have little to say about Zaid ibn Khalifah of Abu Dhabi. Rather are they bent, in their account of the last quarter of the nineteenth century, upon showing how narrowly circumscribed was the power of the Al Bu Sa'id in Oman at this time, and how it could not possibly have reached to Buraimi. Whatever the merits of this argument—the Al Bu Sa'id had, in fact, entrusted their interests in this quarter to the care of Zaid ibn Khalifah—it is more than a little incongruous, seeing that the Al Sa'ud could not even hold on to their homeland of Najd in these years.

[1] *Saudi Memorial*, I, Chapter IV, para. 240. For Mahbub ibn Jauhar, see above, p. 89.

The Saudi Memorial of 1955

The methods by which the authors attempt to disprove the Shaikh of Abu Dhabi's title to Khaur al-Udaid are the usual ones employed throughout the chapter. The sources cited are, in the main, those used in the account given in the present work of the attempts of Shaikh Jasim Al Thani of Qatar to wrest Khaur al-Udaid from Zaid ibn Khalifah.[1] Despite their endeavours, the authors have been unable to turn up any evidence that Khaur al-Udaid was ever under Saudi control, and they are reduced to making statements such as this (in paragraph 258): '. . . Qatar would claim al-'Udaid in the absence of a Saudi claim, and the temporarily weakened condition of the Saudi State at this time justified Qasim [Jasim] in taking this position.' The period referred to is that from 1881 onwards. Since Jasim Al Thani was, after 1876, Ottoman *qaim-maqam* of Dauhah, any claim that he might have made to Khaur al-Udaid would ultimately have been made, albeit vicariously, on behalf of the Ottoman Sultan. The authors explain in the text that their assertion is based upon a letter, dated 28 March 1955, from the then Ruler of Qatar, Shaikh Abdullah ibn Jasim Al Thani, to the Amir Ibn Jiluwi, which is printed as Annex 112 to the *Memorial*. The letter states:

'With reference to your enquiry concerning what we know of the status of al-'Udaid and its population, may God keep you, there is no doubt that all those who lived in al-'Udaid in the past were subjects of the Al Sa'ud, and that al-'Udaid belongs to Al Sa'ud.'

It is an unusual statement to come from a ruler who for years had been disputing the ownership of Khaur al-Udaid with the Shaikh of Abu Dhabi. It is not, however, the only unusual feature of Shaikh Abdullah's account of the history of the inlet.

'. . . The first who lived there were people called Bani Hammad and al-'Ubaidal who came from Najd and lived in (al-'Udaid) for a long time. . . . Afterwards they became afraid and departed and stayed on for a time in Qatar, from which they moved to the Persian side (of the Gulf). . . . After that they settled in al-Kubaisat, until a dispute arose between them and Khalifah Ibn Zayid, (when) they packed up and moved away and settled in al-'Udaid for a long time. They were subjects of Al Sa'ud, and Khalifah could not oppose them.'

The passage raises a number of questions. When did the Bani Hammad and Ubaidil first migrate to Khaur al-Udaid? How long did they stay there before moving to Qatar and then to the coast of

[1] See above, pp. 92–4. Cf. *Saudi Memorial*, I, Chapter IV, paras. 235, 236, 242 and 249–51.

The Saudi Memorial of 1955

Persia? Where is 'al-Kubaisat'? Could the name refer to the Qubaisat section of the Bani Yas who seceded to Khaur al-Udaid in 1836, and again thirty years later? If so, does this mean that the Bani Hammad and Ubaidil were transformed into the Qubaisat? Who was 'Khalifah Ibn Zayid'? Was he possibly Khalifah ibn Shakhbut of Abu Dhabi who compelled the Qubaisat in 1837 to abandon Khaur al-Udaid and return to Abu Dhabi? Or was he the son of Zaid ibn Khalifah who went to Qatar in 1880 and persuaded the Qubaisat to return to Abu Dhabi after their second secession to Khaur al-Udaid and their expulsion from there by Zaid ibn Khalifah in 1877? Seeing that the Qubaisat were compelled by both Khalifah ibn Shakhbut and Zaid ibn Khalifah to abandon Khaur al-Udaid, is it likely that they were really 'subjects of Al Sa'ud and Khalifah could not oppose them'?

Nowhere in Chapter IV do the authors attempt to make out a case for the attribution of the western areas in dispute to the Saudi state, either during the Wahhabi occupations of Buraimi up to 1869, or after that date. They confine themselves, instead, to denying that these areas historically form part of the Shaikhdom of Abu Dhabi. Their efforts at denial, however, are limited to an attack upon the accuracy of what Lorimer had to say about the Dhafrah and Liwa in the geographical volume of his *Gazetteer*, issued in 1908. In paragraph 307 they imply, on the sole authority of an article by Colonel F. F. Hunter, who prepared the map of Arabia to accompany the *Gazetteer*, that British officials in the Gulf were unaware of the existence of Liwa before the *Gazetteer* was compiled.[1] It is not an opinion that is supported by the facts. The existence of Liwa was known in the first half of the nineteenth century, and was even better known in the second half. For instance, Major Sidney Smith, the assistant Political Resident, reported in December 1870, after a visit to Abu Dhabi and the Arabian coast: 'When called upon regarding the outstanding claims of British subjects Sheikh Zaid "regretted that he could not enforce those that were against people who had left Aboothabi and settled in Liwah", although this town is within the Chief's own territory.'[2]

[1] See also Vol. I, Chapter II, para. 51: 'Al-Jiwa was completely unknown to the Western world until the first part of the twentieth century when the Acting British Political Resident in the Persian Gulf, Captain P. Z. Cox, learned of its existence through interrogation of a former inhabitant.'
[2] [I.O.] India For. Proc. (Pol.), Vol. 761, December 1871, no. 378, Smith to Pelly, 19 December 1870. For mention of Liwa in an 1848 report, see above, p. 72.

The Saudi Memorial of 1955

The scholarly caution employed by Lorimer in describing Liwa and the Dhafrah is seized upon by the *Memorial*'s authors as an excuse for calling the information that he gives 'extremely tentative and uncertain'. They also declare it to be untrustworthy because it was derived from British officials, like Sir Percy Cox, 'all of whom relied on native sources; in other words, none of them visited the region, their data being drawn from Arabs having some acquaintance with it'.[1] One is curious to know how much of the authors' description of Liwa in Chapter II, paragraphs 46–52, of the *Memorial*, which is not taken from Thesiger's reports, is based upon personal knowledge, and how much upon hearsay, culled from 'Arabs having some acquaintance with it'.

The reason for the authors' irritation with Lorimer emerges later in paragraph 307:

'The tendency of all this faulty information is to show that Bani Yas have a much closer connection than the Manasir with al-Dhafrah and the villages of al-Jiwa. . . . (All the tribes ignored by him are Saudi tribes.) Lorimer concludes the article on al-Dhafrah by saying that "the whole of it falls within the political sphere of the Shaikh of Abu Dhabi to whose principality it may accordingly be considered to belong". . . .'

If this is meant to imply that Lorimer was deliberately ignoring the presence of Saudi tribes in the Dhafrah in anticipation of a future Saudi claim to its sovereignty, then one can only say that he was acting with remarkable prescience. In contrast to the obloquy to which he is treated in paragraph 307, he is accorded praise in paragraph 308 for calling Buraimi 'a remarkable oasis in the district of Jau, in a tract situated between the 'Omān Sultanate and Trucial 'Omān which may be described as Independent 'Omān'. Lorimer is not quoted fully. In Volume II, p. 264, of his *Gazetteer*, a page cited also by the authors in paragraph 308, he writes:

'Baraimi is independent, but the influence of the Shaikh of Abu Dhabi is strong and increasing. . . . A regular tribute, of which the form and amount are mentioned in the article on the Abu Dhabi Principality, is paid him by the Dhawahir who are numerically a majority in the oasis.'

It might be added that the authors have also had recourse in paragraph 308 to Lorimer's article on Abu Dhabi, but they make no mention of the tribute from the Dhawahir.

[1] *Saudi Memorial*, I, Chapter IV, para. 307.

The Saudi Memorial of 1955

The authors' description of the disputed region in the period of the Second World War (paragraph 359) may serve as a final illustration of the general quality of their work.

'Under the aegis of Saudi rule, lightly but firmly exercised, security was guaranteed to all. Violations of the law, inevitable in any society, were punished by officials of the Saudi Government with despatch and certainty in a manner which may be considered remarkable indeed in view of the difficulty of travel through the region. Every year, as is shown by the documents in Volume III of this Memorial, the people of the region paid the fundamental tax of Islam, the *zakah*, to the collectors sent out by the Saudi administration. The chiefs of the various Saudi tribes, officiating by virtue of the authority conferred upon them by the Central Government, settled many of the local disputes and guided their followers in the observance of the precepts of Islam. More important cases were referred to the learned and highly respected Qadhi of Buraimi, Shaikh 'Abd Allah ibn 'Abd al-'Aziz Al Sulaiman, a native of the town of al-Hariq in Najd, who issued judgements in accordance with the Shari'ah as generally interpreted in the Saudi courts.'

It is a beguiling picture but hardly an accurate one. The *Saudi Memorial* has nothing to offer in the way of evidence of the punishment of 'violators of the law' in the disputed region by Saudi officials other than the statements of Ibn Jiluwi and his subordinates and questionable depositions obtained from a few tribesmen.[1] The tax registers in Volume III certainly do not prove that the people of the region paid *zakat* to Saudi collectors 'every year'. Nor is any proof offered in the *Memorial* that the chiefs of the tribes officiated 'by virtue of the authority conferred upon them by the Central Government'. One might well ask which tribes these were. Were the Bani Yas among them? Or the Manasir, Awamir and Al Bu Shamis? If so, it is strange, as remarked earlier, that the Saudi Government took no notice of their participation, on the side of the Al Bu Falah, in the Abu Dhabi-Dubai war of 1945–8. Nor did they complain about the use of Buraimi by Zaid and Hazza' ibn Sultan as their headquarters during this war.

As for Abdullah ibn Abdul Aziz Al Sulaiman, 'the learned and highly respected Qadhi of Buraimi', the principal activity in which he was engaged in these years was the attesting of false certificates of identity for kidnapped slaves destined for Saudi Arabia. As a young

[1] See above, pp. 213–4.

The Saudi Memorial of 1955

man Abdullah ibn Abdul Aziz had been a supporter of the Ibn Rashid in Najd, but on their overthrow he fled the country. After wandering for some years in Turkey, Persia, India and Oman (where he served for a time as a *qadi* among the Bani Bu Ali of Ja'alan), he settled finally at Hamasa in the Buraimi Oasis. According to the *Memorial*'s authors, 'a large number of merchants in the market of Hamasa hail from Najd'.[1] There were, in fact, five, and Thesiger has a little more information to offer about their activities in 1948. 'Now the only Saudis here were a few merchants engaged chiefly in the slave-trade, which still flourished in the two villages [Hamasa and Buraimi] not controlled by Zayid [ibn Sultan].'[2] Rashid ibn Hamad, the chief of Hamasa, was in partnership with two of the merchants, Abdullah ibn Ghurab and Abdullah ibn Ghanim, in the business of shipping slaves to Najd and Hasa. While Thesiger was in the oasis, a slave dealer from Hasa, Ali al-Murri, was in Hamasa, and he later left for Hasa with forty-eight slaves.[3] Rashid ibn Hamad had appointed Abdullah ibn Abdul Aziz Al Sulaiman a *qadi* for the purpose of issuing documents, giving false names to slaves kidnapped from the Trucial Coast, the Batinah and Baluchistan. When Turki ibn Utaishan arrived at Hamasa in 1952 he appointed Abdullah ibn Abdul Aziz Saudi *qadi* of Buraimi, and used him in his contacts with the local shaikhs. Abdullah himself, however, had only three years earlier acknowledged that he was a subject of the Sultan of Muscat, in a letter to the Sultan's Minister of the Interior in which he spoke of 'our lord, the Sultan' and of 'Oman, your country'.[4]

There is nothing in the remaining paragraphs of Chapter IV of the *Memorial* that call for remark. Nor, for that matter, do Chapter V, 'The Diplomatic Background, 1911–1954', and Chapter VI, 'Legal Submissions of Saudi Arabia', add anything of substance to the Saudi case. Chapter VII, the last in the *Memorial*, seems out of place in what is essentially a legal document for presentation to a judicial body. Entitled 'Other Considerations', it is at once a resentful condemnation of Britain's connexion with the littoral states of Eastern

---

[1] Vol. I, Chapter II, para. 64. 'A large number' becomes, seven paragraphs later, 'a small but influential group'.
[2] *Arabian Sands*, pp. 253–4.
[3] *Arabian Sands*, p. 263. Thesiger persuaded Rashid ibn Hamad to release two young Arabs from the Hadhramaut whom Ali al-Murri had bought.
[4] See *U.K. Memorial*, II, Annex F, no. 8.

The Saudi Memorial of 1955

Arabia and a peremptory assertion of Saudi Arabia's 'manifest destiny' to rule the whole of the Arabian peninsula.

It is reasonable to doubt whether the *Memorial* would have been of much help to the arbitration tribunal in arriving at a correct understanding either of the situation in the disputed areas in recent years or of their past history. Taken as a whole, the *Memorial* is little more than a *mille-feuilles* of fact and fiction, in which the fiction greatly exceeds the fact. Much of the material introduced in evidence is irrelevant, notably the tax registers which form Volume III of the *Memorial*, and the 'declarations of allegiance' from tribesmen living outside the disputed areas, which are reproduced in Volume II. Most of these tribesmen, it might be added, were illiterate, and could not have composed the formal statements to which they affixed their thumbprints. Many of the statements from inhabitants of the disputed areas are open to the same objection. Moreover, as the records of the Saudi police detachment at Buraimi clearly show, nearly all of them were obtained by bribery. Some are not what they are claimed to be, while others reveal from their contents that they were composed by outsiders. The arguments offered in the *Memorial* on the subject of Islamic *zakat*, its collection by Saudi Arabia in the disputed areas, and the relevance of these collections to the determination of sovereignty, are, to say the least, unconvincing.[1] As for the chapter on the history of the region, one can only conclude, after examining it closely, that not only are there serious omissions of fact but there has also been tampering with historical evidence. Like the *Memorial* as a whole, it is a sad monument of misdirected scholarship.

[1] See below, Appendix B.

Conclusion

Sir Anthony Eden's hope, expressed in his statement to the House of Commons on 26 October 1955, that the Saudi Government would in time come to look upon the modified Riyadh Line as an acceptable frontier, was doomed to disappointment. That very day the Saudi delegation to the United Nations replied to his statement with the accusation, already referred to,[1] that 'the sabotaging of the efforts of the international tribunal was a deliberate step taken by the Government of the United Kingdom to force the Buraimi issue to an armed conflict and not to settle it by peaceful means'.[2] Four days later the Saudi Government notified the United Nations of the frontier dispute, and reserved the right to bring it before the Security Council. On 9 November they approached the British Government with a proposal that arbitration proceedings be resumed, and a neutral commission be appointed to supervise affairs in the disputed areas. At the same time they tried to bring pressure to bear upon the British Government to accept the proposal. The Saudi Embassy in Cairo, in the second week of November, issued a statement that 82 persons had been killed or wounded in an armed clash in the Buraimi Oasis on 11 November, caused by British action on behalf of the Sultan of Muscat. '. . . The inhabitants of the oasis fought to the last bullet, after which they were forced to surrender.'[3] No such clash had ever taken place, and a few days later the Saudi Deputy Foreign Minister, who was in Cairo for a meeting of the political committee of the Arab League, retracted the statement, explaining with some embarrassment that it was supposed to refer to the events of 26 October.[4] At its meeting of 14 November the political

---
[1] Above, p. 207. [2] *The Times*, 27 October 1955.
[3] *The Times*, 14 November 1955, citing Saudi statement.
[4] *The Times*, 16 November 1955.

Conclusion

committee of the Arab League announced its support of Saudi Arabia's demand for a return to arbitration, and urged Britain to withdraw its troops from the disputed areas.[1] The following day the Saudi Ambassador in Cairo called at the Soviet Embassy to deliver King Sa'ud's reply to a message received from the Soviet President, Marshal Voroshilov, a few days previously. The reply was said to have expressed the King's appreciation of Russia's expression of support on the frontier issue and the offer of 'material and moral help'.[2]

The British reply to the Saudi proposal was made on 22 November. '... The Saudi Arabian Government have by their actions repudiated the arbitration agreement.... Her Majesty's Government cannot but regard the Saudi Government's proposals for a resumption of arbitration and the appointment of a neutral commission as unrealistic. The money distributed by the Saudi Government during the last three years cannot be taken back; nor can the bribery and intimidation of sheikhs and tribesmen be undone.'[3]

Stung by this answer, King Sa'ud publicly charged the British Government on 12 December, when he was on a visit to India, with having withdrawn from the arbitration because they found that they had a losing case. He himself, he declared, would continue to try to establish his right to the Buraimi Oasis by 'diplomatic means'.[4] Only a day earlier, however, a Saudi arms caravan, with a consignment of eighty rifles, had been intercepted on the outskirts of Buraimi.

'The caravan, which during an arduous desert journey of some 400 miles had been delayed by fever and camel sickness, left its jumping-off point in Saudi Arabian territory on October 25 and had no means of knowing that the Sultan of Muscat's authority had been reasserted in the oasis with the help of Trucial Oman levies late in October.'[5]

The rifles may well have been on their way to the Imam Ghalib ibn Ali.[6] If so, they would have arrived too late to be of any use to him, for the Sultan, Saiyid Sa'id ibn Taimur, was on the verge of bringing to an end both his connexions with the Saudis and his pretensions to independence. In the second week of December the Muscat

---

[1] *The Times*, 15 November 1955.   [2] *The Times*, 16 November 1955.
[3] *The Times*, 25 November 1955, citing contents of British Note of 22 November.
[4] *The Times*, 13 December 1955. See above, pp. 207–8.
[5] *The Times*, 12 December 1955.
[6] See James Morris, *Sultan in Oman*, London, 1957, p. 109.

Conclusion

and Oman Field Force moved against the Imam's stronghold, Nizwa, from Ibri in the west and from the Batinah Coast in the east. They captured Nizwa on 15 December without resistance. Ghalib escaped at midnight on the fourteenth by climbing down a rope at the rear of the great fort and fleeing into the mountains. On 19 December the Sultan himself set out from Salalah, the capital of Dhufar on the southern coast, for inner Oman. Five days later he reached Nizwa, where he received the submission of all the principal shaikhs of central Oman, including Sulaiman ibn Himyar of the Bani Riyam. Ghalib he later allowed to return to his home village of Sait. Talib, Ghalib's brother, hid for a time in the mountains, then made his way to Saudi Arabia.[1]

From Nizwa the Sultan proceeded by way of Ibri to Buraimi, arriving there on 28 December. He was joined the next day by Shaikh Shakhbut from Abu Dhabi. It was the first time that an Al Bu Sa'id and an Al Bu Falah ruler had met in the oasis since the meeting of Azzan ibn Qais with Zaid ibn Khalifah in 1870. Then, as in 1955, their meeting followed the recent expulsion of the Saudis from their territory. Not that the Saudis were ready to accept their expulsion gracefully. Throughout December 1955 and January 1956 the Saudi Government kept stating that they intended taking the frontier dispute to the Security Council, and it was not until the end of January that they showed evidence of a change of mind. On 31 January they issued a statement, taking note of a recently expressed desire on the part of the British Government to restore Anglo-Saudi relations to the friendly basis of previous years, and reciprocating that desire.[2]

The change of tone may well have been connected with Sir Anthony Eden's visit to Washington at that time for consultations with President Eisenhower, mainly about the situation in the Middle East. There was a conspicuous lack of support in Washington for Britain's action in helping the Shaikh of Abu Dhabi and Sultan of Muscat to re-assert their control over the Buraimi Oasis. Before Eden's arrival some of the Saudi documents captured at Buraimi had been shown to officials at the State Department, who were said to be inclined to 'smile a little superciliously' at them.[3] Not surprisingly, as Eden found, the disposition to criticize Britain and sympathize with Saudi

---

[1] For a lively account of these events see Morris, *Sultan in Oman*. See also *The Times*, 16, 17, 19 and 23 December 1955.
[2] See *The Times*, 1 February 1956.
[3] *The Observer*, 12 February 1956. See also *The Times*, 23 January 1956.

Conclusion

Arabia went hand in hand with a considerable misunderstanding of the nature of the frontier dispute. As Eden reported it:
'The President told us that we had to take account of world opinion. People in general, he maintained, were very ignorant about Muscat and Buraimi, and tended to think that the whole Arabian Peninsula belonged, or ought to belong, to King Saud. Naturally we contested this, which took no account of the continuous expansion of Saudi claims ever since 1935. It also ignored the Yemen and Muscat, the independent sheikhdoms in the Persian Gulf, and ourselves in Aden. It certainly showed the dangers of over-simplification.

'During the Suez crisis, I learnt that the United States Government had regarded our action during the autumn of 1955 in furthering the reoccupation of Buraimi by the Sultan of Muscat and the Sheikh of Abu Dhabi as an act of aggression. This opinion was expressed to two of our closest friends and allies, Australia and the Netherlands, but not to us. There was no warrant for any such charge. When our Dutch friends asked Mr. Dulles who had ever suggested that there was any aggression by the United Kingdom at Buraimi, Mr. Dulles replied, "Public opinion in Saudi Arabia." He left himself open to the Dutch rejoinder that there was no such thing.'[1]

The Washington talks ended on 1 February with the issuing of a joint communiqué, in which Eden announced his government's readiness to enter into direct discussions with Saudi Arabia to settle the frontier dispute. Privately, however, he had told President Eisenhower that he 'could not feel sanguine about the result, unless the United States Government put considerable pressure upon the Saudis'.[2] He had also informed him, as he told the House of Commons on his return, that 'her Majesty's Government, acting for the Sultan of Muscat and the Ruler of Abu Dhabi, could not return to arbitration after their experience of Saudi Arabian behaviour'.[3] Direct discussions between the British and Saudi Governments were opened in late February, and they continued at intervals for some time thereafter. From the lack of progress made it would appear that the pressure from the United States was not forthcoming. Whether it would have been effective there is no way of knowing, for it is not certain whether the Saudis seriously contemplated settling the

[1] *The Memoirs of Anthony Eden: Full Circle* (American edn.), Cambridge, Mass., 1960, p. 373.
[2] Ibid.
[3] Hansard, *Parl. Debates*, 5th series, H. of C., Vol. 548 (1955–6), 13 February 1956, col. 2083.

Conclusion

frontier dispute by negotiation. The following November they broke off diplomatic relations with Britain because of the Anglo-French intervention in Egypt in that month, and almost immediately resumed their former activities in south-eastern Arabia.

From the time of his defeat in 1955 the Imam Ghalib ibn Ali had been living in obscurity at Sait in central Oman. His confederates, on the other hand, had been most active. An 'Imamate Office' had been established in Cairo in 1955, and in 1956 it was placed in the charge of two brothers of Salih ibn Isa, *tamimah* of the Al Hirth and *amir* of the Sharqiyah, who, together with Sulaiman ibn Himyar, had sponsored Ghalib's election to the Imamate. In Cairo his brothers worked hard to project to the world at large, and to the Arab states in particular, the image of an independent Imamate of Oman, headed by Ghalib, which was threatened by the Sultan of Muscat and his British allies. At Dammam in Saudi Arabia, Ghalib's brother, Talib, recruited a 'Liberation Army' from Omanis who had gone north to work in the oil-fields of Hasa. Arms were smuggled into central Oman from Saudi Arabia in the first half of 1957, mainly through the port of Dubai on the Trucial Coast or on dhows which landed their cargoes at night on the Batinah Coast.[1] Members of the 'Liberation Army' began drifting back to Oman by the same routes in the spring. Talib himself landed secretly on the Batinah Coast in June, and made his way inland to the Jabal Kaur region where he was joined by his brother. Ghalib announced that he had once more assumed the active functions of Imam, and, supported by Talib's men, he re-occupied Nizwa. Revolt broke out in the high Oman against the Sultan in mid-July. Within a few days the white banner of the Ibadi *mutawwa'*, indicating support for the Imam, was flying at Firq, Izki, Bahla, Jabrin, Sait, Birkat al-Mauz, and Tanuf, high up in the Jabal Akhdar, the stronghold of Sulaiman ibn Himyar. Sulaiman, who had been well primed with Saudi gold, now ranged himself conspicuously on Ghalib's side.

Faced with a situation with which he could not cope alone, the Sultan called upon the British Government for aid. They agreed to give it for a number of reasons—the long-standing friendship with the Al Bu Sa'id, the need to re-assure the rulers of the Gulf states under British protection that subversion of legitimate governments from outside would not be tolerated, the security of British strategic and economic interests in the region, especially Petroleum Develop-

---

[1] See, e.g., *The Times*, 20 July 1957.

Conclusion

ment (Oman) Ltd.'s operations in the Oman steppes, and the urgent necessity to suppress a revolt, backed by outside interests, which, if allowed to spread, would undermine the stability and jeopardize the future progress of the Sultanate. Within three weeks from the date of British intervention the rebellion had been put down, Nizwa and the other towns had submitted to the Sultan, and Ghalib, Talib and Sulaiman had retreated to the remote heights of the Jabal Akhdhar. From there they kept up a running fight with the Sultan's forces and tribal supporters until January 1959, when a special detachment of British troops, supported by a Sultanate regiment, forced its way to the top of the Green Mountain and dislodged the insurgents from their eyrie. Ghalib, Talib and Sulaiman had, by this time, deserted their followers and slipped out of Oman, eventually to find refuge in Riyadh and Cairo.

On the surface, the fact that British intervention had again disrupted Saudi plans in south-eastern Arabia seemed hardly likely to improve the chances either of a resumption of Anglo-Saudi diplomatic relations or of a settlement of the frontier dispute. In reality, however, it had little effect on the situation, for the two governments were a long way from finding any common ground for a resolution of their differences. In the summer of 1957 the British Government had made a direct approach to the Saudi Government for a restoration of diplomatic relations, but the approach had been rejected on the grounds that the solidarity of the friendship existing between Saudi Arabia and Egypt would not permit of such a development until Britain had reached a settlement with Egypt.[1] This condition was dropped in April 1958 when the Amir Faisal, the Saudi Prime Minister, stated that his government were prepared to re-establish diplomatic relations provided that the frontier question was settled, either by arbitration or by a British withdrawal from the disputed areas.[2] The British Foreign Secretary, Mr. Selwyn Lloyd, rejected this condition in a statement to the House of Commons on 23 April. 'Our position', he said, 'is that problems like that of the Buraimi Oasis would be much better handled if we could restore diplomatic relations.'[3]

Since the close of 1955 the Saudis had been insisting that the arbitration was still in force, and the British, with equal insistence, had been saying that it was not. The British refusal to consider arbi-

[1] *The Times*, 24 April 1958.   [2] *The Times*, 21 April 1958.
[3] Hansard, *Parl. Debates*, 5th series, H. of C., Vol. 586 (1957–8), col. 934.

Conclusion

tration again as a means of solving the frontier problem was restated by Selwyn Lloyd in the House of Commons on 8 April 1959, when he declared that Britain could not accede to the repeated Saudi demand for a return to arbitration as a precondition for the resumption of diplomatic relations.[1] Further statements by members of the British Government in May and July of that year made it clear that the Sultan of Muscat and the Shaikh of Abu Dhabi were equally opposed to a renewal of arbitration. Not only that, but they also refused to allow the dispute to go to the International Court.[2] A much more serious difficulty, however, was that caused by an apparent Saudi belief that some territorial concession would be made by the British both to help settle the frontier dispute and to facilitate the resumption of diplomatic relations. To some extent the Saudis would seem to have been encouraged in this belief by the United States Government, who were reported in June 1957 to have urged the British Government to surrender the Buraimi Oasis to Saudi Arabia as a means of inducing the Saudis to co-operate in countering subversion in the Middle East. The diplomatic correspondent of *The Times*, in drawing attention to these reports, commented:

'The British Government are strongly opposed to any sacrifice of the rights of the States protected by Britain, and in any event have no right to surrender territory of theirs without their consent. Any proposal for a settlement of the oasis dispute and of the final frontier —to have any chance of success—would clearly require the most strong and explicit international guarantees.'[3]

The British attitude did not change. As the Marquess of Lansdowne, Joint Parliamentary Under-Secretary of State for Foreign Affairs, said in reply to a question in the House of Lords in July 1959, '... We cannot consider "buying back" ... our diplomatic relations by making concessions at other people's expense.'[4]

Informal talks were begun in New York in September 1959, in the presence of the then Secretary-General of the United Nations, Dag Hammarskjöld, between King Sa'ud's special representative, Abdur

---

[1] Hansard, *Parl. Debates*, 5th series, H. of C., Vol. 603 (1958–9), cols. 175–6.
[2] See Hansard, *Parl. Debates*, 5th series, H. of C., Vol. 605 (1958–9), col. 846, Statement by Minister of State for Foreign Affairs, 11 May 1959; and H. of L., Vol. CCXVII (1958–9), col. 1087, Statement by Joint Parliamentary Under-Secretary of State for Foreign Affairs, 13 July 1959.
[3] *The Times*, 8 June 1957.
[4] Hansard, *Parl. Debates*, 5th series, H. of L., Vol. CCXVII (1958–9), col. 1086, 13 July 1959.

Conclusion

Rahman Azzam, and the deputy head of the British mission to the United Nations, Harold Beeley. The talks went on intermittently until August 1960, when it was announced that the British and Saudi representatives had agreed that a personal representative of the Secretary-General should go to Buraimi on a fact-finding mission. He was to be especially charged with investigating the question of the shaikhs who had been Saudi supporters before 1955 and who had removed to Saudi Arabia on the re-assertion of control over the oasis by Muscat and Abu Dhabi in October of that year.[1] The representative chosen by Hammarskjöld was Herbert de Ribbing, Swedish Ambassador to Spain. He left for Buraimi in the middle of September, stopping at Riyadh on the way for discussions with King Sa'ud. After four days spent in the disputed areas, and after conversations with the rulers of Muscat and Abu Dhabi, de Ribbing returned to New York in late October to report to the Secretary-General.

Although the contents of de Ribbing's report remained confidential, it became known that the Saudi Government were maintaining that the refugee shaikhs and tribesmen should be allowed to return before any progress could be made towards a settlement of the frontier dispute or a resumption of diplomatic relations with Britain.[2] Abdur Rahman Azzam said, at the conclusion of de Ribbing's visit to Arabia, that the Saudi Government would take the issue to the Security Council if the British Government were not willing to reach a solution on the basis of the Secretary-General's personal representative's recommendations.[3] The diplomatic correspondent of *The Times* commented a day or so later, after de Ribbing had talked with officials at the Foreign Office in London before going on to New York:

'There is a good prospect that if Mr. Hammarskjöld were to arbitrate on the dispute, the British Government would be willing to accept his view, and to encourage the Shaikh of Abu Dhabi and the Sultan of Muscat, for whom it is acting in this matter, to accept it also. What it does not want is a further tribunal.'[4]

There was some doubt, however, whether the Sultan and the Shaikh could be persuaded to take back the refugees, some of whom were living under Ibn Jiluwi's protection at Dammam.[5] Rashid ibn Hamad of Hamasa, formerly the Saudis' chief agent in the Buraimi Oasis, had

[1] *The Times*, 11 August 1960.
[2] *The Times*, 20 September and 14 November 1960.
[3] *The Times*, 19 October 1960.
[4] *The Times*, 20 October 1960.
[5] See *The Times*, 20 September 1960.

Conclusion

died, but all the other actors in the conspiracy to subvert Muscat and Abu Dhabi authority in the oasis were alive—Saqr ibn Sultan, the ex-*tamimah* of the Na'im, Ubaid ibn Juma', the ex-chief of the Bani Ka'ab, Sa'id ibn Rashid of the Baluchis of the Dhahirah, and the Al Darmaki and Al Hilal shaikhs of Qattarah and Jimi villages. The Sultan and the Shaikh were hardly likely to dismiss their past activities lightly.

Diplomatic relations between Britain and Saudi Arabia were eventually resumed in January 1963. The Foreign Office, in announcing the resumption on 16 January, stated that the two governments had agreed that discussion of the Buraimi question and other problems connected with it should proceed without delay under the supervision of the Secretary-General of the United Nations, acting in his personal capacity.[1] Whether he will be any more successful in finding an agreed basis for solution of the frontier issue is problematical. The Saudi Government, by making Buraimi the focal point of the issue over the past decade, have, to a large extent, become prisoners of their own strategy. Having staked all upon gaining possession of the oasis and lost, they may now find themselves faced with the rejection of their claim to the other disputed areas. Events have largely overtaken them. Abu Dhabi, as *The Times* put it on 28 April 1961, 'has joined the winning lists in the oil sweepstakes and expects great riches from the fields on shore and at sea'. The chances of Saudi Arabia's succeeding to the sovereignty of the southern shore of the Gulf, or to any substantial part of its hinterland, seem remote. Nor is there any good reason why she should so succeed, if her claim to these areas, and to Buraimi itself, is to be judged on its legal and actual merits.

It is reasonable to contend, as the British Government contended in their *Memorial* to the arbitration tribunal in 1955, that the burden of proof in the frontier dispute rests upon Saudi Arabia. At the time of the conclusion of the Anglo-Turkish Conventions of 1913–14, which established the Blue Line as the eastern boundary of the Ottoman *sanjaq* of Najd, Ibn Sa'ud, who was then an Ottoman subject, possessed no territory to the east of Najd and Hasa, i.e. to the east of the Blue Line. In his treaty of 26 December 1915 with the British Government, which recognized him as an independent ruler, he listed as the ancestral dominions of the Saudi dynasty and the dominions

[1] See *The Times*, 17 January 1963.

Conclusion

over which he ruled, Najd, and three towns in Hasa, together with their dependencies and territories. Twenty years later, he put forward as the eastern frontier of his dominions the Red Line, which took in large tracts of territory to the east of Najd and Hasa to which he had not previously laid claim. Finally, in 1949, he advanced a second frontier claim, embracing territory as far east as, and including, the Buraimi Oasis. It would seem to be incumbent upon the Saudi Government, therefore, not only to show upon what grounds Ibn Sa'ud can be held to have acquired sovereignty over the area to the east of Najd and Hasa after 1915, but, more particularly, in view of their express statement in 1935 that the Red Line had been arrived at 'after the most careful investigation into the actual situation',[1] to demonstrate the grounds upon which Ibn Sa'ud can be held to have acquired, between 1935 and 1949, sovereignty over the territory between the Red Line and the frontier claimed in 1949.

According to the principles of international law relevant to the determination of sovereignty, which were invoked by both the Saudi and British Governments in their *Memorials* as being applicable to the frontier dispute,[2] a state may trace its right of sovereignty to a territory by showing root or origin of title by such means as a treaty of cession or proof of continuous and peaceful display of authority since ancient times. Where no such root or origin of title can be shown, effective possession, as manifested by a continuous and peaceful display of authority, will suffice to establish title. A title founded upon effective possession comprises two elements, both of which must be shown to exist, viz., the intention and will to act as sovereign, and some exercise or display of sovereignty. The primary criterion for determining sovereignty is the continuous and peaceful display of state activity in relation to other states. In thinly populated areas little actual exercise of authority is needed when there are no competing acts of authority by another state. Sovereignty need not be exercised throughout the territory so long as it is exercised in the principal parts, in particular, the settled areas.[3]

Saudi Arabia cannot show root or origin of title to the disputed

---

[1] See above, p. 125.
[2] See *Saudi Memorial*, I, Chapter VI, and *U.K. Memorial*, I, Part IX. The principles are embodied in the decisions given in three cases before the Permanent Court of Arbitration or the Permanent Court of International Justice, viz., the *Island of Palmas Case* (1928), the *Case Concerning the Legal Status of Eastern Greenland* (1933), and the *Minquiers and Ecrehos Case* (1952).
[3] See *U.K. Memorial*, I, 113–14, and *Saudi Memorial*, I, Chapter VI, paras. 4–19.

Conclusion

areas. Her claim to them, as the Saudi Government concede, is based upon the doctrine of effective possession.

'... For all present purposes, it is sufficient to view Saudi Arabia's title as based essentially on effective possession *longi temporis*.'[1]

'... Effective possession is, in the view of Saudi Arabia, the most important single factor to be taken into account in resolving the present dispute.'[2]

According to the argument set forth by the Saudi Government in their *Memorial*, effective possession of the disputed areas by Saudi Arabia began with the first Wahhabi occupation of the Buraimi Oasis in 1795, and it has continued down to the present day, even though the Wahhabi occupations ceased in 1873. The Saudi Government object to these occupations being termed, as they have been by the British Government, 'brief interludes of temporary conquest'.[3] 'Three-quarters of a century of orderly and almost uninterrupted administration', they say, 'can hardly be described as a "brief interlude"....'[4]

The first Wahhabi occupation of Buraimi began in 1800; the last ended in 1869. Between these two dates the Wahhabis occupied the oasis on five separate occasions for a total period of 45 years. Far from being characterized by 'orderly and almost uninterrupted administration', these occupations were little more than military incursions, prompted by a desire for plunder and sustained by the exploitation of tribal and religious factionalism in northern Oman. At one time or another in their 45-year tenancy of Buraimi the Wahhabis were opposed by the Al Bu Sa'id Sultans of Muscat, the Al Bu Falah Shaikhs of Abu Dhabi, the Qasimi Shaikhs of Sharjah, and every major tribe in the region—Na'im, Dhawahir, Bani Yas, Manasir, Awamir, Bani Ka'ab and Bani Qitab. The first occupation ended with the surrender of the Wahhabi commander to the Sultan of Muscat; the other four were all terminated by the forcible expulsion of the Wahhabi garrison. If the primary criterion for determining territorial sovereignty is the continuous and peaceful display of state authority in relation to other states, Saudi Arabia cannot be said to have acquired any rights of sovereignty in the Buraimi Oasis as a result of the occupations of the nineteenth century.

The case made out by the Saudi Government in their *Memorial*

---

[1] *Saudi Memorial*, I, Chapter VI, para. 7.
[2] *Saudi Memorial*, I, Chapter VI, para. 8.
[3] See above, p. 146.   [4] *Saudi Memorial*, I, Chapter VI, para. 24.

Conclusion

for the connexion of the western areas to the Saudi state during the Wahhabi occupations of Buraimi is even less convincing.

'From 1795 to 1873, with three scattered exceptions all prior to 1849, a Saudi governor held Buraimi. . . . For approximately the same period a colleague held Hofuf and the province of Hasa. Between the two of them, they held for their master in Najd the whole expanse of territory—including all the "western areas" of the present proceeding—which separated their respective headquarters.'[1]

No evidence is produced in the *Memorial* to substantiate this assertion, nor can any be found in the available sources for the history of the region. The Wahhabis never established themselves anywhere in the western areas during the nineteenth century. They did not maintain a single outpost between the Qatar peninsula and the Buraimi Oasis, and they exercised no control whatever over the coastal tract, the Dhafrah, or the Liwa Oasis. Indeed, during their later occupations of Buraimi, they preferred to maintain communication with Najd and Hasa by sea, rather than to risk crossing the Dhafrah in the face of the hostility of the Bani Yas and their allies, the Manasir. Bani Yas and Al Bu Falah authority over Liwa, the Dhafrah and the coast as far as Qatar was not relinquished during the Wahhabi period, or at any time thereafter.

In the period after 1869 there is even less substance to the Saudi Government's argument that Saudi Arabia has continuously enjoyed effective possession of the disputed areas. Hasa was lost to the Turks in 1871, and for the next twenty years the Al Sa'ud were preoccupied with fighting among themselves and battling to retain their hold on Najd. They lost their homeland to Ibn Rashid of Jabal Shammar in 1891, and the Saudi state suffered extinction for a decade thereafter. Despite a painstaking sifting of the available historical sources the Saudi Government have not been able to produce in their *Memorial* a single instance of the exercise of authority by the Al Sa'ud in the region east of Qatar in the half-century following the Wahhabis' expulsion from Buraimi. Instead, they are reduced to offering assertions such as these, unsupported by any factual testimony:

'. . . The tribe of Nu'aim remained the dominant local group [in the Buraimi Oasis], and its leaders regarded themselves as in some sense officiating there on behalf of the House of Sa'ud pending the restoration of its direct authority.'[2]

[1] *Saudi Memorial*, I, Chapter VI, para. 23.
[2] *Saudi Memorial*, I, Chapter VI, para. 62.

Conclusion

'... While ... Saudi authority in the disputed areas was enfeebled [after 1869], this interval was not such, under the circumstances, as to impair the Saudi title validly acquired years before.'[1]

'... No other State during the interval established over the region an effective possession sufficient to overcome the prior rights of Saudi Arabia.'[2]

It is absurd for the Saudi Government to claim that the Na'im were loyal subjects of the Al Sa'ud. On no fewer than four occasions—in 1839, 1848, 1850 and 1869—they had helped to expel the Wahhabis from Buraimi. After 1869 they regarded themselves as subjects of the Sultan of Muscat, although their *tamimah* was, in actuality, a client of Zaid ibn Khalifah, the greatest of the Al Bu Falah rulers. After Zaid's death in 1909 the *tamimah* remained on good terms with his successors, shared in the allowance paid by the Sultan to the Al Bu Falah for the protection of the northern frontier, and acted increasingly as the Sultan's representative in Buraimi and its vicinity. How the alleged understanding between the Na'im and the Al Sa'ud can be fitted into this picture it is difficult to see. The Saudi Government's statement that no other power established effective possession of the disputed areas after 1869 is equally unrealistic. Zaid ibn Khalifah was the foremost ruler in Eastern Arabia for the thirty years preceding his death, and the fulcrum of his power was the Abu Dhabi-Liwa-Buraimi triangle. From there his authority reached westwards to the foot of Qatar, eastwards to the watershed of the western Hajar, and southwards into the Dhahirah. He even raided Uqair in Hasa in 1889, in company with some of the Murrah. In the Buraimi Oasis he not only controlled the Dhahiri villages through the paramount shaikh of the tribe, but he also established two Al Bu Falah settlements there. Al Bu Falah dominion over the greater part of the western areas—Liwa, the Dhafrah and the coast—had never been interrupted, and it was not diminished during Zaid's reign, despite the Shaikh of Qatar's raids on Liwa in the eighteen-eighties and his threats at various times to occupy Khaur al-Udaid. Abu Dhabi's title to Khaur al-Udaid was recognized by the British Government on several occasions after 1871, and both the Shaikh of Qatar and the Ottoman Government were cautioned against trying to wrest it from him.

To say, as the Saudi Government do, that 'Saudi authority in the disputed areas was enfeebled' after 1869 is an understatement. It

[1] *Saudi Memorial*, I, Chapter VI, para. 65.   [2] Ibid.

Conclusion

ceased entirely in the Buraimi Oasis and it had never existed in the western areas. Nor was the situation changed by the recovery of Najd by Ibn Sa'ud in the first decade of this century, or by his conquest of Hasa in 1913. The Blue Line laid down in the Anglo-Turkish Convention of that year as the eastern boundary of the *sanjaq* of Najd accurately reflected the limits of his authority in the east. Ibn Sa'ud was an Ottoman subject at the time of the convention's conclusion, and though the convention itself never attained legal validity through the failure of the Porte to ratify it, its definition of the Blue Line is, in itself, evidence of what was considered at that time to be the extent of Ottoman and Saudi jurisdiction in Eastern Arabia. Ibn Sa'ud's position as Ottoman *vali* of Najd was recognized in his agreement with the Porte on 15 May 1914, and it was confirmed shortly thereafter by an Imperial *firman*. The agreement forbade him to conclude treaties with foreign powers, and the *firman* bound him to respect treaties concluded by the Ottoman Empire with such powers. On 5 June 1914 the Anglo-Ottoman Convention of 9 March 1914, incorporating the Blue Line, was ratified by the Porte. The Blue Line thus attained legal force as an international frontier, and Ibn Sa'ud was bound to respect it as the eastern boundary of his dominions.

That obligation remained with him after he achieved his independence of the Porte, since he succeeded to Ottoman sovereignty in Najd and Hasa, and, therefore, to the treaty obligations of the Porte regarding the Blue Line as an international frontier. That Ibn Sa'ud freely recognized that his actual dominions comprised only Najd and Hasa is clear from his description of the latter to Sir Percy Cox on 13 June 1913 as 'the country of our fathers and grandfathers',[1] and from his styling himself, in the treaty of 26 December 1915, 'Ruler of Najd, El Hassa, Qatif and Jubail, and the towns and ports belonging to them'.[2] His obligation in international law was not changed by the Treaty of Jeddah on 20 May 1927, which recognized him as 'King of the Hejaz and of Nejd and its Dependencies'.[3] Moreover, in the treaty of 1915 he undertook to refrain from aggression upon or interference with the littoral states in treaty relations with the British Government, and in the treaty of 1927 he agreed to maintain friendly and peaceful relations with them.

It was not until 1925 that the Saudis manifested any interest in the disputed areas, after a lapse of more than half a century. Such an interval, the Saudi Government now contend, is not sufficient,

---

[1] See above, p. 108.
[2] Aitchison, *Treaties*, 5th edn., XI, 207-8.   [3] See above, p. 121.

Conclusion

'under the circumstances, as to impair the Saudi title validly acquired years before'.[1] 'Under the circumstances' includes the collapse of Saudi power in Eastern Arabia, the occupation of Hasa by the Turks for forty years, the extinction of the Saudi state itself for a decade, the Anglo-Turkish Conventions of 1913–14, Ibn Sa'ud's term as Ottoman *vali* of Najd, the legal obligation that devolved upon him to respect the Blue Line, and his recognition in 1915 that his sovereignty in Eastern Arabia was limited to Najd and Hasa. The activities of Saudi agents in the disputed areas in 1925, and in the years that followed, were not such as to impress one with Ibn Sa'ud's determination to extend his rule over them. They consisted of four visits by Saudi *zakat*-collectors to the Buraimi Oasis between 1925 and 1929, occasional similar visits to the Liwa Oasis from 1926 onwards, and the recovery of some stolen camels by these agents, mainly in the western Dhafrah. Whether or not Ibn Sa'ud felt inhibited from interfering in the areas in question by the obligations he had assumed in the treaties of 1915 and 1927 towards the littoral states, the fact remains that his interest in the region east of the Blue Line in these years was chiefly focused upon the Jafurah and the Rub' al-Khali, and upon bringing their tribes, in particular the Murrah, under his control.

The real test of Ibn Sa'ud's view of the extent of his territorial rights in Eastern Arabia is his frontier claim of 1935. As he had granted an oil concession for his eastern dominions to the Standard Oil Company of California in 1933, he was well aware that it was to his advantage to stipulate the furthest boundary that he could reasonably uphold. He was also aware that the British Government were prepared to waive, for the sake of reaching agreement on the frontier, their strict rights under the Anglo-Turkish Convention of 1914. The frontier that he proposed, therefore, can be presumed to be a definitive statement of his claims. That frontier, the Red Line of 3 April 1935, did not take in the Mijan, the Sabkhat Matti, the Bainunah, the Dhafrah, or the Liwa Oasis, in other words, nearly all the western areas now being claimed by Saudi Arabia. What is more, the Red Line did not come within 100 miles and more of the Buraimi Oasis, thereby clearly showing that Ibn Sa'ud did not regard the oasis as part of his rightful territories.

Saudi activities in the disputed areas in the decade after 1935 do not reflect any change of outlook on the part of Ibn Sa'ud. They con-

---

[1] *Saudi Memorial*, I, Chapter VI, para. 65.

Conclusion

sisted solely of occasional *zakat*-collecting and the recovery of stolen camels, and they were confined to the Bainunah and the area at the foot of the Qatar peninsula, with the exception of a visit by *zakat*-collectors to the western end of Liwa in 1941. The tax registers from the office of the Governor of Hasa, which are reproduced in the *Saudi Memorial* and which commence with the year 1935–6, reveal plainly how haphazard and infrequent these collections were. In like manner, the Amir Ibn Jiluwi's statement of May 1955 in the *Memorial*, concerning his exercise of criminal jurisdiction in the disputed areas, reveals that this amounted to four instances of the apprehension of camel thieves between 1935 and 1955. It is surprising, therefore, to find the tax registers and his statement being made the basis of a claim that Saudi Arabia has regularly and systematically collected *zakat* and administered justice in the disputed areas since 1913. It is even more surprising to find this *zakat* being labelled the classical *zakat* of Islam, and its collection being interpreted as an assertion of temporal sovereignty on the part of Saudi Arabia, and its payment as an acknowledgement of political allegiance. Such an interpretaton finds little support in Islamic law according to the Hanbali rite, which is officially in force in Saudi Arabia. The *zakat* in question may more correctly be described simply as payments from tribesmen to the agents of a ruler, in this case, Ibn Sa'ud, in whose territory they spend part of the year for grazing purposes, and whose protection they enjoy for that time. The first such payments by inhabitants of the disputed areas were made in 1925 by tribesmen who had earlier sought the protection of the Governor of Hasa during the tribal fighting in northern and Trucial Oman in the early nineteen-twenties. The payments continued for a few years thereafter.

The final grounds on which the Saudi Government have sought to prove that Saudi Arabia has enjoyed effective possession of the disputed areas are the declarations of allegiance from tribal leaders and others which are reproduced in the *Memorial* of 1955. These were secured either after Turki ibn Utaishan's arrival in the Buraimi Oasis in 1952 or in the months following the signing of the arbitration agreement in 1954, and they are said to demonstrate the adherence of the tribes of the region to Saudi Arabia. They are practically worthless for this purpose. Half of them are irrelevant because they come from tribesmen living outside the disputed areas; several are riddled with inaccuracies or inconsistencies; and nearly all were secured by bribery. The fact that the Saudi Government felt it

Conclusion

necessary to dictate the contents of these statements and to pay to have them signed is sufficient indication, in itself, of their worth as evidence and of the worth of the Saudi claim as a whole to the allegiance of the tribes.

Nothing that the Saudi Government have been able to produce in the way of evidence of tribal affiliations in the disputed areas is of sufficient weight to offset the preponderance of historical and contemporary opinion that the Bani Yas and the bulk of the Manasir, the two major tribes inhabiting the western areas, have, for at least a century and a half, been loyal to the Al Bu Falah Shaikhs of Abu Dhabi. In the case of the Baduin division of the Awamir, who roam the Dhafrah and the eastern Rub' al-Khali, and frequent the vicinity of the Buraimi Oasis, the Saudi Government have neither demonstrated their current allegiance to Saudi Arabia nor laid claim to their historical loyalty. They could hardly have done so, since the Baduin Awamir have, for a century past, followed the leadership of the Al Bu Falah when they were in the disputed areas. In the Buraimi Oasis the Dhawahir have, for the same period and longer, been subjects of the Al Bu Falah, and for forty years, until his death in 1936, their paramount shaikh served as the Al Bu Falah representative in the oasis. All that the Saudi Government have been able to offer in substantiation of their claim to the loyalty of the Dhawahir are some trumped-up statements purchased from four minor Dhahiri shaikhs. The same is true of their claim to the allegiance of the Na'im in this century. Saqr ibn Sultan of Buraimi village, the Na'imi *tamimah*, and Rashid ibn Hamad of Hamasa both forsook their traditional allegiance to the Al Bu Sa'id Sultan of Muscat and declared themselves Saudi subjects in return for lavish bribes from the Saudi Government.

Though the formulation of the Saudi frontier claim of 1949 doubtless owed something to the historical ambition of the Al Sa'ud to dominate the whole of the Arabian peninsula, it would appear to have been occasioned primarily by Petroleum Development Ltd.'s prospecting activities in the western areas and the Buraimi region after 1945. ARAMCO's discovery and successful exploitation of the Hasa oil-fields may well have encouraged a hope on the part of the Saudi Government that further reservoirs of oil might lie in the Dhafrah, around Buraimi, or along the coast east of Qatar. There

Conclusion

was also the possibility of striking oil in the sea-bed off that coast, and in May 1949 Saudi Arabia had been the first state in the Middle East to proclaim its right to the subsoil and sea-bed adjacent to its coasts. If the Saudi Government had really believed that their right to the territory claimed was incontestable, then it is scarcely conceivable that they would have employed the means that they did after 1949 to secure possession of it. As it is, their actions leave little room for doubt that they were unsure of the strength of their case. While they negotiated on the frontier between 1949 and 1952 they also made contact with tribal leaders in the Buraimi area to pave the way for a *de facto* occupation of the oasis. The occupation of Buraimi was the key to the Saudi Government's plan to gain control of the disputed areas. By effecting a lodgement there not only would they have an advanced base for operations in Oman, but they could also hope that, with the passage of time, the occupation would be accepted as a *fait accompli*, and that considerations of equity would ultimately work to secure to them the territory intermediate to Hasa. When the Dammam Conference at the beginning of 1952 showed that the British Government were not prepared to admit any of their extravagant territorial claims, the Saudi Government decided to put the plan into operation.

The dispatching of Turki ibn Utaishan and his *fidawis* to occupy Hamasa in August 1952 was a violation not only of Muscat sovereignty in the Buraimi Oasis but of Abu Dhabi sovereignty as well; for Turki travelled to Hamasa through both disputed and undisputed Abu Dhabi territory. Having secured their foothold in the oasis, and having been saved from the consequences of their action by the good offices of the United States Ambassador at Jeddah and by the intervention of the British Government to restrain the Sultan of Muscat, the Saudi Government were prepared to allow time to work to their advantage. It took seven months and the imposition of a blockade upon Turki to get them to agree to a British proposal to submit the frontier dispute to arbitration. It took another year to settle the terms of the arbitration, a delay caused primarily by the Saudi Government's attempts to enlarge the extent of territory to be made subject to arbitration. Barely was the ink dry on the arbitration agreement when they began to disregard its most fundamental provision, viz., that both sides should refrain from interference with the tribes of the disputed region and from any act which might prejudice a just and impartial arbitration.

Conclusion

The deliberate and systematic campaign of bribery and subversion initiated by the Saudi Government in the disputed areas, and more particularly the Buraimi Zone, in August 1954 undermined the whole basis of the arbitration. It began with the corruption of the *tamimah* of the Na'im and it was eventually extended to every tribe in the Buraimi Zone and to others far removed from it. The tribes of the Wadi al-Jizzi, to the east of Buraimi, were given money and arms, smuggled in from Saudi Arabia, to induce them to rise against the Sultan. Money and arms were also smuggled to the Imam Ghalib ibn Ali to help him overthrow Al Bu Sa'id rule in inner Oman and to convert the region into a Saudi satrapy. The hub of the system was the Saudi police detachment stationed in the Buraimi Oasis, under the terms of the arbitration agreement, to maintain peace and good order among the tribes but otherwise not to interfere with them. At the specific orders of his superior, the Amir Ibn Jiluwi, Governor of Hasa, the detachment's commander disbursed bribes, distributed arms, and tried to incite a general uprising of the tribes in favour of Saudi Arabia. From February 1955 onwards he received his consignments of arms and money from Hasa mainly by the aircraft which the Saudi Government had been permitted by the arbitration tribunal to use to supply the detachment. Other illegal uses to which the supply aircraft was put during 1955 were the flying out of tribesmen to Saudi Arabia as a means of influencing their loyalties, and the flying in of Saudi officials to obtain declarations of allegiance from prominent tribal leaders. So contemptuous of the arbitral process had the Saudis grown by the spring and summer of 1955 that they even tried to suborn Shaikh Zaid ibn Sultan, the Ruler of Abu Dhabi's brother and his representative in the oasis. An equally clumsy attempt to dislocate the government of the shaikhdom had been made late in 1954, when the Saudis had provided two disaffected members of the Al Bu Falah, living in exile, with funds to overthrow the Ruler, Shaikh Shakhbut.

When these breaches of the arbitration agreement were brought to the notice of the arbitration tribunal by the British Government in August 1955, the Saudis reacted in a manner that can fairly be called characteristically disingenuous. They handed in a dossier of counter-complaints against British activities in the disputed areas, but omitted to include the answers that the British Government had given in previous months to these charges. Their *Memorial* was an even more misleading document, especially the volume of tax registers, the

Conclusion

arguments on *zakat*, the historical section, and the declarations of allegiance obtained by bribery. The conduct of the Saudi member of the tribunal, Shaikh Yusuf Yasin, at the sittings at Geneva did nothing to increase confidence in the Saudi Government's willingness to abide by the terms of an impartial arbitration. Not only did he communicate with the Agent for Saudi Arabia in open tribunal, but there is little doubt that he instructed the one witness produced by Saudi Arabia before the tribunal on the evidence that he was to give. He then revealed to the tribunal that he was the Saudi minister in charge of activities at Buraimi. Finally, it became plain that not even the tribunal itself was to be safe from Saudi methods. It is small wonder that the British member felt compelled to resign; and when, within a few days, his resignation was followed by that of the president, and a month later by that of a third member of the tribunal, it appeared as though the dispute, given the unusual circumstances which had developed, did not lend itself to arbitration.

In the face of their conduct at Geneva, and of their violation of the conditions of arbitration, conditions that they themselves had helped lay down, the Saudi Government's proposal, only a few weeks after the breakdown of proceedings at Geneva, that arbitration be resumed can only be regarded as cynical in the extreme. The repeated refusal of the British Government in the months that followed to consider a return to arbitration may be attributed not only to Saudi Arabia's conduct at Geneva but also to the discovery, in the correspondence of the Saudi police commander captured at Buraimi, of ample proof of Saudi Arabia's violation of the conditions of arbitration in the disputed areas. Yet Saudi Arabia has not lacked for apologists for her behaviour or advocates of her case in the years since 1955. Even among those who are prepared to accept the facts of bribery, subversion and misconduct, there is a disposition to argue that Western standards of probity are not to be expected in the Middle East, that Western judicial procedures are not understood there or fully subscribed to, and that bribery and other underhand practices are a commonplace of life in the area. It is hardly a convincing argument, nor is it quite fair to the inhabitants of the Middle East in general. Whatever may be said in extenuation of the Saudi Government's conduct, the fact remains that they accepted arbitration and the rules by which it was to proceed. If at any time they overlooked or transgressed these rules, the Western legal advisers whom they had retained should have been in a position to remind them of them.

Conclusion

Certainly St. John Philby, perhaps the most ardent Western advocate that Saudi Arabia has had, warned them as early as 1953 of the necessity to behave honestly in the frontier dispute.[1]

The ultimate test of the Saudi Government's behaviour after 1953, and of the excuses offered in condonation of it, is to ask whether the late King Ibn Sa'ud would have sanctioned it. It hardly needs saying that he would not. Indeed, one may doubt whether the exaggerated frontier claim of 1949 would have been put forward if, at that time, he had not been in failing health, if his mind had not been less vigorous than in the past, and if his capacity for rule had not seriously weakened. As it was, he was guided by bad counsel, both from those who led him to believe that the extension of his rule over the southern shore of the Gulf was feasible, and from those who, by fabricating a basis for the claim, persuaded him that it was justified.

[1] See *Forty Years in the Wilderness*, p. 3.

APPENDIX A

The Arbitration Agreement of 30 July 1954[1]

Jedda, July 30, 1954

The Government of the United Kingdom of Great Britain and Northern Ireland and the Government of the Kingdom of Saudi Arabia;

Considering that there is a dispute as to the location of the common frontier between Saudi Arabia and Abu Dhabi and as to the sovereignty in the Buraimi oasis; that Abu Dhabi is a State for the conduct of whose foreign relations the Government of the United Kingdom is responsible and that His Highness Sultan Said bin Taimur has appointed the Government of the United Kingdom to conduct all negotiations and proceedings on his behalf for the settlement of the dispute in so far as it relates to territory in the Buraimi oasis claimed by him to belong to Muscat and Oman;

Considering that it has proved impossible to settle the dispute by direct negotiations;

Desiring nevertheless to find a permanent solution by peaceful means in accordance with the Charter of the United Nations[2] and with the tradition of friendship and goodwill that has long existed between them;

Have accordingly decided to submit the dispute to an independent and impartial Tribunal for arbitration; and, for this purpose,

Have agreed as follows:

[1] Cmd. 9272, Treaty Series No. 65 (1954), *Arbitration Agreement between the Government of the United Kingdom (acting on behalf of the Ruler of Abu Dhabi and His Highness the Sultan Said bin Taimur) and the Government of Saudi Arabia*, Jedda, 30 July 1954.
[2] Treaty Series No. 67 (1946), Cmd. 7015.

The Arbitration Agreement of 30 July 1954

Article I

The Tribunal shall consist of five members selected as follows:

(a) Each of the two Parties to the present Agreement shall nominate one Member, provided that, if either Party fails to nominate its Member within 60 days from the date on which this Agreement comes into force, the other Party may ask the President of the International Court of Justice to make the nomination.

(b) The three remaining Members, none of whom shall be a national of either Party, shall be chosen by agreement between the two Members nominated under paragraph (a) of this Article; of the three, one shall be designated by the selecting Members as President of the Tribunal. If within a period of 90 days from the date on which the appointment of the last-named Member under paragraph (a) is notified to the other Party, the membership of the Tribunal is still incomplete or the President has not been designated, either Party may request the President of the International Court of Justice to make the appointments or designation required.

(c) If any Member of the Tribunal should die, resign, or become unable to act before the Award has been given, the vacancy shall be filled by the method laid down in this Article for the original appointment.

(d) If the President of the International Court of Justice is a national of either Party or is prevented from acting as requested in paragraphs (a) and (b) of this Article, the Vice-President of the Court may be requested to take the necessary action. Any nomination, appointment or designation made by the President or Vice-President of the Court under this Article shall be final and binding on both Parties.

Article II

The tribunal is requested to decide:

(a) The location of the common frontier between Saudi Arabia and Abu Dhabi, within the line claimed by the Saudi Arabian Government in 1949 and that claimed on behalf of Abu Dhabi at the Dammam Conference in 1952;

(b) Sovereignty in the area comprised within a circle whose centre is in Buraimi village and whose circumference passes through the point of junction of latitude 24 degrees 25 minutes North and longitude 55 degrees 36 minutes East.

The Arbitration Agreement of 30 July 1954

ARTICLE III

Each party shall be represented before the Tribunal by an Agent, who shall be responsible for its part in the proceedings. Each Agent may be assisted by such advisers, counsel and staff as he deems necessary.

ARTICLE IV

In conducting its proceedings and in formulating its Award, the Tribunal shall have due regard to all relevant considerations of law, fact and equity brought to its attention by the Parties under Articles V and VI or disclosed through the exercise of the powers conferred upon it by Article VII. In particular, but without being limited thereto, it shall take into account the following factors in so far as it deems them relevant:

(*a*) Historical facts relating to the rights of His Majesty the King of Saudi Arabia and his forefathers and the rights of the other Rulers concerned and their forefathers;

(*b*) The traditional loyalties of the inhabitants of the area concerned;

(*c*) The tribal organisation and the way of life of the tribes inhabiting the area concerned;

(*d*) The exercise of jurisdiction and other activities in the area concerned;

(*e*) Any other considerations brought to its attention by either Party.

ARTICLE V

(*a*) Within a period of six months from a date to be fixed by the President of the Tribunal as soon as possible after the organisation of the Tribunal, each of the two Parties shall present simultaneously to the Tribunal a Memorial setting out its submissions regarding the territories and frontiers in dispute, and the considerations on which its submissions are founded.

(*b*) After the period fixed in paragraph (*a*) of this Article, each of the two Parties shall have the right, within a further period of six months, to present to the Tribunal a Reply to the Memorial presented by the other Party.

The Arbitration Agreement of 30 July 1954

(*c*) On the application of either Party, the Tribunal may, if it thinks fit, grant an extension of either or both of the periods fixed by paragraphs (*a*) and (*b*) of this Article.

(*d*) The Tribunal shall be responsible for communicating the Memorial and the Reply of the one Party to the other Party and shall inform the Parties how many copies are required.

(*e*) After the submission of the Reply of each Party, there shall be no further written submissions, except as provided in Article VII (*b*) or Article X (*b*), unless the Tribunal otherwise directs, and then only within such limitations as the Tribunal may prescribe. If either Party is permitted to make further written submissions under this paragraph, the other Party shall have an opportunity of commenting upon them and of submitting documents in support of its comments.

Article VI

(*a*) Subsequent to the conclusion of the written proceedings called for in Article V, the Tribunal shall sit for the purpose of hearing oral argument by the Parties. Subject to the provision that each Party shall have equal opportunity to be heard, both on principal argument and in rebuttal, the Tribunal shall prescribe the procedure and time-limits to be observed.

(*b*) With the consent of both Parties, the Tribunal may dispense with oral arguments.

Article VII

(*a*) In addition to considering the submissions of the Parties, the Tribunal shall have power on its own initiative to call witnesses (other than the Ruler of any of the territories concerned) to conduct enquiries, and to visit particular localities in the area in dispute whenever it deems such proceedings useful. Any such examination of witnesses, enquiry or visit may be delegated by the Tribunal to one or more of its Members or to one or more other impartial persons whom it may appoint for that purpose. The 'area in dispute' means the area referred to in Article II (*b*) of the present Agreement and all other land claimed both by Saudi Arabia and Abu Dhabi between the Saudi 1949 claim and the claim put forward on behalf of the Ruler of Abu Dhabi at the Dammam Conference in 1952.

(*b*) The Tribunal shall inform each Party whenever it resolves to exercise any of the powers specified in paragraph (*a*) of this Article,

The Arbitration Agreement of 30 July 1954

and each Party shall have the right to appoint representatives (not exceeding four in number for visits to the area in dispute) to be present at the proceeding; to put questions to any witness, under the control of the Tribunal or person or persons conducting the enquiry; and to receive any reports of enquiries or visits and to comment thereon orally or in writing.

(c) Either Party may request the Tribunal to exercise, with respect to any particular witnesses, localities, or subjects of inquiry, any of the powers specified in paragraph (a) of this Article, but the Tribunal may decline at its discretion to accede to such a request.

Article VIII

(a) Any written submission by either Party shall contain a statement certifying the authenticity of the documents quoted or referred to therein and copies of all such documents shall, where possible, be annexed to the submission.

(b) At the request of the Tribunal, either Party shall, if possible, produce the original or an authenticated copy of any document referred to in its written submissions or oral argument, and if unable to do so shall explain to the Tribunal the reasons for such inability. Inability to produce the original or an authenticated copy of any document shall not preclude its consideration by the Tribunal, but shall be taken into account by the Tribunal in determining the weight to be given to the document concerned.

(c) The Tribunal shall satisfy itself as to the authenticity of any documents disclosed in the course of any proceedings which it may conduct under the powers conferred on it by Article VII.

Article IX

(a) The Parties shall present their written submissions and any documents annexed thereto in both English and Arabic, together with a translation into such other language or languages as the Tribunal may request.

(b) The Parties shall present their oral arguments in either English or Arabic. The Tribunal shall make such arrangements for translation and interpretation as it deems necessary.

(c) The Tribunal shall provide for the keeping of a verbatim record of each of its sittings, other than its private deliberations. Copies shall be made available to the Parties as soon as possible.

The Arbitration Agreement of 30 July 1954

Article X

(*a*) If the Tribunal considers it necessary, it shall have the right to arrange for an expert opinion to be given by any person or persons selected by it.

(*b*) Any expert opinion given under paragraph (*a*) of this Article shall either be in writing and communicated to the Parties, or be given orally before the Tribunal in the presence of the Parties. In either case the Parties shall have the right to comment upon the opinion and, under the control of the Tribunal, to put questions to the person or persons responsible for it.

Article XI

The Tribunal may, if it thinks fit, determine the location of the frontier in dispute section by section and may give its award in respect of each section when it is ready to do so without waiting until it is in a position to give its Award in respect of the whole frontier in dispute.

Article XII

The Tribunal shall have power to determine all questions of procedure not regulated in the present Agreement, including the power to fix the dates and places of its sittings and to decide upon the public or private character of each.

Article XIII

(*a*) The Award of the Tribunal, and all decisions on questions of procedure, shall be given by majority vote.

(*b*) The Tribunal shall give the reasons for its Award.

(*c*) The Award shall be given in the language selected by the Tribunal and shall be printed and communicated to the Parties simultaneously. There shall be communicated to the Parties at the same time translations of the Award into English or Arabic or, if the Award be given in some other language, into both English and Arabic. The Tribunal shall state which text or texts are to be regarded as authentic. The original of the Award and all official translations thereof shall bear the certification of the President of the Tribunal.

The Arbitration Agreement of 30 July 1954

(*d*) The Award of the Tribunal shall be final, binding upon both Governments (including the Rulers on whose behalf the Government of the United Kingdom is acting), and without appeal.

Article XIV

(*a*) As part of its Award, the Tribunal shall appoint an expert commission, composed of one member nominated by each of the Parties and a neutral chairman nominated by the Tribunal, to direct the demarcation on the ground of the frontier line fixed by the Tribunal. If either Party fails to nominate its member of the commission within 90 days after the Tribunal has requested it to do so, the right to make the nomination shall pass to the Tribunal.

(*b*) The demarcation commission thus appointed shall erect such markers and take such other steps as it deems necessary to demarcate the frontier line adequately in relation to the needs of the various areas through which it may pass. The chairman of the commission shall have power to authorise slight deviations from the line defined by the Tribunal, not to exceed at any one place one kilometre to either side or five kilometres in length, where the nature of the terrain presents unusual difficulties to demarcation.

(*c*) The demarcation commission shall endeavour to complete its work within two solar years from the date of the Award of the Tribunal. On completion, it shall submit to both Parties a full report of its activities, including such maps, photographs and other data as will enable the frontier line to be accurately maintained thereafter.

(*d*) The members of the demarcation commission shall be remunerated at a rate to be fixed by the Tribunal at the time of their appointment. The remuneration and all expenses of the commission and its work shall be borne by the two Parties in equal shares, to be paid in such manner as may be arranged between the Parties and the commission.

(*e*) In the event of the death, disability or resignation of either the Saudi or the British member of the commission, his Government shall name a successor within 90 days after receiving notice thereof, and if it fails to do so the other Party may request the President of the International Court of Justice to make the nomination. In the event of the death, disability, or resignation of the neutral chairman, either Party may request the President of the International Court of Justice to appoint a successor. If the President of the International

The Arbitration Agreement of 30 July 1954

Court of Justice is a national of either Party or is unable to act for the purposes of this paragraph, the Vice-President may be requested to take the necessary action.

Article XV

After the Tribunal has given its award, either Party may publish any of the proceedings in the case.

Article XVI

(*a*) The Tribunal shall have the power to engage such staff, and at such remuneration, and to rent such premises and purchase such equipment, as it considers necessary, and to make all such arrangements as may be requisite for the holding of any oral hearings or for visits to any particular localities by the Tribunal or by any person or persons appointed by it under Article VII (*a*).

(*b*) The records and papers of the Tribunal and the personal effects of its Members, as well as the records, papers and personal effects of each Agent, shall be considered inviolate, and shall be exempt from all dues, inspections or border formalities.

Article XVII

(*a*) The President and the other Members of the Tribunal shall be entitled to payment of their expenses and to remuneration on a scale to be agreed by the Parties.

(*b*) The remuneration of the President and Members of the Tribunal and the expenses of the Tribunal shall be borne by the Parties in equal shares, and shall be paid in such manner and at such times as may be arranged between the Parties and the Tribunal. The Tribunal shall, subsequent to its Award, deliver a final account of all the expenses incurred.

Article XVIII

Each Party shall pay the expenses of the presentation and conduct of its own case before the Tribunal.

Article XIX

The Tribunal shall have the power to decide any question that may arise as to the interpretation of any provision of the present Agreement.

The Arbitration Agreement of 30 July 1954

ARTICLE XX

The present Agreement shall come into force on the date of signature.

In witness whereof the undersigned, being duly authorised by their respective Governments, have signed the present Agreement.

Done in duplicate at Jedda this thirtieth day of July, 1954, corresponding to the twenty-ninth day of Dhu'al-qada, 1373, in the English and Arabic languages, both texts being equally authentic.

G. C. PELHAM,
Her Britannic Majesty's Ambassador Extraordinary and Plenipotentiary.

FAISAL,
Minister for Foreign Affairs of the Kingdom of Saudi Arabia.

EXCHANGE OF NOTES

No. 1

Her Majesty's Ambassador at Jedda to the Saudi Arabian Minister for Foreign Affairs

British Embassy, Jedda,
July 30, 1954.
(*Dhu'al-qada 29, 1373.*)

Your Royal Highness,

I have the honour to inform you that Her Majesty's Government, acting on behalf of the Ruler of Abu Dhabi and His Highness the Sultan Said bin Taimur, agree to submit the dispute on the common frontier between Saudi Arabia and Abu Dhabi and the question of sovereignty over the Buraimi zone to arbitration—without prejudice to the claims of any of the parties—on the following conditions:

(i) Turki bin Ataishan and his party shall withdraw from the Buraimi zone to undisputed Saudi territory; the Trucial Oman Levies, other armed forces, and officials introduced into the zone after August 1952, shall withdraw therefrom to undisputed territory in the Trucial States; and local armed groups shall be disbanded.

The Arbitration Agreement of 30 July 1954

A small police force to which each side shall contribute a party of up to 15 men shall be substituted for the forces that are withdrawn for duty in the zone;

(ii) the police force referred to in (i) shall be stationed in the Buraimi zone in tents at any mutually agreeable place which is not inside the villages. The task of the group shall be to maintain peace and good order between the tribes in the Buraimi zone. It shall not interfere in any way in the internal affairs, administration or politics of any tribe and shall take action only in the event of an outbreak or disorder provided that the leaders of the two constituent parties agree;

(iii) the Trucial Oman Levies, other armed forces, and officials introduced into the other disputed areas after August 1952, shall be withdrawn from those areas, and local armed groups shall be disbanded;

(iv) neither side shall introduce additional officials or forces into the Buraimi zone or into the other disputed areas; both parties undertake to refrain from action which would prejudice the holding of a just and impartial arbitration; it is understood that restrictions on entry of additional officials shall not apply to Government officials engaged in the arbitration or to persons asked by the arbitral tribunal to attend it; it is also agreed that the tribunal shall have powers and jurisdiction to supervise the execution of this agreement and to adjudicate on matters arising out of its application and to issue such orders and take such action as it sees fit in this respect;

(v) for the purpose of oil operations only and without prejudice to the rights of the parties to the frontier dispute, the region lying between the Saudi 1949 claim and the claim put forward in 1952 on behalf of the Ruler of Abu Dhabi shall be divided in the following manner:

(*a*) in the area bounded on the west by longitude 51 degrees 35 minutes East, on the south by latitude 23 degrees 15 minutes North, and on the east by a straight line connecting the eastern termini of the Saudi 1949 line and the Abu Dhabi 1952 line, Petroleum Development (Trucial Coast), Limited, and D'Arcy Exploration, Limited, may conduct oil operations during the period of arbitration;

(*b*) in the area bounded on the east and west by the same lines as in sub-paragraph (*a*), on the north by latitude 23 degrees 15 minutes North, and on the south by latitude 23 degrees 00 minutes North, no oil operations shall be permitted during the period of arbitration;

The Arbitration Agreement of 30 July 1954

(c) in the area west of longitude 51 degrees 35 minutes East and in the area bounded on the north by latitude 23 degrees 00 minutes North and on the east by the same line as in sub-paragraphs (a) and (b), the Arabian-American Oil Company may conduct oil operations during the period of arbitration.

It is understood that there shall be no oil operations in any case in the Buraimi zone during the period of arbitration;

(vi) these conditions shall take effect from the date on which the arbitration agreement comes into force and the withdrawals referred to in conditions (i) and (iii) shall be completed within one month from that date;

(vii) for the purpose of implementing the foregoing conditions, 'Buraimi zone' means the area comprised within a circle whose centre is in Buraimi village and whose circumference passes through the point of junction of latitude 24 degrees 25 minutes North and longitude 55 degrees 36 minutes East; 'disputed areas' means the Buraimi zone and all other land claimed by both Saudi Arabia and Abu Dhabi between the Saudi 1949 claim and the claim put forward on behalf of the Ruler of Abu Dhabi at the Dammam Conference in 1952.

If His Majesty's Government also agree to these conditions I am to suggest that this letter, together with Your Royal Highness's reply to that effect, shall constitute an agreement between our two Governments, which shall be binding on all the parties concerned.

Pray accept, &c.
G. C. PELHAM.

No. 2

The Saudi Arabian Minister for Foreign Affairs to Her Majesty's Ambassador at Jedda

Jiddah,
29 Dhu a'l-Qadah 1373.
July 30, 1954.

Your Excellency,

I am pleased to acknowledge receipt of your Excellency's letter of to-day's date which reads as follows:

[As in No. 1]

The Arbitration Agreement of 30 July 1954

In accordance with the suggestion in your Excellency's letter, His Majesty's Government considers that letter and this reply thereto to constitute an agreement between our two Governments which shall be binding on all the parties concerned.

Accept, &c.

FAISAL.

APPENDIX B

The Submissions on Zakat in the Saudi Memorial

The legal arguments put forward in the *Saudi Memorial* of 1955 in support of Saudi Arabia's claim to the disputed areas attach great weight to the collection of taxes as evidence of the exercise of sovereignty. 'Of all the State activities tending to substantiate a claim of effective possession,' say the *Memorial*'s authors, '... those having the greatest probative value are the collection of taxes and the preservation of public security. ... In the areas here in dispute, the power to tax and the power to punish the wrongdoer have long been freely and firmly exercised by Saudi Arabia.'[1] The tax collected is said to be the same as that collected in Saudi Arabia, viz., 'the *zakah* enjoined by Islamic law'.[2] This is described by the authors as:

'... a true tax, leviable only by a sovereign and due from the individual subject. Despite confusion arising from the occasional misapplication of the word to other kinds of payments, *zakah* is not a political tribute, nor is it a voluntary gift to a solely religious leader, such as the Peter's pence received by the Pope. By origin an assessment for the relief of the poor and unfortunate, *zakah* early became the chief general tax imposed on the Muslims. On him who has the right to collect it rests a corollary duty to protect those who pay it: no collection, as has been said, without protection.'[3]

The claims of the Saudi Government to have regularly collected *zakat* in the disputed areas in past years, claims which depend largely upon the evidence of the tax registers reproduced in Volume III of the *Saudi Memorial*, have already been examined in the present work.[4] It is proposed here to comment upon the submissions put

[1] *Saudi Memorial*, I, Chapter VI, para. 37.
[2] *Saudi Memorial*, I, Chapter VI, para. 38.
[3] Ibid.   [4] See above, pp. 237–9.

The Submissions on Zakat in the Saudi Memorial

forward in the *Memorial* on the nature of Islamic *zakat* and its significance as an element in the determination of sovereignty.

The classical Islamic theory regarding *zakat* is briefly as follows. The *zakat*, or alms tax, is the third of the five pillars of Islam, the others being the profession of faith (*shahada*), prayer (*salat*), fasting (*sawm*), and the pilgrimage (*hajj*).[1] The Koran enjoins the giving of alms on Muslims as an outward sign of piety and a means of salvation. During the lifetime of the Prophet the character of *zakat* remained vague: later doctrine was largely, but not wholly, formulated on the basis of the references to it in the Koran.

'After Muhammad's death many Beduin tribes . . . refused to continue to pay *zakāt* as they considered their agreements cancelled by the death of the Prophet, and many believers, among them 'Umar himself, were inclined to agree with this. Only the energy of Abū Bakr made the *zakāt* in its fiscal form a permanent institution, which through the establishment of a state treasury contributed greatly to the expansion of Muslim power. Ardent believers continued as before to regard it as their right to bestow their *zakāt* for themselves as they thought fit; but very soon the development and centralisation of the state made this impossible in practice. When the system of *fikh* [jurisprudence] came to be elaborated the *zakāt* was definitely maintained as a religious tax and regulated in all its details.'[2]

Zakat, as an act of religious worship, requires a formulated intention to be legally valid. 'The condition determining the validity (*ṣiḥḥah*) of the payment of *zakāt* is that the payment be coupled with the intention that it is to discharge the *zakāt* rather than some other obligation. For *zakāt* is an act of worship and as such is not valid unless so intended.'[3] Its forcible exaction only becomes necessary when an individual fails to discharge his religious obligation to pay *zakat*. In this case the exaction by force discharges the obligation.[4]

Only Muslims pay *zakat*. It is paid on (i) crops of the field planted for food, (ii) fruits, (iii) livestock (camels, cattle, sheep and goats), (iv) gold and silver, and (v) merchandise. The first three categories compose the so-called 'visible' (*zahir*) property, the last two, the

---

[1] A. J. Wensinck, *The Muslim Creed*, Cambridge, 1932, pp. 26 ff. Some authorities add a sixth pillar, the holy war (*jihad*).

[2] *Shorter Encyclopaedia of Islam*, ed. H. A. R. Gibb and J. H. Kramers, Leiden, 1953, *s.v.* 'Zakāt'.

[3] Nicolas P. Aghnides, *Mohammedan Theories of Finance*, New York, 1916, p. 323.

[4] Aghnides, pp. 326–7.

The Submissions on Zakat in the Saudi Memorial

'invisible' (*batin*) property. To pay *zakat* one must possess a taxable minimum (*nisab*). The rules governing the calculation of the *nisab* are complicated, and they vary according to the different schools of Islamic law.¹ The rates at which the *zakat* is to be paid are also laid down for the five categories: broadly speaking, they are 10 per cent for the first two categories (5 per cent where the land is artificially irrigated), 2½ per cent for the fourth and fifth. The rates for the third category (livestock) depend upon the numbers and kind of animals.²

The yield of *zakat* is divided among eight classes, which are specified in the Koran (Sura ix, 60): 'The *sadaqas* [alms] are for the poor, the needy, those who work on [collecting] them, those whose hearts are to be conciliated (*muʿallafah qulubuhum*), for slaves, debtors, and for Allah's purposes, and for the travellers, as a duty prescribed by Allah.' 'Allah's purposes' here is taken to mean the waging of the holy war (*jihad*), and the part of the *zakat* revenues set aside for this 'is to be devoted to the fighters for the faith who voluntarily take part in the *djihād* without belonging to the regular troops'.³

The legal authorities are not all agreed on whether it is obligatory or merely recommended that *zakat* should be paid to the collector and not distributed directly by the payee. The generally accepted doctrine is that while it is permitted to hand the *zakat* directly to the persons who have claims on it, it is preferable to hand it to the Muslim authorities for regulated distribution.⁴ If the *zakat* is collected by the government it must be paid to the collector even if the character of the government is no guarantee of a proper distribution. In this case, according to some, and especially Hanafi scholars, to satisfy one's conscience, the *zakat* should be paid a second time and distributed direct. The right of the government to collect *zakat*, however, is limited to its collection on the so-called 'visible' goods, i.e. of the first three categories. The so-called 'invisible' properties, i.e. the last two categories, are expressly withdrawn from this control, and payment of *zakat* on them is left entirely to the conscience of the individual.⁵

The organization of the state treasury, the *bait al-mal*, in early Islamic times also underlines the fact that *zakat* was not a tax in the ordinary sense but a religious obligation. Only those moneys and

---

¹ See, e.g., Aghnides, pp. 203 ff.
² See Aghnides, loc. cit., and *Shorter Encyclopaedia of Islam*, loc. cit.
³ *Shorter Encyclopaedia of Islam*, loc. cit.
⁴ Ibid. But see below, p. 298. ⁵ Ibid.

properties which belonged to the Muslim community as a whole and the purpose to which they were devoted, depending upon the discretion of the Imam or his delegate, were 'assets of the state treasury' (*huquq bait al-mal*). The proceeds of *zakat* and other earmarked revenue, such as that part of the fifth (*khums*) of the booty (*ghanima*) which went to the relatives of the Prophet, orphans, poor, and travellers, although it might be controlled by the officials of the treasury and lodged in the treasury pending the determination of the recipients entitled to it, were not 'assets of the treasury'. From the moment of payment *zakat* vested in the entitled recipients and not the *bait al-mal*. The primary source of the income of the treasury was the revenues collectively termed *fai*, i.e. the taxes of *kharaj* and *jizyah*. The former was originally levied upon all lands held by non-Muslims, but with the conversion of large numbers of these to Islam it became necessary to adopt the doctrine that a change of faith by the holder of the land did not affect the liability to pay *kharaj* on the land. *Kharaj* thus came to be regarded as 'a permanent rent from the land for the benefit of the Muslim community, the supreme owner'.[1] The doctrine of *fai* evolved was that the immovable properties acquired by conquest were 'a foundation in perpetuity for the benefit of successive generations of the community, in contrast to the movable booty, *ghanima*, which was distributed immediately'.[2] *Jizyah*, which like *kharaj* was a term used originally to denote tribute,[3] was the poll-tax levied on *dhimmis*, i.e. 'the people of scripture' (*ahl al-kitab*), Christians, Jews, Sabaeans and Zoroastrians.

This, briefly, is the theory of *zakat* accepted by the Sunni schools of law. It may be compared with the interpretation offered in the *Saudi Memorial*, Volume II, Appendix B, under the headings, 'The Zakah: an Opinion by Shaikh Muhammad Ahmad Abu Zahrah, Professor of Islamic Law in the University of Cairo', 'Tax Collecting in Saudi Arabia', and 'Misuse of the Term *Zakah*'.

The pertinent contentions of Shaikh Muhammad Ahmad Abu Zahrah, which he develops with many repetitions, are as follows:

(i) 'The *zakah*, or Property Tax, is the second of the (Five) Pillars of Islam.'

(ii) 'The Worship (*salah*) is a term used for personal (individual) worship whose basis is expressed intention. . . . The *zakah*, on the

---

[1] *Encyclopaedia of Islam* (new edn.), *s.v.* 'Bayt al-mal'.   [2] Ibid.
[3] For a discussion of this, see D. C. Dennett, *Conversion and the Poll Tax in Early Islam*, Cambridge (U.S.A.), 1950.

The Submissions on Zakat in the Saudi Memorial

other hand, is a social obligation, which is the basis of society's mutual responsibility in Islam, for it takes from the rich to give to the poor. It does not involve expressed intention; it requires payment, even forcibly.'

(iii) 'The second respect in which the *zakah* differs from the *salah* is that the Ruler collects the Property Tax, which is the evidence of one's submissiveness to authority. . . . The Property Tax is evidence of obedience to rulers who carry out the Law of Allah Most High.'

(iv) 'The Caliphs who followed the Prophet were wont to take the payment to the Ruler to be a proof of obedience (loyalty), and of submission to the rule of the community. They inferred from the refusal to pay it a proof of unruliness and disloyalty and rebellion against the government of the Ruler, just as it was inferred that refusal to pay the taxes was a proof of rebellion against the government.'

(v) '. . . [The *zakah*] is a tax on property and a right pertaining to it. It is to the Muslim as the *kharaj* (land tax) and the *jizyah* (poll tax) are to the non-Muslim. If these two are a tax, without doubt, it (the *zakah*) also is a tax whose payment indicates loyal obedience.'

(vi) 'The conclusion about all of it is that the *zakah* is a social tax which the Ruler collects, not an individual beneficence. Rather, it is for the security of the State through its army, and it is a co-operative arrangement between the rich and the needy. The State in this is the representative of the needy and deals with the rich in their name, to save them from humiliation and scorn. The payment of the *zakah* . . . is a proof of loyal obedience and a perfection of the authority of the State.'[1]

These propositions differ materially from the accepted doctrine of *zakat* in Islamic law, which has been outlined above. It is of interest to note, moreover, in view of the fact that the Hanbali rite is officially observed in Saudi Arabia, that nowhere in his opinion does Shaikh Abu Zahrah cite the most authoritative texts of the Hanbali school, viz., the *Mughni* of Muwaffaq al-Din ibn Qudama and the *Sharh al-Kabir* of Shams al-Din ibn Qudama.[2] *Zakat* is not, strictly speaking, a property tax but an alms tax.[3] Like the *salat*, it is classed, along with purification (*tahara*), fasting, the pilgrimage, and, some-

---

[1] *Saudi Memorial*, Appendix B, part 1.
[2] Both were published, in 12 volumes, at Cairo in A.H. 1346-8 (1927-30) at the expense of the late King Ibn Sa'ud.
[3] See, e.g., *Shorter Encyclopaedia of Islam*, s.v. 'Zakāt'.

The Submissions on Zakat in the Saudi Memorial

times, warfare for the faith, as one of the ordinances of divine worship (*ibadat*).[1] 'It is to be exacted from all who, whether voluntarily or under constraint, enter into the brotherhood of Islam; but it is not a tax. Rather is it to be regarded as a loan made to God, which He will repay many-fold.'[2]

To claim that *zakat* is 'a social obligation, which is the basis of society's mutual responsibility in Islam' is to read back into the early Islamic community a modern conception for which there is no evidence in Islamic law. The contention that the collection and payment of *zakat* is evidence of submissiveness to authority and obedience to rulers, if by this is meant non-resistance, may be correct. But the collection and payment of *zakat* is not a condition of submission; nor does it necessarily involve submission. Some authorities of the Shafi'i school, including al-Shafi'i himself, hold that it is preferable for an individual to distribute his *zakat* personally.[3] What is perhaps more relevant here is that this doctrine is stated emphatically in the authoritative Hanbali texts, the *Mughni* and *Sharh al-Kabir*, with respect both to the *zakat* on 'visible' property and to that on 'invisible' property. The handing-over of one's *zakat* to the government's agents for disbursement is regarded as a valid alternative, in so far as it discharges the religious obligation to pay *zakat*, but also as a less desirable one.[4]

Since *zakat* was, from the beginning of Islam, a religious obligation recognized by all, and, therefore, had to be paid, it was, except to the scrupulous Muslim, probably largely immaterial to whom it was paid. Thus, it was not unnatural that when a *zakat* collector visited an area or a tribal group, *zakat* was paid to him. Such payment, however, did not carry with it any implication of political submission. It is noteworthy that in both early Islamic and modern times there have been cases of rulers sending out *zakat*-collecting expeditions beyond their frontiers; and also of *zakat* being paid indiscriminately to the collectors of different rulers according to their relative proximity at a given moment. The crucial point was that the *zakat*, as a

---

[1] *Shorter Encyclopaedia of Islam*, s.v. ' 'Ibādāt'.
[2] H. A. R. Gibb, *Mohammedanism*, 2nd edn., Oxford, 1953, p. 64. Cf. *Shorter Encyclopaedia of Islam*, s.v. 'Zakāt': '. . . The religious obligation to pay *zakāt* is everywhere recognized and where the peasant is not overburdened with other taxes, he pays it at least on *ẓāhir* property as far as circumstances permit, although with many abuses in details.'
[3] Aghnides, *Mohammedan Theories of Finance*, pp. 296–301.
[4] *Mughni*, II, 507–9, and *Sharh al-Kabir*, II, 673–6.

The Submissions on Zakat in the Saudi Memorial

religious duty, had to be discharged; its collection *per se* gave no proof of the existence of an effective exercise of governmental authority.

Shaikh Abu Zahrah, in discussing the implications inherent in the payment of *zakat*, slips quickly from the concept of 'submission' to that of 'loyalty'. Thus he states that payment was 'a proof of obedience (loyalty) and of submission to the rule of the community', and that, conversely, the refusal to pay was 'a proof of unruliness and disloyalty and rebellion against the government'. This is not strictly accurate. Legally Muslims were bound to pay *zakat*, and on failure to do so could be constrained to pay—but the disobedience involved was to the ordinances of Allah and not to those of a temporal ruler. The payment of *zakat* was not, in itself, evidence of loyalty and submission; nor was the withholding of payment evidence, in itself, of unruliness and disloyalty. But because of the theocratic nature of Islamic government it is difficult to distinguish between disobedience to Allah and rebellion against his viceregent. The conception of loyalty in a political sense does not apply to the classical theory of the Islamic state: in so far as loyalty existed at all it was a religious sentiment. No political loyalty to a ruler, therefore, can be inferred from the payment of *zakat*. Submission to rulers is enjoined on Muslims by the *Shari'ah*, whether the ruler be 'just', that is to say, rules according to the law, or 'unjust'. Likewise, the *zakat* on 'visible' property is to be paid to his agent, even though the character of the government offers no guarantee of its proper distribution. This holds true even if the ruler is a tyrant, a rebel, or a schismatic.[1] Obviously, in such cases the question of political loyalty does not arise; and the payment of *zakat* is evidence of submission only if by 'submission' is meant non-resistance.

For Shaikh Abu Zahrah to say that the *zakat* is to Muslims as the *kharaj* and *jizyah* are to non-Muslims, and to conclude from this that if these two are taxes then *zakat* is a tax whose payment implies loyal obedience, is to argue from a false analogy. The payment of *zakat* by a Muslim is an individual obligation which he owes to Allah, whereas the payment of *kharaj* and *jizyah* by the 'people of scripture' was not an individual religious obligation but an

---

[1] Aghnides, pp. 298–302 and 335–7; *Shorter Encyclopaedia of Islam*, s.v. 'Zakāt'. In these cases, as indicated above (p. 295), some authorities, particularly of the Hanafi school, hold that the *zakat* should be paid by the individual a second time and distributed direct to the beneficiaries.

The Submissions on Zakat in the Saudi Memorial

arrangement between the Muslim state and the non-Muslim community.

The final submissions of Shaikh Abu Zahrah are all, for reasons already indicated, of doubtful validity. The *zakat* is not 'a social tax': it is an obligatory act of worship, the performance of which is a form of purification.[1] To depict it as 'a co-operative arrangement between the rich and needy' is to introduce a concept unknown in Islamic law. The statement that the *zakat* is designed to achieve 'the security of the State through its army' is at variance with the theory of Islamic law, which maintains that it is those who voluntarily undertake *jihad*, not the regular troops, who are to receive part of the proceeds of *zakat*.[2]

Shaikh Abu Zahrah's opinion is used by the *Memorial*'s authors to support their submissions on the practice and significance of *zakat*-collecting in Saudi Arabia today. They write:

'The Saudi Arabian Government is and always has been a true Islamic government, founded firmly on the principles of the Shari'ah law. As such, it has always taken *zakah* from its subjects in the manner prescribed by that law. For the purposes of the present discussion, it is not necessary to go at length into all the various aspects of this complex subject; the significant point in the present connection is the character of the *zakah* as a true tax, implying on the part of the taxpayer an allegiance in secular as well as religious matters, and on the part of the government an assertion of temporal sovereignty. It is the view of the Saudi Arabian Government that the paying and taking of *zakah* implies precisely this. ... Those who pay *zakah* are devout Muslims, and the Imam has as his duty the protection of the Faith and the Faithful. Thus the payment of *zakah* is an act which puts the taxpayers under the protection of the collector. In effect, this amounts to a sealing of allegiance through the joint performance of an obligatory religious act.'[3]

The payment of *zakat*, as pointed out in the foregoing pages, is not of itself a manifestation of political allegiance to the ruler whose agents collect it, nor is its collection an assertion of temporal author-

---

[1] Shaikh Abu Zahrah's definition of *zakat* as 'a social tax' may be compared with the definition of it given by the *Memorial*'s authors later in Appendix B as 'an obligatory religious act'.

[2] *Shorter Encyclopaedia of Islam*, loc. cit.

[3] *Saudi Memorial*, II, Appendix B, part 2.

The Submissions on Zakat in the Saudi Memorial

ity on his part. The proposition that 'the payment of *zakah* is an act which puts the taxpayers under the protection of the collector' is untenable in Islamic law. What theories of 'protection' exist have been used by the Hanafis, not the Hanbalis, to justify the payment of *zakat* on 'visible' property to the government's collectors, and they apply to the property, not to the person of the owner.[1]

The *Memorial*'s authors go on to quote from H. R. P. Dickson's *Arab of the Desert* (p. 441) to the effect that, in Eastern Arabia, a ruler is bound to protect a tribe that pays *zakat* to him, and that he has no right, therefore, to take *zakat* from a foreign tribe which visits his territory for grazing purposes only. The authors, however, do not quote Dickson fully. He says also (p. 441): 'Should the visiting tribe, however, ask for and obtain permission to settle for the summer on wells in the local Ruler's state, then the latter has the right, by unwritten law, to take full *zakāt* from it. The idea underlying this custom is that the foreign tribe eats up his grazing and drinks his water to the detriment of his own tribe.' What Dickson has to say is in keeping with what is being contended here, viz., that the tax collected under the name of *zakat* in Saudi Arabia, and Eastern Arabia generally, is something other than the classical *zakat* of Islam.

This is further borne out by the description given by the *Memorial*'s authors of the procedure followed in Saudi Arabia—or in Hasa, at least—for disposing of the *zakat* revenues.

'After collection, the receipts are gathered together and taken to the Governor, who, after disposing of the stock and deducting the wages of the officials concerned in accordance with the law, forwards the balance to the Department of *Zakah* and Income Tax of the Ministry of Finance and retains the registers in his files.'[2]

An Islamic government, if it is to be regarded as 'just', must adhere strictly to the rules governing the collection and distribution of the *zakat*. All the schools of Islamic law are agreed that the *zakat* revenues must be expended for the purposes for which they were intended, and that the claims of the local poor and indigent must be met before any surplus can be transferred to the public treasury.[3] In Saudi Arabia the distribution of the *zakat*, if it is *zakat* in the

---

[1] See, e.g., Aghnides, p. 298: 'The right of the state itself to collect the *zakāt* in order later to disburse it to its lawful beneficiaries, according to the Hanifite doctors, is based on the protection (*himāyah*) afforded by the state to the property.'
[2] *Saudi Memorial*, II, Appendix B, part 2.
[3] See, e.g., Aghnides, pp. 423-64.

The Submissions on Zakat in the Saudi Memorial

classical sense, should conform to the precepts of Islamic law. It does not appear, from what the *Memorial*'s authors have to say, to do so.

As has been remarked before in the present work, the authors of the *Saudi Memorial* are at pains to distinguish between what they call 'true *zakah*' and the sums collected under the name of *zakat* by Saudi rulers from the littoral states of Eastern Arabia in the nineteenth century. In Appendix B, part 2, for instance, they write:

'For a number of years between 1808 and 1869, several rulers of the Persian Gulf paid annual sums to the Saudi State, ranging upwards to 40,000 Maria Theresa dollars. Contemporary accounts in both Arabic and English refer to these payments variously as presents, tribute, *zakah*, *jizyah*, *kharaj*, *qanun*, *qaʻidah*, *rasm*, *madda*, alms and tithe. . . .

'The large sums paid to the Saudi State during the nineteenth century were lump payments made by the political head of a foreign state as a form of tribute; they bore no relation to true *zakah*. . . . As Ibn Bishr, the Arab historian, points out, the collecting of the true *zakah* was carried out faithfully by the Saudi State during the same period in which revenue, sometimes called *zakah*, was being obtained from the tributary states of the Persian Gulf.'

To illustrate the use of the term *kharaj*, the authors quote this sentence from the *Tuhfat al-Ayyan* of the Ibadi historian, Abdullah al-Salimi (II, 187): 'The Sultan (of Muscat) paid him (Mutlaq al-Mutairi) the *kharaj* to keep him away from the country.' They give no example of the use of the term *jizyah* to describe the payments made to the Saudi Amir, yet the same page of al-Salimi states: '. . . True Muslims were treated as polytheists and made to pay the *jizyah* and the *kharaj*.' It is clear from this, and from the context in which the sentence occurs, that al-Salimi is expressing astonishment that taxes of this nature should have been imposed by the Saudis upon fellow Muslims, viz., the Ibadiya of Oman. Another Omani historian, Salil ibn Raziq, likewise considers it worthy of mention that the Persians, after their invasion of Oman in 1737, imposed the *kharaj*.[1]

[1] *Imâms and Seyyids of 'Omân*, p. 143. Cf. Aghnides, pp. 360–1: 'The land of the Arabs has been considered as tithe land, because the Prophet, and after him the four "righteous" califs, did not impose on it the *kharāj*, and because the payment of *kharāj* involves humiliation, and the lands of the Arabs do not deserve *kharāj* any more than their persons deserve slavery.'

The Submissions on Zakat in the Saudi Memorial

As for *jizyah*, the poll-tax on subject Christians, Jews, and other 'people of scripture', it is scarcely conceivable that the Muslim rulers and inhabitants of the Persian Gulf states in the nineteenth century would have applied the term to the tribute they paid the Saudis—unless, perhaps, with acerbity. The terms *qa'idah*, *rasm* and *madda* occur only in two letters from the Residency Agent at Sharjah in 1854 and 1856, cited by the authors in Volume I, Chapter IV, paragraph 195 of the *Memorial*. Generalizations concerning their use cannot properly be made from isolated instances of this kind. *Qanun* is taken by the authors from Ibn Raziq's history of the Al Bu Sa'id, translated by Badger. But Badger defines it in a note as 'tribute (in the shape of *Zakât*, or Obligatory Alms for religious purposes) . . . paid to the Wahhâbis by Máskat and Sohâr'.[1]

Contrary to what the *Memorial*'s authors say, *zakat* was the term commonly used by the inhabitants of the littoral states of Eastern Arabia and Bahrain to describe the payments made to the Saudis in the last century, and it was employed by the Saudi Amir himself.[2] This is not to say that the *zakat* collected was the classical *zakat* of Islam, any more than the tax collected in Saudi Arabia today under the name of *zakat* is, strictly speaking, Islamic *zakat*. In the cases of Muscat and Bahrain, in particular, the *zakat* paid to Riyadh was, as has been observed earlier, little more than *Danegeld*. But it never entirely lost its religious attributes, and the excuse often made by the Saudi Amir for enforcing its payment was that it was his duty as Imam to do so. No distinction was drawn at the time between the *zakat* collected from tribesmen and that exacted from Muscat and Bahrain, and it is misleading of the *Memorial*'s authors to suggest, as they do in the passage quoted above, that Ibn Bishr drew such a distinction. The only difference lay in the varying degrees of coercion required to exact payment. Thus, converts to the Wahhabi practice of Islam, like the Qawasim of the Trucial Coast—and, for a time, their kinsmen on the Persian shore—paid *zakat* to Riyadh more or less willingly, while the rulers of Bahrain and Muscat did so with great reluctance.

But this *zakat* did not carry with it any implications of political or territorial sovereignty. The Persian Qawasim, for example, did not regard their payment of *zakat* to the Saudi Amir as an acknowledgement of his temporal authority over them.[3] The *zakat* paid by the

[1] *Imâms and Seyyids of 'Omân*, p. 364, n. 1.
[2] See above, p. 84.
[3] See above, pp. 77–8.

The Submissions on Zakat in the Saudi Memorial

Shaikh of Bahrain to the Amir Faisal in the eighteen-fifties was 'purely of a religious character . . . [and] its payment was not held to imply any territorial jurisdiction'.[1] If it had, then it is highly unlikely that the British Government would have advised the Shaikh, as they did on several occasions, to continue its payment to the Amir. It is even less likely, if such had been the nature of this *zakat*, that they would have accepted the Amir Abdullah's declaration in 1866 that he would not 'injure or attack the territories of the Arab tribes in alliance with the British Government, specially on the kingdom of Muscat, further than in receiving the zukat that has been customary of old'.

The *Memorial*'s authors, however, argue in the opposite sense. Since, they say, the collection of 'true' *zakat* is an assertion of temporal sovereignty, the 'zukat' of the 1866 declaration could only have been 'political tribute, paid by one State to another'. '. . . It amounted to a license to the Saudi ruler to collect tribute in areas not his own without affecting thereby the "independent status" of those areas. . . . The term was not used to mean the true *zakah*, the payment of which by every individual Muslim is enjoined by the Koran.'[2] Leaving aside the question of whether the payment of political tribute implies a degree of political subjection or not, it is clear that here, as elsewhere in the *Memorial*, the authors have misunderstood the true character of Islamic *zakat*. The 'zukat' of the 1866 declaration, in fact, more closely resembled Islamic *zakat*, in that its payment was not held to constitute an acknowledgement of the secular authority of the Saudi ruler, than it did political tribute.

The authors' general argument concerning the significance of the *zakat* collected by Saudi Arabia in the disputed areas in this century is similarly unacceptable. If, as they assert, this *zakat* is the classical *zakat* of Islam, then its collection cannot form a legal basis for a claim to sovereignty over these areas.

[1] See above, p. 79.
[2] *Saudi Memorial*, I, Chapter VI, para. 26. See also, II, Appendix B, part 2.

Index

Abbas Pasha of Egypt, 79
Abbas ibn Abdullah, 132
Abdul Aziz, Shaikh, 79
Abdul Aziz ibn Abdur Rahman Al Sa'ud, King of Saudi Arabia, 21–2, 43, 44, 45, 149, 151, 152, 216; recovers Najd, 104; Hasa, 108; designs on Oman, 104–5, 109, 115–16, 119–121; overtures to British, 105, 108; to Turks, 110–11; *vali* of Najd, 110–111; legal position, 268–9, 273; treaties with Britain, 112–14, 121–2, 273; raids Iraq, 114; conquers Hijaz, 115; collects taxes at Buraimi, 116, 119–20, 274; at Liwa, 121, 274; grants oil concession, 122; 1935 frontier claim, 124–6, 157–8, 269; 1949 frontier claim, 144–5, 269; and Buraimi O., 159, 161, 167, 269; and Churchill, 170; death, 176; character, 280. *See also* Saudi Arabia
Abdul Aziz ibn Ghardaqah, 56, 248
Abdul Aziz ibn Sa'ud, Wahhabi Amir, 246
Abdul Aziz ibn Sa'ud ibn Jiluwi, acting Governor of Hasa; and Buraimi O., 187–8, 191–2, 225–6, 229
Abdul-Ghani ibn Ali, 132
Abdul Latif, Saudi official, 188, 194
Abdul Mejid, Ottoman Sultan, 81 n. 1
Abdullah al-Quraishi, Saudi official at Buraimi O., 175, 194; attempts bribery of Zaid ibn Sultan, 194, 200–1; before arbitration tribunal, 194–5, 201–3
Abdullah ibn Abdul Aziz Al Sulaiman, Saudi *qadi* at Buraimi O., 257–8
Abdullah ibn Ali Al Mahmud, 152
Abdullah ibn Baruk, chief of Al Bu Hamir section of Manasir, 41, 214
Abdullah ibn Faisal, Wahhabi Amir, takes Buraimi O., 75; threatens Oman, 75; exacts tribute, 76; and Thuwaini ibn Sa'id, 83–4; succeeds father, 84; and 1866 undertaking, 84–5, 108, 147, 158, and Appendix B; Ottoman subject, 84, 85; contemplates recapture of Buraimi O., 87–8; deposed, 89; *qaim-maqam* of Najd, 89; Amir of Najd, 95; deposed, 95
Abdullah ibn Humaid al-Salimi, Ibadi historian, 55 and Appendix B
Abdullah ibn Jasim Al Thani, Ruler of Qatar; and Khaur al-Udaid, 254
Abdullah ibn Jiluwi, Governor of Hasa; and Al Bu Falah, 115
Abdullah ibn Nami, Saudi police commander at Buraini O.; arrives, 175; suborns *tamimah* of Na'im, 176–7; distributes money, 178–9, 181–3, 195–6, 198, 202, 204, 222, 225, 233–4; and arms, 178–9, 191–3, 202; to Imam Ghalib, 186, 193, 204; and Sulaiman ibn Himyar, 186; aircraft incident, 184; obtains declarations, 188, 195–6, 223, 226–7, 234; expelled, 205–6
Abdullah ibn Salim, *tamimah* of Bani Ka'ab; becomes chief, 177–8; assassination plotted, 180; and Saudis, 232
Abdullah ibn Sa'ud, Wahhabi Amir, 57
Abdullah ibn Thunaiyan, Wahhabi Amir; threatens Buraimi O., 67
Abdur Rahman, Haji, Residency Agent, Sharjah, 89–90
Abdur Rahman ibn Faisal, Amir of Najd; raids Liwa O., 94; exiled, 95; returns, 104; *qaim-maqam* of Najd, 105
Abdur Rahman ibn Ibrahim, 70, 78
Abu Dhabi shaikhdom; described, 20; early history, 51, 58–62; relations with Qatar, 94–5; with Saudis, 104, 108–9, 118–19, 121, 159, 180; strength, 106; confines, 131–3, 141; war with Dubai, 31, 42, 154, 156, 220; Saudi claims on, 144, 146;

Index

Abu Dhabi—*continued*
1952 frontier claim, 153–4; oil discovered, 268. *See also* Al Bu Falah, Bani Yas.
Abu Isa, 83
Abu Sandan, 119–20
Abu Zahrah, Shaikh Muhammad Ahmad, Appendix B
Aden Protectorates, 124, 128, 145
Aflaj, Bani Qitab, 98, 187, 233
Ahmad ibn Hilal, *see* Ahmad ibn Muhammad ibn Hilal
Ahmad ibn Ibrahim, Muscat Minister of Interior, 138; at Buraimi O., 140, 160 n. 1, 164
Ahmad ibn Muhammad al-Salf, chief of Khawatir, 48 n. 1; and Sultan of Muscat, 139–40, 224; and Saudis, 164, 195–6, 224
Ahmad ibn Muhammad al-Sudairi, Wahhabi *naib* at Buraimi O., 70 n. 3, 75–6; tries to seize Himriyah, 82, 251
Ahmad ibn Muhammad ibn Hilal, chief of Dhawahir, 46, 48, 116, 119, 189; Abu Dhabi *wali* at Buraimi O., 96, 133–4, 228; settles tribal disputes, 97–102; death, 135
Ahmad ibn Muhammad ibn Thani; and Ibn Sa'ud, 104
Ahmad ibn Sa'id, Imam of Oman, 21; elected, 53; reign and death, 53
Ahmed Tewfiq Pasha, *vali* of Baghdad, 81 n. 1
Ain village (Buraimi O.), 33, 34, 45, 46, 135, 161, 230; taken by Zaid ibn Khalifah, 96
Ain Baiwa, 142
Ajman shaikhdom, 22, 47, 60–1, 104
Al Badr section of Awamir, 44
Al Bu Falah dynasty, 20, 31, 37, 42, 46, 49, 51, 106, 217; jurisdiction, 131–3, 141, 220, 272; and Buraimi O., 60–1, 66, 95–6, 108–9, 133–5, 230–1, 256, 272, 276; relations with Qawasim, 60–1, 91; with Al Bu Sa'id, 60–1, 75–6, 133; with Wahhabis, 65, 67, 71; with Al Thani, 94; with Na'im, 65–6, 89, 95–8, 100, 133–5; with Dhawahir, 45–7, 60, 66, 71, 96, 247–8, 256, 272, 276; with Manasir, 41–2, 66, 72, 99–100, 154, 156, 212, 236, 276; with Awamir, 44–5, 72, 95, 97, 165, 236, 276; *Saudi Memorial* on, 244. *See also* Abu Dhabi, Bani Yas
Al Bu Falasah, 36
Al Bu Hamir section of Manasir, 39, 40–1, 42, 46, 214

Al Bu Khail section of Manasir, 39, 40–1, 46, 211 n. 3, 214, 236
Al Bu Khuraiban section of Na'im, 47–8, 66, 69, 71, 96, 165
Al Bu Muhair section of Bani Yas, 36, 46, 218
Al Bu Mundhir section of Manasir, 39, 40, 41, 121, 180, 214–15, 236, 242
Al Bu Rahmah section of Manasir, 39, 40, 41, 188, 214–15, 235, 236, 242
Al Bu Sa'id dynasty, 21, 23; founded, 53; fortunes, 81–2; *Saudi Memorial* on, 244, 253. *See also* Muscat and Oman
Al Bu Sha'ar section of Manasir, 39, 40, 41, 211 n. 3, 214, 236, 242; raid Qatar, 94; Ifar, 100
Al Bu Shamis tribe, 47–8; and Wahhabis, 56 n. 1, 63–4, 69, 74, 82, 246–247; and Al Bu Falah, 42, 66, 72; and Al Bu Sa'id, 136, 137, 138; and British, 68, 82; of Wadi al-Jizzi, 97, 178–9; and Zaid ibn Khalifah, 101–102; and Saudis, 115–16, 165, 168, 171, 178–9, 182, 196
Al Hajariyin tribe, 57, 63
Al Hamuda clan of Na'im, 48, 66, 120
Al Hirth tribe, 86, 109, 116, 185
Al Kathir tribe, 42, 43, 125, 126
Al Khalifah dynasty, 79. *See also* Bahrain
Al Mishaghin section of Bani Yas, 36, 37
Al Murrah tribe, 28, 31, 42–3; at Khaur al-Udaid, 93; raid Abu Dhabi, 94, 115; Uqair, 273; allegiance, 124, 125, 126, 144, 154, 210, 213, 274; tax paying, 212, 237–238, 243; *dirah*, 126, 127, 129, 210
Al Murur section of Bani Yas, 36, 37 n. 2
Al Rimal, 26, 28
Al Sa'ud dynasty, 211–12, 236; early history, 53–4, 57, 62, 64, 67, 89, 91; overthrown, 95, 271; *Saudi Memorial* on, 244. *See also* Wahhabis
Al Thani dynasty, 20, 22, 91; and Al Bu Falah, 94–5
Al Ya'aqib tribe; and Saudis, 182–3
Alexandria, Convention of, 67
Ali Aba al-Rus al-Dhu'ayyif of Awamir; and Saudis, 188, 221–2, 235
Ali ibn Abdullah Al Thani, Ruler of Qatar, 153
Ali ibn Barak, 200
Ali ibn Ghanim, *wali* of Jimi village, 135

306

Index

Ali ibn Hamud, 66
Ali ibn Hilal, *tamimah* of Duru', 183
Ali ibn Mudhaffar, 138
Ali ibn Muhammad, 132
Ali ibn Muhammad ibn Rubayyi', Bani Qitab shaikh; and Saudis, 191–2, 226
Amin al-Raihani, 122, 145
Amir ibn Mubarak, chief of Al Bu Khail section of Manasir, 41, 214; allegiance, 236
Amirah, 144
Anbak, 125
Aqaila, 168, 213 n. 3, 239
Aqal, 27, 154
Aqil, Saudi official, 204
Aqlat Manasir, 153
Arab Information Centre, 208
Arab League, 260–1
Araiqi, 151, 181, 231
ARAMCO (Arabian-American Oil Company), 38, 145, 174, 212, 216, 217, 276; in the Dhafrah, 142–3
Arbitration; suggested on frontier question, 149, 166; agreement negotiated, 170–2; terms, 172–4, and Appendix A; tribunal, 23, 47, 187; composition, 172, 174; sitting at Nice, 184; permits use of aircraft, 184, 188; sitting at Geneva, 180, 199–203; suspended, 203–4
Ash Shora newspaper, 117
Asir, 121
Awamir tribe, 31, 40; origin, numbers and distribution, 43–4; leadership and allegiance, 43–4, 125, 126, 222; past history, 52, 71, 72, 138; and Al Bu Falah, 44–5, 72, 95, 97, 214, 276; and Saudis, 115–16, 119, 160, 165, 168, 179, 180; tax paying, 221, 238–9; claimed as Saudi subjects, 144, 221–2, 235–6
Azzam, Abdur Rahman, Saudi adviser and agent; before arbitration tribunal, 145 n. 4, 201, 203; and Buraimi question, 266–7
Azzan ibn Qais, Ruler of Muscat and Oman, 53 n. 1, 83, 95, 96; elected Imam, 86; expels Wahhabis from Buraimi O., 87, 251–2; alliance with Zaid ibn Khalifah, 88, 101, 262; defeat and death, 89

Badger, Rev. G. P., Arabist and British official, 53 n. 2, 246–7, 252, and Appendix B
Baghdad, 89
Baghdad Railway, 107
Bahlah, 35, 264

Bahrain, 58, 122, 150, 176, 183; and Wahhabis, 62, 74, 84–5; pays *zakat*, 78–9, 249, and Appendix B
Bainunah, 29, 30, 40, 132, 161, 168, 239, 242; Saudi claims to, 146, 213, 274, 275
Bait al-Falaj, 248
Ba'ja wells, 217, 218
Baluchi tribe, 210, 268; and Bani Qitab, 99; and Saudis, 151, 181, 191, 231
Bandar Abbas, 57, 88
Bandar al-Mirfa, 19, 141, 144, 145 n. 1, 146, 159
Bandar al-Mughairah, 144
Bani Bu Ali tribe, 57, 68, 258
Bani Ghafir (Miyayihah) tribe, 52, 99, 100, 125, 126
Bani Hajir tribe, 94, 144, 154–5, 213
Bani Hasan tribe, 179
Bani Hina tribe, 52, 185
Bani Jabir tribe, 33, 53, 136
Bani Ka'ab tribe, 56 n. 1, 66, 71, 97, 98, 99, 210, 268; and Saudis, 118, 152, 160, 171, 177–8; claimed as subjects, 231–2
Bani Kalban tribe; and Saudis, 182–3
Bani Qitab tribe, 42, 66, 71, 72, 95, 98, 210, 241, 246, 247; and Zaid ibn Khalifah, 98–100; and Saudis, 165, 171, 191; claimed as subjects, 231, 232–3, 234
Bani Riyam tribe, 109, 116, 185, 262
Bani Ruwaihah tribe, 116
Bani Yas tribe, 20, 27, 29, 115, 121, 132, 154, 180, 211; origin and distribution, 36, 216–17; numbers and sections, 36–7, 217, 219; way of life, 37–8, 217–18; early history, 51–2, 56, 59–60, 61, 71, 72, 74, 95, 246–8; allegiance, 38–9, 154, 156, 216–18, 236, 276. *See also* Abu Dhabi, A Bu Falah
Baruni, Sulaiman, 117
Basra, 57, 110
Batin, 29, 30, 132
Batinah Coast, 34, 35, 43, 56, 58, 75, 83, 98, 101, 102, 262, 264
Battal al-Mutairi, Wahhabi *naib* at Buraimi O., 57
Beeley, Harold, 267
Bir Aziz wells, 28
Bird, Richard, 140
Birkat al-Mauz, 264
Bitanah, 29, 30, 132
Blue Line, 145, 149; defined, 107–8; significance of, 111, 113–14, 268, 273–4; Saudi view of, 123; British view of, 148

Index

Bombay Marine (Indian Navy), 59, 61
Britain; and Trucial Shaikhdoms, 22, 105; and Sultanate of Muscat, 23; past policy towards Wahhabis, 68, 74, 80, 82; towards Turks in P. Gulf, 93; early relations with Ibn Sa'ud, 105, 108, 109; 1913 Convention with Turks, 107–8, 109; 1915 Treaty with Ibn Sa'ud, 112–13; Convention of Uqair, 113; Treaty of Jeddah, 121–2, 273; 1934–7 frontier negotiations, 123–9, 157–8; 1949 negotiations, 143–4; opposes new Saudi claim, 146–7, 148; proposes frontier commission, 149–50; London discussions, 150–1, 155; Dammam Conference, 153–8 opposes Saudi occupation of Buraimi O., 161; concludes Standstill Agreement, 163; proposes arbitration, 149, 166, 169; abrogates Standstill Agreement, 169; blockades Hamasa, 169; concludes arbitration agreement, 170–2; protests breaches, 177, 193–4, 199–200; and Hamasa fire, 199; and arbitration tribunal, 204; discontinues arbitration, 205; ends Saudi occupation, 205; declares frontier, 205; Saudi accusations against, 207–9, 260–1; *Saudi Memorial* on, 244; refuses return to arbitration, 261, 263, 265; suppresses Oman revolt, 264–5; agrees to fact-finding mission, 267; resumes diplomatic relations, 268. *See also* East India Company
British Imperialism in Southern Arabia, 208–9
British India Steam Navigation Company, 103
Bullard, Sir Reader, British Minister to Saudi Arabia; and Sufuq well, 129, 130–1; and Red Line, 157–8; British member of arbitration tribunal, 174; resigns, 203–4; Saudi accusations against, 204, 207–9
Bunaiyan well, 28, 126, 127, 128
Buraimi Oasis; described, 33–5; population, 45; early history, 52; Wahhabi occupations, 54–7, 62–4, 68–71, 73–4, 75, 81–3, 87, 246–8, 249–50, 251–2, 270; and Abu Dhabi, 60–1, 66–8, 71–2, 74, 96, 103–4, 109, 133–5, 231; and Muscat, 60–1, 87–89, 95, 101, 133, 136, 139–40, 147, 252–3; Miles's visit to, 95–6, 252; Cox's 102–4; Lorimer on, 244, 256; Saudi tax collectors at, 116, 119–20, 274; and Saudi 1935 claim, 129;

oil exploration, 139–40; claimed by Saudi Arabia, 159, 161, 245; occupied, 159; Standstill Agreement on, 163; Saudi tactics over, 166–8; British response, 169; arbitration agreement on, 171–3; interim régime in, 175–204; Saudi occupation ended, 205; fact finding mission, 266–7; refugees, 267–8
Buraimi village, 33, 34, 47, 95, 103, 116, 133, 246
Buraimi Zone, 172, 173, 178, 179, 191, 193, 194, 197, 198, 202, 223, 231, 278
Bushire, 57, 73, 84
Buti ibn Khadim, chief of Qubaisat; at Khaur al-Udaid, 93–4

Californian Arabian Standard Oil Company, 129
Cheesman, Major R. E., 26, 28
Churchill, (Sir) Winston; and Ibn Sa'ud, 170
Clayton, Capt. P. H., 201
Cox, Capt. P. Z. (Sir Percy), Political Resident in P. Gulf; on Zaid ibn Khalifah, 102–3; visits Buraimi O., Dhahirah, 102, 103–4; and Ibn Sa'ud, 104–5, 108, 109, 112, 119, 273
Curzon, Marquess, 17

Dalma Island, 29, 35, 36, 93, 131–2
Dammam, 23, 79, 83, 175, 183, 188, 194, 198, 214, 215, 216, 222, 235, 236, 264, 267
Dammam Conference, 41, 42, 153–8, 162, 215, 240, 277
Danegeld, 78, and Appendix B
Dar es Salaam, 21
Dara'iya, early capital of Najd, 53, 57, 118, 248
D'Arcy Exploration Company, 174; in Oman, 116, 118, 136
Dariz, 99, 117, 161
Dauhah, 20; Turks at, 92–3; Qubaisat at, 94
Dauhat al-Nakhlah, 27
Dauhat al-Salwah (Bay of Salwah), 19, 20, 26, 122, 124, 125, 127, 144, 145, 153
Dauhat al-Sila', 27
Dawasir tribe, 144
De Dihigo, Dr. Ernesto, member of arbitration tribunal, 174; resigns, 204
De Ribbing, Herbert, Swedish Ambassador to Spain, investigates Buraimi O. question, 267

Index

De Visscher, Dr. Charles, president of arbitration tribunal, 174; resigns, 203–4
Desert Locust Survey, 32 n. 2
Dhafrah, 28, 29–33; Thesiger on, 29; history, 51, 56, 59, 71, 72, 94, 106, 246; Saudi tax collecting in, 121, 148, 213, 239; Saudi claim to, 49, 129, 131, 146, 148, 156–7, 211, 217–218; assessed, 271, 274–5; Abu Dhabi claim to, 132–3, 154, 157, 244, 255; Lorimer on, 154, 157, 244, 255–6; *Saudi Memorial* on, 255–6
Dhahirah province of Oman, 33, 51, 53, 89, 91, 96, 97, 101, 102, 106, 116, 138, 171, 210, 268; Saudi activities in, 151–2, 164, 233–4
Dhank, 35, 47, 69, 89, 96, 117, 118, 139, 160, 182, 223, 233
Dhawahir Collection, 97
Dhawahir tribe, 33, 45; allegiance, 46–7, 276; past relations with Al Bu Falah, 60, 65–6, 71, 95, 247–8, 256, 272; with Na'im, 65; with Wahhabis, 246–8; and Saudis, 116, 171, 188–90; claimed as subjects, 228–30, 236
Dhiban ibn Ali al-Rubayyi', Bani Qitab shaikh; and Saudis, 187; sent money and arms, 191–2, 233; declares allegiance, 188, 226, 233
Dhiyab ibn Isa, Ruler of Abu Dhabi, 51
Dhiyab ibn Saqr, Al Bu Falah, 134; and Saudis, 180, 223
Dhufar, 27, 34, 138, 262
Dickson, Col. H. R. P., 114, and Appendix B
Dirah; defined and discussed, 18, 35, 126–7; of Bani Ka'ab, 231; of Bani Qitab, 232–3; of Bani Yas, 35, 37, 38, 211, 217; of Duru', 182; of Manasir, 35, 39–40, 156, 211, 217; of Murrah, 42–3, 126, 127, 129, 210; of Na'im, 47
Dubai shaikhdom, 22, 34, 36, 38, 74, 98, 99, 104, 106, 176, 178–9, 180, 190, 264; and Saudis, 108–9, 117; war with Abu Dhabi, 31, 42, 154, 156, 220
Dulles, John Foster; and Buraimi O. question, 263
Duru' tribe; and Awamir, 44–5; and Saudis, 115–16, 119, 125, 126, 168, 182–3, 185, 186
Duwaihin well, 217, 218

East India Company; and P. Gulf, 57–8; and piracy, 58–9

East India Company's Islands, 30
Eden, Sir Anthony; on frontier question, 205–6, 260; at Washington, 262–3
Eastern Reaches of al-Hasa Province, 216, 217–18, 219, 221
Eccles, Capt. G. J.; travels in Oman, 116, 118, 136, 232
Egypt; French occupation, 58; and Wahhabis, 57, 64, 67; and Oman, 186
Eisenhower, President Dwight D.; and frontier question, 262–3
Encyclopaedia of Islam, 212, 231, and Appendix B

Fadhil ibn Muhammad, Al Bu Shamis shaikh; and Wahhabis, 82, 251
Faisal ibn Abdul Aziz Al Sa'ud, Saudi Foreign Minister; and Riyadh Line, 129; and Red Line, 158; at London discussions, 150–1, 155, 159, 162; at Dammam Conference, 153–8; and breach with Britain, 265
Faisal ibn Sa'ud; raids Oman, 56
Faisal ibn Turki, Sultan of Muscat; and Zaid ibn Khalifah, 101–2
Faisal ibn Turki, Wahhabi Amir, 64, 67, 89, 94, 158; and Oman, 68, 69, 70, 71, 72, 82, 83; and Buraimi O., 72, 73, 74, 75; seeks British support, 72, 73, 74, 80; and Bahrain, 74, 78–79, and Appendix B; Ottoman dependant, 73, 79–81; death, 83
Faris ibn Ghanim, Mazari', 220, 226
Firq, 264
Frontiers; principles and problems of definition, 17–19, 126–7, 143–4, 166, 269; proposed commission, 149–50; Anglo-Turkish Blue Line, 107–8; Anglo-Turkish Violet Line, 111; Saudi-Iraq, 113; Saudi-Kuwait, 113; Saudi Red Line, 124–5, 157–8; British Green Line, 125; British Riyadh Line, 127–8, 205; Saudi 1949 Line, 144–5; Qatar 1952 Line, 153; Abu Dhabi 1952 Line, 145, 153–4; British 1955 Line, 205
Fuad Bey Hamza, Saudi Foreign Minister; and 1934–7 frontier negotiations, 123–7, 130, 145, 151, 157
Fujairah, 20, 22, 97, 98, 241

Gazetteer of Persian Gulf, 36, 46, 154, 157, 243–4, 249–50, 251, 255–6
Ghafalah tribe, 66, 72, 98, 99
Ghafiri tribal faction of Oman, 52–3, 55, 96, 104, 109, 116, 139

309

Index

Ghaghah Island, 29, 142
Ghalib ibn Ali, Imam of Oman; and Saudis, 185–6, 193, 204, 278; and Egyptians, 186; and Sultan of Muscat, 261–2; revolts, 264–5; defeated, 265
Ghanim ibn Juraiw, 214 n. 3
Ghar al-Buraid, 153
Gharbiyah province, 51
Ghaus al-Kabir, 38
Glubb, Sir John, 115 n. 1

Hadhramaut, 25, 43, 124, 126, 210
Hafit village, 34, 47, 139, 160, 164, 165, 196, 223
Hafiz Wahba, Saudi Ambassador to Britain, 153
Hajar mountains, 18, 25, 34, 35, 47, 232
Hakki Pasha, Turkish Ambassador to Britain, 110
Hamad ibn Abdullah, Shaikh of Fujairah, 98
Hamad ibn Ahmad al-Yahyayi, Al Bu Shamis chief of Dhank, 48 n. 1; and Saudis, 118
Hamad ibn Futaim, 178, 181
Hamad ibn Mubarak, chief of Al Bu Rahmah, 40, 214
Hamad ibn Rashid al-Hajari, 186
Hamad ibn Saif, Al Bu Khuraiban shaikh, 66
Hamad ibn Saif, Bani Kalban shaikh; and Saudis, 182
Hamad ibn Salim Al Rakkadh, chief of Awamir, 115
Hamad ibn Salim al-Wahshi, Al Bu Shamis shaikh of Dhank, 48 n. 1; and Saudis, 233–4
Hamad ibn Uwais, 192
Hamasa village (Buraimi O.), 33, 47, 116, 151, 152, 181, 186, 188, 189, 191, 204, 222, 223, 246, 258, 267; Saudi occupation, 159, 164, 175; blockaded, 169; fire at, 198–9
Hamdan ibn Khalfan, Al Bu Shamis shaikh; and Saudis, 195, 224–5, 227
Hamdan ibn Zaid, Ruler of Abu Dhabi, 115, 133
Hamerton, Capt. Atkins; visits Buraimi O., 65–6
Hammarskjöld, Dag, 266–7
Hamra Duru', 34
Hamud ibn Azzan, Ruler of Sauhar; and Buraimi O., 64, 67; and Wahhabis, 68–9, 71
Hamud ibn Sarur, Al Bu Shamis chief, 66, 68, 72

Hanafi school of Islamic law, **Appendix B**
Hanbali school of Islamic law, 154, 157, 240, and Appendix B
Harab tribe, 115 n. 1
Hariq (Salim ibn Bilal al-Hariq), Wahhabi general, 54, 246–7
Harith ibn Musallim al-Umairi, 186
Hasa province, 17, 22, 50, 52, 54, 68 n. 2, 70, 71 n. 1, 112, 126, 145 n. 4, 179, 249, 268, 269; annexed by Turks, 89, 91, 158; recovered, 108, 143, 148; tax collecting in, 212–13, 215, 221, 242
Hassan, Mahmud, member of arbitration tribunal, 174
Hawamil section of Bani Yas, 36, 37, 121, 154, 218, 220
Hay, Sir Rupert, Political Resident in P. Gulf; at Dammam Conference, 153, 158
Hazm Sauda Nathil, 153, 154
Hazza', Bani Yas shaikh, 247–8
Hazza' ibn Sultan, Al Bu Falah, 119, 134, 142, 214; before arbitration tribunal, 180, 201
Hennell, Col. Samuel, Political Resident in P. Gulf; initiates Trucial System, 62; and Buraimi O., 64–5; on Bani Yas, 71; on *zakat*, 78, 85; on Faisal ibn Turki, 79
Hijaz, 22, 55, 57, 114, 121, 249
Hili village (Buraimi O.), 33, 45, 46, 96, 135, 229
Himriyah; and Wahhabis, 82, 251
Hinawi tribal faction of Oman, 52, 55, 96, 104, 109, 116
Howard, Bushrod, 209 n. 3
Hufuf, 26, 50, 271
Humaid ibn Ali ibn Hashilah, Duru' shaikh; and Saudis, 182–3.
Humaid ibn Dahnan, 132, 220
Humaid ibn Rashid, Al Bu Khuraiban shaikh, 224, 226
Hunter, Col. F. F., 128, 255
Huqf, 34
Husain, Mullah, Residency Agent, Sharjah, 66 n. 2, 67 n. 1, 71 n. 2, 72 n. 1 and n. 2, 74 n. 1 and n. 3
Huwaishil ibn Ali, Duru' shaikh; and Saudis, 186

Ibadiya sect of Islam, 21, 52, 69, 77, 96, 109, 167
'Ibn Azdakah,' *see* Abdul Aziz ibn Ghardaqah
Ibn Battal, Wahhabi *naib* at Buraimi O., 73, 74
Ibn Bishr, *see* Othman ibn Bishr

310

Index

Ibn Jiluwi, *see* Abdul Aziz ibn Sa'ud ibn Jiluwi, Abdullah ibn Jiluwi, Sa'ud ibn Jiluwi
Ibn Nami, *see* Abdullah ibn Nami
Ibn Rashid dynasty, 21, 91, 112, 258. *See also* Muhammad ibn Rashid
Ibn Sabhan, Rashidi Governor of Riyadh, 94
Ibn Sa'ud, *see* Abdul Aziz ibn Abdur Rahman Al Sa'ud
Ibrahim Pasha, 57
Ibrahim ibn Othman, Abu Dhabi *wali* at Buraimi O., 46, 135
Ibrahim ibn Sulaiman ibn Ufaisan, 246
Ibri, 35, 100, 102, 117, 139, 182, 185, 262
Ifar tribe, 99–100, 210
Ikhwan, 114–15, 125
Imamate of Oman, 21, 185; origins, 52; in eighteenth century, 52–3; lapses, 53 n. 1; revived, 109
Imâms and Seyyids of 'Omân, 53 n. 2, 246–8, 252, and Appendix B
Iraq, 17, 113, 114, 127, 248, 249. *See also* Turkish Arabia
Iraq Petroleum Company, 138
Isa ibn Salih, *tamimah* of Hirth; and Imamate, 116; and Saudis, 116–18
Izki, 264

Ja'alan province of Oman, 57, 118, 258
Jabal Akhdhar, 34, 35, 109, 185, 264, 265
Jabal Dukhan, 27
Jabal Hafit, 33, 34, 103
Jabal Kaur, 34, 264
Jabal Nakhsh, 27, 124, 127, 128
Jabal Shammar, 21, 22, 89, 91, 121
Jabrin (Oman), 264
Jabrin Oasis, 26, 28, 29
Jaddat Harasis, 34
Jafurah desert, 26, 28, 71, 108, 112, 115, 122, 140
Jahili grove (Buraimi O.), 46, 96
Jahiliyah (Dhafrah), 213 n. 3
Jahiliyah (Hasa), 212
Jasim ibn Muhammad ibn Thani, Ruler of Qatar; and Turks, 92, 93, 107; and Khaur al-Udaid, 94, 254; raids Abu Dhabi, 94–5; and Ibn Sa'ud, 104
Jau plain, 33, 96, 256
Jaub depression, 28
Jiban, 26; lesser, 28
Jihad, 124, and Appendix B
Jimi village (Buraimi O.), 33, 45, 46, 96, 103, 133, 228, 268

Jizyah, 55, and Appendix B
Jeddah, 23, 115, 163, 169, 183, 191, 199, 205; Treaty of, 121–2, 145, 147
Jubail, 110, 112

Kahil (Buraimi O.), 183–4, 191
Karab tribe, 31
Karbala, 54
Kashf al-Ghummah, 51, 53 n. 2
Kemball, Capt. A. B., Political Resident in Gulf; and Wahhabis, 75–6, 79, 80; concludes perpetual maritime truce, 75; on *zakat*, 79; and Al Bu Shamis, 82, 251
Khalid ibn Sa'ud, Wahhabi Amir, 67
Khalid ibn Sultan, Al Bu Falah, 134
Khalifah ibn Shakhbut, Ruler of Abu Dhabi, 60, 62, 68; and Buraimi, 65–67; and Khaur al-Udaid, 62, 255
Khalifah ibn Zaid, Al Bu Falah, 98, 102, 134
Khamis ibn Rashid ibn Nasir, chief of Awamir, 43–4
Khanchiyah, 38 n. 1
Kharaj, 55, and Appendix B
Khashabah, Lieut.-Col. Ali; visits Oman, 186
Khatam, 33, 40, 72, 242
Khaur al-Duwaihin, 27, 142, 146, 217
Khaur Kantur, 141
Khaur al-Udaid, 19, 20, 27, 142, 153, 217; Qubaisat settlement at, 37, 62, 92–4, 255; attacked, 94; Abu Dhabi claim to, 92–3, 128, 132, 154, 155–6, 272; Qatar claim to, 91, 94, 254–5, 272; Saudi claim to, 124, 126, 127, 128, 146, 155–6, 158, 254–5; surveyed, 141; *Saudi Memorial* on, 254–5
Khawatir section of Na'im, 47, 48, 98, 139, 196, 241
Khazail tribe, 114
Khidama quarter of Buraimi village, 104
Khurshid Pasha, 64, 66
Kidan, 29, 30, 153
Koran, 76, 77, 239, 240, and Appendix B
Kuwait, 17, 19, 21, 104, 105, 107, 110, 113, 114, 122, 150, 156, 242

Labat section of Duru', 182
Lakmat al-Shu'ub, 111
Lansdowne, Marquess of, 266
Lingah, 60, 131
Liwa Oasis, 17, 20, 25, 30; Thesiger on, 31–2; settlements and population, 32, 35, 36, 37, 218–19; administration, 32–3, 132–3, 220; past

311

Index

Liwa Oasis—*continued*
history, 72, 94, 255, 272; Saudi tax collectors at, 121, 148, 213, 239, 274, 275; Saudi claims to, 125, 129, 130, 146, 148, 218–19, 271, 274; *Saudi Memorial* on, 255–6

Lloyd, Selwyn, 265, 266

Lorimer, J. G., 36, 104, 154, 157, 243–244, 249, 251, 255–6

Ma'aliya section of Bani Qitab, 233

Madinah, 115

Mahadhah, 118, 152, 171, 177, 178, 191, 231

Maharibah section of Bani Yas, 36, 37, 38, 121, 132, 154, 218, 220

Mahbub ibn Jauhar, 89–90, 253

Majid ibn Sa'id, Sultan of Zanzibar, 81

Maliki school of Islamic law, 154, 157, and Appendix B

Manahil tribe, 31, 43, 125, 126, 210

Manasir tribe, 27, 31; numbers, sections and distribution, 39, 214, 217, 219; way of life, 39–41, 215, 218–19; past history, 52, 59, 65, 66, 72, 73, 94, 95, 99–100, 247–8; and Al Bu Falah, 41–2, 59, 66, 72, 94–5, 99–100, 154, 156, 212, 214, 247–8, 276; and Saudis, 115, 121, 180, 212, 214; tax paying, 41, 121, 212–13, 237–9, 242; claims on allegiance, 124, 125–6, 144, 148, 154, 156, 211–15, 217, 235–236, 247–8

Mani' ibn Muhammad, chief of Dhawahir, 45, 47, 201, 228, 229; allegiance, 189, 236; attempted bribery of, 189–90

Maqabil tribe, 102; and Saudis, 178–9

Mardini, Omar Fauzi Beq, *vali* of Basra, 110

Maritime truces, *see* Trucial System

Markhiyah, 161, 213 n. 3

Masfut, 98

Mas'udi grove (Buraimi O.), 96, 103

Matar ibn Salim al-Azizi, Al Bu Shamis chief of Dhank, 48 n. 1; and Saudis, 165, 224, 233–4

Mazari' section of Bani Yas; numbers and distribution, 36, 37, 38, 46, 132, 154, 218–20; early history, 65, 66, 71, 72, 73; and Saudis, 115, 121; allegiance, 156, 219–20; tax paying, 238–9, 242

Mazim, 99

Mecca, 54, 115

Mehemet Ali, 57, 64

Midhat Pasha, *vali* of Baghdad; annexes Hasa, 89; further claims, 91–2

Middle East Journal, 208

Mijan, 27, 125, 126, 130, 146, 154, 217, 274

Miles, Col. S. B., Political Agent at Muscat, 53 n. 4; visits Buraimi, 95–6, 231, 252

Mirfa, *see* Bandar al-Mirfa

Miyayihah tribe, *see* Bani Ghafir

Mubarak ibn Sabah, Ruler of Kuwait, 105

Mubarak ibn Umair, 193

Mudhaffar ibn Sulaiman, *wali* of Sauhar, 136–7, 138, 139

Mughairah (Maghira), *see* Bandar al-Mughairah

Mughni, Appendix B

Mughshin, 31

Muhammad al-Sahili, Saudi tax collector; at Liwa, 121

Muhammad ibn Abdan, Wahhabi *naib* at Buraimi O., 247

Muhammad ibn Abdul Aziz, Wahhabi *naib* at Buraimi O., 63

Muhammad ibn Abdul Aziz al-Ausaji, Wahhabi *qadi* at Buraimi O., 249

Muhammad ibn Abdul Wahhab, religious reformer, 53–4

Muhammad ibn Abdullah, Al Bu Shamis chief, 66, 68

Muhammad ibn Abdullah al-Khalili, Imam of Oman; campaigns in Dhahirah, 116–17; and Saudis, 116, 147, 161, 162; death and succession, 185

Muhammad ibn Abdullah al-Najadi, 188 n. 2

Muhammad ibn Abdullah ibn Manah, Wahhabi envoy; signs 1866 undertaking, 84–5

Muhammad ibn Ahmad al-Yahyayi, Al Bu Shamis shaikh of Dhank; and Saudis, 182–3, 233–4

Muhammad ibn Ali Al Hamuda, *tamimah* of Na'im, 96; and Azzan ibn Qais, 88; and Ibn Rashid, 94

Muhammad ibn Ali ibn Awwad, Al Bu Khuraiban chief, 48 n. 1; and Saudis, 165, 224–5

Muhammad ibn Ali ibn Huwaidan, Bani Qitab shaikh, 233

Muhammad ibn Aun, Sharif of Mecca, 73, 81

Muhammad ibn Hamad, Al Bu Shamis shaikh of Hamasa, 160, 226

Muhammad ibn Hamad ibn Rakkadh, shaikh of Awamir; and Saudis, 195–6, 222, 226

Muhammad ibn Haufan, 180

Index

Muhammad ibn Khadim, chief of Al Bu Sha'ar, 40, 214; allegiance, 236
Muhammad ibn Khalifah, Ruler of Bahrain: and Wahhabis, 78–9
Muhammad ibn Khila, *tamimah* of Ifar, 183 n. 5
Muhammad ibn Mansur, Saudi tax collector; at Buraimi, 119, 188, 194, 196, 226; at Liwa, 121, 148; at Sunainah, 168
Muhammad ibn Nasir, Imam of Oman, 51
Muhammad ibn Rashid, Amir of Hail (Jabal Shammar), 94; captures Riyadh, 95, 158
Muhammad ibn Sa'id ibn Tinah, *tamimah* of Duru', 183
Muhammad ibn Saif, Al Bu Falah, 72
Muhammad ibn Saif al-Ajaji, Wahhabi *naib* at Buraimi O., 70, 71
Muhammad ibn Salimin ibn Rahmah, *tamimah* of Baduin Al Bu Shamis, 48 n. 1, 182, 187; and Sultan of Muscat, 136, 138, 140, 225; and Saudis, 151, 160, 164, 224–6; sells allegiance, 188, 225–6; defects, 196–197, 225
Muhammad ibn Sa'ud ibn Arar, 229, 230
Muhammad ibn Sayyah, chief of Mazari', 220
Muhammad ibn Shakhbut, Ruler of Abu Dhabi, 60
Muhammad ibn Sulaiman, *tamimah* of Bani Ghafir, 99, 100
Muhammad ibn Sultan al-Darmaki; and Saudis, 188, 198; bribed, 188, 228; declares allegiance, 188, 195, 227, 228–9, 235; refugee, 268
Muhammad ibn Sultan Al Hamuda, *tamimah* of Na'im, 120, 133, 137
Muhammad ibn Thani, Ruler of Qatar, 92
Muhammad ibn Zaid, Al Bu Falah, 134
Muhammad Salih Abdul Karim al-Ajami, Saudi agent at Hamasa, 175, 176, 177, 181, 187, 191, 225
Munba'aj wells, 217
Muntafiq tribe, 114
Murabba'at al-Ain (Buraimi O.), 34
Muraikhat tribe, 132
Musandam peninsula, 18, 25, 59 n. 2
Muscat and Oman Field Force, 261–2
Muscat and Oman, Sultanate of, 21, 23; and Wahhabis, 54, 62–3, 68–9, and Appendix B; frontiers, 51; revolt in, 264–5; *Saudi Memorial* on, 244. *See also* Al Bu Sa'id
Mutair tribe, 115 n. 1
Mutawwa', 69, 86; of Oman, 86, 109, 264
Mu'tiridh village (Buraimi O.), 33, 45, 46, 96, 230
Mutlaq al-Mutairi, Wahhabi *naib* at Buraimi O., 55, 56, 57, and Appendix B
Muwafaqah, 214
Muwaffar al-Din ibn Qudama, Muslim jurist, Appendix B
Muwaiqi' settlement (Buraimi O.), 33, 44, 46, 135, 230

Nadir Shah of Persia, 53
Na'im tribe, 33, 34, 42, 45, 46, 268; divisions and distribution, 47; principal shaikhs, 48; allegiance, 48–9, 224; past relations with Wahhabis, 55, 56, 63–4, 69, 71, 77, 87, 89, 246–247, 248, 251–2, 253, 272; with Al Bu Falah, 60–1, 65–6, 89, 95–6, 97–98, 100, 133–5, 272; with Al Bu Sa'id, 60–1, 95, 101, 133, 136, 137, 139–40, 252–3, 272; Hamerton's description of, 66; ask for British protection, 68, 82, 251; oppose Azzan ibn Qais, 88–9, 252; Miles's description of, 95–6, 252; Cox's, 103–4; relations with Saudis, 116, 118, 120, 176–7, 271; claimed as subjects, 222–4, 233–4, 236, 276
Najadat tribe, 33
Najd, 21, 22, 53, 158, 248, 269; *sanjaq* of, 107; sultanate of, 112–13; frontiers of, 113, 268–9, 273
Najd al-Hadith wa Mulhaqatahu, 122, 145
Nakkut wells, 217
Nasir al-Hudhaili, Saudi agent, 179, 225
Nasir ibn Ali Nabhan, 55
Nasir ibn Sa'id ibn Suwaid, chief of Al Bu Rahmah, 40, 214, 216, 235, 236
Nasser, Gamal Abdul, 186
Nizari tribes, 52
Nizwa, 35, 43, 262

Oil concessions, 122, 138, 141, 274; companies, *see* ARAMCO, Californian-Arabian Standard Oil Company, D'Arcy Exploration Company, Iraq Petroleum Company, Petroleum Concessions Ltd., Petroleum Development (Oman) Ltd., Petroleum Development (Trucial Coast) Ltd., Qatar Petroleum Com-

313

Index

Oil concessions—*continued*
  pany, Standard Oil Company;
  operations restricted, 150–1, 158,
  171–2, 173–4
Omar ibn Omair, 152, 160 n. 1
Oppenheim, L. F. L., 113
Othman ibn Bishr, Wahhabi historian, 56 n. 2, 70 n. 3, 76, 77, 246, 248–9, and Appendix B
Ottoman Empire, 111, 113; 1913 convention with Britain, 107–8. *See also* Sublime Porte, Turks

Palgrave, W. G., 83–4
Pearling, 35, 37–8, 106, 131–2
Pelly, Col. Lewis, Political Resident in P. Gulf; and Wahhabis, 83, 84–5, 212; and Khaur al-Udaid, 92–3
Petroleum Concessions Ltd.; in Oman, 138, 139, 140; in Abu Dhabi, 139, 141, 142, 159
Petroleum Development (Oman) Ltd., 264–5
Petroleum Development (Trucial Coast) Ltd., 38, 174
Philby, H. St. J. B., 26, 28, 54, 112, 209, 280
Piracy, 22, 55, 58
Pirate Coast, 54, 55, 56; British expeditions to, 58. *See also* Trucial Shaikhdoms
Political Agent at Muscat, 88. *See also* Miles, Way
Political Officer, Trucial Oman, 142, 159, 160 n. 1, 162, 167, 189–90. *See also* Stobart
Political Resident in P. Gulf, 58–9, 69, 70, 74, 75, 78, 93, 108, 139, 150, 153, 161, 185. *See also* Cox, Hay, Hennell, Kemball, Pelly

Qabil village (Buraimi O.), 34, 117, 160, 223
Qadhib, Shaikh of Lingah, 77
Qahtan ibn Saif, 67
Qahtani tribes, 52
Qala, 44
Qasim; Turks in, 105
Qasr al-Hillah (Buraimi village), 34
Qasr al-Khandaq (Buraimi O.), 33–4, 71, 73, 89, 95
Qasr al-Subarah (Buraimi O.), 71, 73; erected, 54, 246
Qasr al-Sudairi (Buraimi O.), 34; constructed, 83; destroyed, 95
Qatar, 17, 18, 19, 20, 22, 25, 26, 27, 52, 122, 141, 217, 246; war with Abu Dhabi, 94–5, 272; and 1913 Anglo-Turkish Convention, 107; frontiers of, 20, 123–5, 127, 144, 145, 146; 1952 claim, 153; *zakat* collecting in, 239, 242–3
Qatar Petroleum Company, 38, 243
Qatif, 108, 110, 112, 248
Qattarah village (Buraimi O.), 33, 45, 46, 96, 135, 188, 204, 228, 229, 230, 268
Qawasim tribe, 55; and piracy, 58; and Bani Yas, 60–1; and Al Bu Sa'id, 55, 60–1; and Wahhabis, 55, 63, 74, 77, and Appendix B; of Persian coast, 77–8; decline, 106
Qirran ibn Mani', chief of Al Bu Mundhir, 40, 121, 214–15
Qubaisat section of Bani Yas, 29, 36, 37, 132, 154, 218, 220; settlement at Khaur al-Udaid, 62, 92–4, 255
Qubiyat tribe, 134
Qufa, 29, 30, 132
Quff oases, 43
Qumzan section of Bani Yas, 36
Quraini, 153

Rabadh, 31
Raddah, 38 n. 1
Ramlat al-Hamra, 29, 33, 40, 42, 132, 242
Ramlat al-Su'aidan, 153
Ras al-Hadd, 56
Ras al-Hala, 93
Ras al-Hamra, 154
Ras al-Hazra, 142, 217
Ras al-Khaima shaikhdom, 22, 25, 58, 103, 106, 241
Ras al-Qaliyah, 145
Ras Asqhaila, 129
Ras Mushairab, 217
Ras Tanura, 159
Rashid tribe, 31, 37 n. 2, 43, 210, 214, 233
Rashid ibn Abdullah ibn Zuraiq, Al Bu Shamis shaikh of Dhank, 224
Rashid ibn Ahmad, Ruler of Umm al-Qaiwain, 99
Rashid ibn Hamad, Al Bu Shamis chief of Hamasa, 48, 49; and Sultan of Muscat, 137, 138, 140, 152, 226; and Saudis, 151–2, 159, 160, 164, 165, 258; bribed, 177, 195–6, 226–7, 276; subversive activities, 175, 178–179, 181–3, 186, 188–90, 192, 198, 199, 229, 233–4; changes allegiance, 187–8, 222–3, 225–7, 235, 236; leaves Hamasa, 205; dies, 267–8
Rashid ibn Khadim, chief of Al Bu Sha'ar, 40, 214
Rashid ibn Sa'id, Baluchi chief; and Saudis, 151, 160

Index

Rashid ibn Sa'id al-Darmaki; and Saudis, 229, 230
Rashid ibn Saqr, Al Bu Falah, 134
Rawashid section of Bani Yas, 36, 37, 46
Red Line, 145; defined, 124–5; significance, 129–31, 269, 274; disowned, 157–8
Rendel, G. W. (Sir George); and 1934–7 frontier negotiations, 126–7, 128–9, 130, 157
Rentz, George, 212, 216, 231
Residency Agent, Sharjah, 60 n. 2, 63, 66, 72, 89, 94, 117, 131, 132, 134, and Appendix B. *See also* Haji Abdur Rahman, Mullah Husain
Riyadh, 21, 144, 151, 161, 164, 165, 212; capital of Najd, 62; falls to Ibn Rashid, 95; recovered by Ibn Sa'ud, 104
Riyadh Line, 127–8, 129–31, 157
Ross, Lieut.-Col. E. C., 51 n. 1
Rub' al-Khali, 18, 22, 25–6, 27, 28, 29, 30, 31, 107, 108, 111, 126, 127, 128, 145, 153, 210, 213
Rumaithat section of Bani Yas, 29, 36, 37, 154
Ruwaihah, 42
Ruwais, 141
Ryan, Sir Andrew, British Minister to Saudi Arabia; and 1935 frontier negotiations, 125–8, 157, 158

Sa'ad al-Omani, 192
Sa'ad ibn Mutlaq, Wahhabi *naib* at Buraimi O.; defeated by Al Hajariyin, 63; barred from Buraimi O., 64–6; returns, 68; ravages Oman, 68–9; conduct and recall, 69–71; defeated by Bani Yas, 72, 250; final stay at Buraimi O., 73
Sa'ara village (Buraimi O.), 33, 47, 95
Sabkhat Matti, 26, 27, 29, 109, 142, 153, 217, 246; Thesiger on, 28; and Saudi claims, 125, 126, 127, 130, 146, 211, 274
Sadlier, Capt. G. F., 57 n. 2
Safa well, 168
Sahail ibn Khamis, chief of Mazari', 220
Sa'id al-Sahali, Saudi tax collector; at Liwa, 121
Sa'id ibn Ahmad, Imam of Oman, 53 n. 1
Sa'id ibn Buti, 117
Sa'id ibn Huwaidin, Bani Qitab shaikh, 233
Sa'id ibn Khalfan al-Khalili, Ibadi *mutawwa'* leader, 86, 87
Sa'id ibn Maktum, Ruler of Dubai, 31; and Saudis, 117, 118
Sa'id ibn Mubarak, chief of Al Bu Rahmah, 40; visits Saudi Arabia, 188; gives statement, 188, 214–15, 222, 235
Sa'id ibn Muhammad al-Hilal; and Saudis, 188–9, bribed, 189, 228; declares allegiance, 188–9, 195, 227, 228–9, 235; refugee, 268
Sa'id ibn Rashid, Baluchi shaikh; and Saudis, 151, 198; bribed, 181, 191, 195–6; declares allegiance, 187–8, 195, 226, 227, 231; sent arms, 191; refugee, 268
Sa'id ibn Sultan, Sultan of Muscat; and Buraimi O., 57, 60–1, 64; and Wahhabis, 62–3, 75–6; death, 81
Sa'id ibn Sultan al-Darmaki; and Saudis, 188, 198, 204; bribed, 188, 228; declares allegiance, 188, 195, 227, 228–9, 235; refugee, 268
Sa'id ibn Tahnun, Ruler of Abu Dhabi; expels Wahhabis from Buraimi O., 71–2; permits their return, 73, 250; retakes oasis, 74; mediates between Wahhabis and Muscat, 75–6; and Bahrain, 74, 78; deposition and death, 81, 91
Sa'id ibn Taimur, Sultan of Muscat, 21, 48; and Buraimi tribes, 137–8, 140, 224, 236; grants oil concession, 138; and Rashid ibn Hamad, 152, 236; and Saudis, 161–3, 182–3; retakes Buraimi O., 205, 262; and Imam Ghalib, 261–2; suppresses revolt, 264–5
Saif ibn Hamud ibn Azzan, 71
Saif ibn Sulaiman al-Bishari, 83 n. 1
Saif ibn Sultan, Shawamis shaikh, 102
Sait, 262, 264
Salalah, 262
Salifat al-Ghaus, 132
Salih ibn Ali, *tamimah* of Hirth, 86
Salih ibn Aziz, 214, 216
Salih ibn Isa, *tamimah* of Hirth, 185, 264
Salil ibn Razik, Omani chronicler, 53, 56, 246, and Appendix B
Salim ibn Dhiyan, chief of Bani Ka'ab, 118
Salim ibn Hamad ibn Rakkadh, *tamimah* of Awamir; deposed, 44, 222; and Saudis, 160, 165; bribed, 195–6, 222, 236; declares allegiance, 187–8, 195, 221–2, 226, 227, 235
Salim ibn Jahaman, 192–3
Salim ibn Muhammad ibn Ali Al Hamuda, 96

Index

Salim ibn Musallim ibn Hamm, *tamimah* of Awamir; elected, 44, 222; and Al Bu Falah, 165, 236; and Saudis, 160, 179
Salim ibn Rashid al-Kharusi, Imam of Oman, 109, 116, 185 n. 1
Salim ibn Thuwaini, Sultan of Muscat; murders father, 83; overthrown, 85–6
Salwah oasis, 27, 104, 129, 140, 142, 145 n. 4, 239
Saqr ibn Dhiyab, Al Bu Falah, 59
Saqr ibn Khalid, Ruler of Sharjah, 98
Saqr ibn Sultan Al Hamuda, *tamimah* of Na'im, 48, 49, 133, 135; and Bertram Thomas, 120; and Sultan of Muscat, 137–9, 140, 227, 276; and Saudis, 160, 165, 169, 192; bribed, 176–7, 187, 195, 227; changes allegiance, 187–8, 195, 222–223, 226, 235, 236; leaves Buraimi, 205; refugee, 268
Saqr ibn Zaid, Ruler of Abu Dhabi, 119, 133, 134
Saruq, 29, 30, 132
Sa'ud ibn Abdul Aziz, Wahhabi Amir, 248
Sa'ud ibn Abdul Aziz Al Sa'ud, King of Saudi Arabia, 41; and Buraimi O., 176, 190, 192, 207–8, 261
Sa'ud ibn Faisal, Wahhabi Amir; revolts, 88; becomes Amir, 89; dies, 95
Sa'ud ibn Jiluwi, Governor of Hasa, 31, 134, 142, 152, 153, 213–14, 254, 267; and Abu Dhabi, 117–19; and *zakat* collecting, 120–1, 213, 242; and Buraimi shaikhs, 159–60; directs subversion at Buraimi O., 175–7, 187, 190, 195–6, 197, 202, 225, 235, 278; and in Oman, 178–80, 181–3, 186–7, 193, 202, 204; smuggles arms, 192–3, 202; and Hamasa fire, 199; and arbitration agreement, 177, 178; and Zaid ibn Sultan, 194; and declarations of allegiance, 195, 214, 216, 222, 225, 227, 231, 236
Saudi Arabia, 21–2, 122; 1935 frontier claim, 124–6, 129–31, 157–8; 1949 frontier claim, 19, 20, 49, 144–5, 147–8; examined, 145–7, 268–76; and London Agreement, 150–1, 155; and Omani leaders, 151–2, 277; and Dammam Conference, 153–8; claims Buraimi O., 159, 161, 166; occupies Hamasa, 159, 277; seeks U.S. intervention, 163; concludes Standstill Agreement, 163; persists with claim, 166–8; suggests plebiscite, 166, 170; accepts arbitration, 170–2; intrigues at Buraimi O., 175–7, 191–2, 197–8, 199, 202, 204, 278; and in Oman, 178–83, 185–7, 193, 202, 204, 264–5, 278; rejects protests, 177, 181, 206; misuses aircraft, 183–4, 188, 197–8, 215, 222; purchases allegiances, 187–8, 195–6, 198, 235–6; complaints and counter-complaints, 191, 194–5, 199; and arbitration tribunal, 204, 278–9; accuses Britain, 207–8, 260–261; proposes return to arbitration, 260, 265–6; smuggles arms, 261; breaks off diplomatic relations, 264; agrees to fact-finding mission, 267; resumes diplomatic relations, 268. *See also* Abdul Aziz ibn Abdur Rahman Al Sa'ud
Sauhar, 34, 75, 83, 103, 136, 161, 164
Seton, Capt. David, Resident at Muscat, 78 n. 1
Shabib ibn Muhammad al-Hilal; and Saudis, 188–9; bribed, 189, 228; declares allegiance, 188–9, 195, 227, 228–9, 235; refugee, 268
Shafi'i school of Islamic law, Appendix B
Shakhbut ibn Dhiyab, Ruler of Abu Dhabi, 51; deposed, 60; position at Buraimi O., 60
Shakhbut ibn Sultan, Ruler of Abu Dhabi, 20, 41, 46, 119, 134, 190; grants oil concession, 141; jurisdiction, 132–3, 135, 141, 142–3; 1952 frontier claim, 153–4; resists Saudis, 161; attempted overthrow, 180, 278; retakes Buraimi O., 205, 262
Shamal province, 51
Shams al-Din ibn Qudama, Muslim jurist, Appendix B
Sharh al-Kabir, Appendix B
Shari'ah, 76, 77, 156, 240, 241, and Appendix B
Sharif of Mecca, 73, 250. *See also* Muhammad ibn Aun
Sharif Ali, 73
Sharjah shaikhdom, 22, 34, 36, 82, 86, 97, 104, 106, 141, 165, 171, 189, 210, 233, 241
Sharqiyah province of Oman, 57, 109, 185
Shawamis tribe, 102, 178 n. 1
Shawcross, Sir Hartley; before arbitration tribunal, 200–2
Shinas, 58
Sikak, 125
Sila' (Ras al-Sila'), 142, 217

316

Index

Sir Bani Yas Island, 30, 93
Sirhan ibn Sa'id, 51 n. 1
Slave trade, 21, 22, 23; at Hamasa, 258
Smith, Maj. Sidney, Assistant Political Resident in P. Gulf; at Khaur al-Udaid, 92–3; on Liwa, 255
Standard Oil Company, 122, 129, 274
Stobart, P. D., 142–3
Su'ayyid Al Arafa (Su'ayyid Al Faisal), Saudi *amil*, 214; at Buraimi O., 115–16, 118, 119
Subais section of Bani Yas, 36
Sublime Porte, 79, 92, 105, 107, 110, 273. *See also* Ottoman Empire, Turks
Sudan tribe, 36
Suez crisis, 263, 264
Sufuq well, 126, 128, 143; position of, 128–31
Suhail ibn Buti, 117
Sulaiman ibn Abdullah, Al Bu Shamis chief, 66
Sulaiman ibn Himyar al-Nabhani, *tamimah* of Bani Riyam, 185; and Saudis, 185–6, 193; and Sultan of Muscat, 262; revolts, 264–5; defeated, 265
Sulaiman ibn Suwailim, *wali* of Sauhar; and Zaid ibn Khalifah, 101–2; death, 136
Sultan ibn Ahmad, Ruler of Muscat, 58, 247
Sultan ibn Ali al-Salf, 224
Sultan ibn Muhammad al-Darmaki, headman of Qattarah village, 133, 229
Sultan ibn Muhammad Al Hamuda, *tamimah* of Na'im; and Al Bu Falah, 96–100, 133–4
Sultan ibn Rashid al-Ya'aqubi, shaikh of Ibri, 100
Sultan ibn Saif, 66
Sultan ibn Saqr, Ruler of Sharjah and Ras al-Khaima, chief of Qawasim (*ob.* 1866); and Buraimi O., 60–1, 72, 74; death, 91
Sultan ibn Saqr, Ruler of Sharjah, 152
Sultan ibn Surur, chief of Dhawahir, 45, 47, 201, 228, 229; declares allegiance, 189, 236; attempted bribery of, 189–90
Sultan ibn Zaid, Ruler of Abu Dhabi, 133; opposes Saudis, 115–16, 117–119; death, 119, 134
Sunainah, 47, 66, 151, 168–9, 196, 223
Sur; raided by Wahhabis, 83
Surveys; of the Arabian coast, 30, 59, 141

Taff, 29, 37, 40
Tahnun ibn Shakhbut, Ruler of Abu Dhabi, 59, 60; and Buraimi O., 61
Tahnun ibn Zaid, Ruler of Abu Dhabi, 115, 133
Talib ibn Ali; and Saudis, 185; and Sultan of Muscat, 262; revolts, 264–265; defeated, 265
Tanuf, 264
TAPLINE, 238
Tarif, 159, 168
Tawwam, 53, 246. *See also* Buraimi Oasis
Taylor, Capt. Robert, 40 n. 1
Tharwaniyah, 31, 211 n. 3
The Country of Saudi Arabia, 145
The Resolving of Doubts, 247
The Times, 266, 267, 268
Thesiger, Wilfred; crosses Jafurah and Sabkhat Matti, 28–9; crosses Rub' al-Khali, 31; on Liwa O., 31–2, 218; on definition of Oman, 34; on Al Bu Falah, 39, 42, 231; on Awamir, 43–4; on Zaid ibn Sultan, 135; on Na'im, 139; on Tuwairish ibn Hamudah, 182; on Sulaiman ibn Himyar, 185; on slave trade at Hamasa, 258
Thomas, Bertram, 27, 28; and Buraimi O., 119–20; on *zakat*, 120–1; and Bani Ka'ab, 232
Thuwaini ibn Sa'id, Sultan of Muscat, 68–9, 81; concludes treaty with Wahhabis, 75–6; opposes them, 83; murdered, 83
Treaties, conventions, agreements:
Anglo-Muscat Agreements, 1798/1800, 58
Anglo-Persian Treaty, 1801, 58
General Treaty of Peace with Piratical Shaikhs, 1820, 58
First Maritime Truce, 1835, 62
Ten Years' Maritime Truce, 1843, 62
Treaty of Maritime Peace in Perpetuity, 1853, 22
Wahhabi undertaking of 1866, 84–85, 112, 147
Anglo-Turkish Convention, 1913, 107–8, 111, 146, 149, 268, 273
Anglo-Turkish Convention, 1914, 111, 113, 146, 149, 268, 273
Saudi-Turkish Agreement, 1914, 110, 149
Anglo-Saudi Treaty, 1915, 112–13, 268–9
Anglo-Qatar Treaty, 1916, 22
Treaty of Muhammarah, 1922, 113
Convention of Uquair, 1922, 113

Index

Treaty of Jeddah, 1927, 121–2, 145, 147
Anglo-Saudi Agreement on Kuwait, 1942, 156
Buraimi chiefs' agreement, 1948, 140
London Agreement, 1951, 150–1, 155, 158, 159, 161, 162, 167, 169
Standstill Agreement (Buraimi O.), 1952, 163, 165, 167, 168, 169
Anglo-Saudi Arbitration Agreement, 1954, 23, 171–4, and Appendix A
Trevor, Maj. A. P., Political Agent, Bahrain, 110 n. 2
Trucial Oman Levies, 150, 158, 161, 168, 169, 172, 173, 174, 201, 205, 232, 261
Trucial Shaikhdoms (Trucial Coast, Trucial Oman, Trucial States), 17, 18, 19, 20, 91, 99, 102, 108, 115, 156, 220, 232, 241; relationship with Britain, 22, 34, 105, 141; economy, 35–6; and Wahhabis, 73, 74, 75, 80, 82, 84–5; frontiers, 18, 124
Trucial System, 22, 62, 93, 105, 132
Tuhfat al-Ayyan fi Sirat Ahl Oman, 55 n. 1, and Appendix B
Turki ibn Abdullah, Wahhabi Amir, 62–4, 249
Turki ibn Abdullah ibn Utaishan, Saudi official; occupies Hamasa, 159–60, 161, 163, 277; subsequent activities, 164–5, 166, 167, 169, 188, 232, 258; withdrawn, 172–4; continues subversion, 175, 176–7, 181, 195
Turki ibn Ahmad al-Sudairi, Wahhabi *naib* at Buraimi O., 82–3; killed, 86
Turki ibn Sa'id, Sultan of Muscat, overthrows Azzan ibn Qais, 89; at Buraimi O., 88–9, 252; and Na'im, 88–9, 95, 252–3
Turki ibn Sa'ud; raids Oman, 56
Turkish Arabia (Turkish Iraq), 54; British Assistant Political Agent in, 52. *See also* Iraq
Turks; at Dauhah, 92; and Khaur al-Udaid, 93; occupy Hasa, 89, 91; Qasim, 105; and Ibn Sa'ud, 105; lose Hasa, 108. *See also* Ottoman Empire, Sublime Porte
Tuwairish ibn Hamudah; Thesiger on, 182; and Saudis, 182–3

Ubaid ibn Juma', *tamimah* of Bani Ka'ab; and Sultan of Muscat, 137, 138, 140; deposed, 177; and Saudis, 152, 160, 164, 177–9, 187, 195; declares allegiance, 195, 227, 231–2; flees, 205; refugee, 268
Umar ibn Muhammad ibn Ufaisan, Governor of Hasa, 62–3, 249
Umm al-Qaiwain shaikhdom, 22, 99
Umm al-Qura, 122 n. 3, 145 n. 2
Umm al-Samim, 33
Umm al-Zamul, 33, 153
United Nations; Secretary-General of, 24, 266–8 (*see also* Dag Hammarskjöld); Saudi delegation to, 207, 260
United States; and Blue Line, 122; Army survey unit, 141; ambassador at Jeddah, 163, 277; and Buraimi question, 207, 262–3, 266
Uqair, 26, 110, 272
'*Uqud al-Juman fi Ayyam Al Sa'ud fi 'Uman,* 245, 246, 248, 253
Uraiq wells, 104, 213, 238

Violet Line, 124, 125, 128, 149; defined, 111
Voroshilov, Marshal, 261

Wadi al-Jizzi, 34, 35, 47, 71, 75, 95, 97, 102, 118, 140, 160, 161, 171, 231; Saudi activities in, 177–80, 278
Wadi al-Qaur, 35, 231, 232
Wadi Hatta, 98
Wahhabis, 34, 44, 46, 104, 109; origins and beliefs, 53–4; first seizure of Buraimi O., 54, 246–7; early invasions of Oman, 55–7, 247–8; defeated by Egyptians, 57; recover, 62; second occupation of Buraimi O., 62–3, 249–50; ended, 64, 251; second defeat by Egyptians, 64; recover, 67; return to Buraimi O., 68; ejected, 71; fourth occupation, 73, 250–1; ends, 74; fifth occupation, 75; reimpose *zakat* on Oman, 75–6; raid Sur and Batinah, 83; expelled from Buraimi O., 87, 251–2; defeated by Turks, 89; eclipse by Ibn Rashid, 91, 95
Wahibah tribe, 186
Wakra, 93
Wasit, 160, 224
Way, Capt. A. Cotton; Assistant Political Resident in P. Gulf, 86; Politica lAgent, Muscat, 88
Wellsted, Lieut. J. R.; explores Oman, 63

Ya'ariba Imams of Oman, 53
Yanqul, 139
Yasat Island, 30

318

Index

Yemeni tribes, 52
Young, Richard; before arbitration tribunal, 197, 202
Yusuf Ibrahim, 193
Yusuf Yasin, Saudi Foreign Minister, 151; and Red Line, 128–9, 130, 157–8; at Dammam Conference, 153, 155 n. 3, 156–8; member of arbitration tribunal, 174, 184, 201–203, 279; and Buraimi O., 184, 190, 203

Zaid ibn Khalifha, Ruler of Abu Dhabi, 46, 48, 91, 95, 133, 136; and Azzan ibn Qais, 88, 262; and Buraimi O., 88–9, 96, 272; and Na'im, 97–8, 100, 272; and Ifar, 99–100; and Baluchis, 99; and Bani Qitab, 99–100; and Khaur al-Udaid, 92–4, 254–5; and Manasir, 99–100; and Al Bu Sa'id, 100–1, 101–2; and Al Bu Shamis, 101–2; Miles on, 96; Cox on, 102, 104; opposes Ibn Sa'ud, 104; dies, 106; his power assessed, 106, 272; *Saudi Memorial* on, 253

Zaid ibn Saqr, Al Bu Falah, 134; and Saudis, 180, 223
Zaid ibn Sultan, Al Bu Falah *wali* at Buraimi O., 34, 42, 44–5, 46, 48, 135–6, 139, 161, 165, 182, 188, 189–190, 191, 204, 230–1, 257, 258; Thesiger on, 135; attempted bribery of, 194, 200–201, 278; before arbitration tribunal, 180
Zakat (zakah); defined and discussed, 62, 120–1, 148, 156–7, 215, 240–3, 248–9, 275, and Appendix B; as imposed by Wahhabis, 76–9, 85, 240, 246–7, 248–9; in 1866 declaration, 84–5; as collected by Saudis, 116, 119–20, 121, 131, 148, 156–7, 212–213, 215, 220–1, 223, 228–30, 237–9, 273; by Al Bu Falah, 132–3, 135, 148, 156, 220, 229, 241; in Trucial Oman, 156–7, 215, 241; in Qatar, 221, 242–3; registers, 212–13, 220, 221, 222, 237–9, 275; as interpreted in *Saudi Memorial*, 76, 85 n. 3, 237, 239–42, 275. *See also* Appendix B
Zakhnuniyah Island, 107–8
Zanzibar, 21, 64; Sultanate of, 81
Zwemer, Samuel, 104 n. 1

319